Gender and Heresy

Women and Men in Lollard Communities, 1420–1530

Shannon McSheffrey

D0223661

University of Pennsylvania Press

Philadelphia

Library of Congress Cataloging-in-Publication Data
McSheffrey, Shannon.
    Gender and heresy : women and men in Lollard communities,
1420–1530 / Shannon McSheffrey.
        p.   cm. — (Middle Ages series)
    Includes bibliographical references and index.
    ISBN 0-8122-3310-7 (alk. paper). — ISBN 0-8122-1549-4 (alk. paper)
    1. Lollards.   2. Heresies, Christian — England — History — Middle
Ages, 600–1500.   3. Sex role — Religious aspects — Christianity — Case
studies.   4. Sex role — England — History.   5. England — Church
history — 1066–1485.   I. Title.   II. Series.
BX4901.2.M37   1995
284′.3 — dc20   95-37249
                                                            CIP

Gender and Heresy

University of Pennsylvania Press
MIDDLE AGES SERIES
Edited by
Ruth Mazo Karras
Temple University

Edward Peters
University of Pennsylvania

A listing of the available books in the series
appears at the back of this volume

Contents

Illustrations

Abbreviations

A&M	John Foxe, *Acts and Monuments*. Edited by George Townsend. 8 vols. London: Seeley, Burnside and Seeley, 1843.
BCRL	Birmingham City Reference Library
BIHR	*Bulletin of the Institute of Historical Research*
BL	London, British Library
Bodl.	Oxford, Bodleian Library
BRO	Aylesbury, Buckinghamshire Record Office
BRUO to 1500	A. B. Emden, *Biographical Register of the University of Oxford to 1500*, 3 vols. Oxford: Oxford University Press, 1957–59.
Bucks. Muster	*The Certificate of Musters for Buckinghamshire in 1522*. Edited by A. C. Chibnall. Royal Commission on Historical Manuscripts, Joint Publication 18, 1973.
Bucks. Subsidy	*The Subsidy Roll for the County of Buckingham Anno 1524*. Edited by A. C. Chibnall and A. Vere Woodman. Buckinghamshire Record Society, 8, 1950.
Cal. Inq. Hen. VII	*Calendar of Inquisitions Post Mortem . . . Henry VII*, 3 vols. London: Public Record Office, 1898–1955.
CPR 1494–1509	*Calendar of Patent Rolls, 1494–1509*. London: Public Record Office, 1916.
EETS, e.s.	Early English Text Society, Extra Series
EETS, o.s.	Early English Text Society, Original Series
EM	John Strype, *Ecclesiastical Memorials . . . under King Henry VIII, King Edward VI, and Queen Mary I*, 3 vols. Oxford: Clarendon, 1822.
ERO	Chelmsford, Essex Record Office

EWS	*English Wycliffite Sermons*, 3 vols.: vols. 1 and 3, ed. Anne Hudson; vol. 2, ed. Pamela Gradon. Oxford: Clarendon, 1983–90.
FZ	*Fasciculi zizaniorum Magistri Johannis Wyclif cum tritico*. Edited by W. W. Shirley. Rolls Series. London: Public Record Office, 1858.
HT	*Heresy Trials in the Diocese of Norwich, 1428–31*. Edited by Norman P. Tanner. Camden Society, 4th ser., 20, 1977.
JEH	*Journal of Ecclesiastical History*
KAO	Maidstone, Kent Archives Office
L&P	*Letters and Papers, Foreign and Domestic, of the Reign of Henry VIII*. Edited by J. S. Brewer et al. 21 vols. and addenda. London: Public Record Office, 1862–1932.
Lich. Ct. Bk.	Lichfield, Lichfield Joint Record Office, MS B/C/13, Court Book of Bishop Geoffrey Blyth of Coventry and Lichfield (1511–12).
ORO	Oxford, Oxfordshire Record Office
PCC	Prerogative Court of Canterbury
PRO	London, Public Record Office
REED	*Records of Early English Drama*
Reg. Audley	Trowbridge, Wiltshire Record Office, Reg. Audley, Register of Bishop Edmund Audley of Salisbury (1502–24).
Reg. G. Blyth	Lichfield, Lichfield Joint Record Office, MS B/A/1/14i, Register of Bishop Geoffrey Blyth of Coventry and Lichfield (1503–31).
Reg. J. Blythe	Trowbridge, Wiltshire Record Office, Reg. John Blythe, Register of Bishop John Blythe of Salisbury (1494–99).
Reg. Chedworth	Lincoln, Lincolnshire Archives Office, Episcopal Register XX, Register of Bishop John Chedworth of Lincoln (1452–71).
Reg. Chichele	*Register of Henry Chichele* (Archbishop of Canterbury, 1414–43). Edited by E. F. Jacob. 4 vols. Canterbury and York Society, 42, 45–47, 1938–47.

Reg. P. Courtenay	Winchester, Hampshire Record Office, MS A1/15, Register of Bishop Peter Courtenay of Winchester (1487–92).
Reg. W. Courtenay	London, Lambeth Palace Library, Reg. W. Courtenay, Register of Archbishop William Courtenay of Canterbury (1381–96).
Reg. Fitzjames	London, Guildhall Library, MS 9531/9, Register of Bishop Richard Fitzjames of London (1506–22).
Reg. Fox, vols. 2, 4	Winchester, Hampshire Record Office, MSS A1/18, A1/20, Register of Bishop Richard Fox of Winchester (1501–28).
Reg. Hales	Lichfield, Lichfield Joint Record Office, MS B/A/1/12, Register of Bishop John Hales of Coventry and Lichfield (1459–90).
Reg. Longland	Lincoln, Lincolnshire Archives Office, Episcopal Register XXVI, Register of Bishop John Longland of Lincoln (1521–47).
Reg. Morton	London, Lambeth Palace Library, Reg. Morton, vol. 1, Register of Archbishop John Morton of Canterbury (1486–1500).
Reg. Warham	London, Lambeth Palace Library, Reg. Warham, vol. 1, Register of William Warham of Canterbury (1503–32).
R.S.	Rolls Series
Salisbury Reg. Langton	Trowbridge, Wiltshire Record Office, Reg. Langton, Register of Bishop Thomas Langton of Salisbury (1485–93).
SCH	*Studies in Church History*
TCD	Dublin, Trinity College
TRHS	*Transactions of the Royal Historical Society*
Winchester Reg. Langton	Winchester, Hampshire Record Office, MS A1/16, Register of Bishop Thomas Langton of Winchester (1493–1501).

Acknowledgments

It is my pleasure to thank the following people who offered their help at various stages in the preparation of this book: the late and sadly missed Michael Sheehan, Joseph Goering, Jane Abray, Anne Hutchison, Joel Rosenthal, Jane Harrison, Paul Deslandes, my colleagues at Concordia University (particularly Robert Tittler and Elizabeth Seddon), Judith Bennett, Anne Hudson, Norman Tanner, and the anonymous readers at the University of Pennsylvania Press. I have greatly profited from their assistance and advice; it should go without saying, however, that any blemishes that remain are my own responsibility only. My thanks are also extended to the ever-helpful librarians and archivists at these institutions: the Library of the Institute for Mediaeval Studies at the University of Toronto, the Records of Early English Drama Project at the University of Toronto, the Buckinghamshire Record Office, the Essex Record Office, the Lichfield Joint Record Office, the British Library, the Corporation of London Record Office, the Guildhall Library, the Public Record Office, the Westminster Diocesan Archives, the Kent Archives Office, the Hertfordshire Record Office, the Bodleian Library, and the Oxfordshire Record Office. This project would not have been possible without that great patron of Canadian academics, the Social Sciences and Humanities Research Council of Canada. My parents, Brian and Grace McSheffrey, and my sisters, Maureen McSheffrey and Jeanne Parker, have supported and encouraged my intellectual pursuits from my early schooldays and at the same time reminded me how esoteric it all is. Most important of all, I would like to express my appreciation to my husband, Eric Reiter, for his patience in reading seemingly endless drafts, his help with theology and canon law, his map-drawing skills, his critical acumen, and his sharp eyes. This book is for him.

Montreal
April 1995

Note: Spelling in transcriptions of Latin and English has been maintained, except that *u*'s and *v*'s have been regularized and abbreviations have been silently expanded. Punctuation has been modernized. Dates are Old Style, except that the year begins January 1.

1. Introduction

Gender and Religious Deviance

Ideas about sexual difference shape, and in turn are shaped by, religious culture. This is as true of Christianity, the dominant European religion, as of any other faith. Despite St. Paul's declaration of radical spiritual equality for all, regardless of ethnicity, status, or sex — "There is neither Jew nor Greek, there is neither slave nor free, there is neither male nor female; for you are all one in Christ Jesus" (Gal. 3:28) — gender has been both a theoretical and a practical factor in the organization of religious life throughout the history of Christianity. The historical relationship between gender and religion has recently attracted the attention of many scholars, especially those studying the medieval and early modern periods, the paradigmatic "ages of faith" in the Western past.

This book seeks to examine how the gender identities of women and men affected their participation in one Christian movement. Over the last two or three decades the scholarly study of gender, growing as it has out of feminist theory and women's history, has naturally focused mainly on women. Yet, as Natalie Zemon Davis commented almost twenty years ago, gender is a fundamentally relational construct; to understand it fully we must examine masculine as well as feminine identities.[1] In this study I endeavor to shift both the general direction of scholarship on late medieval and early modern religion, as well as a particular field of historical inquiry — the study of women in heretical or sectarian religious groups — toward a consideration of both sexes. My contention is that neither women nor men partook of religious activities in gendered isolation and so any study of gender roles must be comparative and relational. Bonds between adherents of a religious movement and community dynamics are central to understanding these issues.

This book studies women and men in communities of Lollards, heretics active in England between about 1380 and 1530. In choosing to focus on religious deviance in my examination of gender and Christianity, I follow in the footsteps of a number of earlier scholars. Heretical or sectarian groups offer the opportunity both to examine a small community as a case study and to consider such a heterodox movement as a variation on, or perhaps even a kind of mirror image of, orthodoxy. Most previous explorations of the theme of gender and heresy, however, have examined women's roles only; few case studies have systematically compared the participation of both sexes in a single sect. Yet close study of a heterodox religious movement, as I have undertaken here, is necessary to consider fully the range of factors affecting participation in religious culture.

An examination of women and men in Lollard communities underscores that gender was indeed a crucially important variable in participation in a heterodox movement — but not necessarily in the direction often assumed. This particular religious deviance tended to attract men, particularly of the artisanry or petite bourgeoisie, more than it did women of any station. Heterodoxy did not mean sexual equality: challenges to orthodoxy did not lead inexorably to questioning of patriarchal gender categories. Late medieval and early modern Christianity (both orthodox and heterodox) and the gender norms with which it interacted were complex cultural phenomena experienced differently by people according to their sex, social station, geographical context, and a host of other factors.

This claim runs counter to much that has been written on the subject: scholars have often assumed that women were particularly attracted to deviance, perhaps especially religious deviance.[2] Despite a number of challenges to the conventional association of women with heterodoxy,[3] the magnetism of deviant religious groups for medieval women is textbook orthodoxy: two popular women's history surveys, *Becoming Visible* and *A History of Their Own*, as well as the medieval volume of the French series *A History of Women in the West*, repeat the notion, giving it a kind of canonical status.[4] Behind this generalization lies the assumption that women, as marginal members of their societies, are unsuited to or excluded from the dominant religious order, made by and for men. Heretical sects drew women more than men because such groups provided women with more opportunities for religious activity and expression than they could find in orthodoxy.

There are a number of problems with this hypothesis. Perhaps the most fundamental difficulty is its failure to take account of "women" and "men" as internally differentiated groups. Gender was an important factor, but recognition of that need not lead us to see all women as having the same gender identity. Other variables, such as socioeconomic status, family position, age, geography, and occupation, acted together with femaleness and maleness to create a range of gender identities: in essence all these elements were gendered at the same time as gender identity depended on them. As feminist theorists like Denise Riley have recently argued, "women" is in effect too large a category;[5] to say that women *qua* women were drawn to deviance is overly simplistic. This is not to argue that gender is an unimportant factor in historical analysis, indeed, quite the opposite. Historians have only begun to scratch the surface of the complexities of gender identity in the past.

Moreover, the assumption of male dominance in religion fails to consider the subtle but important ways that the relatively less powerful also participate in the development of culture. Recently some scholars have emphasized the creative contributions of subordinate groups to premodern religious cultures. Caroline Walker Bynum, for instance, shows how important aspects of late medieval piety (such as eucharistic devotions) were particularly the creation of women, albeit unusual and exceptional women.[6] Robert Scribner's work on popular religion during the Reformation period shows the dialectical process of the creation of religious culture and the ways in which ordinary lay believers may choose to interpret to their advantage practices that the ecclesiastical elite intended to be used differently. We can no longer see women as outsiders to the dominant religious cultures of the medieval and early modern period; even peasant women could shape and employ orthodox practices, such as those associated with the blessing of candles, in ways completely outside the understanding of bishops and theologians.[7]

The assumption that it is marginalized groups like "women" who are attracted to deviance thus oversimplifies both the too-large category of women and the interactive process through which religious culture develops. It also oversimplifies deviance itself, assuming that it is precisely its heterogeneity, its otherness, that attracts followers rather than the character of the deviance. Certainly rebellion against authority for rebellion's sake was one of the drawing cards of heterodox religious groups, but by no means was it the only one. We should not rob heretical sects of their own particularity: different sorts of heresies appealed to different sorts of people. To assume, as some have, that Catharism and Lollardy — to mention two very different heretical movements of the later Middle Ages — appealed in similar ways[8] is to fail to understand the nature of their followings. The dualist rejection of the flesh embraced by the Cathars contrasts strikingly with Lollard exhortations to marry and bring forth children, for instance; such differences in doctrine and practice must have affected the composition of the sects' memberships.

Finally, we should examine what we mean by deviance: deviance or disorderliness in one sense is conformity in another. While in an ideal world all authorities might seek to create the same social and religious configurations, medieval people were often faced with contradiction. Some who became involved in a Lollard community—who subscribed to a deviant religious sect—did so in order to comply with traditional structures of authority. In participating in a Lollard conventicle a wife might obey the wishes of her husband or a son the command of his father; at the same time as they complied with expected behavior within the family, they transgressed the orders of such higher authorities as bishops and kings. On the other hand, those who followed the dictates of higher powers regarding religious orthodoxy might challenge the supremacy of more immediate figures. Participation in a deviant religious movement was by no means a simple, straightforward act.

In this volume, I analyze the activities, relationships, and beliefs of women and men in the Lollard movement. This book is the only full-length treatment of gender in the Lollard movement. What little writing there has been on the subject has seen Lollard women participating almost equally with men, but I argue the opposite, that Lollardy, both as a creed and as a social movement, appealed much more to men than to women. Men—drawn mostly from among artisans and husbandmen in south and central England—were overwhelmingly dominant in the movement, both in numbers (they made up two-thirds of reported adherents) and, more importantly, in influence and participation. Women Lollards were usually related to a Lollard man, and it seems likely that most women came to be involved in the movement because of their male relatives' influence.

Male and female members of the communities played roles that reflected rather than overrode late medieval gender expectations. Although some have seen medieval heresy as an escape for women from patriarchy, Lollardy did not serve this function. The sect affirmed in theory and practice the norm of the male-dominated family, where women were restricted to roles that kept them close to the domestic center and where men were the public leaders. A marginalized religious group like the Lollards illustrates the complex interaction between religious culture and gender ideology in late medieval society.

Crucial to this study is the concept of "gender." Theorists and historians are currently grappling with the meaning of gender and its role in historical causation or our interpretation of past (and present) societies. Many scholars have used gender to designate the cultural, as opposed to the biological, constructions of femininity and masculinity—another variant of the classic Aristotelian binaries nature and culture, biology and socialization. Historians have been particularly influenced by the work of Joan Wallach Scott, whose 1986 article, "Gender: A Useful Category of Historical Analysis," in many ways established that consideration of gender was integral to the historical enterprise.[9] Her understanding of gender, shaped by the postmodern interest in language and discourse, is that the term denotes "the knowledge that establishes meanings for bodily difference."[10] Recently, however, feminist theorists have been troubled by the "denial of the body" inherent in the dichotomy between sex and gender.[11] Judith Butler in particular has led feminists to attempt to understand how the very physicality of sexual difference is itself integral to gender.[12]

"Gender" in this study means identity as a sexed being. This identity is not fixed; as Denise Riley suggests, gender identity fluctuates.[13] The meaning of "women," for instance, differs both over time and even at a particular temporal and spatial point.[14] Women in late medieval England did not have the same identity as women in late twentieth-century Canada. Nor did all late medieval women have the same gender identity: to be a woman, to act in a feminine way, was differently constituted for a noblewoman than for a peasant, for an adolescent than for an elderly widow. Gender is not the only aspect of identity — it converges with social position, ethnicity, family status, age, occupational grouping, and a myriad of other elements.[15] I do not see gender as something that can be superseded by another facet of identity (such as social status), but as an elastic concept, one that moves and adjusts according to other aspects of identity. Behavior that others would accept as appropriate and consistent with womanliness in the wife of a mayor, for instance, might have been unsuitable and unwomanly in the wife of a rural carpenter.

At the same time as identities are individually constituted, they nonetheless draw from cultural norms and expectations. Butler's idea of gender as "performance" is a useful way to think about what "identity" means — that is, a person's actions constantly *create* that person's gender identity (rather than expressing an underlying, unchanging norm or essence).[16] This does not happen in a vacuum, but in relation to the "performances" of others; as Butler says, the repeated performatory action of gender "is at once a reenactment and reexperiencing of a set of meanings already socially established."[17] While gender, then, is not a fixed norm perfectly or imperfectly reflected by people in a society, people forge their gender identities within the framework of the gender identities created by others.

The Lollard movement lies on the cusp of one of the great divisions in current historiography, the gulf between medieval and modern. While the sect was born in a period most historians still consider safely "medieval" — the late fourteenth century — evidence of its coherence as a movement does not disappear until about 1530, when European society is supposed to have entered a new era, the "early modern" period. One of the aims of this book is to attempt to bridge the too-often separate historiographies of these two eras. I also want to suggest, following a recent exploration of this problem by Judith Bennett, that the "Great Divide" separating these two chapters of the Master Narrative exists much more strikingly in the minds of historians than in the actuality of the lives of people in this period.[18]

The approaches of both medieval and early modern historians to the question of gender and religious culture contribute to this study. Here it is worth pointing out the rather different preoccupations of these two branches of historical inquiry. Within medieval historiography in the last several decades, scholars have emphasized religious practice rather than doctrine in their analyses of women's place in the medieval Catholic Church. Varying evaluations of the lives and activities of nuns, mystics, Beguines, and devout laywomen (especially those of high estate) have emphasized how open, or closed, the late medieval Church was to participation by the female half of the population.[19] This literature has emphasized opportunities available to the exceptional women who wished to live a life wholly dedicated to religion, rather than the devotional life of the ordinary laywoman of middling or low status who led a full life as a worker, wife, mother, or daughter.[20]

Scholarship on gender and Reformation religion[21] has had a rather different focus. It has centered on the laity and in particular on the effect of doctrinal changes on women's and men's views of themselves. Historians have interpreted Protestantism's affirmation and praise of the married state and its insistence on the priesthood of all believers, male or female, in divergent ways. Some scholars see these theological teachings as beneficial to women, legitimizing their position in the domestic sphere and emphasizing their spiritual equality. But others argue that the confirmation and even strengthening of patriarchy in Protestant teaching was detrimental to the status of women, limiting their options both in religious and secular life and reinforcing their subordination. Recently some Reformation scholars have turned to the question of how doctrinal change, particularly the eradication of the cult of saints, affected women's religious practice. In her important book on women in Reformation Augsburg, Lyndal Roper argues that late medieval Catholicism nurtured a peculiarly "feminine mode of religious experience" that was absent in Protestantism.[22]

Lollardy was a late medieval heresy, but as sixteenth-century Protestants themselves recognized, the Lollards and their creed had a good deal in common with Reformed Christianity. This study will emphasize continuity rather than disjuncture in the periods we have designated as medieval and early modern. I consider below issues that affected Lollard, Protestant, and pre- and post-Reformation Catholic communities. The importance of the family and its constitution of authority, popular creativity in religious practice, and the implications of doctrine for women and men are questions central to the examination of both medieval and early modern religion.

The roles of Lollard women and men are considered through community studies of the largest groups uncovered by fifteenth- and sixteenth-century episcopal inquisitions and through analyses of the activities and beliefs of members of those groups. This method allows for a closely focused picture of the activities of Lollards in the context of their own communities. Through a wide-ranging examination of how Lollards functioned in groups, I find that a person's gender affected to a great extent how or even if he or she would participate in different Lollard activities. Other factors, particularly family situation and socioeconomic position, also affected attraction to the sect and consideration of Lollard activities as possible or appropriate for women and men.

That men and women tended to respond differently to matters spiritual and secular needs recognition and examination. Close investigations of medieval men's and women's activities can help add to our general knowledge about how people interacted and how they expected others to behave. Lollard communities were a microcosm of English society in the fifteenth and early sixteenth centuries or at least of certain parts of English society. Through a study of Lollards we can learn much about how gender shaped the lives of late medieval men and women outside as well as inside the heretical group.

Lollardy

The Lollard movement had its genesis in the 1380s at Oxford University, inspired and perhaps encouraged by the theologian John Wyclif, who died in 1384.[23] Itinerant preachers, followers of Wyclif, spread from the university in the 1380s and 1390s, disseminating Lollard doctrine around several parts of southern and central England. By the turn of the fifteenth century, Lollardy was established as a small but tenacious sect with continued connections to Oxford and substantial gentry support. Purges of Oxford Lollards around 1410 and Oldcastle's Revolt against the monarchy in 1414 severed the Lollard movement's associations with the gentry and academe, and the sect was thereafter primarily associated with artisanal groups and the bourgeoisie. Prosecution of the sect was sporadic — several investigations in the 1420s were followed by a lull of more than fifty years during which bishops uncovered few heretics. But the establishment of the Tudor dynasty coincided with a renewal of prosecution, and between the 1480s and the 1520s authorities sought and found Lollards in most of the dioceses in the ecclesiastical province of Canterbury. With the advent of the Reformation in England, Lollardy dropped from view, probably blending with the various streams of Protestant thought with which it had much in common.

The most striking aspect of Lollard doctrine to contemporaries and to modern historians is its virulent anticlericalism. Lollards not only condemned the clergy for their wicked lives but also denied that they had any special powers conferred upon them as a result of their ordination. Some held the extreme view that priests were not able to effect any of the seven sacraments, and they saw any such claims on the part of the clergy as an illegitimate assumption of God's role. Lollards repudiated other elements of medieval Catholicism, such as fasting, pilgrimages, the adoration of images, the invocation of saints, and the keeping of holy days, as "inventions" that had no basis in scripture. These practices were instituted by the clergy, they thought, for the purpose of seducing Christians into idolatry and enriching the Church. There was also a strong streak of apocalypticism in Lollard anticlericalism: the clergy represented for some the clear sign of the Antichrist's presence in the world.

While Lollard doctrine consisted to a large extent of attacks on orthodoxy, the central core of the creed was a conception of a new church fundamentally different from the old, based on the primacy of scripture and the congregation of the predestined. The Lollards also had a distinctive notion of the priesthood and its role. Ordination was not what made a priest: it was pious living and faithfulness to God's precepts. The priest's role was not to perform the sacraments but to preach and teach the word of God. The gap between priest and layperson was considerably narrowed by the Lollard belief in a direct relationship between God and the true Christian, which obviated the intermediary role of the clergy. Emphasis on the scriptures and the layperson's understanding of them resulted in a stress on vernacular devotional works and on the ability to read them.[24]

This picture of Lollardy owes much to the interpretation of Anne Hudson. Her approach to the study of Lollardy, blending the skills of the scholar of English with those of the historian, has led her to challenge the standard interpretations of the movement. Hudson has argued that to understand Lollardy as a creed, one must look not only at the prosecutions against those suspected of heresy or at the writings of those attacking the Lollards but also, and perhaps more importantly, at the writings of the Lollards themselves. Hudson has been a pioneer in discovering and editing Lollard English texts; in recent years she has also made forays into the historical end of Lollard studies. In her 1988 book, *The Premature Reformation*, Hudson blended the two approaches and synthesized the diverse literature on Lollardy.

The result of Hudson's work is an affirmation of Lollardy as a movement with a coherent creed and a continuous inheritance from the time of Wyclif to the Reformation. This has challenged both the received opinion on Lollardy[25] and some recent work on late medieval religion in England.[26] Hudson's work has provided an important reinterpretation of Lollardy's origins and its continued vitality and coherence as a set of beliefs, and it will remain the standard piece of scholarship on the Lollard movement. For the enterprise of looking at later Lollard social organization, however, Hudson's picture of the Lollards, drawn largely from texts, may overemphasize the scholarly end of the movement. The academic Wycliffite books written in the late fourteenth or early fifteenth century do not necessarily reflect the views of the movement a century later, made up then of laypeople uninterested in the particulars of scholastic theology.

How do we define adherence to Lollardy? Some historians have found Lollard doctrine to be so vague and variable that they have questioned that "Lollardy" existed at all: J. J. Scarisbrick characterizes it as a "disparate [and] dispersed" movement that cannot "be fully distinguished from pre-Christian survivals" and R. N. Swanson suggests that "the Lollard 'movement' may be no more than an historians' construct."[27] From our point of view, ascription of doctrinal heresy can indeed seem difficult: what the dominant religion (or "orthodox" church) defined as incorrect (or "heretical") altered over time (even assuming unanimity within the Church hierarchy regarding orthodoxy). While some Lollards held beliefs that were clearly outside orthodoxy as defined by fifteenth- or early sixteenth-century Catholic officials, others were condemned for holding to notions that were in fact consistent with official dogma (for instance, regarding vernacular scripture or private marriage). Specific problems of doctrine are largely beside the point, however, when determining adherence to Lollardy. Lollards' status as heretics was for the most part self-defined: they rejected the Catholic Church's claim to authority and held themselves to be outside it. As Richard G. Davies, in a 1990 address to the Royal Historical Society,[28] remarked, the debate about the "existence" of Lollardy as a movement has rested almost entirely on the criterion of doctrinal coherence to the exclusion of all other factors. But recruitment to and solidarity of sects such as Lollardy depend on social factors as well as matters of belief.

There is, as Hudson points out, still work to be done on the social basis of Lollardy. Several important articles have appeared that reconsider the socioeconomic status of the movement's adherents.[29] But the social interactions between members of Lollard communities, and particularly the impact of gender on these relationships, remain little investigated. Although female participation has received extensive consideration from historians of continental medieval heresies (particularly Catharism),[30] the role of women or gender in Lollardy has been given scant attention. Two articles by Margaret Aston and J. F. Davis have examined specific aspects of women's place in Lollardy, while making no attempt to assess their overall impact on the movement.[31] Only Claire Cross's 1978 survey article, " 'Great Reasoners in Scripture,' " directly addresses the question of women's roles in the sect.[32] Cross's work has served to introduce the question of women in Lollardy and makes some important observations, such as the significance of married couples and the centrality of the family unit. But Cross by no means treats the subject fully in this short essay. Her conclusion, that women were very active in Lollardy and that their roles "must have exceeded" those attained by their counterparts in orthodoxy,[33] is problematic; she does not, in fact, effectively compare the activities of heretical women to the activities of those in orthodoxy. Nor does she make the more telling comparison between the roles of women and men in the movement.

Sources

As is the case with most heterodox movements, our knowledge of Lollard communities comes mostly from the records of their enemies: the ecclesiastical authorities of the late medieval English church, especially at the episcopal level.[34] While Lollards did indeed produce a considerable corpus of writing themselves (in the form of sermons and treatises),[35] that writing, mostly anonymous, tells us relatively little about individuals or social relationships within the communities. Instead we must rely upon the records of prosecution, the bishops' registers and the court books into which scribes entered the testimony of suspects and witnesses.

Testimony and other sorts of legal evidence are, of course, by no means straightforward records of the thoughts and actions of people in the past.[36] The inherent bias of the court as a whole and the recorder of the documents in particular must be considered when using the records of ecclesiastical courts. Scribes who organized Lollards' heresies into discrete articles to be abjured, for instance, may have either simplified the beliefs of the suspects or made them more sophisticated and uniform than they actually were. Even the simple translation of responses delivered in English into the Latin in which they were usually recorded may have altered meanings significantly.

The question of gender is also critical. Some scholars have suggested that there may have been a systemic bias in the all-male, clerical court which led those investigating Lollardy to regard male heresy with more seriousness than female heresy.[37] It is clear that there was some bias in reporting the activities of a community. It is not clear, however, that that bias inaccurately reflects power realities within that community. Not only did the courts disregard the activities of women, so also did Lollard witnesses. There is ample evidence that the prejudice against seeing women as prominent participants in a community such as a Lollard group went beyond the courts into English society as a whole. Lollard men in their testimony were even more likely than the courts to ignore the activities of women.

Analysis of testimony — particularly different versions of a single situation or event — can also bring into relief the limitations of this sort of source as a record of "fact."[38] We have few ways of knowing at this remove who told the "truth" and who deliberately or unconsciously testified falsely or incompletely. This can, however, be turned to advantage. Questions about the prominence of women or the leadership of a community, for instance, are all about perception rather than about actual activities. I have carefully considered such issues in the evaluation of documents.

The most valuable sources for the history of Lollard communities are court books, which record, usually in Latin, the extended depositions and examinations of those brought before the bishop or his designated representatives on charges of heresy. Almost all who testified in proceedings against Lollards were themselves implicated in the movement—witnesses from outside the community were rare.[39]

A closer look at a fragment of the evidence these books provide will show both the richness of the material and some of its limitations. In December 1511 a young woman accused of heresy was brought before the court of the bishop of Coventry and questioned about her activities:

> Juliana, daughter of Agnes Yong, age twenty, born in Coventry, sworn and examined. Questioned whether she knew how to read, she answers negatively. At length, after Silkeby affirmed in her presence that she could read perfectly, she admitted it. She said also that she heard Alice Rowley speaking against pilgrimages, veneration of images, and the sacrament of the altar, saying that that which was offered was nothing but bread and wine. She asserts that she believed these things. Asked about the book that she got from Alice Rowley, she denies that she has such a book, affirming that she gave the book back to Alice Rowley. She says that she brought the book to the house of the afore-named Alice and together with a book of the commandments she put it under the mattress of a bed in *the chapell chambre*, and, as she asserts, she told Alice about it. She says moreover that she did this because Silkeby had extracted from her an oath, warning her that if she had any books she should hide them or else they might be found in her possession.[40]

Although some witnesses were apparently given more free rein than others to testify what they would, the depositions as recorded were usually in response to standardized leading questions. As this example shows, the judge's interrogation of a witness was often based on information gathered in previous depositions: Robert Silkby, for instance, had previously testi-fied that Juliana Yong could read.[41] In this case, Juliana's attempt to deny previous testimony proved fruitless. The Coventry judge's relatively un-usual tactic of producing the prosecution's witness in person to confront the recalcitrant offender was no doubt an effective means of breaking her down. Clearly once one member of a community had given a full confes-sion—as had Robert Silkby, a leading member of the group[42]—the others were in a difficult situation. The contents of Juliana's deposition are rela-tively typical, focused as they are around occasions when she and her fellow sectarians discussed Lollard doctrine and around the possession and trading of books.

Juliana Yong's evident reluctance to offer testimony was, on the other hand, somewhat unusual; witnesses' garrulous willingness to name names, describe events, and above all to forswear their beliefs always remains something of a surprise to the modern observer. Although there is no evidence that English authorities used or even threatened torture in heresy prosecution, some offenders (including a number of leading Coventry Lollards) were imprisoned for a period.[43] Bishop Geoffrey Blyth of Coventry and Lichfield in fact advised the use of "the payne of imprisonment" to extract confessions.[44] The discomfort and danger of late medieval prisons and, of course, the ever-present threat of execution may have led many witnesses to say more than they intended when brought before the court.

The evidence offered by court books is fascinating and suggestive; unfortunately, only two such books survive intact, while passages from a third come to us only in a seventeenth-century transcript.[45] I have used all three extensively in this study for the light they shed on the Lollard communities in the diocese of Norwich between 1428 and 1431 and in the cities of Coventry and London in the early sixteenth century. Other material from court books and bishops' registers that has not survived to the twentieth century was transcribed in the sixteenth century by John Foxe in his Protestant martyrology *Acts and Monuments* (sometimes called the *Book of Martyrs*), first published in the 1560s.[46] Foxe's transcriptions provide invaluable evidence, particularly regarding the Chiltern Hills Lollards of the early sixteenth century. The problem of biased sources doubles, though, when considering the material provided in the *Acts and Monuments* — Foxe used Catholic sources for Protestant polemical purposes.[47] While Foxe's transcriptions are accurate for the most part where they can be verified against surviving sources, not all details can be trusted, because Foxe occasionally mistranscribed names or dates (so that Elizabeths are called Joans and their trials are dated both 1521 and 1541)[48] and because he sometimes suppressed information he evidently considered to be unsatisfactory for his Protestant mission.[49] Where the original records are extant, I have used them in preference to Foxe.

For other communities, records of episcopal investigations survive only in the bishops' registers, where scribes recorded proceedings in a more concise and (for us) less informative way.[50] These accounts almost always show us only the end product of the prosecutions: that is, the suspects' abjurations of their heretical beliefs and the penances enjoined on them for their sins. Again, an extended example of this sort of document, written in Latin and English:

> 29 November 1463, John Qwyrk, layman, denounced and detected of the crime of heretical perversity, was examined concerning the charges written

below by the reverend men Masters John Botuler, Doctor of Canon Law, Thomas Edmunde, Physician and rector of the church of St. Andrew in Holbourne, London, and the Prior of Blackfriars, Oxford, Doctor of Theology. He admitted those charges before the Reverend Doctors, judicially presiding in this matter as Commissaries of the Reverend Father Lord John [Chedworth], by the grace of God Bishop of Lincoln.

First, he admitted that he was familiar with James Wylly, burned for the crime of heresy, who had taught him the epistles of St. Paul in English.

He admitted also that he taught and preached that the sacrament of the altar is only in memory of Christ and that nothing remains there except the substance of bread.

He admitted also that he taught and preached that the ecclesiastical judge cannot for any reason separate a man and woman between whom marriage has been solemnized, because what God had joined together man cannot separate.

He admitted and recognized also that he taught and preached that offerings should not on any account be made to vicars or priests or given to saints or holy places, but rather that they should be distributed to the poor. And that the images in church are not to be venerated but that it suffices for a man simply to say the Our Father, the Hail Mary, and the Creed only to God and the Blessed Mary.

He admitted also that he held and preached that Peter and the Apostles submitted themselves voluntarily to poverty and thus they attained God's kingdom. But modern bishops have excessive possessions.

He admitted also that he taught and preached that there is no such place as purgatory, but each person goes either to heaven or to hell after death.

In the name of god Amen. Before you Reverend fader in god John by the grace of god bisshop of Lincoln, I John Quyrk laborer of your diocise, not lettered, make opyn confession and knowlege in your presence and the presence of wittenesse here beyng at the tyme, that I have holden, taught, and affermed certayn false articles and opynionse of heresy, agaynse diverse sacramentis and the trew Cristen faith and the determinacion of holy churche. . . . Assone as I have doon my penaunce which is injoyned me I shall departe owte of the diocise of Lincoln never after to come therin during my lyff, under payne of relapse, as god me help and theis holy evaungelies. In wittenesse of theis premisses, I, John Qwirk forsaid, subscribe my selff with my nowne handis and he made this sign +.[51]

Abjurations are notoriously difficult to use as a reflection of a person's beliefs: they were formulaic and likely followed a standardized list of questions administered to each suspect.[52] Some abjurations were unique, however, providing quotations of the suspect's own words. Others record interesting information — as John Qwyrk's does — about a deponent's activities and those of his or her family and neighbors, and about the suspect's attitudes toward other Lollards. Here we learn about John's own preaching activities and about his familiarity with the infamous James Wyllys.

Other material related to Lollard prosecutions survives only as embedded in polemical works, both pro- and anti-Lollard. The trial of the important East Anglian Lollard William White, for instance, was recorded by the anonymous author of the mid-fifteenth-century anti-Lollard collection *Fasciculi zizaniorum*.[53] Information that Foxe gathered for his *Acts and Monuments* but did not use is preserved in his papers, deposited in the British Library; the proceedings recorded there were used by John Strype, another Protestant polemicist, in his *Ecclesiastical Memorials* (originally published in 1721) and by the editors of *The Letters and Papers . . . of Henry VIII*.[54]

For these community studies, I have made every effort to uncover any evidence about the Lollards beyond what appeared in the heresy proceedings. I consulted government documents (including state papers, muster rolls, civic records, and subsidy rolls) and ecclesiastical documents (such as visitation records, archdeaconry court proceedings, and wills) to collect any biographical details about those who were involved in Lollard communities. Wills proved especially useful in establishing relationships between Lollards (although not for determining confessional leanings), and I employed them along with subsidy rolls and muster rolls to determine the socioeconomic status of suspected adherents.

In order to consider Lollards' attitudes toward social relationships, I also examined other, textual sources, some originating from hostile observers of the movement and some written by Lollards themselves.[55] Sermons proved to be most fertile.[56] I remain convinced, however, that a social study of Lollard attitudes must also employ depositions and abjurations. Despite their shortcomings as reflections of Lollards' beliefs, and mediated as they are through hostile ecclesiastical questioning and recording, they remain our only window into the opinions of the individual men and women who made up the Lollard communities. Lollard writings may provide a truer picture of the sect's doctrine as it was conceived by its teachers, but the writings were produced in an academic environment by clerical males of considerable education, who must have had a perspective different from that of humbler laymen and laywomen who made up the bulk of the sect's membership in the years following Oldcastle's Revolt.

The Communities

This study examines eight Lollard groups, some communities being more clearly cohesive than others. The word *community* is used here in the sense

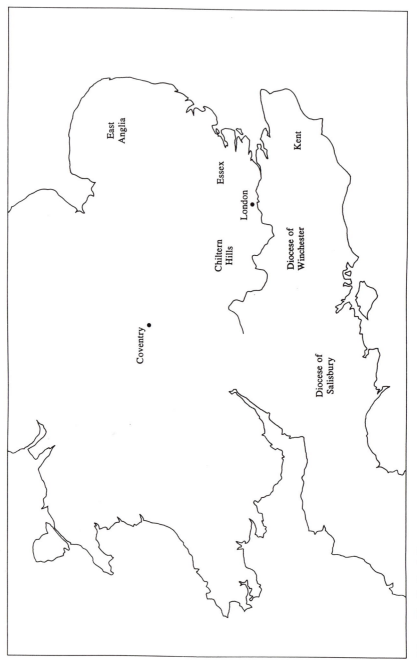

Map 1. The Lollard Communities, 1420–1530.

of a "complex of social relations" between people from a particular locality who shared an adherence to the Lollard creed and participated in Lollard activities with other heretics.[57] As sociologists point out, communities are stratified groups and can often mean different things to different members.[58] Ties within Lollard communities were established through web-like networks, so not all members may have known one another; the thread that bound a community together was contact with its leaders.

I have selected the particular Lollard groups studied here for the amount and quality of information available about individual adherents and about the relations between the individuals; I aimed to examine a Lollard's activity in the context of the activity of other Lollards. Because there is little information for the early period that allows the historian to see Lollards as part of a larger community — surviving records concentrate on individuals rather than groups — the emphasis in this study is on the later period of Lollard activity, between 1420 and 1530.[59]

Among the eight Lollard groups are two fifteenth-century communities, the Lollards of East Anglia, detected between 1424 and 1431, and their fellows uncovered in the Chiltern Hills in 1462 and 1464. Authorities discovered and prosecuted the remaining six groups in the late fifteenth and early sixteenth centuries: they pursued a second community from the Chiltern Hills between 1506 and 1532; a group of dispersed Lollard communities, loosely connected, in the dioceses of Salisbury and Winchester between 1486 and 1522; a community in the city of Coventry between 1486 and 1522; a group centered in London between 1490 and 1530; a community in the nearby county of Essex, closely related to the one in London, likewise prosecuted between 1490 and 1530; and, lastly, a group in Kent in 1511 and 1512. These communities represent all the larger Lollard groups for which we have evidence. Chapter 2 presents a case study of a particularly interesting community, the Coventry Lollard group uncovered between 1486 and 1522. A short description of the others will be useful here.

The group uncovered in Norfolk and Suffolk by Bishop William Alnwick of Norwich in 1428 was the first to be systematically prosecuted in East Anglia, although the community had thrived for perhaps as much as a decade before Alnwick began his proceedings.[60] Sometime between 1424 and 1428 an influx of new members fleeing from prosecution in Kent reinforced this community.[61] Among these Kentish émigrés was the man who became the group's leader, William White, a disaffected cleric and possible academic Wycliffite who wrote one or more Lollard texts.[62] White and the other Kentish heretics joined a community centered in the area of Loddon,

Norfolk, and in the Waveney Valley along the border between Norfolk and Suffolk. Alnwick's prosecution of this community between 1428 and 1431 implicated eighty-three people from his diocese in the Lollard heresy; in the fall of 1428 secular authorities burned three of these for their heresy, including William White.[63] Alnwick had completed his investigations by 1431, and there are no signs of Lollardy in this area again until much later in the fifteenth century.

The next community studied is a group uncovered in the Chiltern Hills of Buckinghamshire by Bishop John Chedworth of Lincoln between 1462 and 1464. Geography made this area a difficult one for ecclesiastical officials to investigate properly — it lay at the extremes of four dioceses, London, Winchester, Lincoln, and Salisbury — and there was likely a continuous tradition of heresy there from at least the time of Oldcastle's Revolt in 1414 to the Reformation.[64] The most important teacher in the group discovered by Chedworth was probably James Wyllys, formerly of Bristol, who taught men in Wycombe, Amersham, Chinnor, and Henley (including John Qwyrk). Officials tried Wyllys along with another man in 1462 and burned him later that year; another Lollard was brought to court in 1463, and then thirty-four suspects appeared before the bishop in 1464.[65] Local clergy may have been involved in the community, perhaps under the patronage of a local gentry family, the Cheynes.[66]

Despite Chedworth's prosecutions, this Lollard group almost certainly survived and was the direct ancestor of another community uncovered in the same area fifty years later.[67] The town of Amersham was evidently well known for its heretical group; according to Foxe, when the traveling teacher Thomas Man spoke to Lollards in the Windsor area, they told him of the large number of Lollards in Amersham and, moving there about 1500, he found "a godly and a great company, which had continued in that doctrine and teaching twenty-three years."[68] Soon after Man's arrival, the bishop of Lincoln, William Smith, began to prosecute the heretics in the Amersham area. Unfortunately, almost all the original records of sixteenth-century prosecutions in Buckinghamshire have been lost, but Foxe had access to some of this material and used it extensively in his *Acts and Monuments*. His picture of proceedings led by Smith in the first decade of the century is unclear: some heretics were burned at Wycombe some time prior to 1503, and a more intense prosecution known as the *magna abjuratio*, dated by Foxe to 1507 but probably better ascribed to 1510–11,[69] involved a large number of people from the Amersham area.[70] Much more detailed is Foxe's account of the proceedings of Bishop John Longland of Lincoln about 1521.[71] Longland evidently made a concerted effort to uncover all heretical activities in this part of his diocese, and the resulting proceedings, used by Foxe, implicate almost 300 people from the diocese of Lincoln and a further hundred or more from neighboring dioceses. This very large community was connected with Lollard groups eastward, in London and Essex, and westward and southward, in Oxfordshire, Berkshire, and Wiltshire.

A picture of a "community" of the Lollards south and west of the Chiltern Hills, prosecuted by the bishops of Salisbury between 1485 and 1521, is more difficult to build. Pockets of heretics, probably but not certainly connected to one another and to Lollards in the Chiltern Hills, were uncovered in Berkshire (centered around Maidenhead, Windsor, Reading, Newbury, and Wantage[72]) and in Wiltshire (centered around Devizes). Thomas Langton prosecuted them between 1485 and 1491, John Blythe in 1499 (his proceedings were finished after his death by Archbishop Morton), and Edmund Audley between 1502 and 1521.[73] Abjurations of repentant heretics in the registers of these bishops are all that remain of the proceedings against these groups. John Longland uncovered some material about heretics in Oxfordshire in examination of Buckinghamshire Lollards, and this closes some of the gaps.[74]

Even more shadowy is the community in the kingdom's largest city. Although it is probable that London was the center of Lollard activity in England from the fourteenth century, we can draw no clear picture of the heretical group in that city from surviving records.[75] Although other documents indicate that London bishops made some effort to prosecute their heterodox constituents, only scattered cases survive in the registers. Depositions from the few cases that we have, however, indicate that London's anonymity was a refuge for some who fled the authorities in other dioceses and that it was a center from which books were bought.[76] It seems likely that the Lollard and Protestant communities in London were intertwined to some extent in the 1520s, although the makeup of both groups is obscure.[77]

The London Lollard community was closely connected with another group of Lollards outside the metropolis in Essex. Lollards had been holding conventicles in the city of Colchester and in several towns west of there, especially Steeple Bumpstead and Braintree, from at least the 1490s on. While scattered evidence exists for prosecutions in the 1490s and the first two decades of the sixteenth century, fairly full information of a prosecution Bishop Tunstall undertook in the late 1520s was preserved by Foxe and used by John Strype in his *Ecclesiastical Memorials*.[78] Long depositions by John

Hacker of London, John Pykas of Colchester, and John Tyball of Steeple Bumpstead provide a detailed picture of Lollard activities in Essex. Surviving wills and government documents reveal further information about these Lollards and their relationships to one another.

The records for the Lollard community in Kent are unfortunately less full. As with the Chiltern Hills, Kent may have had a continuous tradition of heresy from the early fifteenth century. There is some evidence for heresy in the Weald in the 1420s; investigations in the same villages in 1511, almost a century later, found that Lollards were still active there. The Lollard community in Kent was centered in three areas: the Weald, especially the town of Tenterden; Maidstone and surrounding villages; and the city of Canterbury. Warham dealt seriously with the heretics in his diocese, burning five (one for relapse, four for contumacy) and incarcerating another five.[79]

I develop my arguments about gender and Lollard communities over the next five chapters. Chapter 2, "The Lollards of Coventry," presents a case study of the heretics uncovered in that important Midland city at the beginning of the sixteenth century. Serendipitous survival of evidence allows us not only to see the inner workings of this community's conventicles and other activities but also to examine the frontiers between Lollardy and orthodoxy and the importance of gender and social status in religious choices.

Chapters 3, 4, and 5 investigate themes that arise from the case of the Coventry Lollards, as the study broadens outward to consider other groups as well. Chapter 3, "The Lollard Communities," explores the composition, activities, and authority patterns of the sect's communities, examining both the more formal conventicles (conventionally the purview of men) and less formal situations (the sphere of most medieval women's activity). I argue that women and men tended to participate in Lollardy in different ways, because of the social and economic construction of male and female lives in late medieval England, and the prevailing ideology about women's and men's proper spheres of action.

Chapter 4, "Lollards and the Family," considers in detail one important social factor in men's and women's participation in Lollard communities: family relationships. Women most often took part in Lollard activities in the context of their families; the familial nature of the sect paradoxically both favored and restricted their involvement. Men, on the other hand, were much less likely to be related to another heretic, but, as fathers and husbands, the sect's teachings conferred upon them a commanding and responsible role.

Chapter 5, "Gender and Social Status," examines the more prominent Lollards, female and male, in order to probe in wider perspective questions about social rank raised by the example of the Coventry Lollard group. Influential Lollard women tended to come from relatively higher socioeconomic backgrounds than those of other members of the sect; leading men, by contrast, came from a range of stations. Indeed, evidence from various communities suggests that the prominence of men of the artisanry in the Lollard sect reflects both the heresy's political and religious incompatibility with elite men and its suitability for men of lower estate. This chapter also looks at how far women's activities and authority in Lollard communities could stretch; with the exception of an extraordinary Coventry woman, Alice Rowley, even the most active and influential female Lollards confined their endeavors to informal situations rather than public teaching roles.

The sixth and concluding chapter, "Lollardy, Gender, and Late Medieval Religious Culture," considers the spiritual as well as social factors behind male predominance in the Lollard movement. The century before the Reformation, which historians have traditionally viewed as characterized by corruption at the higher levels of the Catholic Church and lassitude at the tier of parish clergy, was a period of profound lay creativity. The nature of late medieval religiosity varied considerably according to gender, social status, geography, and a host of other factors. To some extent, Lollardy may represent an attempt by artisan men to partake in a book-centered, self-directed piety just as their social superiors did. The Lollard creed also represented a rebellion against another type of religiosity, that which revolved around the cult of saints, a devotional style particularly characteristic of women of lower status. Lollards despised pilgrimages, images, and the invocation of saints; these practices were not scriptural and thus, they argued, had no divine sanction. But in denigrating the cult of saints, Lollards attacked the aspect of late medieval Catholicism that was most open to individual creativity, especially for the relatively powerless; it also erased any specifically female figures from the pantheon of the divine and quasi-divine. Due in part to the creed's lack of attractions for women of the lower orders, few women became involved independently in Lollard communities.

2. The Lollards of Coventry

The records of the prosecution depict especially vividly the Lollard community active in the city of Coventry in the early sixteenth century. The court book recording the depositions of those brought before Bishop Geoffrey Blyth in 1511 and 1512 brings to life the people of this important Midlands town as they went about their heretical business. While in many respects the Coventry Lollards were unusual as compared to their counterparts in other communities, a case study of this Lollard group provides a useful basis on which to ground further discussion. Just as we can study the heterodox in order to reveal hidden facets of the orthodox, so can the Coventry Lollard community's atypical aspects highlight and give nuance to our understanding of other Lollard groups.

Lollardy in Coventry was marked by three relatively unusual aspects. First, the community, while essentially unified at the level of its leadership, practiced its faith in three segregated groups: married couples, men, and women. The various groupings within the Coventry Lollard community and the activities that defined a person's identity as a Lollard underline the importance of social dynamics in religious life. Second, probably because of the existence of all-female conventicles, unparalleled elsewhere in the Lollard movement, women played a much greater role in Coventry Lollardy than in other communities. The depositions in the Lichfield Court Book provide us a full picture of the range of these women's religious lives. Third, while a few socially elite women participated in the heretical sect, men of that station did not, although strong suspicions were cast in their direction. The religious leanings of men of the civic oligarchy had much in common with Lollard ideas, but the men's social and cultural milieu predisposed them to orthodoxy. The borders between the devotional styles and preoccupations of the Lollard groups and of a certain part of the orthodox world — the male bourgeois elite — shed light on the interaction of gender, politics, and modes of religious observance in the late medieval English town.

The Lollard Prosecutions in Coventry

Coventry was one of the most important cities in England in the late Middle Ages, ranking perhaps third or fourth in the kingdom in size and economic importance. Ironically, it flourished in the wake of the dislocation of the Black Death and acted from the second half of the fourteenth century as a central hub of the commercial network of the Midlands. Coventry was also a center of ecclesiastical administration: it shared an episcopal see with Lichfield and was the site of a number of important religious houses, including a large Benedictine priory. From 1451 it constituted a county unto itself. Although Coventry was still one of the most important cities at the time of the accession of the Tudors, by then the city had entered into a serious decline.[1]

The city's prosperity had been built on a single industry, textile manufacture, and when the cloth trade began to falter in England generally, so did Coventry's economy. The decline began in the 1440s as the city suffered under the combined assault of a general slump in the textile industry, the diversion of needed capital to royal coffers for the wars of the period, and the era's ever-present famine and disease. A short-lived recovery in the 1490s was followed by a much more serious and ever-worsening decline in the first three decades of the sixteenth century, capped by a particular crisis between 1518 and 1525. The most obvious signs of this "desolation" (as Charles Phythian-Adams called it) were severe depopulation and a reluctance to invest in the city's industries.[2]

Coventry was thus still an important city but one whose fortunes were seriously deteriorating in the period for which we have evidence of significant Lollard activity. As in the rest of the Midlands, little or no Lollardy was uncovered in Coventry between the early 1430s and the 1480s.[3] The first sign of a Lollard revival in the city (or, perhaps more properly, a revival in the prosecution of Lollards) came in March 1486. Bishop John Hales brought a number of suspected Lollards before his court, including Roger Brown; John Phisicion, alias Blumston; and John Smyth.[4] They were charged with various Lollard heresies against the eucharist and the veneration of images; their vilification of a local shrine, the image of the Virgin in the Tower, was especially noted.

The limited scope of Hales's prosecution in 1486, however, did not succeed in crushing Coventry's Lollard community. At least one of the most prominent Lollards in 1511, Roger Landesdale, was already active in

1486, and the court book recording Blyth's prosecution of 1511 shows that Brown, Phisicion, and Smyth continued to proselytize others after their abjurations. Another important Lollard from Blyth's prosecution, Alice Rowley, was also active by the early 1490s, although no direct connection can be drawn between her and the Lollards of Brown's generation.[5]

The next significant attempt to eradicate heresy in the city was made by Bishop Geoffrey Blyth in 1511–12,[6] coinciding with similar investigations in their dioceses by Bishop Fitzjames of London, Bishop Smith of Lincoln, and Archbishop Warham of Canterbury. Blyth began his pursuit against the group of heretics centered in Coventry in the autumn of 1511.[7] The proceedings continued until early December, resumed mid-January, and ended in March. While according to surviving ecclesiastical records only Joan Warde was handed over to the secular authorities to be burned (in March 1512), two annalists (obviously copying from the same tradition) record that seven heretics were burned that year in Coventry, including Joan Warde.[8]

In all, sixty-four suspected Lollards were brought before the bishop and his commissaries in 1511 and 1512. Most were willing to abjure their heresies, although some were obstinate and did not admit them until the second or third appearance.[9] Others, for whom the evidence was incomplete, were dismissed so that officials could make further inquiry against them, and they apparently never returned.[10] Sometimes, if the accused refused to admit their heresies, their fellow heretics who had deposed against them were brought back to the court to repeat their testimony.[11]

As in 1486, the prosecution of 1511–12 did not deter all those who abjured from continuing their Lollard practices. According to evidence in the city annals and that preserved by Foxe, authorities prosecuted seven members of the group a second time in 1520.[12] These included leading figures from 1511–12 (Robert Hachet, Thomas Bowen, and Joan Smyth) as well as others whom officials had not perceived to be as dangerous in the earlier prosecution (William Hawkyns, Thomas Wrixham, and John Archer).[13] The Bodleian annal also identifies Thomas Landesdale, hosier, brother-in-law to Joan Smyth; he was not named in the early prosecutions, although Richard Landesdale (his brother, formerly husband to Joan Smyth) and Roger Landesdale were.[14] Robert Silkby, another central figure from 1511–12, was burned in December 1521 or January 1522.[15]

The community uncovered in the 1511–12 prosecution had connections with Lollards in other towns or cities. Some Lollards who formed part of the Coventry group lived in nearby Birmingham and Leicester.[16] Coventry Lollards also had connections with two other centers of heresy in the early sixteenth century, Bristol and London, and received a visit from a "knowen man," a prominent Lollard, who stayed in the city for six days.[17]

The court book and the bishop's register implicate about 110 people in the group, 37 women (about one-third) and 73 men. As Fines notes, most of the adherents of the Coventry community were artisans.[18]

The Coventry Conventicles

The unusually full evidence for the Lollard community in Coventry gives us a great deal of valuable information about the inner workings of Lollard conventicles and gatherings, particularly the way in which the members of the community grouped themselves. The Lollards in the city divided by sex and marital status into three subgroups that met separately, for the most part. Interestingly, there are hints that orthodox parish life may have witnessed the same divisions.[19] The first two groups, married couples and men, had counterparts in virtually all the other Lollard communities; the all-female group, however, was unique.

CONVENTICLES OF MARRIED COUPLES

When both husband and wife were interested in Lollardy, they usually participated in the sect together. A witness testified that Thomas Archer and his wife (unnamed), for instance, went often to the home of John Phisicion to receive instruction, while John Holbache and his wife (again unnamed) had conversations with Roger Landesdale. Deponents also referred to William and Katherine Revis most often in tandem, as if they customarily took part in Lollard activities together. None of these heretics was judged to be prominent: neither Archer, his wife, Holbache's wife, nor Katherine Revis appeared before the bishop; William Revis did appear but denied the charges against him; and Holbache was judged by the bishop's commissaries not to have participated fully in the Lollard group.[20]

One group of interrelated couples was nearer to the inner circle of the Coventry community and merits a closer look. At the core of this group were three siblings: Thomas Villers, Thomasina Bradeley, and the wife of Thomas Banbrooke (whose first name we are never told). The husbands of the two sisters, Richard Bradeley and Thomas Banbrooke, were also active Lollards; whether they were already adherents of the sect when they married is unknown.[21] At least two of the three Villers siblings, Thomas and

Thomasina, learned their heresies from their mother, Mother Villers, a literate and active Lollard who at one time had abjured at Leicester.[22] Mother Villers may have been dead by 1511, as she did not appear in court.

Mother Villers had taught Thomasina by reading to her, as Margaret Landesdale related:

> Eight or nine years past [1502 or 1503], the mother of Thomas Villers, together with her daughter who is now the wife of Bradeley, entered into her house and remained there from noon until six o'clock. The said mother read in a certain large book, while her daughter was present there and listened, as Margaret's husband [Roger] lay ill in his bed.[23]

Although Thomasina Bradeley proved to be an unusually intransigent witness, denying all the charges against her when brought before the bishop, she had apparently followed in her mother's footsteps. Margaret Landesdale reported that several years after Thomasina had come to the Landesdales' with her mother, she came on her own in order to communicate with Margaret's husband, Roger, and she enthusiastically listened to him read at gatherings at the Banbrookes' or her own home.[24]

Thomas Villers, her brother, was a twenty-seven-year-old spicer who received instruction first from his mother and then from Robert Silkby. Like Thomasina, he at first refused to give testimony when he was initially brought before the court, but when he was confronted in the courtroom by Robert Silkby, Richard Bradeley, Thomas Banbrooke, William Lodge, Roger Landesdale, and John Jonson, he broke down and admitted that he had indeed associated with Lollards. He had not told the truth before, he said, because he had promised the others, especially Silkby, not to divulge their secrets. Most testimony regarding his activities linked him to Robert Silkby and his brothers-in-law, Richard Bradeley and Thomas Banbrooke. Interestingly, in light of the "family" nature of Lollardy among the Villers, there is no sign that Thomas Villers's wife (identified in his deposition as the daughter of Thomas Redhell of Birmingham) was involved in the group.[25]

The commitment to Lollardy of the third sibling, the wife of Thomas Banbrooke, is less clear than the adherence of her brother and sister. She was reported several times to be of the sect, in each case coupled either with her husband or her sister. But other evidence indicates that she may have been only reluctantly involved in the movement: Thomas Wrixham reported that she told her brother-in-law Richard Bradeley that he should hand over his book of heresy to the bishop so it could be burned. She did not appear personally before the bishop; her husband denied the charges against her on her behalf, and the bishop appears to have accepted this.[26] Certainly the evidence does not indicate as strong a connection as her sister's with the Lollard community.

Her husband, Thomas Banbrooke, however, and her sister's husband, Richard Bradeley, participated fully in the community; they were said to have held meetings in their houses where the Gospels and other books were read. Banbrooke, like his sister- and brother-in-law, was at first unwilling to admit his heresy when examined. He ultimately received a lighter penance than Bradeley, although this cannot always be used as a reliable gauge of guilt.[27]

It was in some ways natural for couples of married Lollards to participate in the movement together. In the case of the Villers siblings, the shared Lollard convictions of at least Thomas, Thomasina, Thomasina's husband Richard Bradeley, and their brother-in-law Thomas Banbrooke served to provide a ready-made context in which to discuss their beliefs. Nonetheless, it is striking that both the third sibling, Thomas Banbrooke's wife, and Thomas Villers's wife were less enthusiastic. Notwithstanding the example of Thomasina Bradeley and a few other women like her, it was common for husbands to be more zealous about Lollardy than their wives.

MEN'S CONVENTICLES

Coventry also had conventicles that were made up primarily of men, most of whom were not married to known Lollards. The core of this group included Roger Landesdale, Robert Silkby, Robert Hachet, Balthasar Shugborow, Thomas Ward, Thomas Bowen, Robert Peg, John Atkynson, Thomas Flesshour, Thomas Lieff, John Longhald, William Hawkyns, John Davy, David Clerc, and Thomas Abell. They ranged in age from twenty-two to sixty-seven, and all except Shugborow were craftsmen. They were by no means prominent men in an economic, social, or political sense.[28]

The most influential among this all-male group were the older men whose heretical careers were long-lived enough to connect them to those Lollards prosecuted by Bishop Hales in 1486. Thomas Flesshour (a sixty-seven-year-old whose trade is not recorded) hosted many conventicles and had a connection to Roger Brown, who had given him heretical books around 1493. The home of Robert Hachet, leather-dresser, age sixty, also served as a meeting-place for heretical men, according to the reports of his servant Rose Furnour.[29]

Roger Landesdale and Robert Silkby were leading figures of the male conventicles and the community as a whole. Many of the gatherings of men were held in the home of Roger Landesdale, a sixty-three-year-old tailor. Landesdale, first taught his heresy by Roger Brown, had been active in the community from at least the 1480s. He taught many in Coventry, especially through public reading, with which he was particularly associated. He read often in his house and others came there to consult his library, much of which he had inherited from his relative Richard Landesdale.[30] He was keenly concerned with secrecy, perhaps affected by witnessing the prosecution of others of his kind. The judge asked him about "secret words" that the Lollards used, and he replied that they were, "May we all drinke of a cuppe and at the departing, god kepe you and god blesse you."[31] Other evidence points to the use of a password: Thomas Wrixham reported that John Davy was able to enter a meeting of Thomas Abell, Robert Silkby, and Thomas Bowen "by means of a certain word."[32] Landesdale also attempted to prevent others from overhearing him by reading in a room with a closed door, and he often taught and discussed Lollard doctrine out of doors, while walking "in the park."[33] Landesdale was one of the kingpins of the Lollard community in Coventry. He knew everyone there, and he was also acquainted with others outside the city, such as the "foreign painter" named Dowcheman who lived at Leicester.[34]

Robert Silkby was another leader in the Coventry Lollard community —Bishop Blyth, in a letter to his fellow Bishop Smith of Lincoln, referred to him as "one of the chieff heretikes here."[35] He was a shoemaker by trade, originally from Leicester, and had lived in Coventry for the previous eighteen years. He was among the first brought before the bishop, and his arrest sent waves of panic into the community. The Coventry Lollards had reason to worry, for Robert Silkby gave a great deal of information to the bishop. He also appeared at least twice as witness for the prosecution when others denied the allegations made in his depositions.[36]

Robert Silkby was a valuable witness for the bishop because he was at the heart of the community and had had contacts with almost all its members, both women and men. To admit to conversation with Silkby was treated by the court and by the deponents as tantamount to a confession of heresy. He taught many and converted at least William Hawkyns, John Atkynson, and Robert Peg. He also acted as librarian for the community: his activity in distributing and trading books to different parties (even in different towns) must have been invaluable. He had connections with Lollards outside Coventry—he knew heretics in Bristol and Leicester and, perhaps on his way to the latter city, apparently visited the heretical parish priests of Leicestershire, Dr. Alcock, Ralph Kent, and William Kent.[37]

He abjured his heresy in 1511 when brought before Bishop Blyth, but he, like some of the others, continued his heretical activities. When seven others were arrested and executed in 1520, he fled Coventry. He was able to live elsewhere under the pseudonym of Dumbleby for about two years, but finally he was apprehended and burned as a relapsed heretic in December 1521 or January 1522.[38]

Largely because of the greater freedom late medieval English society accorded to men's activities, the men in the Coventry community were at greater liberty than were the women. Connections with Lollards outside of Coventry, such as Silkby's with the heretical priests of Leicestershire, were also almost entirely the province of men. We shall see, however, that women could take advantage of the men's network when they had to.

Women's Conventicles

Coventry's conventicles made up of married couples and men were fairly typical of other Lollard communities. The women's group and its most prominent member, Alice Rowley, made Coventry unique. A group of about fourteen women, mostly widowed or single, participated in Lollard activities almost always in an all-female environment, with occasional visits from leading men like Landesdale or Silkby. This phenomenon has no parallel in other Lollard communities; women Lollards outside Coventry apparently took part in mixed conventicles or did not attend gatherings at all. There are, however, analogues in other religious movements. Quaker women met separately from men in order to discuss "women's concerns"; mixed meetings were run by and for men, and women were to be present but remain silent.[39] Weekly "class meetings" of eighteenth-century Cheshire Methodists were segregated by sex and marital status, and all-female bands were led by women.[40]

While Lollardy has sometimes been seen as an arena in which vigorous women were able to act prominently and publicly alongside men,[41] only one woman can be said to have truly fulfilled that role: Alice Rowley. As a woman of high social standing and unusual charisma, she was able to achieve a position within her Lollard community that no other female Lollard could.

In 1511 Alice Rowley was the widow of a prominent mercer, William Rowley, who had been a merchant of the Calais Staple and a landowner and who had acted as sheriff, mayor, justice of the peace, and Master of the Holy Trinity Guild (the senior merchant guild) before he died in 1505.[42] Historians have sometimes depicted William Rowley as a Lollard,[43] but Joan Warde's deposition shows that he was not favorably disposed toward his wife's activities.[44]

Alice Rowley's early Lollard activities may have been curtailed by the influence and authority of her Catholic husband, as her most active days were apparently in the years after his death in 1505. As a widow, she was unencumbered by a non-Lollard husband and was without male Lollard relatives who could claim to speak for her within the heretical community. A strong group of other women who were similarly without male Lollard relatives (although often with female relatives) allowed Alice Rowley an environment in which she could be active and authoritative. Perhaps as a result of her activities among women, she was able to extend her authority to male groups as well; unlike most other women in the Lollard sect, her contributions to the community in Coventry were respected by both men and women.

Alice Rowley was a charismatic and intelligent woman; she was also literate, which was unusual for a woman, even a Lollard. Perhaps most important, her socioeconomic status was high, more elevated than that of any man in the community. This in itself did not give her authority—another female Lollard, Joan Smyth, shared Alice Rowley's high social background but not her position in the community.[45] In combination with her personality, her literacy, and her widowhood, however, Rowley's elite status allowed her a role no other woman was able to play.

Alice Rowley was the most prominent of the female Lollards in Coventry. Her career as a heretic will be discussed in more detail,[46] but here it is important to understand the context from which she came. Her success was due to her social status, her own intelligence and charisma, and the cohort of active female Lollards.

At the core of the women's group in Coventry were Alice Rowley, Joan Warde, Joan Smyth, Agnes Jonson, Agnes Yong, Juliana Yong, Agnes de Bakehouse, Margaret Grey, Elizabeth Gest, Agnes Corby, Agnes Brown, the wife of Bromley, Rose Furnour, and Mother Margaret. Many of the women in this group were single or widowed[47]—all but Joan Smyth, Margaret Grey, and Elizabeth Gest fall into this category. Others were married, but only two women who had strong connections to this group were married to other Lollards (Joan Gest and the recently widowed wife of Roger Bromley). Bromley's wife had been Alice Rowley's servant and was often present with Alice, Agnes de Bakehouse, and Robert Silkby in the home of Mother Margaret, and her husband communicated often with male Lollards, including Roger Landesdale and Robert Silkby.[48] Other women, Joan Smyth, Elizabeth Gest, Margaret Grey, Margery Locock, the wife of Bluet, Isabella Trussell, and Katherine Edmund, were married to men not known to be suspected of Lollardy. Some of these women became involved in Lollardy because of family connections rather than through their current husbands: Joan Smyth's first husband, Richard Landesdale, had converted her; Elizabeth Gest's mother was Agnes Corby; and Margaret Grey's mother was Agnes Jonson.[49]

The story of Joan Warde, alias Wasshingbury, is particularly interesting. She first became a Lollard about 1491, under Alice Rowley's instruction, but soon after her conversion she was forced to flee from Coventry "out of fear of William Rowley,"[50] who apparently did not approve of his wife's association with heretics. Using the Lollard network, she was escorted by Robert Bastell to Northampton, where she stayed with a leather-dresser for about five months. After that she moved on to London and lived there for about the same length of time at the home of a certain bedder named Blackbury, whose wife, Joan, was a Lollard. Through Lollard connections in London, she married Thomas Wasshingbury, a heretical shoe-maker.[51] Thomas and Joan stayed in London for three years. They then moved to Maidstone, where both were arrested and questioned about heresy along with fifteen others. In August 1495, before Dr. Cambreton, commissary of the Archbishop of Canterbury, the Wasshingburys and the others abjured their heretical opinions. The authorities then released the heretics, but not before they had been branded ("signati") with the letter *h* on their jaws. They performed penance in Maidstone, Canterbury, and London.[52]

Sometime after 1495 Joan returned to Coventry, apparently without her husband, who may have been burned in Kent.[53] Once she returned to the place where she had first learned her heresy, she resumed her contact with Alice Rowley and other Coventry Lollards, becoming one of the most important female Lollards, teaching Wycliffite doctrines and passing around books. She was brought before the bishop several times in 1511 and 1512: one appearance was undated and the others were on 16 November 1511 and 11–12 March 1512. Her final trial was the last in Blyth's round of prosecutions in 1511–12; the tardiness of this proceeding was probably due to Blyth's having sent to Canterbury for information about her first abjuration.[54] Joan's status as an abjured heretic would have been obvious from the beginning from the mark on her jaw.

Joan admitted her heresies in all her appearances. She acknowledged that her errors were due to "lack of grace" ("carentia gracie"), and she said that she was contrite. As was customary, authorities gave her an opportunity to give a reasonable cause for her relapse, but she could do no more than submit herself to the mercy of the judge. Judge Robert Canlyn, the bishop's commissary, gave her the penalty of the relapsed, and the sheriffs of Coventry, being present, accepted her into their custody.[55] The procession of Joan Warde and her fellow Lollard Alice Rowley through the streets was recorded by one of the city's annalists:

> Then were certaine persons peched of heresy whereof some bare faggott's before ye procession on the markett day. The principall were Mrs Rowley & Ioan Ward.[56]

The same annalist records that Joan was burned, along with six others.[57]

Unlike Alice Rowley, Joan Warde was not the wife of a prominent man, but nonetheless she was able to achieve some prominence in the Lollard group, especially among its female members. Her career is a testament to the ability of a Lollard (even a woman) to travel extensively around southern England using the sect's connections.

While Joan Warde had contacts with men and women in the community, her friend Agnes Jonson (also known as "little moder Agnes")[58] exemplifies the tendency among most of the female Lollards to associate mostly or exclusively with women. Agnes Jonson was an active Lollard: she was literate (Rose Furnour said she "knows best how to read"),[59] she owned books, she was involved in the conversion of new members to Lollardy, and she had at least one contact with a Lollard in London. But her known connections were solely with women such as her daughter Margaret Grey and her friends Alice Rowley, Joan Warde, Rose Furnour, and Agnes de Bakehouse. The only suggestion that she had any contact with the men in the community was Agnes de Bakehouse's report that Balthasar Shugborow had heard that she taught her daughter.[60]

Rose Furnour's example is also instructive. Rose was twenty-four years old when she was brought to court; until just before her appearance, she had been the servant of Robert Hachet, a prominent heretic. Although she was in Hachet's employ, she said that Agnes Jonson and Joan Warde, two women, had instructed her in her opinions. Hachet also later taught her, but her deposition shows that she belonged to the circle of women, not to Hachet's cohort. The information that she gave the court about who came and went from Hachet's home indicates that she was not a participant in their activities.[61]

Other women were perhaps not as exclusive in their contacts, but the readings and discussions that these women attended were either all-female or mostly female gatherings.[62] The bishop's court seems to have thought of these women as a discrete unit as well. Six women appeared together before the bishop on 22 January 1512: Agnes Jonson, Agnes de Bakehouse, Agnes Yong, Agnes Corby, Agnes Brown, and Elizabeth Gest.[63] Similarly, Alice Rowley and Joan Warde were to perform their penances together, although Joan's was more severe.[64]

These groups of men and women in Coventry by no means existed in isolation from one another; chief heretics tended to have contacts with all groups. Robert Silkby, for instance, was frequently in the presence of the women. He often met with Alice Rowley, Agnes de Bakehouse, Bromley's wife, Mother Margaret, and Agnes and Juliana Yong. Thomas Bowen also had contacts with some women in the group. Agnes de Bakehouse said that she often communicated with him in the Benedictine priory church of Coventry, and Alice Rowley and Joan Warde also had meetings with him. Moreover, the chief women, especially Alice Rowley, tended to become involved with the men's groups. Rowley went to Landesdale's house often to hear him read, and she herself read there. She also frequently went to Thomas Acton's house over a period of four years. Joan Warde, too, admitted that she had had contact with Roger Landesdale, Robert Silkby, Robert Hachet, Thomas Bowen, and Thomas Abell.[65]

As one might expect, women played a large part in the conversion of other women. Alice Rowley was, again, particularly prominent. She taught at least Joan Warde, Juliana Yong, and, together with Joan Warde, Agnes Corby; one suspects that she was also a great influence on other women, such as her servants Bromley's wife and Margaret White. Alice taught men as well: Thomas Acton said that it was she who had first led him into the sect, while Thomas Bowen said that she and Landesdale taught him about the sacrament of the altar. Alice's pupil, Joan Warde, taught Agnes Corby and Isabella Trussell and, as already seen, she and Agnes Jonson converted Rose Furnour.[66]

WOMEN'S RELATIONSHIPS AND ACTIVITIES
WITHIN THE LOLLARD COMMUNITY

Two significant relationships that had a bearing on conversion to Lollardy — family and servant-employer — recur in the records. They offer clues as to how the heresy was spread, particularly, in the case of Coventry, among women.

Many of the Lollards in the Coventry community were related to one another. The number of female Lollards who had children also involved in the movement is especially striking. Besides Mother Villers and her three children, other mother-child relationships include Agnes and Juliana Yong; Agnes Corby and Elizabeth Gest; Agnes Jonson and Margaret Grey; Joan Smyth and two daughters, one of whom was the wife of Northopp; Alice Lye and William Lodge; and Agnes Brown and daughter.[67] There were other family relationships as well: John Harris and Bluet's wife were brother and sister; Thomas Lieff was son-in-law to Margaret Landesdale; John Bull was the nephew of John Phisicion; Joan Smyth was probably the sister-in-law of Roger Landesdale; and Agnes Brown was possibly the sister-in-law of Roger Brown.[68] The Coventry Lollard community was unusual in that women were more likely than men to have a family member involved in the movement; other Lollard communities show the opposite pattern.[69] This reflects and explains the relatively strong role women played in Coventry Lollardy, as family relationships may have been particularly important for bringing women into the community.

Another potentially influential relationship that recurs in the records is that between servant and employer. Some Lollards were converted or taught by their employers: Katherine Baker was reportedly instructed by her mistress Alice Flexall (otherwise unknown); Joan Gest learned her heresy from her master, John Smyth; and Robert Hachet had a hand in the instruction of Rose Furnour. Other Lollards had servants who were Lollards, although no indication is given as to whether they were converted by their employers or were already Lollards when they went into service. Alice Rowley had two servants, the wife of Bromley and Margaret White. Joan Smyth's son-in-law Richard Northopp, mercer, used to be her servant (or perhaps more correctly, the apprentice of Joan's husband, draper Richard Smyth).[70]

The activities of the women were no different from those of the men: gatherings of Lollards, big or small, revolved around the reading of books and discussions about the sacrament of the eucharist, images, pilgrimages, and giving alms to the poor. Reading was particularly important, and at least five of the women amongst the Coventry Lollards—Agnes Jonson, Alice Rowley, Mother Villers, Juliana Yong, and Thomasina Bradeley[71]— were literate. This was a remarkably high rate of literacy among women; unlike most women in other communities, Coventry women did not have to rely on men to read their texts to them.[72]

Many more than these five women possessed books, which they passed around to one another and to others in the community. Some Lollards possessed books without being able to read them; Thomas Abell, for instance, who received a book from Joan Warde, was unable to read it and wanted to arrange for someone else to read it to him.[73] But unsurprisingly, the literate were most deeply involved in the book trade. Alice Rowley, Thomas Acton deposed, had given him a book, while she herself said Thomas Banbrooke had loaned her a book of the Gospels which she in turn loaned to "a certain Dawson."[74] Alice also had a book from Roger Landesdale entitled "De vita Thobie"; he borrowed from her "another book of the entire old law in English made to be carried around by hand" and a book of the Epistles of Paul.[75] Landesdale reported that she brought the book of the Pauline Epistles over to his house for him to read three months before his examination, and then she took it home again.[76] As we saw earlier, Juliana Yong, frightened that a book would be discovered in her possession, used Alice Rowley's "chapell chambre" as a hiding place.[77]

Joan Smyth, a wealthy woman like Alice Rowley, also had a number of books, although she could not read. She had inherited the books of her first husband, Richard Landesdale, who died about 1502–3. She kept these books, the Acts of the Apostles, the Epistles of Paul, and the Commandments, for three months after her husband's death. But, as she feared they would be discovered in her custody, she gave them to Roger Landesdale, probably her husband's brother.[78] She seems, however, to have had other books later. Alice Rowley said that she had given Joan a Psalter and a book of the Commandments.[79] Joan borrowed "a certain book of the Passion of Christ and Adam" from Master Longland for three weeks, which Roger Landesdale read to her in a closed room.[80] She presumably then gave the book to Alice Rowley to return to Master Longland, for when Alice came to visit her while she was lying sick in bed, she asked Alice whether she had returned the book to him. Alice replied that she had not because she had decided there was no need.[81]

Joan Warde also had at least two books of her own: a book "de mortuo et egrotante" that Silkby had given her two years before, which she subsequently traded to Thomas Abell, and a book of the Commandments, which Agnes Jonson read in for three years.[82] Agnes Jonson admitted that she had a book "de Thobia" and that her daughter Margaret Grey had another such book. This same book (or perhaps another) Agnes traded to Joan Blackbury, a Lollard living in London.[83] Isabella Trussell was also reported to own an Old Testament that had belonged to Thomas Forde, and she admitted that she had had "librum pessimum."[84]

The women not only owned books but also discussed various elements of Lollard doctrine among themselves, as did the rest of the Lollard community.[85] Alice Rowley, Joan Ward, and Agnes Yong were charged with dogmatizing against the sacrament of the altar, pilgrimages, and the veneration of images.[86] Alice Rowley was particularly active in preaching her ideas about the sacrament of the altar. She told Agnes Corby that the host was not the real body of Christ but was only offered in memory of Christ's passion.[87] She also admitted to saying "How can the preiste make god?"[88] and discoursed on giving alms to paupers rather than paying tithes or making offerings to images. Agnes Corby said that Alice often spoke on the Gospel "Noli timere pusilus grex" (Luke 12:32); the verse that followed told readers of the Wycliffite Bible, "Selle ʒe tho thingis that ʒe han in possessioun, and ʒiue ʒe almes."[89] Rose Furnour, perhaps learning from Alice, admitted she, too, often spoke about the same gospel.[90]

Coventry had the most active women in the Lollard movement for a number of reasons. The urban context allowed women to form all-female conventicles; these afforded women the opportunity to take prominent roles in gatherings without contravening social and biblical conventions that women should not publicly teach in the presence of men. Outside Coventry, evidence for women's participation in Lollard conventicles is rare, as we will see in the next chapter. Involvement of high-status women such as Alice Rowley and Joan Smyth probably lent legitimacy and perhaps cachet to the community. The women of Coventry were also more likely than women in other communities to be literate, and there is evidence that they taught each other to read. More women without male relatives also participated in the Coventry community than elsewhere: the role of widows in particular is much higher in this group than in other communities. Women who became involved in the sect outside familial and especially marital bonds were more likely to play independent roles in the movement. These factors reinforced one another, probably attracting more women to the sect, which in turn made the female gatherings stronger.

Nonetheless, it must be emphasized that the situation in Coventry was, as far as we know, unique to the Lollard movement and, even in Coventry, the role of women was not as great as that of men. While many Coventry women were apparently drawn to the movement either independently or through female relatives rather than in the context of a patriarchal family, men still dominated the community as a whole. Women were able to create in Coventry an enclave for themselves, in which they could be more active than women in other communities. With the exception of the remarkable Alice Rowley, though, they did not reach out to become authoritative in men's groups as well. The social restrictions on women's public activities, their more limited mobility, and, perhaps above all, the difficulty of obtaining the respect and recognition necessary for authority and influence prevented them from ever becoming truly equal participants.

Coventry's Civic Oligarchy and the Lollard Community

One of the central differences between the men's and the women's groups in Coventry was the social status of their leaders. While women like Alice Rowley and Joan Smyth were of the city's oligarchical elite, men like Roger Landesdale and Robert Silkby were humble tailors and shoemakers. But some of the depositions in the court book also implicate men of much higher standing, albeit almost always by rumor or hearsay. Were these accusations justified?

Some historians, especially Imogen Luxton, have argued that several important men as well as women from the city's governing elite were intimately involved in the Lollard community. They were not brought before the authorities, Luxton contends, because of their wealth and influence.[91] But while these men (more numerous even than Luxton notices) were connected to one another and implicated by deponents in the heresy, the balance of evidence indicates that they remained on the orthodox side of the divide, even while two women of their social level crossed the line into Lollardy.

First, the case for the prosecution. The argument Luxton makes for the involvement of the male civic elite in Lollardy has some support. A number of men, prominent in the civic oligarchy[92] of Coventry and closely associated to one another, were named as Lollards by those examined in the court book, although they were not brought before the bishop.

A central figure in the clique was James Preston, D.Th. (1479–80), who was admitted as vicar of St. Michael's parish, Coventry, in 1488 and died by 1507.[93] Alice Rowley said that he had borrowed a book of the "new law" from her and had later returned it, and she was of the opinion that Preston favored her and her sect.[94] Preston was evidently a learned and pious man, and his contributions to the Lollard community would have been considerable if he had indeed favored it.

Deponents reported that other prominent men were rumored to be Lollards. Two Lollards said they had heard that Banwell was of the sect; a William Banwell, mercer, was fairly prominent in civic affairs from 1501 until his death in 1531.[95] The Coventry Lollards also thought Thomas Forde and possibly his brother William were suspect. Two people suggested that Roger Bromley must be of the sect because he was apprenticed to Master Forde (either Thomas or William), while another reported that Isabella Trussell had an Old Testament that had belonged to Thomas Forde. Both Thomas and William Forde were important citizens; Thomas was active from 1461 to 1510, and William was active from 1474 to 1508, serving in the mayoralty in 1497.[96]

Some Coventry Lollards had actually spoken about religious matters with these men. Roger Landesdale said that he had often had communication with Derlyng, and Alice Rowley said that she had heard the same man speaking against the church. They perhaps referred to John Darlyng, capper, whose name recurs in the Leet Book between 1483 and 1510.[97] Roger Landesdale was specifically asked about Master Thomas Bayly, and he answered that he had discussed the Gospel of Matthew with him once, six years before, but since then had had no communication with him, although he had heard that Master Bayly had many books. Others said they too thought Bayly was a heretic. Thomas Bayly, mercer, was prominent in civic affairs from 1481; he was mayor in 1487 and justice of the peace and Master of the Holy Trinity Guild in 1494. He continued to be active in city politics until 1510.[98] Thomas Bonde was also cited twice by deponents—Thomas Flesshour said, for instance, that Bonde communicated with a number of Lollards about the book *The Life of Thobia*. A man of the same name was a prominent civic figure in Coventry from about 1485 to 1507, holding the position of mayor in 1498.[99] A Mistress (Magistra) Coke was mentioned twice in the court book: Thomas Clerc said that Acton's wife was friendly with Mistress Coke and that Mistress Coke had a husband, now dead, who was of the sect. Alice Rowley said that Mistress Coke "knows her secret" because she (Alice) had confided to her that she was going to destroy all her books. Mistress Coke may have been the widow of Richard Coke, mercer, who died in 1507—Jane Coke, "thridmaker," is referred to as his executrix in 1509.[100] Richard Coke was very prominent in the civic affairs of Coventry: he was sheriff in 1480, mayor in both 1486 and 1503, member of Parliament in 1491–92, and member of the commission of gaol delivery in 1500 and 1501 and of the commission of oyer and terminer in 1506.[101]

Even the two most prominent families of Coventry, the Wigstons and the Pysfords, were implicated by the Coventry Lollard community.[102] Thomas Bowen claimed to know them; Thomas Wrixham said that he had heard Bowen saying that Masters Wigston and Pysford had "very beautiful books of heresy," while Atkynson had also heard Bowen saying that Master

Pysford was of the sect.[103] The bishop followed up on this by asking Robert Hachet, a leading heretic, whether he had heard anything suspicious about Pysford or his daughter, who was married to Wigston (that is, William Pysford the Elder and his daughter Agnes, wife of William Wigston the Younger), but Hachet said that he knew nothing about them.[104]

Those prominent men who were named as "of the sect" by the Coventry Lollards were tied to one another through family relationships, intermarriage, and business partnerships. James Preston's will shows his connections to the oligarchy of the city: he describes William and Thomas Forde as "my kinsmen" and named William Pysford and William Forde as supervisors, while Richard Coke and Thomas Forde were witnesses.[105] William Pysford had two daughters who married into other families in the clique — Agnes married William Wigston, and Joan married into the Forde family, probably the son of William Forde.[106] William Pysford Jr. referred to another Joan Forde, daughter of Master William Forde, as his cousin.[107] William Pysford had ties with several other men in Coventry: he was the supervisor of the will of Richard Coke; he, John Padland, Richard Coke, and William Rowley were members of the commission of gaol delivery together in 1500 and 1501; and he and William Forde oversaw the founding of a hospital by the will of Thomas Bonde in 1507.[108] William Forde also founded a hospital, giving William Pysford and William Wigston power to change its provisions.[109] Other evidence indicates that Richard Coke, John Padland, and Thomas Bonde, along with a number of other men, owned property together.[110] Richard Coke named Agnes Banwell as his sister and left bequests to the children of William and Thomas Banwell; William Banwell, probably his brother-in-law, was also witness to the will.[111] Other ties between these men are illustrated in their testaments.[112]

There is no question that the deponents from the Coventry Lollard community identified a group of elite men who were tied to one another. But what do the court book allegations of their involvement in Lollardy really say? The accusations are based either on hearsay and rumor or on short conversations about vernacular books. There is no indication that any of the deponents, even Alice Rowley, widow of one of their number, was well acquainted with these substantial and important citizens. Certainly there is no evidence that these men participated in the community's conventicles. The connections between the men of the elite and the Coventry Lollards of the court book were tenuous. The testimony indicates one of two things: either these men were, in fact, Lollards (operating in a separate community of their own), or the deponents were mistaken.

Fortunately, further evidence survives outside the court book. Luxton first brought attention to two aspects of this evidence that she saw as corroborating the accusations in the court book: the terminology used in the wills of these men and their ownership of English scripture and other vernacular devotional material. But more recent scholarship has re-evaluated these two "indicators" of religiosity in the period before and during the Reformation, and they can no longer be taken as proof that these men were Lollards.

The wills of members of the Wigston and Pysford families and other men associated with them contain terminology that Luxton describes as anticipatory of Protestant tendencies.[113] Recent assessments of the use of testamentary terminology to determine confessional leanings, however, have warned that such use is problematic,[114] and these wills illustrate the pitfalls into which a scholar can fall. A full reading of the wills Luxton described as proto-Protestant places men of this clique squarely in the orthodox rather than the Lollard camp.

A number of the men named in the court book, James Preston (1506), William Forde (1508), Thomas Bonde (1507), William Pysford (1518), William Pysford Jr. (1518), Henry Pysford (1525), and William Wigston (1536), used similar preambles in their wills.[115] Although they closely resembled one another, these preambles were phrased unusually (although not as unusually as Luxton claimed[116]) when compared to the great majority of other wills written during this period, indicating that the standard formulas were eschewed in favor of something more personal. Some of the language prompted Luxton to make comparisons to Lutheran justification by faith. But while part of William Forde's 1508 preamble (which is an English version of Preston's Latin) bequeaths his soul to God in a way that anachronistically calls to mind solafideism—he hoped to be saved "not by my meritis but by the habundaunt goodnes of hym and his grete mercy in the which I have moost singlerly trustid"—the text viewed as a whole makes it clear that Forde was orthodox:

> And in the meritis and prayers of that moost singler comforte and helper of all wretchis and needy persons the clene virgyn and moder of God our lady seynt Mary. Also in the meritis of that gloryous Archangell seynt Mighell and in all the holy company of heven. And in the suffragis of the holy church.[117]

The wills of Thomas Bonde and the Pysfords, William Sr., William Jr., and Henry, similarly reflect a desire to partake in the merits of Christ through the intercession and prayers of Mary and all the blessed virgins, martyrs, apostles, confessors, and the whole company of saints.[118] The will of William Wigston, William Pysford Sr.'s son-in-law, has a preamble that without reflection might be classified as "Protestant":

> When yt shall pleas allmighty god to call me to his mercye I bequeth my soule to his infynyte goodnes, beseching hym to Receve it in to the nombr of them that shall be savid. And to be oone of the partetakers of the meritis of his blessed and bitter passion.[119]

But there is nothing inherently un-Catholic in these sentiments. Furthermore, and perhaps more importantly, Wigston's legacies — bequests for twenty trentalls and the maintenance of a chantry — were orthodox, showing that he did believe in the efficacy of prayers for the dead.[120]

The identification of Richard Coke as a Lollard similarly rests heavily on his will.[121] But the provisions of Coke's will indicate orthodoxy: the usual torches and tapers were to be provided, including one at the "high awter to geve light to the Sacrament." Bequests were made to the religious orders of the city to say *Dirige* and Mass for his soul (in opposition to the usual Lollard aversion to religious orders and to the doctrine of purgatory). He wanted a simple funeral, writing in his testament, "I will that there shall be as litell coste doon for me as may be with honestee."[122] Though, according to K. B. McFarlane, this request might indicate Lollard leanings, in fact it was not unusual among the orthodox.[123]

One of the bequests made by Coke in his will was of two English Bibles to two parish churches, and this brings us to the second plank in Luxton's platform: ownership of English scripture as a clear sign of heresy.[124] Again, recent scholarship has determined that this equation of ownership of an English Bible with Lollardy is faulty. Anne Hudson remarks that over 250 manuscripts of the Wycliffite translation of the Bible survive (most of them incomplete copies); this is a larger number than is known for any other English medieval text, with the nearest rival, *Prick of Conscience*, at 117 copies. Unless the number of Lollards is very much greater than has been previously thought, not all who owned Lollard Bibles were Lollards. In fact, as Hudson points out, Wycliffite Bibles were owned by religious houses, individual priests, nobles, and other laypeople whose orthodoxy was never brought into doubt.[125]

Other evidence points to the Wigstons' and the Pysfords' orthodoxy. William Pysford's will provided that a chantry be founded for one priest to sing mass daily;[126] in 1511, three Wigstons (William Wigston the Younger, husband of Agnes Pysford; Thomas Wigston, clerk, brother of William the Younger; and Roger Wigston, perhaps a cousin) also founded a perpetual chantry to sing mass in the collegiate church of St. Mary, Newark, in Leicester.[127] Members of both families were clergymen.[128] John Wigston, who, a chronicler noted, strove against Mariolatry while mayor of Coventry, was nonetheless Master of the Holy Trinity Guild (a bastion of late medieval pious orthodoxy) six years later.[129] William Pysford was also interested in the religious life of the crafts and guilds: he bequeathed in his will money and gowns to several crafts in Coventry for their pageants.[130] Two others suspected of Lollardy also had close relationships to the Guild of the Holy Trinity: Thomas Bayly was Master of the Guild in 1494 and Thomas Bonde left land to the Guild in order to maintain a chaplain, twelve poor men, and one woman, "to pray for the king, the gild, and especially the soul of Thomas Bonde, late of Coventry, draper."[131] Richard Coke was mayor of Coventry during the 1486 prosecution of Lollards.[132]

Another piece of evidence adduced for heresy among the Wigstons and Pysfords was the marriage between Agnes Pysford, daughter of William Pysford Sr., and William Wigston.[133] While William's Lollardy is uncertain, there is even less evidence for Agnes's: the only indication that she favored the heresy was the bishop's inquiry about her to the Lollard Robert Hachet, who said that he did not know her.[134] Her later actions indicate that by the 1530s, at least, she was a piously, even conservatively, orthodox woman. After her husband died in July 1536, she appeared before Bishop Longland of Lincoln and took a vow of widowed chastity before God, the Virgin, and all the saints.[135]

Altogether, the picture we have of the clique at the summit of Coventry society is of men who were active in religious affairs, pious, and interested in vernacular devotion, but who were orthodox, not heretical. How, then, to explain the allegations in the court book? The evidence of the testimony does not indicate anything certain except that the Coventry Lollards thought—mistakenly, I would argue—that these men had the same beliefs they did. They confused the similarities in the impulses behind active orthodox spirituality practiced by the civic elite with their own heretical piety.

Many of the rumors reported in the court book involved the ownership of English Bibles or devotional works; it seems likely that the Lollards were guilty of the same sort of assumption that some modern historians have made, namely that interest in vernacular scripture and devotional literature indicated heresy. Roger Landesdale, for instance, identified Lollards as those who owned English Bibles:

> When asked further why he believes that John Spon was a heretic, Roger says because John brought to him a certain book concerning the old law, translated into English.[136]

But not all Englishmen would have had the same reaction. When Dr. Preston borrowed a book of the new law from Alice Rowley and said that he favored her and her kind,[137] did he approve of her sect or of her reading of the scriptures? Were the "very beautiful books of heresy" that Thomas Wrixham said the Pysfords and Wigstons owned really heretical or were they copies of the scriptures or orthodox works of devotion?[138] I argue that the ownership of vernacular scripture by these families indicates less that they were heretics than that they were zealous Catholics eager to learn more about their faith.

Yet, clearly, investigators against heresy did see possession of English works by some people as evidence for Lollardy.[139] The distinction, I think, is one of social status. For people of the social groups from which Lollards came, literacy and ownership of books were signs of heresy. For those higher in status, possession of devotional works in the vernacular was a sign of respectable, "honeste" (as English civic records continually say), orthodox piety.[140] Thirty years later, Henry VIII's government was still willing to make such distinctions of gender and social status: the 1543 Act for the Advancement of True Religion forbade public or private reading of scripture by "woomen [noble and gentle women excepted] . . . artificers, prentises, journeymen, serving men of the degrees of yeomen or undre, husbandemen, [or] laborers."[141] Reading the Bible was appropriate and pious for some social groups, but unseemly and possibly even seditious when practiced by women or tradesmen.

Thomas More's attitude toward the English Bible is illuminating. He did not object to biblical translations *per se*, but said that one must guard against "faulty" translations (such as, More would say, Wyclif's version).[142] "Other" English Bibles are perfectly acceptable if approved by the authorities:

> But my self haue sene & can shew you bybles fayre & old wryten in englyshe / whych haue ben knowen & sene by ye byshop of ye dyocyse / & left in ley mennys handys & womens to suche as he knew for good & catholyke folke / yt vsed it with deuocyon & sobernesse. But of trouth all suche as are founden in the handys of heretykes / they vse to take away. But they do cause none to be burned as farre as euer I coulde wytte / but onely suche as be founden fautye.[143]

As there was no other English translation of the Bible until Tyndale's,[144] More can only be referring here, unknowingly, to copies of the Wycliffite Bible, without the prologue. He demonstrates that "good & catholyke folke" — and one suspects that More means people like him — could own English Bibles without necessarily being suspect of Lollardy. Richard Coke's bequest of his English scriptures to two parish churches indicates that he saw nothing inherently heretical in them.[145] Indeed, to early sixteenth-century elites, heresy inhered more in the mind that read the English scripture than in the scripture itself. Lollards and prominent Coventry burghers may have shared an interest in reading scripture, but this does not mean that both interpreted the act of reading an English Bible in the same way.

Another point of intersection between the Lollards and the members of this elite clique was a concern with the issue of poverty. Lollards like Alice Rowley often preached that it was better to give offerings to the poor than to shrines of saints.[146] The poor in their midst were also a matter of concern for William Forde, Thomas Bonde, William Pysford, and William, Thomas, and Roger Wigston, who all founded hospitals or almshouses for paupers.[147] While mayor of Coventry, William Pysford established a "Comien box," where money for the poor could be donated or bequeathed.[148]

While Lollard religiosity thus had much in common with that practiced by these men, such interests could easily be met within the bounds of orthodox piety as practiced by English elites in the late fifteenth and early sixteenth centuries. Moreover, there were considerable political disadvantages associated with adherence to heresy. Prominent men had more to lose by becoming Lollards than did either women of the same social station or men of lesser status. Participation in the civic life of a city like Coventry was inextricably intertwined with participation in the orthodox church, at least outwardly.[149] The economic crises that Coventry underwent during the decades around 1500 may have served to make it even less likely that the men of the oligarchy would challenge orthodoxy. The mayor was expected to be an upstanding Catholic — part of the ceremony of the office in Coventry included a twice-daily procession, accompanied by all his officers, from his house to his parish church where he heard morning mass and evensong.[150] In many urban centers, involvement in the most important religious fraternities was also essential to civic life; the Holy Trinity Guild and the corporation of the city of Coventry, for example, were interdependent, to the extent that one automatically became master of the guild after serving a term as mayor.[151]

Was this intimate connection between the Catholic Church and the corporation of a city a matter of form, or were members of the civic elites really expected to be devout Catholics? Would a man hide his Lollard inclinations in order to succeed in the outside world? Or would the bishop and society in general turn a blind eye to prominent members of the elite who were known to be Lollards?[152] This latter scenario always remains a possibility—the Cheynes of Buckinghamshire and the Durdants of Middlesex may have escaped prosecution because of their status[153]—but the cases of Coventry (where Bishop Geoffrey Blyth showed little hesitation in pursuing women of the elite such as Alice Rowley and Joan Smyth) and Colchester (where Thomas Mathew, a city councillor, was forced to abjure[154]) must also be noted.

Ultimately, the evidence for the lives of the men in the Coventry elite leads to the conclusion that Catholicism suited them better than Lollardy, for spiritual as well as political reasons. While similar attitudes toward activism in religion characterized both Lollardy and orthodoxy,[155] the social distinction between the members of the oligarchies and the artisan men who made up the leadership of most of the Lollard communities may have been crucial to their religious choices. The kind of orthodox devotion that characterized the urban elite tied into their social, political, and even economic roles and was to a great extent their own creation. But an active orthodox lay piety that revolved around the reading of scripture and devotional works was unavailable to those farther down the social scale. Artisan men, in joining a Lollard community, may have been seeking to partake in the same sort of independent religious activity that characterized those several rungs up the social and political ladder.

Social distinctions were also gendered. Women of the elite (at least in the cases of Alice Rowley and Joan Smyth) may have been attracted to the Lollard community because it offered them, as social superiors, a leading role that they were unable to play inside orthodoxy among others of their social level. In contrast, women of the lower orders apparently did not find the same advantages in the heresy, which presented them only with roles that accorded with generally prescribed feminine behavior, as we will see later. Lollard groups enabled artisan men and a few elite women to undertake independent religious activity and community leadership, already available to elite men in orthodoxy. Artisan women did not find these elements anywhere.

The Coventry Lollard Community in Perspective

A gray area lay between orthodoxy and heresy in late medieval England; for those whose religious feelings fell into this margin, inclination toward Lollardy or toward Catholicism depended upon a host of factors. Certainly adherence to Lollardy was partly about religiosity, about a search for a more meaningful approach to religious life and expression. It was also about belonging. The sect's social aspects and the sense of community it offered were sometimes key aspects of its attraction.[156] The women's conventicles in Coventry, for instance, gave a number of widows as well as other women the opportunity to participate in communal activities and socialize together. Adherence to the sect was also about belonging in another sense: some who participated may have done so at least partly because their husbands, wives, parents, or employers did. On the other hand, commitment to Lollardy also meant dissociation from orthodox life; belonging to one group could entail exclusion from another.

Attraction to Lollardy's spiritual offerings and the appeal of the sect's social side were shaped by various aspects of an individual's identity. Gender was clearly important: as we will see in more detail, Lollard communities drew significantly more men than women and extended different roles to the sexes. In Coventry, men and women did not always participate together in heretical activities; we will see similar segregation in other Lollard communities, although women's roles elsewhere were much more curtailed than in Coventry.

Social status also played a significant role. Male Lollards tended to come from the artisan classes, while their fellows farther up the social scale were uninterested in the sect. Most women, too, were of the lower orders, of course, but the Coventry community also drew a few women of the civic elite. The complex interactions of gender and social status within Lollard communities will be the subject of a later chapter; as suggested here, for some the Lollard sect met needs that orthodox Catholicism did not provide those of their gender or station, while for others orthodoxy offered more choices.

Personal networks, family, occupation, and neighborhood bonds also affected recruitment to the sect. In Coventry, as elsewhere, Lollards tended to be tied to other Lollards through blood, trade, or parish. The leverage these relationships brought to bear were not themselves simple or unidirectional; through such bonds an individual might be encouraged or influenced to become involved in heresy, or might be pressured or impelled. An individual's involvement in a Lollard group was altogether a complex matter.

3. The Lollard Communities

A Lollard community was not a strictly defined association. While all adherents of the sect from a particular locality may be said to belong to the same Lollard community, they did not meet together in large community groups, and almost certainly they created no membership lists or other written signs of affiliation (as did later Protestant sects).[1] The practice of the Lollard faith — which most often involved discussion of doctrine — took place in formal and informal situations, in almost ritualized gatherings and in casual conversations between neighbors in the street. The cement that made a Lollard community cohere was in most cases its leadership: knowing and conversing with a noted Lollard teacher (Robert Silkby of Coventry is a good example) was the thread that connected all members of the sect in a particular locality.

Lollards did congregate in formal gatherings, known among themselves and to their prosecutors as conventicles, or schools, as they were often called. All members of the community did not, however, participate in these meetings, as some practiced their faith exclusively through informal conversation and private or familial reading and talk. The style of Lollard religious practice differed from person to person; a number of factors influenced this style, of which gender was often the most important. Participation in formal gatherings was more appropriate and more convenient for men than for women. Such gatherings involved formal speaking and group discussion of religious matters, usually defined as male activities in medieval society. On a more basic level, the logistics of participation in the schools, particularly the extent of travel that was often involved, also favored men over women.

The sociologist Mark S. Granovetter has devised a model to describe how members of communities interact with one another which can help us understand the dynamic of Lollard groups. The ties between people who make up communities, Granovetter argues, vary in strength according to the amount of time spent together, the emotional intensity and intimacy of their relationship, and the services they have performed for one another.

Cliques (groups of people connected to one another by strong ties) are linked to other cliques through weak ties (or bridges or conduits); these cliques together make up a community. The vital bonds of the community are thus the weak ties rather than the strong ones, since it is along the bridges between cliques that new information flows and connection with the community is made.[2] In a Lollard community, conventicles brought together those who were linked primarily by weak ties, whereas informal or familial relationships represented strong ties.

Women's relationships in Lollard communities were concentrated among those with whom they had strong ties: their families, close neighbors, and friends. Men's lives, on the other hand, brought them more frequently into contact with people outside their immediate familial and social acquaintance, providing them with greater access to information and thus making them more pivotal to the Lollard communities. This accords with what some historians have written about men's and women's social networks in the late Middle Ages: men's circles of contacts radiated outward from the household whereas women's tended to concentrate inward.[3]

This sort of division in men's and women's lives — often termed public and private spheres — has been a troublesome concept in the literature on historical gender roles. A traditional interpretation saw a rigid dichotomy between the (male) public sphere and the (female) domestic or private sphere, but historians of medieval women (and others) have recently challenged this. Gender cannot be so easily defined: historians must also take into account, for instance, a man's or woman's social position. Not all men participated fully in public life, as political roles, for instance, were defined according to social position and ability. On the other hand, noblewomen, especially widows, frequently acted for themselves in the "public" legal and economic spheres.[4]

Other scholars have noted that the clear physical demarcation between "public" and "private" marked by the boundaries between the home and the outside world, described by historians of the late eighteenth- and nineteenth-century English middle class, does not accurately portray late medieval or Tudor English society.[5] The physical space of the home was not the boundary; public and private were confounded there as the patriarchal household, headed by a male, was not only the domestic center but also the unit of social, economic, and political organization.

Nonetheless, while eschewing rigid dichotomies or absolute laws, there can be no doubt that late medieval society regarded certain activities as more appropriate for a man than for a woman. Men dominated the more formal or "public" activities of late medieval social, economic, and (as I argue here) sectarian life. Informal, unofficial activity, on the other hand, was generally open (though not limited) to female participation. Men's wider networks — a reflection of their social roles — gave them a commanding position in the Lollard movement.

Schools and Conventicles

GENDER AND TRAVEL

Lollard conventicles, or schools, as they were often called, were important arenas for the learning and discussion of Lollard ideas.[6] Their centrality to the heretical communities makes it all the more significant that men overwhelmingly dominated these gatherings. Indeed, in some communities, women only rarely attended Lollard schools, and there are few records of women's participation in discussion. Conventicles, despite their clandestine and secret nature, were formal and in a sense public events; late medieval people were accustomed to regard such gatherings as a sphere of male activity.

The one conventicle in which women took part fully helps us understand the parameters of this phenomenon. As we have seen, Coventry women formed their own schools, and in these all-female meetings they played a much more extensive role than did women in other groups. While women were not full participants in conventicles of mixed gender, women-only gatherings allowed them to teach and discuss Lollard doctrine without fear of breaching norms that forbade public teaching of men. The Coventry community's urban situation also made women's gatherings more possible. Attendance at conventicles in rural communities often entailed a significant journey, which was both easier to fit into the rhythm of many men's jobs and more acceptable in social terms for men than for women. Such questions of travel and the spatial or geographic aspects of gender have been little investigated, but bear consideration. Ideology and logistics together militated against women's participation in conventicles: with the exception of the roles of Coventry women, female roles in Lollard gatherings were remarkably limited.

Lollards assembled in conventicles in the private homes of adherents of the sect. There they discussed Lollard ideas and listened to readings from the scriptures or from Lollard books. William Baker of Cranbrook gave a description of such an event that took place in 1509:

At Cristmas was xii monethes, upon Childermas nyght, this deponent [Baker], John Bampton, William Ryche, and another yong man of Bamptons acquayntaunce came togider to the house of Edward Walker of Maideston. At whiche tyme the said William Baker, John Bampton, William Riche, and the said yong man of Bamptons acquayntaunce and everyche of theym commyned, held, concluded, and beleved that the sacrament of the aulter that the preest did hold above his hede at the sacryng tyme was not Cristis body, flesshe and bloode, but oonly brede. Also this deponent saith that he dide redde unto John Bampton, William Riche, Edward Walker, and to the same yong man, Walkers acquayntaunce, upon the said Childermas nyght in the house of the said Walker, a booke of Mathewe, where yn was conteyned the gospellis in Englisshe; with the whiche redyng the said John Bampton, William Riche, Edward Walker, and the said yong man were contentid and pleasid, saying that it was pitie that it might not be knowen openly. The whiche redyng in the said booke as they understood it was ayenst the sacramentis of thaulter, baptisme, Matrymony, and preesthode.[7]

Such gatherings also sometimes took place out of doors, probably for greater secrecy: for example, William Sweeting, a cowherd, met James Brewster, John Woodrof and his wife, his brother-in-law, and Thomas Goodred in a field where he was keeping beasts.[8] Reports of attendance at schools and conventicles, such as that given by William Baker, suggest certain patterns in which gender and geography were factors: while men dominated most conventicles, the gender imbalance was most pronounced if participation involved significant travel.

In rural Lollard communities in which adherents of the sect were geographically scattered, conventicles were made up almost exclusively of men. It is no surprise that reports of conventicles among the Lollards uncovered in the Chiltern Hills by Bishop Chedworth in the 1460s involved only men. Chedworth prosecuted only one woman, and she was not named by any of the other Lollards, nor is there any evidence that she participated in schools.[9] Those who taught in the conventicles in this community — James Wyllys, formerly of Bristol, John White of Chesham, a man named Pope, the rector of Chesham Bois, and William Belgrave of Stokenchurch — were all men, and their reported pupils were also all male.[10]

But even other communities with a greater proportion of women had all-male meetings. Although over a third of those implicated in the Kentish group were female, these women reportedly played almost no part in the conventicles, and the extent of travel involved was an important factor in their exclusion from these gatherings. The evidence indicates that men from the three main concentrations of Lollards in the diocese of Canterbury

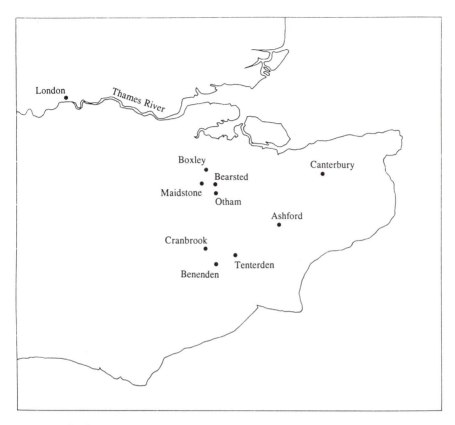

Map 2. Lollard Centers in Kent, c. 1511–12.

(around Tenterden, Maidstone, and Canterbury) visited one another regularly to discuss Lollard opinions. The considerable distance between these centers may have prevented women from making the same trips. William Baker of Cranbrook, for instance, met informally to discuss Lollard matters with John Browne of Ashford in a garden at Charte, roughly halfway between Ashford and Cranbrook.[11] He also traveled to Maidstone with Robert Reynold of Cranbrook and Stephen Castelyn of Tenterden to attend the gathering at the home of Edward Walker described in the quotation.[12]

Reports of another conventicle hosted by Edward Walker in the depositions of William Riche of Benenden and Robert Bright of Maidstone illustrate the distances from which men gathered to discuss Lollard doctrine and the all-male character of their meetings. Riche testified that on 26 December 1510 John Bampton, who had traveled south to the Weald from his home in Boxley or Bearsted (just outside Maidstone), came to Riche's house in Benenden along with William Baker of nearby Cranbrook. Both men stayed the night, and the next day, Riche, Baker, and Bampton traveled the considerable distance of twenty-five kilometers back to Bampton's house. There they met Robert Bright of Maidstone, Richard Bampton of Boxley, Thomas Feld of Boxley, Stephen Castelyn of Tenterden, and a young man whose name neither Riche nor Bright knew. That night they all proceeded to Edward Walker's house in Maidstone, three or four kilometers from Bampton's house. At Walker's home they "satt drynkyng and began to comyne of their matiers furthwith they came thidder." But all was not safe—Walker's wife, who was present and listened to their conversation, stopped to warn them as they were talking:

> Sires, it is not good that ye talke moche here of thies maters, for the Jaylours will take hede to you yf ye comme hider. And also be ware, for som folkis will commyn hider anon.

Soon after this, the jailer's wife and another woman came into the house and the men stopped talking and left soon after.[13]

The descriptions of these conventicles in Kent give them the air of men's clubs. The participants noted were all men, many of whom had traveled from some distance to attend. While Walker's wife was present for their discussion in her house and may have listened approvingly, there is no indication that she contributed, and it seems unlikely that she would have been included had the gathering been held elsewhere. Women of the household in which the gathering took place were probably frequently present, even if they were ignored in depositions. Perhaps they were not considered important enough: John Bampton's wife, who later abjured Lollardy,[14] may well have been at the gathering held at her house earlier that same evening, but neither Riche nor Bright mentioned her. Walker's wife herself enters the narrative only when she becomes an active player, warning the men of the impending visit of the jailer's wife. But even she is not included in both versions of the story. Only Bright mentions her; in Riche's version, it is Walker himself who warns them about speaking in front of the jailer's wife and the other woman.[15]

Accounts of the more informal visit of Joan and Thomas Harwode to the home of John Browne of Ashford similarly illustrate how women could be overlooked in depositions. Joan, Thomas, and John "sittyng all togider ther by the fyre, etyng and drynkyng, had communicacion ayenst worshipping of imagis of seynt<s> and goyng on pilgremagis."[16] Joan Harwode remarked that Elizabeth, John Browne's wife, was present and assented to all they said, but Thomas Harwode did not refer to Elizabeth Browne at all, stating only that he and his wife discussed doctrine with John Browne.[17] Even when women were present and spoke at conventicles or even more informal gatherings, men sometimes disregarded them.

Similarly, in East Anglia, we know from their own abjurations that Sybil Godesell and Hawise Mone were present at the schools held in their own homes, while Matilda Fleccher probably also attended the conventicle in her house organized by her husband, although she was never accused of it. Neither Sybil nor Matilda, however, was ever cited as a Lollard by any other of the accused, and Hawise Mone was mentioned by only three deponents, one her servant.[18] The court asked East Anglian Lollards to list the Lollards with whom they were familiar,[19] and among those lists, only one woman, Batild Burrell, dead by the time of Alnwick's investigations, was ever named.[20] This indicates either that women in East Anglia (with the lone exception of Batild Burrell) attended conventicles only when they were held in their own homes, or that any women who were present at such gatherings were included among the "and others" often appended at the end of such lists. Evidence is rare for women's attendance at the Kent and East Anglia conventicles, especially those held outside their own households. Women may have been present even if it went unreported, but such disregard is significant in itself and tacitly says much about women's roles in these gatherings.

The Kentish and East Anglian Lollard communities were rural as well as geographically scattered, and this inhibited women's participation in their conventicles. A trip such as that described in the records for Kent would have been difficult for women in the fifteenth or sixteenth century; although women could (and did)[21] travel with their husbands, this was difficult, and it was virtually impossible for them to travel on their own.[22] Even the unusual Margery Kempe, convinced though she was of God's protection, always traveled in a group or under the care of a man. She experienced many difficulties on her pilgrimage to the Holy Land because her companions continually abandoned her, leaving her without escort.[23]

Different geographical circumstances could make it easier for women to attend Lollard schools, but this never led to gatherings where men and women participated equally. All-male groups were common in all communities. In Hampshire, Thomas Andrew of Woodhay deposed that he went to the home of William Lye, also of Woodhay, where there was a gathering of twelve men discussing transubstantiation.[24] Among the London Lollards at the beginning of the sixteenth century was a core of men who sometimes met in Shoreditch at the house of Lawrence Swaffer and sometimes at the house of William Russel in Coleman Street.[25] Some of the meetings of these groups involved long-distance travel, as did the conventicles of the Kent Lollards: the house of Thomas Man of Amersham, Bucks., for instance, was the site of a number of gatherings that included Londoners Thomas Grove, Christopher Glasbroke, and William Tilseworth as well as William Glasbroke of Harrow-on-the-Hill.[26]

There are, of course, examples of conventicles made up of both men and women. Robert Bartlett of Amersham, for instance, testified against a number of "known-men," who he said gathered together often to read about and discuss the worship of images. This group included not only "known-men" but women too: Bartlett mentioned Elizabeth Dean of West Wycombe, William Tylsworth, Emma Tylsworth (William's wife), William Grinder and his wife, John Scrivener, Alexander Mastal, Thurstan Littlepage, and John Bartlett.[27]

But men and women did not take part in conventicles on an equal basis. Men came alone to these gatherings, while women rarely did; in most cases when men and women participated together, the women were part of a married couple. Descriptions such as Robert Pope's deposition before Bishop Longland in 1521 are typical of conventicles involving women: he notes that Thomas Harding and his wife, John Scrivener and his wife, Thomas Man and his wife, and another Thomas Man and his wife used to gather together often to speak about matters of religion.[28] The husband-wife relationship was the most frequent context in which Lollard women participated in the movement; the implications of this will be discussed fully in the next chapter.

Here let us examine the other side of the problem: the difficulties inherent in single women's participation in conventicles. An unattached woman's involvement in a clandestine meeting made up mostly of men would have been unwise in a culture that closely guarded women's reputations; such an act could easily have been interpreted as unchaste. A single woman's attraction to a creed would have had to be strong indeed to overcome the powerful psychological and social inhibitions attached to her participation. Women in most Lollard commmunities were able to participate in the sect, particularly in its formal aspects, only with the support of male relatives.

Among the Coventry Lollards, however, this problem was obviated by the formation of all-female conventicles alongside the usual all-male and mixed conventicles. The phenomenon of all-female groups allowed women (especially single women) to take part in discussions more fully than they were able in mixed conventicles. Indeed, Wycliffite sermons praised separation of the sexes in religious worship, since this kept men and women "fro lecherye."[29] The existence of a cohort of unattached women in Coventry created an environment in which women could participate without the company of male relatives.

Evidence for conventicles made up entirely of women cannot be found for any of the other Lollard communities studied here. The closest example is given by Roger Bennet of Amersham before Bishop Longland about 1521: he said that William Smith, the wife of John Milsent, the wife of William Rogers, Robert Stamp and his wife, and the wife of Robert Bartlet used to meet together. "These good *women* here named," as Foxe tells it, "were detected to the bishop by Roger Bennet, for that upon the holidays, when they go and come from the church, they used to resort unto one J. Collingworth's house, and there to keep their conventicle."[30] While William Smith and Robert Stamp were obviously not women, Foxe's report of the story suggests that the meetings were dominated by the women rather than the men. Such gatherings may indeed have existed in all the communities studied, but it is also conceivable that the phenomenon was confined to the urban Lollards of Coventry. This community was concentrated in a smaller geographical space, making travel to attend conventicles much easier for women than, for instance, in the rural community in Kent. But other factors, discussed earlier, also contributed to the unique situation in Coventry, allowing for greater participation by women.

LEADERSHIP OF LOLLARD CONVENTICLES: WOMEN PRIESTS?
Regardless of the involvement of women, leadership of Lollard conventicles was almost always in male hands, following both a clerical model and prescribed gender roles that subordinated women to men.[31] Lollards challenged the authority of the office of the Catholic clergy, but they nonetheless retained for their teachers a clerical idea of authority based on two criteria: first, participation in the power of the sacred (although certainly to a lesser extent than Catholic priests) and, second, expertise, knowledge, and skill. While the second criterion was probably more important among Lollards, expertise alone cannot translate into authority unless the social environment predisposes others in the group to recognize that person's proficiency or ability.[32]

Late medieval people were unlikely to acknowledge women's leadership of a late medieval mixed religious community. Women found it more difficult than men to acquire skills needed for leadership, especially literacy. Furthermore, the prevailing culture did not generally view women's authority in public situations as legitimate. And, lastly, Lollard leadership retained from Roman Catholicism at least a residue of the idea of priest (always male) as participant in the sacred.

Indeed, the clerical model of authority was not always just a model; in many cases the leaders of conventicles were in fact members of the Catholic clergy. Some Lollard leaders, like Richard Fox of Steeple Bumpstead, were accorded respect and authority because, not in spite, of their clerical status.[33] The two main teachers in the East Anglian community, William White and Hugo Pye, were both chaplains.[34] The rector of Chesham Bois was an important leader of the Buckinghamshire community uncovered by Chedworth in the 1460s.[35] Other great teachers of the Lollard tradition, such as John Hacker, Thomas Man, John Pykas, and John Tyball (whose influence will be discussed in the following chapter),[36] were apparently members of the laity, but all were men.

Nonetheless some Lollards, albeit few, held the unusual tenet that women as well as men could be priests.[37] As some fifteenth-century Norfolk Lollards put it,

> every man and every woman beyng in good lyf oute of synne is as good prest and hath [as] muche poar of God in al thynges as ony prest ordred, be he pope or bisshop.[38]

This doctrine was not an element of mainstream Lollard thought—the evidence for those expressing this view is all early and even then comes from the more extreme fringe.[39] What Lollards who claimed this extraordinary power for women meant by priesthood is unclear and was perhaps not fully articulated in their own minds; while all holy men and women, by virtue of that holiness, had the same powers as an ordained priest, Lollards also believed that ordained priests' powers were negligible.[40] The assertion that even women could be priests may in fact have been nothing more than an expression of contempt for the clergy.[41] In practice there is no evidence that women acted as priests in the orthodox sense: there were rumors in London in the early days of the movement, possibly apocryphal, of women performing sacraments,[42] but no such activities are reported for the later communities.[43]

The evidence for women acting as public teachers and leaders of con-

venticles, a minimalist definition of "Lollard priest," is slim. The only concrete evidence that women did function as teachers in conventicles comes
from the unusual community in Coventry. Alice Rowley, Joan Warde, and
Agnes Yong were all charged with discoursing against the sacrament of the
altar, pilgrimages, and the veneration of images.[44] While women taught
each other, they also had instruction from one of the chief male heretics,
Robert Silkby, who often met with Alice Rowley, Agnes de Bakehouse, the
wife of Roger Bromley, Mother Margaret, and Agnes and Juliana Yong.[45]

While women taught other women at least in the context of the Coventry conventicles, the evidence for female leadership of mixed conventicles
and public instruction of men, a striking breach of gender norms, is clear in
only one case and ambiguous in two others. The two indefinite possibilities
regard the wives of two wandering Lollard teachers, Joan White (wife of
William White) and the wife of Thomas Man. John Foxe claimed that Joan
White converted many in East Anglia after her husband's death in 1428.
According to Foxe, she followed in

> her husband's footsteps according to her power, teaching and sowing abroad
> the same doctrine, [and she] confirmed many men in God's truth; wherefore
> she suffered much trouble and punishment the same year at the hands of the
> said bishop.[46]

No other record survives, however, of the trial Foxe alludes to here,[47] and
Joan appears in the extant records only in passive roles: William Baxter
reports that she was escorted from Martham to Seething by one Lollard to
stay with another, and in William White's trial she is seen only as the
instrument by which he defied the Church's doctrine of clerical celibacy.[48]
No Lollards ever cited Joan as a fellow heretic. Although Foxe's report
should not be dismissed out of hand, it remains curious that no evidence of
Joan's influence on the group survives apart from his report.

Similarly obscure is the reference to the participation of the wife of
Thomas Man in her husband's activities. Thomas Man, who was burned at
Smithfield in 1518, was said to be one of the four great teachers of the early
sixteenth century in the Chiltern Hills; he was active throughout southeast
England and was cited by many Lollards.[49] His wife, who is unnamed,[50]
appears in the records twice. Robert Pope said that she was present with her
husband at an Amersham gathering where the scriptures and other matters
of religion were discussed.[51] The other reference is more tantalizing: at
Thomas's trial, transcribed from Fitzjames's lost register by Archbishop
Ussher in the early seventeenth century, it was recorded that

ye and your wife have turnyd 5. 6. or 7. hundreth people to your law and opinions in points and articles as ye wer abjured of, and oder also that be contrary to Crists faith and to ye determination of our moder holy churche.[52]

Although this report indicates that Thomas and his wife operated as a missionary team converting hundreds of people, Man's wife's role is not reflected in other records as her husband's was. The evidence indicates that Thomas often traveled alone, without his wife.[53] In the cases of Joan White and the wife of Thomas Man, their prestige and authority appears to have been a reflection of the activities of their husbands.

Only one woman, the extraordinary Alice Rowley of Coventry, clearly played a public teaching role in conventicles of mixed gender. Rowley admitted in her trial that she had been in the home of Roger Landesdale and had taught there against pilgrimages and oblations to images in the presence of several men; she also confessed that she had read publicly before a number of Lollards, including Roger Cutler, Joan Smyth, Thomas Banbrooke, and Robert Bastell.[54] Thomas Flesshour also deposed that he had heard Alice reading in the book of the commandments in the home of Roger Landesdale.[55] Two men at least credited her with their conversions: Thomas Acton said that it was she who first led him into the sect, and Thomas Bowen said that she and Landesdale taught him about the sacrament of the altar.[56] Alice clearly played an influential role in the Coventry Lollard community, but it was also unparalleled; she is the only Lollard woman for whom there is clear evidence that she instructed men publicly. As we have seen, Alice Rowley's place in the Lollard movement was due to a number of unusual factors, including her high social status; her prominence in Lollardy was anomalous and cannot be taken as typical.

Women's ability to lead conventicles was inhibited not only by social and religious conventions about authority but also by their illiteracy. Among the most important Lollard activities, both formal and informal, was reading books. In Brian Stock's terms, Lollards formed textual communities, groups whose activities are formed around texts and their interpretation.[57] Literacy, the ability to interpret the written word to the group, was clearly an important skill in a book-centered sect like Lollardy. As Stock notes, illiteracy did not prevent access to a text; others could relay the information it provided.[58] But the purveyors of written information were in a position of power. Margaret Aston argues persuasively that those who were literate were most influential in Lollard communities,[59] and important members of the movement were often described as "principal readers or instructors."[60] Literacy was a significant factor in attraction to and participation in the movement, especially in the conventicles, which functioned primarily around reading and discussion of written texts.

The extent of lay literacy in the fifteenth and early sixteenth century is a matter of considerable debate. While some scholars have posited a swiftly rising rate of literacy in the late Middle Ages, especially after the introduction of print, others have suggested that what concrete evidence we have presents a much more pessimistic picture.[61] Moreover, historians and literary scholars have paid relatively little attention to an apparent gender gap in late medieval literacy, where men were much more likely than women to acquire the ability to read.[62]

Lollard evidence — which is, admittedly, likely to be incomplete — supports the hypothesis of a generally low level of literacy at the middling and lower reaches of society in late medieval England and a particularly low level among women. The prosecutors of the sect attached a good deal of significance to the fact that an accused person could read; his or her literacy was seen to be so unusual as to be evidence for Lollardy.[63] Deponents thus sometimes reported to the authorities that particular Lollards were literate or had read a particular book or text. While this evidence is somewhat haphazard and incomplete, it does point to a sizable difference between men's and women's abilities to read.

Our sources indicate that only seven women (five of them from Coventry) were certainly literate. Of those few, most or perhaps all learned to read through Lollard instruction.[64] Lollard men were by no means usually literate but were much more commonly reported to be able to read than their female counterparts. According to depositions and abjurations, at least one-fifth of all Lollard men in the communities studied could read.[65] A significant gender gap in evidence for Lollard literacy thus emerges: about one in thirty-three women could read, whereas about one in five men could. If the literate were much more likely to be leaders than the illiterate, women were severely disadvantaged.

This differential probably reflects general rates of literacy and the contexts in which fifteenth-century people learned to read. Not all men learned to read through their occupations, but many did, and more occasions to obtain literacy presented themselves to men than to women. Women were much less likely in their economic lives to have any need to attain literacy skills, and they had many fewer opportunities to do so, outside or even inside Lollard communities.[66] Women's illiteracy reinforced their subordinate position in the Lollard movement — inability to read effectively excluded almost all women from leading roles.

While women's illiteracy did not cut them off from the contents of

Lollard books, as we will see later, the evidence indicates that almost all women were forced to rely on others to read the material in the books to them. This was undoubtedly a handicap in any attempts they may have made to teach and surely inhibited their opportunities to take leading roles in the communities. It also limited their attraction to a sect that was so firmly based on the written word.

Even when women could not read, though, recitation of scripture or Lollard texts offered them another sort of opportunity to speak before gatherings. Women were conspicuous among those in the sect who had memorized passages of scripture or prayers, and Claire Cross has seen this as a significant element of women's power in the movement.[67] Recitation was not, however, equivalent to leading conventicles.

Certainly, women were thought to be (and were) capable of memorizing passages of scripture or prayers. Learning scripture by heart was by no means limited to Lollards and was a common orthodox practice at least among the gentry. Margaret Rocliffe, for instance, granddaughter of Sir William Plumpton, had, according to her father-in-law, "near hand learned her sawter [psalter]."[68] Among Lollards, Marion Westden Mathew, according to John Pykas, often spoke of the Gospels and Epistles, which she knew by heart.[69] Thomas Westfelde said that he had heard Elizabeth Sampson of London reciting in English the chapter that begins "Primum quidem sermonem feci de omnibus O Theophile, etc." (Acts 1).[70] Agnes Wells of Amersham learned the Epistle of James from Thurstan Littlepage, as did her brother Richard Bartlett.[71] At least one woman, Alice Colins of Ginge, even publicly recited her memorized passages at conventicles. But this activity did not confer upon her the status of a Lollard teacher or leader. Foxe describes her recitation thus:

> This Alice likewise was a famous woman among them, and had a good memory, and could recite much of the Scriptures, and other good books; and therefore when any *conventicle of these men* did meet at Burford, commonly she was sent for, to recite unto them the declaration of the Ten Commandments, and the Epistles of Peter and James.[72]

Alice Colins apparently was not a regular attendant of the conventicle, which was made up of men. She made appearances at the group to act as a kind of living book, but there is no indication that she proceeded to explain the readings to the gathering after she had recited; rather, her recitation was like that of a child called upon to recite before guests.

Further examples show that others who memorized passages were

indeed children and that it is very unlikely that such activity could have
given them leadership roles. Elizabeth, daughter of a cooper named Blake,
aged about thirteen, could recite by heart many Gospels and Epistles, according to Elizabeth Mathew.[73] Similarly, the daughter of a man named
Wily could recite chapter twenty-four of Matthew's Gospel and a Lollard
book called "the Disputation between the clerk and a friar."[74]

Men also memorized and recited passages of scripture or Lollard writings. Robert Best of Colchester knew the Epistle of James by heart; a
mysterious Lollard named Tuck who visited Coventry knew the Apocalypse
completely and by memory; William Pykas of Colchester, like Wily's daughter, was able to recite the same disputation between a clerk and a friar for the
edification of Lollards meeting at his employer's home; John Gest of Birmingham memorized part of an Epistle of Paul.[75] But none of these men
were otherwise teachers in the schools of their communities. A London
Lollard with an uncertain role in the movement, the goldsmith John Bar-
rett, knew the letter of James "perfectly without book,"[76] and may be an
example of a more prominent Lollard who recited texts. Even so, recitation
cannot be seen as a direct avenue to authority within the movement. While
memorization and recitation undoubtedly gave women and girls as well as
some men a significant role in evangelization, this activity in itself did not
confer upon them the power and authority of leadership.

Lollards, like Protestants later, wished to express the radical spiritual
equality of women and men without challenging the social hierarchy, also
divinely ordained, which placed women under the authority of men and restricted their public activity.[77] Other religious sects that ostensibly preached
gender equality, such as the Shakers, also maintained in practice communities in which authority was organized along patriarchal lines.[78]

HOSTING CONVENTICLES

While women did not lead conventicles or even often actively participate in
them, there is one significant role they did play in these gatherings: that of
host or facilitator. Although most schools were hosted by men, a notable
number of women provided space for Lollard meetings.

Hawise Mone of East Anglia, for instance, seems to have been particularly active in this respect. Conventicles were regularly held in the home
of Hawise and Thomas Mone, at which the heresiarch William White
and others taught.[79] Hawise also hosted a ritual fast-breaking ceremony in
defiance of the Church's ordinances. One of the Mones' servants, John
Burrell, testified to the court that Hawise Mone and several men prema-

turely broke the Lenten fast on Easter Saturday, 1428. Burrell saw Hawise, his own brother Thomas Burrell, John Pert (another servant of Thomas Mone), and a man clad in a russet gown[80] secretly shut themselves up in "le chesehous chambr" where they ate a quarter of cold pork. Thomas Mone, Hawise's husband, did not participate, as he was at the market in Horning on that day.[81] Hawise's facilitation of gatherings was apparently independent of her husband's adherence to the sect.

Other women also hosted Lollard gatherings. John Pykas of Colchester said that he had taught in "the houses and presences" of a number of townspeople, including Dorothy Long, Katherine Swayn, Margaret Bowgas, and Margaret Cowbridge.[82] In Steeple Bumpstead, Essex, a number of women provided houses for Lollard meetings: Mother Bocher and Mother Charte (both probably widows) supplied space for Richard Fox, John Tyball, John Smyth of Steeple Bumpstead, Friar Topley, Friar Gardiner, and sometimes John Smyth of Redgwell to meet.[83] The same group also met at Bower Hall, said Thomas Hilles, in the home of a woman named Joan Agnes, alias Smyth, who probably lived there as a servant.[84] But it should be noted in these rural Essex examples that while women hosted these events, those who attended, according to the witnesses' reports, were all men; if women apart from the hosts were present, they were not considered to be important enough to mention.

Women's most significant role in the Lollard conventicles in some communities, then, was as receivers of heretics, an important function in a movement that held its conventicles in private households. But while women who received heretics were often charged with learning from them, there is no evidence that their role in conventicles in their own houses was more than passive or that they attended conventicles elsewhere.

Men overwhelmingly dominated Lollard conventicles. In some communities, only men attended such gatherings; in others, women were sometimes present—as hosts, sometimes as pupils, but only very rarely as teachers. The exception to this pattern is the Lollard group of Coventry, where the concentration of the community in an urban area made women's participation in conventicles more possible. Even there, however, men's and women's involvement in Lollard conventicles was by no means equal.

WOMEN AND MEN AS VIEWED BY DEPONENTS AND BY THE COURTS
Although some women were clearly able to be active in Lollardy, their overall role in the movement was much more limited than that of men. Their lack of a public role in the movement meant that the activities of

women were not taken as seriously as those of men, both in the estimation of the ecclesiastical authorities and of their fellow Lollards.

Generally, the chronology of cases presented before the courts indicates that ecclesiastical officials saw the heresy of women to be less dangerous than that of men. The example of the prosecution of the Lollards in Essex by Cuthbert Tunstall, Bishop of London, between March and July 1528[85] shows this clearly. The course of prosecution for men in Essex ran for several months in a geographical pattern. Most women, on the other hand, were brought before the court on a single day.

John Hacker, a great Lollard teacher who became an important informant for the bishop, likely abjured and deposed before the main prosecutions began in March 1528. In that month, men of Colchester and nearby East Donyland were summoned and examined. Men from Steeple Bumpstead appeared before the court in late April and May, along with one other Colchester man. During this period, only one woman, Alice Gardiner of Colchester, appeared before the court.

Not until several months later, on July 15, were twelve women (along with five men) summoned to appear. Nine of the twelve were married to men who had previously appeared or been implicated; there was no apparent evidence against four of these except their relationship to their husbands, and the charges against at least one were dropped for default of proof. Four more women appeared between 17 and 22 July.

This Essex material shows that the officials had less interest in women's activities than men's and that they did not perceive women to be among the dangerous Lollards. Women were prosecuted (when prosecuted at all) apparently as an afterthought; the cases viewed to be most serious were investigated in March, April, and May, while the male Lollards who were prosecuted in July along with the women were evidently on the fringes of the community. The surviving records for the July prosecutions are much abbreviated; the July 15–17 segment, for instance, records the names of the men and women who were summoned, indicates those who appeared, inscribes the names of the compurgators of the women who purged themselves, and registers nothing about several other women who may not have even appeared.

A telling example of the authorities' attitude toward women are the cases of John Girling and his wife Joan Girling. John Girling was summoned before the bishop on March 19, probably after John Pykas had given evidence against both him and his wife in an undated deposition. Joan Girling, on the other hand, was not cited to appear until July 15, along with the other women, despite the fact that evidence was given against her not only by Pykas but also by William Raylond, probably also in March. Indeed, on the face of it, Joan Girling was more dangerous than her husband. As the court knew from Raylond's testimony and her husband's examination, she had previously abjured heresy at Lambeth and performed penance at St. Paul's Cross in London; before this, she had been married to three men—a man named Bishop in Eccles (Norfolk), John Vincent, and John Adams (none known specifically to have been Lollards)[86]—before she became the wife of John Girling in Colchester. In 1528 she was thus a relapsed heretic, yet officials made no special attempt to bring her into custody when her husband was prosecuted in March. She did appear in court when summoned in July; the record, however, states only that she was to return the following day to answer the charge, and we do not know the result.[87]

The authorities prosecuting Lollard communities clearly did not take women as seriously as men. The court focused on men, and officials made greater efforts to prosecute and punish them. This may have been due to the prejudices of the court: the bishop and his officials perhaps wrongly assumed that women could not play important roles.[88]

The assumptions of the court about women's importance, however, were shared by the members of the sect. We have already seen witnesses' tendency to exclude women from their narratives about Lollard activities. A close look at testimony and the court's prosecution of women shows that the courts were overall no more or less likely to summon women who were named in depositions than men. In communities for which registers or court books survive, women were named as suspected heretics in depositions in almost exactly the same proportion as they appeared in court.[89] In East Anglia, the authorities took women more seriously than did the Lollards themselves: while six women accused of Lollardy were brought before the bishop, only one woman (Batild Burrell, dead by the time of the bishop's proceedings) was included in the defendants' lists of Lollards with whom they were familiar.[90] All the main teachers acknowledged by the accused were men.[91]

The propensity to regard women as unimportant was the result of systemic societal attitudes, not simply a clerical bias. Generally, the accused of both sexes showed a tendency to disregard the activities of female Lollards, although male deponents were more guilty of this. The courts' views of women's importance in the movement thus reflected not only their own prejudices but also the prejudices of the accused.

PUBLIC AND PRIVATE: MEN AND WOMEN IN LOLLARD CONVENTICLES

It should not surprise us that women were, for the most part, inactive in Lollard conventicles. Although conventicles were by their nature private, secret affairs, they were the most public of Lollard activities. Prevailing social norms demanded that women be less active in this sphere than men, who were to act as the public representatives of their families. Women, if they were present at all at formal Lollard gatherings, for the most part fulfilled their society's expectations of feminine behavior, that they "keep silence in the churches" (1 Cor. 14:34), as St. Paul told them, and let men speak for them.

Historians interested in gender and the public-private dichotomy have examined most closely the economic roles of late medieval men and women. They have found that, below elite levels of society, the work of the male head of the household (the patriarch) defined the occupation and status of the household. Men's occupations in the late Middle Ages varied much more than those available to women, and virtually all work that carried prestige and high remuneration was restricted to men. Women's work was to complement the work of the head of the household; it tended to be ill-paid, low-status, flexible, and part-time.[92]

Social and political roles reflected and reinforced this economic division. Women's contacts were much more centered on the household than were men's; men's networks were larger and less kin-centered than women's.[93] Households were represented in the official functions of late medieval society (in politics, in guilds) by their male members, particularly by the head of the household; women generally had no direct voice in official, formal procedures, although in exceptional circumstances they could sometimes exercise the same rights as men.[94] Women could and did act in the world outside their households as long as they did so unofficially and not in a "public" way.

A "public" woman was in some ways an unchaste woman. Speaking or acting publicly could be seen as improper; a woman's reputation for chastity and respectability depended not only on her physical integrity but also on her quiet demeanor and her representation in public by a male guardian, a relative or employer.[95] Wandering in the streets unescorted was a dangerous and suspect activity.[96] In some cities, single women were forbidden to live outside the structures of a male-headed household for moral reasons. In Coventry, unmarried women were not to set up house by themselves or with other women but were to live with their families or go into service until they married; otherwise it was feared they would fall into prostitution and endanger their souls and the moral fiber of the city.[97]

Religious teaching addressed the formal/informal divide. Paul had forbidden women to speak in the churches, and Gratian said that "a woman, no matter how learned or holy, may not presume to teach men in a gathering."[98] But not all medieval theologians interpreted the ban as extending to individual, informal tutoring. Thomas Aquinas said in his *Summa theologiae*, "A woman is not permitted to teach publicly in a church, but she is permitted to instruct others in private by personal suggestions."[99] Pauline restrictions on women speaking publicly or debating religious matters continued to influence Christian religious practices for centuries after the Reformation.[100] Women such as mystics or prophets who went beyond these boundaries did so on the basis of special powers given them by God, which allowed them to transcend normal expectations of womanly behavior; even so, they often faced popular hostility.[101] Protestant and Reformed Catholic leaders in the sixteenth century also agreed that the proper role of women was in the domestic and familial sphere, and they regarded female public activity as shocking and outrageous.[102] Lollard women were not prophets or mystics, and they (with the exception of Alice Rowley) acted only in ways that were traditionally open to women.

Lollard Activities Outside the Conventicles

INFORMAL TEACHING

Lollards learned their faith and discussed its tenets in individual conversations among family members, friends, and neighbors (in Granovetter's terms, those to whom an individual was strongly tied) as well as in conventicles. Although social expectations constricted women's participation in the formal aspect of Lollard interaction, informal situations were traditionally much more open to them. Not surprisingly, women were much more active teaching on an individual basis than in conventicles; it seems clear that much of their learning also took place in private. Although men still dominated the informal aspects of the movement as they did its formal gatherings, the emphasis here will be on women's activities. What female activity there was in Lollardy was almost all on this individual, informal plane, and women's interactions tended to be with Lollards to whom they were strongly tied.

Women were particularly active teaching other women. We have seen this in relation to the all-female conventicles in Coventry; it also took place more informally on a one-to-one basis. The redoubtable Margery Baxter of Martham and Norwich lectured her orthodox neighbor, Joan Clyfland, and Joan's servants about the tenets of the Lollard faith. Margery scolded Joan for genuflecting and praying before man-made images: "lewed wrightes of stokkes hewe and fourme suche crosses and ymages," she said, "and after that lewed peyntors glorye thaym with colours." She asked Joan if she would like to see the true cross of Christ, and when Joan replied that she would,

> Margery said "See," and then extended her arms out, saying to Joan, "this is the true cross of Christ and this cross you can and must see and adore every day here in your own house, and it will come to you that you labor in vain when you go to the church to adore and pray to any dead images or crosses."[103]

Margery also invited her neighbors into her home in the evening to hear her husband read the "law of Christ" (possibly a Lollard version of the scriptures).[104] It is notable that Margery saw her instruction of Joan and her servants as preliminary; she was anxious that they come and hear her husband who, she said, "is the best teacher of Christianity."[105]

Women in other Lollard communities also taught each other. Joan Collingborne taught Joan Timberlake and Alice Tredway that saints were not to be worshiped and that pilgrimages were not profitable. She told them not to tell their curate, but nonetheless Alice Tredway immediately caused her to be called before the bishop.[106] Isabel Morwyn tried to teach her sister, Elizabeth Copland, about Lollard doctrine.[107] Alice Harding taught Joan Norman about the wickedness of pilgrimages and worshiping images. Isabel Tracher thought Alice Harding was so wise that she sent her daughter to live with her and to be instructed in the Lollard faith.[108] John Edmunds of Burford also sent his daughter Agnes into service in a Lollard family, the household of Richard Colins of Ginge. Alice Colins, Richard's wife, who recited scripture to conventicles of men, may have been responsible for the instruction of Agnes Edmunds, who learned "the Ten Commandments, the five wits bodily and ghostly, and the seven deadly sins."[109] Alice Colins did teach several other women, including Margaret House of East Ginge, Joan Steventon, and the wife of John Harris.[110] Alice Cottismore of Brightwell tried to teach her servant Elizabeth Wighthill about her Lollard beliefs, particularly those concerning pilgrimages.[111]

Female Lollards sometimes took advantage of gatherings of women on occasions of birth or death to spread their beliefs, particularly when the orthodox practices they so despised were manifest. Elizabeth Sampson of London objected to the invocation of the Virgin to aid a woman in labor, attacking those who called upon the Virgin both at her own and at another woman's childbed.[112] A Lollard named Katherine Cucklewe of Reading actually took the opportunity that her own deathbed offered to tell the women gathered around her that God was conceived in sin. Margaret Symson, a widow who was present, adopted Katherine's opinion and said it "opynly in lyke maner."[113]

Women also taught men, often those who were in some way subordinate to them. Agnes Ashford taught James Morden two passages from scripture; for the first, he went to her five times, for the second, twice. James was the servant and cousin by marriage of Richard Ashford, Agnes's son.[114] Agnes Ashford also instructed her son Thomas Tredway.[115] Batild Burrell of the East Anglian Lollard community taught her young brother-in-law John Burrell some things she had heard read from a book.[116]

Other male pupils were not subject to the women who instructed them: William Raylond of Colchester, for instance, said that in about 1522 or 1523 he heard the wife of John Girling, sitting at her kitchen table, speak of the Gospels and Epistles; she was asked about the sacrament of the altar and said that it was "but an Host" and that the images of saints were but idols.[117] Alice Harding of Amersham coached Richard Bennett about what he should do when the priest came to give him communion.[118] Joan Gun of Chesham taught John Hill about the Epistle of James and other elements of Lollard doctrine.[119] Joan Austy of Essex also instructed Christopher Ravins and his sister Dyonise in the Epistle of James.[120] For medieval women to teach adult men was not unusual; although public instruction was forbidden, teaching men or women privately in an informal way was an activity open to them in orthodoxy as well as in Lollardy.

Women not only taught informally, they learned informally as well. While there is little evidence that women participated even as learners at conventicles, they were certainly taught about Lollardy through private, individual instruction. They learned both from women and from men. In the Kentish community, for instance, in which women made up a significant proportion of the Lollard population although they did not seem to take part in gatherings, women must have learned their heresies somehow, though little evidence survives about their instruction. Agnes Grebill of Tenterden was taught her beliefs in her home by her husband, by William Carder (also of Tenterden), and by John Ive of Canterbury.[121] John Ive's widow Agnes went to Robert Harryson's house along with another woman, Elizabeth White, to learn some Lollard ideas.[122] Other women may have been taught even more informally, particularly in the context of the family.

The record is fuller for the group uncovered by Longland in the Chiltern Hills in the 1520s. James Morden of Amersham taught Alice Atkins. Alice Brown was taught the beatitudes by John Tracher. Robert Cosin and Thomas Man instructed Joan Norman of Amersham not to go on pilgrimages, worship images of saints, confess to priests, or refrain from drinking before Mass on Sunday. Agnes Wells learned the Epistle of James from Thurstan Littlepage. Joan Cocks, the wife of Robert Wywood, husbandman, asked her master, Robert Durdant, and the Butler brothers to teach her something about God's law.[123]

Many examples of women learning about Lollardy in the Chiltern Hills have a family connection. James Morden, in addition to teaching Alice Atkins, also taught his sister Marion about images, "and after these little things he intended to teach her of the sacrament." Marion said that he had taught her the Pater Noster, the Ave, and the Creed in English and told her that she should not go on pilgrimage or worship saints and images. She had not done any of these for the six years before her examination, following her brother's advice. Richard Ashford, James Morden's employer, taught his wife Joan. John Barret, goldsmith of London, taught his wife and his maid the Epistle of James, which he knew by memory. Robert Bartlet taught his sister, Agnes Wells.[124]

Two of the most important teachers in the community centered in London and Essex, John Hacker and John Pykas, each taught a number of women. Hacker, whose career took him throughout Essex and London, deposed that several women had been his "followers" along with a number of men: Cony's wife, Joan Austy, Elizabeth Newman, Dorothy Long, Marion Westden Mathew, the wife of Bully, the wife of Styes, Alice, Mother Bristow, and Mother Beckwyth.[125] Pykas, whose activites were confined to Colchester, also taught Marion Westden Mathew and Dorothy Long; his other pupils included Margaret Bowgas, Margaret Cowbridge, and Alice Gardiner.[126]

The surviving evidence indicates that women's learning and teaching tended to take place in informal, often familial situations rather than in public conventicles. But it must be emphasized that even in these situations, women were altogether less active than men, even in the Chiltern Hills, Essex, or Coventry. No forum of Lollard activity was dominated by women.

THE TRADE IN LOLLARD BOOKS

Books were often passed around from person to person (women as well as men, literate as well as illiterate) as a way of spreading the Lollard word.[127] Illiteracy did not bar a Lollard from participation in the textual culture of the sect, as both men and women, literate or illiterate, had access to Lollard writings through the reading of others. In some cases illiterate Lollards showed great awareness of the written word despite their inability to read.[128] Thomas Boughton, a woolwinder and shoemaker of Hungerford who appeared before Bishop John Blythe in 1499, confessed that he

> had a great mynde to here sermouns and prechynges of doctours and lerned men of the church. And as long as they spack the veray wordys of the gospels and epistles such as I had herd afore in our englissh bookys, I herkned wele unto them and had great delight to here them. But assone as they began to declare scripture after their doctouriss and brought in other maters and spack of tythes and offrynges, I was sone wery to here them and had no favour in their wordys.[129]

For Thomas Boughton and perhaps for most other fifteenth-century lay-people, books were heard rather than read. Nonetheless, although he could not read, Boughton was sophisticated enough to distinguish between the different texts a preacher used to prepare his sermons.

Reading material for the Lollards consisted of a mixture of scripture, heretical Lollard tracts, and orthodox devotional works. The nature of late medieval orthodox books[130] may seem at first glance to be unsuitable for Lollard reading, but Lollards valued any religious work in English, and both they and their prosecutors viewed their possession of such books as a heretical act.[131] Lollards sometimes interpreted the content of orthodox works heretically. Alice Cottismore, for instance, understood her *Legenda aurea* (one of the most popular books of saints' lives, printed in English in 1483 by Caxton) as hostile to images and pilgrimages.[132] Other orthodox texts in English were read by members of the sect, including a book on the art of dying, Alice Rowley's English primer or book of hours ("librum . . . de primario in anglicis"), and several examples of books of a service of the Virgin Mary in English.[133] What Lollards made of these books and how they used them is not obvious; clearly, though, they valued access to religious knowledge in the vernacular however they found it.

As the illiterate Alice Cottismore's example reminds us, not all who possessed books, temporarily or permanently, could read: illiterate men and women who had books arranged for others to read the contents to them.[134] When the illiterate Thomas Abell of Coventry received a book from Joan Warde, he asked her to arrange for someone to come and read it to him.[135] Joan Smyth borrowed a book for three weeks, during which time Roger Landesdale came to her house to read it to her.[136] Robert Benet of London testified that he had bought a small book of the four Gospels from a stationer named Thomas Capon, but since he could not read it, he kept it locked up in his chest for four years. Finally, Capon came to live with Benet, and he read the book to him, explaining its contents. After Capon died, Benet sold the book to Thomas Austy for "a horse lode of hay."[137]

Men were more likely in most communities to have custody of books, but women were by no means excluded. Some of the Coventry women were very active in the book trade, as we saw earlier. Women from other Lollard communities also exchanged books, but not to the extent of the women in Coventry. Mother Bristow of London had a Gospel of Luke, while Joan Barret of London lent John Scrivener of Amersham the Gospels of Matthew and Mark.[138] The wife of Robert Pope of Amersham and West Hendred was said by John Butler to have various books "against the Romish religion."[139] Alice Saunders tried to buy a book in English for her daughter.[140]

Women's custody of books was often transitional. Joan Smyth passed the books she had inherited from her first husband, Richard Landesdale, to his relative Roger Landesdale.[141] Joan Austy of Essex, like Joan Smyth, inherited "Wycliffe's Wicket" and a book of the commandments from her first husband, John Redman, and then about eight weeks after her marriage to her second husband, Thomas Austy, she passed the books to him.[142] Agnes Pykas of Colchester gave her son John a book of Paul's Epistles in order to convert him; later John gave her the book for safekeeping as well as a New Testament he had subsequently bought, as he felt he was under suspicion.[143]

A London woman's experience with a book provides an interesting view of how books were traded around in an attempt to convert. John Woodroff gave Elizabeth Bate of the parish of St. Andrew, Eastcheap, a book of the commandments that belonged to Henry Hert. Hert later visited her and asked her how she liked the book. She replied that she did not much care for it; he asked for it back and told her that he would bring her another one that she would like better. She gave the book back to him, but he never returned.[144]

Women married to other Lollards often had access to the books their husbands owned. For example, Richard, the husband of Alice Colins of Ginge, was called a "great reader" and was said to have had "Wycliffe's

Wicket," the Gospel of Luke, a book of Paul, a gloss of the Apocalypse, a book of Our Lady's Matins in English, a book of Solomon in English, "The Prick of Conscience," "The King of Beeme," and a book of the Ten Commandments,[145] an impressive book list that was typical in its mixture of scripture, Lollard texts, and orthodox devotional texts. Alice Colins apparently could not read, but she undoubtedly benefited from her husband's book collection. Margery Baxter of Martham and Norwich was also read to by her husband in the evenings.[146]

Even when the books were not immediately available, recitation of memorized passages of scripture was another common means of conveying written texts. Hudson notes that memorization was used extensively by the Lollards and that it was a means of evangelization to those without access to books.[147]

Reading Lollard books was a central aspect of the sect's life. As in many of the movement's activities, women played a participatory but usually secondary role. Because their Lollard networks were more limited than men's, women were less likely to receive books from other Lollards. They possessed books less often, relying instead on male relatives and friends. Women were also much less likely to be able to read the texts than men.

Lollards and Recruitment to the Sect

To be a heretic in the Middle Ages was to cut oneself off from the universal church, the community of the faithful. Some historians have interpreted this as leading to a cutting of social ties as well — as Susan Brigden has said regarding Lollards, "utter social ostracism awaited the heterodox."[148] There is some evidence that the taint of Lollardy was sufficient to make a man or a woman a pariah. Margery Kempe, for instance, several times mistaken for a Lollard, was treated with derision both in her hometown of Lynn and on her travels.[149] Those who were Lollards sometimes hid their heresy: Margery Swayne, alias Barnard of Willesford in the diocese of Salisbury, confessed that she "wold not have commyn unto the churche oft tymes but to advoyde the Romour of the <pepul>."[150]

The ecclesiastical courts, seeking to use social pressure to promote religious conformity, assigned humiliating penances to heretics in order to draw public attention to their crimes. The most common involved walking in a public procession, barefoot and with head uncovered, carrying a candle or a faggot to symbolize the burning the penitent would incur on relapse into heresy.[151] Some Lollards were required to wear an embroidered badge depicting a faggot on the sleeve of their outermost garment for a period of a number of years or indefinitely.[152] Another mark of a heretic, more permanent, was branding with the letter *h* on the cheek or hand.[153] One case illustrates both the court's success in using such social pressures to conform and its occasional willingness to temper the penance: one man claimed that wearing the badge of the faggot on his sleeve would impede his ability to get employment, and the vicar-general, recognizing the merit of his claim, dispensed his penance.[154]

Other evidence, however, indicates that the ostracism of Lollards was far from complete. Indeed, the sect seems to have been tolerated to a great extent by the orthodox. No one from any of the East Anglian villages where Lollards were prosecuted by Bishop Alnwick in the 1420s, for example, apparently ever lodged a complaint against the heretics, not even the parish priests. The only depositions against Lollards by witnesses outside the group were made by Margery Baxter's neighbors in Norwich, a city particularly noted for its strongly orthodox lay piety.[155] Alnwick's prosecution was probably a result of an impetus from above (specifically, the exhortations of his archbishop William Chichele) rather than of complaints from below.[156] Similarly, the 1511 investigations into Lollardy by Bishops Fitzjames of London, Smith of Lincoln, and Geoffrey Blyth of Coventry and Lichfield were probably prompted by Archbishop Warham of Canterbury.[157] Few non-Lollards ever appeared as witnesses against those accused of being members of the sect. Lollards were, to some extent at least, benignly tolerated by the orthodox.

Social pressures worked to encourage as well as discourage participation in Lollard communities. In some villages, Lollards may have made up a majority or at least an influential minority, outnumbering "conforming" Roman Catholics. Amersham, where as many as 125 Lollards lived,[158] was such a community. Whether Lollards were a minority or a majority there, they were influential enough to pressure some who wished to stray from the heretical path.[159] The smaller town of Steeple Bumpstead, Essex, had fewer Lollards (only seventeen can be identified), but they included the parish priest, Richard Fox, and two churchwardens.[160] Fox consciously used his position as a religious authority to pressure potential converts, spreading his Lollard views through the confessional. Robert Hemsted said that he became a member of the sect because Fox had so assiduously courted him and "because he [Fox] was Prist."[161]

Even in areas where Lollardy was a minority movement, its very exclusiveness may have constituted an allurement.[162] It is possible that Lollardy was seen in some circles as fashionable, especially in the early fifteenth century when the memory of Lollards such as Sir John Oldcastle gave the movement an upper-class cachet. Certainly a woman such as Margery Baxter of Martham and Norwich felt herself to be among the elect and treated her orthodox neighbors with some disdain.[163] A later Lollard from Amersham was not embarrassed about her reputation: "Men do say, I was abjured for heresy; it may well be a napkin for my nose, but I will never be ashamed of it."[164]

Occasionally men and women were drawn to the Lollard movement because of personal animosity against the Catholic Church or particularly against the clergy. The Hemsted family (Joan, Robert, and Thomas) of Steeple Bumpstead, Essex, for instance, may have harbored a resentment against the Church because of a conflict with a local priest.[165] Another man, Richard Carder of Iver, was perhaps attracted to Lollardy in reaction to his wife's love affair with the local vicar.[166]

Social contacts within the Lollard movement indicate that heretical connections in the neighborhood or occupation could result in attraction to the sect. Interpersonal bonds work hand-in-hand with a group's ideology in recruitment; people are unlikely to become involved in a sect unless they have some prior attachment to its members.[167] Gender affects the ways in which these bonds work. In Lollardy, extrafamilial ties affected both women and men, but men's contacts tended to be much more far ranging than women's.

While little information survives about exactly where Lollards lived (making neighborhood relationships difficult to establish), several examples from the diocese of Norwich indicate that neighbors were sometimes the targets of proselytization. Thomas Mone, according to his servant John Burrell, often taught Lollard doctrines "to many of his neighbors."[168] Margery Baxter of Martham and Norwich made valiant attempts to convert her neighbor, Joan Clyfland, and Joan's servants.[169] According to his 1424 abjuration, Richard Belward had "counselled divers women, that they should not offer in the church for the dead, neither with women that were purified."[170] Both men and women would likely have been affected by neighborhood ties.

Whether Lollards sought to convert their friends or made friends with other converts, records that survive concerning members of the communities indicate that the social life of Lollards often involved people who shared their beliefs. In two communities where a number of Lollard wills survive, it is possible to trace continued connections, long after the prosecutions had ended, between those who were implicated in the movement. Such close relationships (and wills generally named close friends and family)[171] affected both men and women.

In the Chiltern Hills, two men who were apparently active in Amersham life, as well as in the Lollard community there, were named in a number of wills of those implicated in the sect. Robert Andrew (who acted as churchwarden for Amersham in 1519–20, although he was said in the early 1520s to be a man "especially noted to be of that [the Lollards'] side")[172] was supervisor and witness to the will of widow Katherine Bartlett in 1525 and witness to the will of widow Alice Saunders in 1539.[173] He was also appointed in 1524 to conduct an inventory of the goods of Florence and John Hill (the latter implicated in the Lollard community along with Andrew).[174] Roger Bennett was also an active man in town life; he acted as executor for the wills of the Hills and as witness to the will of Robert Fleming, rector of Amersham, who died in 1526.[175] Roger was related to or very friendly with Richard and Alice Saunders, the wealthiest of the Amersham Lollards. Richard Saunders left a bequest in 1524 to John, Thomas, Emma, and Alice Bennett, and in 1539 Alice Saunders left a bequest to Alice, daughter of Roger Bennett. John, Thomas, Emma, and Alice were probably all children of Roger Bennett (who named Thomas and Alice as such in his will of 1544), and it is possible that Alice Saunders was Alice Bennett's godmother.[176]

Wills of Colchester Lollards also illustrate social ties between members of the community. Thomas Mathew acted as witness in 1525 to the will of John Denby Sr. (possibly the husband of the Widow Denby later suspected of Lollardy).[177] Thomas Mathew's own 1534 will was supervised by the Lollard teacher John Pykas, witnessed by John Denby Jr., and included a bequest to Dorothy Long.[178] The 1539 will of Alice Gardiner was executed by John Denby Jr. and witnessed by John Bradley.[179]

While men and women shared relationships with family friends and neighbors equally, more far-flung connections were almost exclusively the territory of men. Lollards, as historians have noticed,[180] established something of a national network connecting the different communities; how extensive and organized this network was is a matter of debate,[181] but it is clear that members of the different communities studied here knew one another. William White and his followers, for instance, fled from prosecution in the diocese of Canterbury in the 1420s, moving from the Kentish Weald to an established Lollard community in East Anglia.[182] Sixteenth-century Lollards in Essex had ties to the communities in London and the Chiltern Hills.[183] The Coventry community also had connections with London and with the obscure but apparently important Lollard center, Bristol.[184] Men from London, Essex, and Middlesex who had regularly traveled to meet one another in the 1510s and 1520s continued their friend-ships into the new religious horizons of the 1530s and 1540s.[185]

Connections between communities were maintained because Lollards traveled to visit Lollards in other towns. With some exceptions, these trav-elers were men rather than women, allowing male Lollards to maintain a wider network of Lollard acquaintances than female Lollards. Men from the Kentish community in the early sixteenth century regularly traveled between the Tenterden area, Canterbury, and the Maidstone area. In one case, a woman traveled with her husband,[186] but for the most part, the women involved in the Kentish community did not participate in gather-ings held in other towns. In Essex, Richard Fox, John Tyball, and John Smyth, all of Steeple Bumpstead, traveled together to Colchester in the 1520s. On their way, they stopped at Braintree, staying one night with Mother Beckwyth and a second with her son William. In Colchester, the three men ate supper at the home of John Pykas and stayed with Thomas Mathew. The same three also traveled to Boxted to visit a man named Johnson.[187] John Tyball and Thomas Hilles traveled to London, where they bought a New Testament from the Lutheran Robert Barnes.[188]

Some men who acted as missionaries traveled extensively, probably using an underground network. Thomas Man traveled all over southeast England in the first two decades of the sixteenth century evangelizing.[189] John Hacker was also a Lollard missionary: he was known in the Chiltern Hills, Oxfordshire, Berkshire, London, and Essex.[190] According to Foxe, two London men, John Stacy and Lawrence Maxwell, "once a year, of their own cost, went about to visit the brethren and sisters scattered abroad."[191]

Margery Baxter was one of the rare women who traveled on Lollard business. She went to Yarmouth, probably accompanied by her husband,[192] and secretly carried back to her home in Martham some heretical books belonging to William White.[193] Nonetheless, it is striking that she appar-ently did not travel south with her husband to visit the main concentration of Norfolk Lollards in Loddon. William, her husband, traveled with Wil-liam White and was well-known in Loddon and other villages south of there, while Margery was not.[194]

Although female Lollards traveled infrequently, two unmarried women were able to use the national network to escape prosecution. Joan Warde, alias Wasshingbury of Coventry, fled that city about 1491 for fear of prosecution and was led by a Lollard to Northampton and then to London, staying in both cities with Lollards. Having married in London, she moved with her husband to Maidstone, Kent, several years later. After an arrest and conviction for heresy there, Joan returned to Coventry and its Lollard community, apparently without her husband.[195] Another woman, Joan Bocher, alias Joan of Kent, also used the network to flee prosecution. She moved from Steeple Bumpstead, Essex, to Frittenden in the Kentish Weald after she had been detected of heresy in Essex in 1528.[196] As these examples show, women's travels in the Lollard network were usually in situations necessitating flight, that is, as the result of exceptional circumstances rather than the rule.

For the most part, the means by which the Lollard network was established are obscure, but one significant way in which Lollards came to know one another was through work. William Riche of Benenden, glover, for instance, met Robert Harryson of Canterbury while in Tenterden on business: "ii yeres passed at Tenterden upon seynt martis day at a feyre kept there, he had communicacion with the said Haryson." They met thereafter at Canterbury as well as at Tenterden.[197] Trade links were important in Norfolk and Suffolk for maintaining contact with other Lollard communities. John Godesell, for instance, a parchment-maker from Ditchingham, had links with others in his craft in London and, through them, to the Lollard book trade.[198] William Baxter's trade as a wright or carpenter may have attracted Nicholas Belward of Earsham to his home in Martham. Nicholas, who converted William and his wife Margery, "wrought with them continually by the space of one year."[199] Locally, trade connections between Lollards living in the same town also indicate that occupational ties were significant for the recruitment of men. Lollardy in Loddon, for instance, was dominated by shoemakers; in the Martham area Lollards were centered in the carpentry trade (perhaps as a result of the influence of Nicholas Belward); and in Beccles the Lollards whose crafts are known were skinners and glovers.[200] Such occupational links,[201] an important factor connecting Lollards to their national community, were probably almost exclusively the province of men. Women's work rarely involved long-distance travel.

One measure of the extent to which women's contacts in the movement tended to be narrower than those of men is women's relationship with the clergy, a group that became increasingly marginal in the later years of the movement. In the early years of Lollardy, clerics were indispensable to its growth and maintenance. They played a leading role in the community in East Anglia, for instance: eight members of the clergy were implicated in Bishop Alnwick's proceedings against the heretics.[202] The two men in the community who were cited most often as teachers, by both men and women, were William White and Hugo Pye, chaplains.[203]

In contrast to the central role played by the clergy in the early period, however, Anne Hudson has characterized their involvement in later Lollardy as peripheral.[204] As the clergy became less central to the community, they had even less contact, proportionately, with the women in the movement. In Coventry, for instance, two priests with cures in Leicestershire were known by some of the men in the community. William Kent, rector of Staunton (now Stoney Stanton), was mentioned by Robert Silkby as being of the sect and was described by Bishop Blyth in a letter to Bishop William Smith of Lincoln as "maistre of divers heretikes." Kent was admitted to the cure of Stoney Stanton in 1465 and died by 1510.[205] His nephew, Ralph Kent, was also a priest, who, Silkby deposed, read to him many times from heretical books.[206] "Doctor Alcock of Ybstock" was also of the sect, Robert Hachet reported, while Silkby said that Alcock was involved in carrying books to William Kent. John Alcock was rector of Ibstock, Leicestershire (north of Stoney Stanton) and was obviously a learned man: he was a doctor of canon law by 1479 from a foreign university and held a number of benefices, including Ibstock, until his death in or before 1507.[207] Less information is available about another possible member of the clergy, a Sir Ralph Shor who was believed to have erroneous books.[208] None of these men advanced beyond the very fringes of the Coventry community, and because of this, they were only indirectly connected to the women in the group, none of whom knew them personally.

The Lollard community in Steeple Bumpstead, Essex, was an exception to the tendency in later Lollardy for clergy to be involved only on the margins of the movement — the curate of the parish and three Augustinian friars from a nearby house were directly involved in the Lollard circles there. But even in Steeple Bumpstead, the curate's and friars' contacts with female adherents appear to have been limited. Richard Fox, the curate, was converted by John Tyball[209] and became one of the leading teachers of Lollardy in the area, using his position as parish priest to convert at least two men in the confessional. The churchwardens of Fox's parish were a Lollard, John Tyball, and a man he hoped to convert to Lollardy, Thomas Hemsted.[210] But women of the Steeple Bumpstead community were apparently taught by lay Lollard teachers such as John Tyball or Gilbert Shipwright rather than by Fox or the three friars active in the town.[211] Family ties were key: Tyball was related to at least three of his female pupils.[212] Since women's contacts with the movement were most often made through their relatives, as we will see in the following chapter, clergy were less likely to be involved in the instruction of women, since they were not members of families in the Lollard communities. Clergy and members of religious orders may also have avoided such contact with women (especially in individual, face-to-face situations) because of potential rumours of sexual indiscretion.

*   *   *

Social factors affected women's and men's participation in the Lollard communities differently, both in extent and in direction. Women were by no means completely confined to their households, but their social contacts tended to be concentrated in the family and neighborhood. Men, on the other hand, had a social network, often based on occupation, that was wider than the household or immediate surroundings. Sensitivity to reputation and chastity could inhibit women without a Lollard family member or close friend from becoming involved in groups made up mostly, sometimes exclusively, of men. Only the community in Coventry, which included an all-female group, provided the sort of environment that welcomed unattached women. Social and ideological considerations rendered membership in a Lollard community and participation in its activities more difficult for and perhaps less attractive to women than to men.

4. Lollards and the Family

Historians studying the social aspects of medieval heretical sects and Protestant movements have approached in various ways the important question of the role of the family, the basic unit of social organization.[1] Scholars of medieval heresy have often tied the patriarchal nature of families in the Middle Ages to Catholicism; a revolt against Catholicism constituted a revolt against patriarchy. The Marxist thesis of Gottfried Koch, for instance, contends that women became involved in heresy (specifically Catharism) as a rebellion against their families and the patriarchal system typified and represented by the medieval Catholic Church. This thesis has been challenged in a number of recent works. Richard Abels, Ellen Harrison, and John Mundy, studying women in Catharism, find that Koch exaggerated the extent of women's participation in the movement. Those women who became involved, they argue, were not revolting against patriarchy but were in fact most often participating as part of a male-headed family. Others, who have also contested Koch's premise that women became adherents of the Cathar faith independently, have nonetheless seen the family-centered nature of heretical communities as promoting women's roles. In his study of the Cathar village of Montaillou, Emmanuel Le Roy Ladurie notes that the importance of the household or *domus* in Cathar organization emphasized family participation. Malcolm Lambert hypothesizes that the confining of Cathar activity to the household in fact made women more influential, suggesting that "the quiet diffusion and implanting of heresy in families was naturally a woman's work."[2]

While Reformation historians have also generally affirmed that the family was at the heart of the social organization of Protestant sects, their evaluation of the implications of this for women are mixed. Some have seen Protestantism's endorsement and praise of the married state and its emphasis on the family as the basis of religious life as beneficial to women, legitimizing their position in the domestic sphere and underscoring their spiritual equality with men. Conversely, others view the confirmation and even strengthening of patriarchy in Protestantism as detrimental to the status of women, limiting their options both in religious and secular life and reinforcing their subordination.[3]

Historians have also seen the Lollard movement as family-centered. The clandestine nature of the communities demanded that conventicles be held in the homes of believers rather than in parish churches or other public places, thus stressing the participation of the entire household.[4] Working in tandem with the sect's organization was its doctrine, which confirmed the importance of family and marriage and their patriarchal[5] structure.

Those who have studied Lollardy, particularly Claire Cross, have tended to view the family orientation of Lollardy as a basis for women's power in the movement.[6] Certainly the Lollard creed regarded the roles of married men and women as conferring the greatest merit, as opposed to orthodoxy where virginity and celibacy were most highly prized. In the Lollard view, family life pleased God best, validating the lives that the majority of men and women led.

While Lollards challenged the social and particularly the religious order in some ways, they did not question the prevailing patriarchal structures of marriage and family, which they saw in the same terms as others around them. The Lollard creed reinforced the familial model in which wives and children were subject to the male head of the household. Moreover, since Lollardy recognized no other roles for women than as wives and mothers, it removed the possibility that at least some orthodox women had of living outside the structures of the patriarchal family.[7]

Lollardy's emphasis on family both encouraged and limited the participation of women in the movement. Women participated in the Lollard movement most often in the context of their families and were more likely to be involved in Lollardy when other members of the family were also Lollards, suggesting that this may have been the main avenue of their recruitment. Although Lollard attitudes toward the family encouraged women's participation, paradoxically they also limited it by constraining women to the roles normally expected of them in the patriarchal family.

For men, the sect centered less on the family. Some men also became involved in Lollardy through their families, but a significantly smaller proportion of men than women had relatives in the movement. Men more often came into contact with and participated in the movement through extrafamilial ties. Nonetheless, within Lollard families male relatives were more likely to be recruited than female. In addition, prevailing patterns of authority within late medieval families conferred upon the men a dominant role.

Thus, while the family was the locus of most women's activity in the Lollard movement, it also predisposed them to subordinate and supporting roles. The family was of less importance to men (whose contacts in the sect often oriented away from the family), but within that structure they were authoritative and dominant.

Lollard Beliefs and the Family

Lollardy's view of family and marriage and the role of both sexes in these institutions affected the participation of men and women in the sect. Unfortunately, the beliefs of the Lollards in the communities studied here were not carefully recorded by the authorities except in the case of the community in the diocese of Norwich in the 1420s. The beliefs of this community, however, along with Lollard writings and occasional echoes in the prosecution of later Lollards, indicate something about their ideas of marriage, although other family relationships are little discussed.

Lollards viewed the married state as both natural and virtuous.[8] In their questioning, the authorities concentrated on suspects' objections to clerical celibacy and the Church's interference in marriage ceremonies, but underlying these beliefs was a positive view of conjugal relations and the family. The ideas of the East Anglian Lollards and their successors ultimately derived from Wyclif and his early followers. The emphases of the later Lollards, however, differed from those of their precursors, probably reflecting the changing social basis of the movement in the fifteenth century, centered in the household rather than in the university. The differences between the views expressed in Lollard writings and those found in abjurations remind us that the ideas of medieval clerics regarding family and marriage should not be taken as typical of lay society.

Wyclif and his disciples held ambivalent views on marriage. Wyclif supported the married state as a natural and positive one for laypeople, but his advocacy of clerical marriage (a more vexed question and thus more discussed) was unenthusiastic. Clerks should be allowed to take wives, he argued, because they fornicate if they are not allowed to marry.[9] The *Twelve Conclusions of the Lollards* (composed by members of the movement and displayed before Parliament in 1395) recommended clerical marriage more strongly than did Wyclif, but again more because of the impossibility of chastity than the positive goods of marriage. The Third Conclusion deplored the law of clerical continence, "þat in preiudys of wimmen was first ordeynid," while the Eleventh objected to the vows of chastity to which nuns were sworn, because such women, "þe qwiche ben fekil and vnperfyth in kynde," commit unspeakable crimes such as abortion and infanticide when subjected to such promises.[10] Lollard sermons pointed out that Christ's followers and other religious leaders in Christ's time were married. But the sermons did not insist upon the issue except as a weapon against the contemporary clergy, who also had wives and children but in a much worse way, "for þei han [them] owt of wedloc."[11]

Lollards in the diocese of Norwich, on the other hand, rejected celibacy not because it inevitably led to fornication, but because it was unnatural not to marry and have children. Edmund Archer of Loddon expressed the view that

> chastite of monkes, chanons, freres, nonnes, prestes and of ony other persones is not commendable ne meritorie, but it is more commendable and more plesyng unto God al suche persones to be wedded and bringe forth frute of hare bodyes.[12]

This may be an echo of the Lollard sermon written for the marriage mass, which outlined Augustine's three goods of marriage (faith, progeny, and chastity) and specifically noted that "God made hem in þis kynde [male and female] to loue, and þus brynge forþ fruyt."[13]

Clerical marriage was of particular interest to the clerics among the East Anglian Lollard community. According to Thomas Netter, William White, the group's leader, wrote "libelli" advocating the marriage of priests, in which he argued that Christ himself had favored it and that the Apostles had taken wives. White, along with another ordained priest among the East Anglian Lollards, put his ideas into practice: White married a young woman named Joan, and Thomas Pert, chaplain, married Katherine Hobbes.[14] Later Lollards also argued for clerical marriage. Thomas Tailour of Newbury, who abjured before Bishop Langton of Salisbury in 1491, said "that the order of pristhod was never ordeyned ne made by god but only matrimony."[15] Richard Sawyer, alias Pytfyn of Newbury, admitted in 1491 that he thought that priests should have their own wives and that they used to have them "in the old days."[16] John Tyball of Steeple Bumpstead, Essex, similarly thought that every priest should have a wife and used as justification a chapter of St. Paul, "where he saithe theis wordes, 'Every Bisshop ouwgt to be husbond of one wif, and to bryng forthe childern' [1 Tim. 3:2]."[17]

Lollards also believed, following Wyclif,[18] that marriage need not be solemnized by a priest in a church. The officials' treatment of this as an error to be abjured was in fact inconsistent with canon law: private or clandestine marriages without the blessing of a priest, while not favored by the Church, were canonically and theologically valid in the late Middle Ages.[19] No doubt the ecclesiastical opponents of the Lollards saw their objection to church weddings as another aspect of Lollard anticlericalism, and this is certainly true to some extent. But the way in which the Lollards expressed their belief reveals also a view of marriage in which mutual love was a necessary constituent part.

Henry Shercot of Devizes, who abjured before Bishop Audley in 1517, held what was apparently a purely anticlerical opinion: "wee shuld doo well ynowgh and have matrimony and baptisme withowte prestis, for crystyn-nyng is but wasshyng of the chylde with watyr and salte, and weddyng is but weddyng."[20] Richard and William Sparke of Somerham abjured a sim-ilarly bald view in 1457: "Only consent between a man and woman makes marriage, and this suffices without any other ceremony to the effect that, for instance, a man and wife may cohabit. The ceremony ordained by the church was constituted because of the avarice of priests."[21] These objections to marriage echo Lollard disapproval of other sacraments and of orthodox practices regarding the veneration of images, which they maintained had also been instituted only to feed the greed of the clergy.

The East Anglian Lollards, whose abjurations more fully express their views than those of their later fellows, show a more refined picture. While anticlericalism was still a factor (William Hardy, for instance, confessed to having believed that church weddings were "but vayneglorie induced be covetise of prestes to gete mony of the puple"),[22] such negativism about the clergy was not the only underlying theme. Baldwin Cowper of Beccles was charged in 1430 with holding that "oonly consent of love in Jhu' Crist betuxe man and woman suffiseth for the sacrament of matrimon, withoute contracte of ony wordis or solempnizacion in churche."[23] The Lollards emphasized the privacy of the act of marriage, which in their view con-cerned only the man, the woman, and Christ. Margery Baxter of Martham said that the "consent of mutual love" was sufficient, "without the expres-sion of any words,"[24] and John Kynget similarly said "thogh the man and the woman never speke."[25] One East Anglian Lollard, Richard Fleccher, envisaged a more public ceremony than did some others, but he still ex-cluded participation by the church: "only consent betuxe man and woman, with consent of the frendys of bothe parties, suffiseth for matrimony, with-oute expressyng of wordis or solennizacion in churche."[26] The emphasis these deponents put on the "speaking of words" reflects the idea that the words traditionally used even in private weddings, where no clergy were present, were nonetheless "canonical" and thus too closely associated with the Church.[27]

Despite the Lollards' rejection of the involvement of the Church, marriage was still in their eyes very much a religious act, a sacrament effected by the two parties "in Jesus Christ." It was also more than the financial or dynastic arrangement envisaged by some modern historians[28] — the consent of the parties was expressed in "mutual love" between them.[29]

The relationship between the married couple and their offspring, the "frute of hare bodyes," is rarely explicitly addressed in the articles abjured by the Lollards. But the Lollards' views regarding the sacraments of baptism and confirmation indicate something about the duty of transmitting the faith from one generation to another. Many Lollards thought that baptism or confirmation was not necessary "if the fadir and modir of the persone whiche shuld be baptized be of Crist' beleve";[30] Christianity could, and should, be directly passed from parent to child, presumably through the parents' instruction. The responsibility of the parents to inculcate Lollard beliefs and virtues in their offspring must have been considerable. Indeed, Lollard parents, both mothers and fathers, did teach their children Lollard beliefs, just as orthodox parents were expected to instill the basic elements of the Catholic religion in their offspring. Again, Lollard doctrine and practice reinforced the importance of family ties.

The emphasis on family and especially marriage in Lollardy affirmed the traditional roles of men and women as spouses and parents. In contrast to orthodoxy, which might lead believers to think that God favored the chaste nun or priest over the married person,[31] the Lollard creed allowed wives and husbands to feel they were fulfilling the role that was most pleasing to God. This also, however, reinforced the woman's traditionally subordinate role as wife under the authority of her husband, and the child's subservient position to the parent, especially the father.

In both theoretical and legal thinking of the Middle Ages, a woman was to be subordinate to a man, most often her husband or father.[32] Lollards, while they implicitly and explicitly challenged the orthodox views of many of medieval society's other institutions and relationships, did not stray from the traditional interpretation of the position of women and men inside the family. Like their contemporaries, Lollards saw the subordination of wife to husband, woman to man, as part of God's divine creation.

Wyclif's assessment of power relationships in a marriage, for instance, repeated with little alteration the Adam's rib analogy used by many medieval theologians, such as twelfth-century writers Peter Lombard and Hugh of St. Victor. As Wyclif wrote,

> The wife must honor her husband more diligently than the reverse; as a sign of this, woman was made from man, not man from woman, as is shown in Gen. iii. Nonetheless, there must be mutual companionable love between them; as a sign of this, the woman was not made from the head nor from the feet of the man, but from his side, to denote that she must not be servant nor mistress to her husband but a companion by his side.[33]

The Lanterne of Li3t puts the matter even more plainly: "For it is writen fro þe bigynnyng. Ge. ii°. þat God ordeyned man. to heed & lord ouir þe womman / & a3enward þe womman to be vndirloute & suget. vnto þis man."[34] Other writers' recognition that higher powers might interrupt these hierarchies serves only to reinforce their normalcy. William Thorpe noted that "þe laawe of holi chirche techeþ in decrees þat no seruaunt to his lord, neiþir child to his father ne to modir, neiþer wiif to her housebonde, ne monke to his abbot owiþ to obeie, no but in leeful þingis and lawful."[35] Lollard sermons emphasize that it is instinctive for a wife both to love her husband and to be glad in "hire herte and her cher" when he is near, and to "do wrchipe to [him] for he is betere."[36] The sermons' frequent use of family relationships as metaphors for God's affiliation with his people further naturalized the authority of husband over wife, father over son, and parent over child.[37]

Emphasis on family in Lollard doctrine thus certainly confirmed the patriarchal structure of the medieval household and perhaps even increased its importance. Lyndal Roper has argued that a similar emphasis on the family in the ideology of the German Lutheran churches narrowed the definition of women's place to the domestic context only, greatly restricting their roles outside the household.[38]

In practice, of course, the balance of power was not the same in every marriage, although it was still usually weighted in favor of the husband.[39] Some historians have suggested that wives in the lower levels of society had more influence in a marriage than at upper levels. Women of the urban artisan classes married in their mid-twenties; their husbands, whom they chose themselves, were roughly the same age. Women of the elite (urban or rural), on the other hand, usually married when teenagers to husbands (often chosen by their parents) who were in their late twenties or early thirties. Thus artisan women, it is thought, had more authority and influence in their households than did wives of the upper classes.[40] Artisan women may indeed have had more equal marriages than their counterparts among the gentry, but the evidence of Lollard marriages indicates that this greater equality was only relative. While some women were able to participate in Lollard activities with a measure of independence from their husbands, almost all marriages appear to have conformed to a model in which husbands were dominant and wives subordinate.

Family Relationships in the Lollard Communities

The Lollard creed's reinforcement of traditional patriarchal family structures is particularly significant for a gender analysis of the movement, because women who became involved in Lollard communities most often participated in the context of a family. Seven of every ten women identified as Lollards were certainly related to another Lollard, while only half as many men had another family member implicated.[41] The figures for both men and women are undoubtedly underestimations; among the Buckinghamshire Lollards, where more information about family relationships is available, the numbers rise to 78 percent of women and 46 percent of men. If an assumption is made that those from the same town with the same surname were related, the figure for women in Buckinghamshire rises to as high as 85 percent.

The large proportion of female Lollards with family ties provides a clue as to how women came to be involved in the movement: although evidence regarding recruitment of women is meager, it seems likely that many women were attracted to the movement through family connections. It also implies that women who participated in Lollardy most often did so in the context of the patriarchal family structure and all that it represented. More than 90 percent of women with family connections in the Lollard movement were related to male members of the sect,[42] a pattern also found in the later Protestant communities.[43] Thus the participation of most women in the Lollard movement was governed by the norms of the late medieval family in which men were dominant, authoritative figures. Only among the all-female conventicle in Coventry was the pattern different — there, three women had Lollard husbands (although two of these husbands were dead by the time of Blyth's prosecution in 1511), but eight women (four mother-daughter relationships) were related only to other female Lollards. The unusual nature of the Coventry community, as we saw in Chapter 2, is no doubt partly a reflection of this.

Proportionately, women were more likely than men to have a relative in the movement, but in absolute terms, more men (233 men vs. 189 women) were part of Lollard families than women. This suggests that while women who joined the movement most often did so as part of a family, male relatives were still more likely to be recruited (or to respond to recruitment) than female relatives.

Husbands, Wives, and Widows

The most important family relationship in the Lollard communities was that between husband and wife. In relative terms, more women than men had Lollard spouses. Of 271 women involved in the communities studied here, 138 (or 51 percent) were married to men involved in the movement; obviously the same number of men, 138, were married to Lollard women, but proportionately this made up only 20 percent of the 682 men implicated in the sect.[44] Half the women, but only one-fifth of the men, participated in Lollardy as part of a married couple.

We saw the importance of a group of married couples in Coventry, which included Thomas Villers and his sisters Thomasina Bradeley and the wife of Banbrook and their husbands. The same phenomenon is seen many times in other communities. The report that the heresiarch Thomas Man led five married couples from the Chiltern Hills to safety in Suffolk and Norfolk during the *magna abjuratio* of 1510–11[45] indicates that to some extent the marital unit was basic to the Lollard communities, just as it was to society as a whole. But the two halves of the marital unit were not equal—wives and husbands played different and asymmetric roles in the movement.

Wives varied in the extent of their activity and commitment to the sect. Some were very active. Although many women took part in Lollard activities only as part of a married couple, some wives functioned independently of as well as in concert with their husbands. As we have seen, Hawise Mone of Loddon, who together with her husband hosted Lollard schools, also invited guests to break the Lenten fast with her while her husband was away.[46] Alice Colins of Ginge, whose husband Richard was said to be "a great doer among these good men," was accused separately from her husband of discussing and teaching Lollard doctrine to several women.[47] In one case, a husband disapproved of his wife's independent activities: Isabel Tracher of Amersham had a Lollard husband, but he was not enthusiastic about his wife's participation. While he was said to have sheltered Thomas

Grove in his house when Grove refused to attend mass, Tracher also apparently rebuked his wife for the same offence of not going to church.[48]

In some rare cases, wives appear to have been more active than husbands. Joan Gest of Coventry and then Birmingham is the most striking example of this. Her employer John Smyth, who had abjured in 1486, first taught Joan her heresy in Coventry before her marriage. She later married John Gest of Birmingham and then taught him her Lollard opinions (as her husband himself affirmed). An important factor in Joan's having taken a leading role may have been their relative ages; John said that Joan converted him in about 1500, when he was about twenty years old and she thirty. Joan and her husband participated in the movement both as a couple and separately. Joan, for instance, went to stay with Agnes Brown in Coventry for three weeks and thus maintained contact with the women in Coventry. Joan and John were assigned penances at the same time on 6 November 1511; they were the only married couple in the Coventry community who were given their penances together.[49] Another case is less clear: testimony indicates that both Isabel and John Morwyn of Amersham were Lollards, but the evidence against Isabel is much more extensive than against John. Isabel Morwyn was still participating in the context of a Lollard family, however; her family of origin (the Bartletts) were prominent Lollards.[50]

More common than wives who were more active than their husbands are cases of wives who appear to have been involved only reluctantly in the movement. Constance Clerc of Coventry, the wife of Thomas Clerc, for instance, was rumored to be of the sect, but Constance herself denied it when brought before the bishop. Her husband Thomas agreed that she was not involved: he said that she had heard him reading various times and knew the books he had were heretical, but that he had not read the books to her and, indeed, that she had wanted him to burn them.[51]

Similarly, Roger Landesdale testified against another Coventry woman, Katherine Hachet, whose husband Robert was a prominent heretic, saying that she had often heard him (Landesdale) reading and that she favored heretical opinions. But Katherine Hachet, like Constance Clerc, denied this when she was brought before the bishop and said that she had tried to discourage her husband from keeping the company of heretical men. Robert Hachet agreed that his wife knew his secrets and opinions, but that she did not favor them. Nor was she mentioned in the deposition of Rose Furnour, a former servant of the Hachets, who informed the court about the Lollard activities of the Hachet household.[52]

Margaret Landesdale, unlike Constance Clerc and Katherine Hachet, admitted that she was a Lollard along with her husband, but her deposition shows her to have been an unenthusiastic one, in some ways a spectator on the side-lines of her husband's activities rather than a full participant. She deposed that she had seen Silkby come to their house two or three times and that she had heard him communicating with her husband, Roger; she also saw Joan Smyth (then the widow of Richard Landesdale, probably Roger's brother) bring books to Roger, and she saw where he hid them; similarly, she saw Thomasina Bradeley come to communicate with Roger, but she was not privy to their conversation. Although Margaret may not have been much involved in her husband's Lollard activities, she did abjure the heresy and served penance.[53]

If some women participated in Lollardy only reluctantly, under pressure from their husbands, this was never the case with men. Even John Gest, whose wife clearly led him into the sect, was an enthusiastic Lollard.[54] The authority that husbands held over their wives might have led women to become involved in the sect somewhat against their own inclinations, while the power relationship between husbands and wives would rarely if ever have worked in the reverse.

The participation of widows illustrates the extent to which married women's activity was curtailed or restricted. Widows, an important element in some communities but virtually absent from others, were in some ways an anomalous group in a movement that centered on the family. In many cases widows were simply part of this family-centeredness — although they had no husbands, they often had other close relatives in the movement. But some widows, particularly those in Coventry, operated outside the patriarchal and especially the marital structure, leaving them able to play roles less available to other women. Because they were not subject to the authority of a husband, widows were freer to participate in Lollardy than were women married to orthodox husbands.[55] They were also freer to take significant roles and often did — their commitment to the movement may in some cases have been greater since involvement was a personal choice rather than a family one.

The part played by widows in Lollardy varied significantly from community to community. In some groups it was virtually non-existent; all women were either married or young single women. This was the case in the East Anglian community in the 1420s (where one woman, Isabella Chapleyn, may have been a widow)[56] and in the Kentish communities uncovered in 1511 (where the Lollard husband of one woman, Agnes Ive, had recently died).[57] Three women from the diocese of Salisbury were widows,[58] but little is known about these women or their roles in the community. Even in the large Lollard community in the Chiltern Hills there were few widows. Only one woman was certainly a widow[59] and another, Agnes Ashford, was probably also widowed. Ashford had Lollard offspring, Richard Ashford and Thomas Tredway, and taught her son Richard's servant various Lollard prayers.[60] Two widows from London, Joan Boughton and her daughter Lady Jane Yonge, may have been important to their community,[61] but their roles are obscure, as is Lollardy in the metropolis generally.

While Lollard widows in East Anglia, Kent, the Chiltern Hills, and London are relatively rare, widows were more commonly involved in the Lollard communities in Essex and Coventry and contributed significantly to them. A number of widows of Colchester, particularly Margaret Cowbridge, Alice Gardiner, Katherine Swayn, and Agnes Pykas, were involved in the Colchester Lollard community, although the extent of their commitment to Lollardy is not always clear.[62] Widows were also implicated in the rural Essex community centered around Steeple Bumpstead, acting particularly as hostesses to Lollard gatherings. Mother Beckwyth of Braintree, probably the mother of Anthony, Robert, and William Beckwyth, hosted John Tyball, Richard Fox, and John Smyth as they traveled from Steeple Bumpstead to Colchester. Other widows in the Steeple Bumpstead area welcomed Lollard schools in their homes: Joan Bocher (who went on to an active career as an Anabaptist); Mother Charte; and another woman who may have been a widow, Joan Agnes, alias Smyth.[63]

Widows were most prominent in the community in Coventry — the all-female groups there attracted widowed women, who made up much of their membership. Alice Rowley, the leader of the group, had been a widow since 1505.[64] Joan Warde was probably also a widow,[65] and Agnes Brown was the widow of a man who had been "the worst" Lollard, Thomas Brown.[66] Other women were presumably also widows since their husbands were never mentioned and they had children. Agnes Yong was the mother of Juliana Yong, who was always identified only as the daughter of Agnes, making it unlikely that her father was still alive.[67] Agnes Corby was the mother of Elizabeth Gest.[68] Agnes Jonson was the mother of Margaret Grey and was known as "Mother Agnes" or "litle moder Agnes," probably indicating her status as a widow.[69] Agnes de Bakehouse was likely also widowed, although she may have been a spinster; again, no husband is mentioned.[70] The prominence of women in Coventry Lollardy may be due to the number of women who participated in the community outside the constraints of marital bonds.

Just as wives' roles in the Lollard sect were restricted by patriarchal family structures, those same structures encouraged husbands to take a more active part than their wives. The examples are too numerous to cite here, but a closer examination of the Lollards in one community, that uncovered by Archbishop Warham in Kent in 1511, vividly shows a pattern where men participated much more vigorously than their spouses.

William Baker of Cranbrook, for instance, attended Lollard gatherings held all over Kent, but the only evidence for his wife Margaret's involvement in Lollardy is her own abjuration. There is no record of their having participated together: all the evidence for William's part in the Lollard group consists of his interaction with other male Lollards.[71] The case of John and Joyce Bampton of Bearsted is similar: although Joyce admitted in her abjuration that she had been a heretic for seven years, no deponents named her as a participant in Lollard gatherings (even those held at her own house). John, on the other hand, was, according to the testimony given by himself and others, a frequent attender of conventicles.[72] Even Agnes and John Grebill fit this pattern, although Agnes's role is much clearer to us because of the amount of evidence required to condemn her as an unrepentant heretic. While John visited other male Lollards and they visited him, Agnes's contacts involved her family and occasional visitors to their house.[73] Because women's Lollard activities in Kent appear to have been confined to domestic and familial situations, they were less recorded than those of their male relatives, but they were also narrower.

The large number of Lollards married to other Lollards suggests that many were converted by their spouses. Husbands probably had greater influence on their wives than the reverse: certainly ecclesiastical officials expected husbands to govern their wives in matters of religion as in other things. In seventeenth-century Strasbourg, it was thought that a woman "would easily let herself be led into error in religion by her husband."[74] On the other hand, medieval clerics thought that wives were able to persuade their husbands to act properly in spiritual matters,[75] indicating that influence within a marriage no doubt traveled a two-way path.

Little specific evidence in fact survives about conversion, especially of women. In the case of the Essex Lollards, for instance, the court made little effort to ascertain how women were converted, although they were more concerned about the question as regards men. Any such evidence usually comes incidentally from a man's deposition about his own activities, the bias arising from the court's greater interest in men's heretical endeavors.[76] Thus there is much less information about what was perhaps a usual pattern of husbands instructing their wives. The only example in the Essex records that explicitly states that a man led his wife into the heresy is John Tyball's conversion of his wife (who was, despite her husband's instruction, reluctant to believe what he taught her about the sacrament of the eucharist).[77]

On the other hand, there are several examples of wives initiating their husbands into Lollardy, although subsequent instruction usually came from men. Joan Hemstead of Steeple Bumpstead, Essex, had learned the Pater, Ave, and Credo in English from Gilbert Shipwright; she then taught her husband Thomas what she had learned. The remainder of Thomas's instruction in Lollardy came from his parish priest, Richard Fox, and from John Tyball, who perceived that he would be interested in the sect when they observed that he knew English prayers. Thomas Hilles, who had lived in Steeple Bumpstead and in Witham, said that he had first been taught his heresy by a woman, Joan Dyer of Finchingfield, to whom he had been betrothed but who had then died. She taught him the first chapter of the Epistle of James; later he too was instructed by John Tyball. Joan Gest of Birmingham instructed her husband John, ten years her junior, in the Lollard creed. He subsequently had heretical conversations with John Jonson and Roger Landesdale.[78] These cases of wives converting husbands may have been more likely to have been recorded than husbands' conversion of wives precisely because they were rather unusual. Nonetheless, the influence of a fervent Lollard wife should not be discounted.

Some Lollards were married to non-Lollards, a situation with different implications for women than for men. While it may have been uncomfortable and perhaps dangerous for a man to be involved in heresy when his wife was not, a woman theoretically could use only her influence or a threat to disclose his activities to the authorities to attempt to dissuade her husband from heresy. Husbands, on the other hand, effectively could (or at least were expected to) forbid their wives from pursuing a course that would take them outside the orthodox church. Although some women in the Lollard communities were married to men who were apparently not Lollards, their course of action was sometimes more difficult than that followed by men whose wives did not participate in the sect.

Many men were married to non-Lollards. Some wives simply tolerated their husbands' activities, such as the wife of Robert Benet of London, who was present when her husband read from the scriptures to Thomas Walker but did not listen to what he said.[79] Others, like Katherine Hachet and

Constance Clerc of Coventry,[80] attempted to persuade their husbands to abandon their activities.

But many orthodox wives were apparently under more pressure from their husbands or their husbands' friends to forsake their Catholic beliefs than they themselves could exert to dissuade their spouses from heresy. Most often this pressure took the form of sarcasm or ridicule. William Sweeting, who had a long and varied career as a Lollard and a parish clerk around various parts of Essex and London, was married, although nothing is known about his wife except that she apparently did not share his beliefs. He censured her for her orthodox devotional practices: "he asked of her, what good she would receive by her going on pilgrimage? adding moreover, that as he supposed it was to no purpose nor profit; but rather it were better for her to keep at home, and to attend her business." He also rebuked her for worshiping images in the church and for setting up candles before them.[81] Similarly, William Dorset of King's Langley scolded his wife, who was about to set off on pilgrimage to Our Lady of Willesdon: "Our lady," said William, "is in heaven."[82] John Bayly of Rolvenden, Kent, ridiculed his wife for making a pilgrimage on "Reliques Sunday," saying that the priests only wanted to make money.[83] When John Bates of Stratford Langthorn hosted the great Lollard teacher Thomas Man at his house in 1515, Bates's wife (apparently not of the sect) asked Man to go with her to hear the Gospel, but Man replied, "I will not go there; go you if you list; ye shall have as much need for it, as to put your finger in the fire and to burn it."[84]

While husbands might fear that their non-Lollard wives would testify against them in the ecclesiastical courts, wives had no direct authority over their husbands and were thus not able to prevent their husbands from practicing heresy. Nor did the courts presume that wives were capable of deterring their spouses from participation in Lollard groups. Husbands, on the other hand, who were expected to rule their wives, were responsible to some extent for their spouses' behavior. Two cases in Kent illustrate these different expectations. John Bukherst of Staplehurst, Kent, appeared before Archbishop Warham in June 1512 and abjured Lollard heresies; his wife, Joan Bukherst, appeared the same day, and the Archbishop gave her a penance (abstaining from fish on the next five successive Fridays) because she had concealed her husband's opinions.[85] Although she was not expected to prevent her husband's errors, she did have a duty to report them to the ordinary. Another couple, Joan Dodde and her husband John Dodde, also appeared the same day before Archbishop Warham; in this case Joan abjured heresy while her husband was given penance for concealing her opinions. John's penance was more severe than that of Joan Bukherst (he was to offer two candles worth 1d. to the image of the Virgin in his parish church), because Joan Bukherst's error in not disclosing heresy in her husband was less serious than that of John Dodde, who theoretically had authority over his wife. John Dodde's responsibility for his wife's behavior was made explicit in the court's admonition "that from this point on he will manage his wife properly and honestly."[86] A later parallel shows that ecclesiastical courts saw it as the duty of the patriarch to ensure proper religious behavior in his household: among Catholic recusants in the 1570s and 1580s, spinsters and widows were seen as responsible for their own conduct, while husbands were expected to answer for the actions of their wives. Courts often ordered husbands to force their wives to conform.[87]

The extent to which a wife recognized her husband's authority over her in spiritual matters is unclear, but in many cases it was in the husband's worldly interests to keep his wife from heresy. An orthodox husband may have felt embarrassment or perhaps even suffered impediments to his business or civic career as a result of the activities of a Lollard wife. In two Coventry cases, at least, husbands were hostile to their wives' Lollardy. Margery Locock, described as recently the wife of Hugo Stubbe, had married Henry Locock, girdler, not long before her appearance in the bishop's court. She admitted that she had been a Lollard while she was married both to Hugh and to Henry and that she was willing to renounce her heresies, and she did so. But rather than enjoining her to do the usual public abjuration and penance, the bishop ordered her to swear corporally instead, because he feared that otherwise she would be repudiated by her husband.[88] The husband of Alice Rowley, William, caused one of Alice's Lollard contacts, Joan Warde, to flee Coventry, perhaps to remove what he saw as a bad influence on his wife.[89]

Because of the difficulties inherent in mixed marriages, it is not surprising to find evidence that Lollards, like the Cathars and Waldensians,[90] practiced sectarian endogamy. The ecclesiastical officials suspected that the Lollards married only one another: Agnes Wells of Amersham was asked "whether she knew such a law and custom among them, that such as were of that sort did contract matrimony only with themselves, and not with other Christians?"[91] While Wells's answer to this question is not recorded, it is clear that Lollards often did marry one another. Joan Warde of Coventry, for instance, married a certain Thomas Wasshingbury of London, shoemaker, also a heretic, through the efforts of two Lollards named Mytilener and Brian.[92] A witness cited William Frank of Amersham as a Lollard partly because he married a woman who had previously abjured heresy.[93] Children of Lollards often married other members of the sect. Joan, the daughter of long-time Lollard Thomas Vincent, married two men who were Lollards, John Redman and Thomas Austy.[94] The daughter of Thomas Parker of Colchester married Lollard John Thompson.[95]

The wedding of two Lollards could be the occasion of a Lollard gathering. John Scrivener of Amersham reported that John Merrywether, his wife and his son, Isabel Harding of Amersham, Hartop of Windsor, Joan Barret of London, Henry Miller, John Stilman, and Nicholas Durdant were all present at the marriage of Robert Durdant's daughter. "They assembled together in a barn, and heard a certain epistle of St. Paul read; which reading they well liked, but especially Durdant, and commended the same."[96] The marriage of Joan and Robert Burges of Burford was also a Lollard event. Roger Dod, Thomas Baker, Robert Livord, John Sympson, Thomas Reiley, John Clemson, James Edmunds, and William Gun were all present at the wedding, which was held at the home of John Harris of Upton.[97]

Some Lollard families were interrelated by marriage, suggesting either that this was the means by which the faith was spread or that families intermarried because they belonged to the Lollard faith. The long-lived Chiltern Hills community in Buckinghamshire illustrates this particularly well: important families such as the Mordens, Ashfords, Bartletts, and Littlepages were related to one another by marriage.

Fully half the women who were involved in Lollardy were married to other Lollards, suggesting that this was a critical element in recruitment of women to the movement. The dynamic in Lollard marriages varied. Some women participated in the movement always with their husbands, while other wives functioned independently of as well as in concert with their husbands, suggesting that they saw their beliefs as more than a wifely duty. In rare cases, wives appear to have been more committed than their husbands, but a more common pattern was greater activity of husbands than wives, especially in interaction with the outside Lollard community. Some wives were involved in the sect reluctantly, perhaps as a result of pressure from their husbands, but no husbands were Lollards against their wills — men who were converted by their wives were apparently all convinced and enthusiastic Lollards. The power relationship in a late medieval marriage made it more likely that women would be influenced or pressured to join the Lollard movement against their inclinations; while women clearly had influence in a marriage, it appears not to have been significant enough to induce reluctant husbands to become Lollards half-heartedly.

When Lollards were married to non-Lollards, the implications were different for women than for men. Women could plead with their husbands not to follow the dangerous path of heresy, but they had little practical or theoretical authority over their spouses. Husbands, on the other hand, were expected by the church courts to ensure their wives' orthodoxy. Although, clearly, women were able to act against the wishes of their husbands if they felt a higher authority calling them, the relatively small number of women married to non-Lollards suggests that this was not common. Some examples show that women experienced hostility from their husbands if they persisted in Lollardy against their wishes.

PARENTS AND CHILDREN

While the marriage bond seems to have been the most important family relationship between Lollards, the parent-child relationship was clearly an important avenue for bringing new Lollards into the group: parents were expected to teach their children their faith. While parents made an effort to bring both daughters and sons into the sect, the structure of the patriarchal family sometimes emphasized the participation in the movement of adult sons rather than daughters, who moved away from their family of origin upon marriage.[98]

The ecclesiastical and secular authorities recognized that the tie between parents and children was a significant means of bringing Lollards into the movement, and they tried in some cases to sabotage it. They saw both male and female children as vulnerable. Joan Clerk was the only daughter of William Tylsworth, who was burned at Amersham about 1506; her penance included setting fire to her father.[99] Similarly, when John Scrivener, also of Amersham, was executed in 1522, his children were compelled to set fire to him.[100] Foxe reports from the remembrances of witnesses that when Laurence Ghest was burned at Salisbury about 1508, his wife and seven children were ordered to be present; Foxe implies that this was meant to stimulate Ghest's recantation,[101] but it could as easily have been a warning to the children, as were the incidents at Amersham. The officials in Kent also feared the transmission of Lollardy from father to child: as John Browne of Ashford was being burned, "one Chilton, the baily-arrant, bade cast in Browne's children also, for they would spring, said he, of his ashes."[102] The bailiff was correct about Browne's children: his son Richard was imprisoned as a Protestant under Queen Mary, and his daughter Alice apparently also became a Protestant and told Foxe the story of her father's last days.[103] Lollards and ecclesiastical officials regarded Lollard parentage as significant.

John Grebill Sr. of Tenterden and Benenden, Kent, deposed that his neighbor William Carder had been born in Lincolnshire

> and that the said Carder shewed to this deponent that his fader and moder were of the same secte, and he saith that the moder of the said Carder fled from Tenterden about xl yeres past for fere of the saide heresies, but whether [whither] he knoweth not.[104]

The court scribe noted at the bottom of the abjuration of William Bocher of Steeple Bumpstead that "he was descended from vicious stock: because the grandfather of his father was burned for heresy, as it is said."[105]

Officials had reason for concern: children did in fact learn heresy from their parents. Young children sometimes became involved in Lollardy simply by being present during their parents' activities.[106] The two adolescent sons of John Forge, John Jr. and Thomas, who deposed against their father, indicated that they had been present when their father's friends James Brewster and William Sweeting read from Lollard books and taught from them.[107] Thomas Love of Rockland St. Mary, Norfolk, directed his six-year-old daughter to give his friend, John Fyllys, meat to eat on the vigil of the feast of St. Thomas the Apostle, thereby making his daughter part of the act of defiance against the Church.[108] Others were more purposefully instructed in the faith. Edward Parker, aged about eleven, the son of Richard Parker of Reading, appeared before Bishop Audley about 1508 because he had been discussing Lollard doctrine with his playmates: "He said publicly when there were others present playing with him that the body of Christ is not in the sacrament of the altar, but is only bread, and also that the images of saints were not to be adored because they were stones and sticks."[109] He was asked by the bishop how he had learned these things; at first he said it had been Lewis John of Reading who had taught him, and then he changed his mind and stated that it had been his father Richard.[110]

Memorization was a means for instruction of children as well as adults. Elizabeth, the daughter of Blake, a cooper of London, was apparently a Lollard by the age of thirteen; she could recite by heart many Gospels and Epistles.[111] Another daughter, Joan Colins, was also being taught by her mother and father, Alice and Richard Colins of Ginge, to memorize various scriptural passages and prayers.[112] The Colins's instruction was seen to be so effective that John Edmunds sent his daughter Agnes into service in their household "to the intent she might be instructed there in God's law."[113] Some children were even taught to read: the son of William Bate of Seething, reported William Baxter, could "read English very well," and the daughter of Hawise and Thomas Mone was "partly of the same sect, and [could] read English" also.[114]

It is interesting to note here that the Mones' daughter was only "partly" a Lollard; was she perhaps rebelling against her parents and refusing to adopt wholeheartedly the Lollard creed? A clearer case of rebellion against Lollard parents is seen in the Grebill family of Kent. John Grebill Sr. deposed that he had started to teach his sons about his beliefs concerning the sacrament of the altar when they were about seven years old, in the presence of their mother Agnes, who was agreeable to their being taught these things. Their sons, Christopher and John Jr., however, both testified that they were not very interested in their parents' beliefs until they were much older. Christopher (age twenty-two) said that he had "no felyng in that maters of errours" until he was taught at age nineteen by his parents' friend, John Ive. John Jr. (age twenty-one) said that his parents had tried to teach him many times from the age of fourteen or fifteen, "but he never cowde perceyve their techingis nor geve any hert therunto tyll this yere last past."[115] John Colins of Burford also objected to his father's instruction: when his father, Thomas Colins of Ginge, taught John the Ten Commandments and various Lollard doctrines, John was "so much discontented . . . that he said he would disclose his father's errors, and make him to be burned; but his mother entreated him not so to do."[116] Although not all children were willing to heed their parents' instruction and follow their example, it is clear that parents heavily influenced their children.

Adult children as well as minors could be converted by parents. John Pykas of Colchester, who was about thirty-three when brought before Bishop Tunstall of London in 1528, said that he had been converted by his mother, Agnes Pykas:

> About a five yeres last past, at a certayn tyme, his mother, then dwellyng in Bury, sent for hym; and movyd hym that he shuld not beleve in the Sacraments of the Church, for that was not the ryght way. And then she delyvered to this respondent one book of Powle's Epistoles in English; and byd hym lyve after the maner and way of the said Epistoles and Gospels, and not after the way that the Church doth teche. . . . And so in contynuance of tyme, by the instruction of his mother, and by reading of the said books, he fell into these errors and heresies ayenst the Sacrament of the Altar.[117]

Parents could also be converted by their adult children. John Tyball both converted his mother, Elene Tyball, and taught his godmother, Alice Gardiner.[118]

The number of parent-child relationships in a community is partly a function of the age and longevity of that community. The Lollard group uncovered in the diocese of Norwich by Bishop Alnwick in 1428, for instance, was fairly young, probably less than ten years old.[119] Several young children in the group (the son of William Bate, the daughter of Hawise and Thomas Mone, and the daughter of Thomas Love of Rockland St. Mary)[120] were involved in Lollard activities, but no adult children are known to have belonged. On the other hand, the community of Lollards in the Chiltern Hills, which went back at least to Oldcastle's Revolt in 1414, encompassed many parents and their adult children.[121] Clearly, the longer a community survived, the greater the number of intergenerational relationships within that community and probably the greater the likelihood that women in these families, born into the sect, would participate in the heresy.

The relative importance of fathers and mothers varied from community to community. The records for Coventry, which show a generally higher importance of women than in other communities, reveal a particularly high number of female parents, who were more likely to have daughters in the movement than sons.[122] Other Lollard communities do not show a similar preponderance of female parents—among the Chiltern Hills Lollards, for instance, fathers were far more common than mothers: there were five mothers and fifteen fathers.[123] Nonetheless, as we shall see, some mothers in Amersham, especially Katherine Bartlett and Agnes Ashford, were very significant in intergenerational Lollard families.

Other Family Relationships

Sibling relationships also appear among Lollards, although they were less common than spousal or parent-child ties. In some families, several siblings were involved in the movement. The Bartletts of Amersham are the most notable example: five siblings were involved in the Lollard community there, while a sixth received some Lollard instruction as well. John, Richard, and Robert Bartlett and Agnes Wells, Isabel Morwyn, and Elizabeth Copland were brothers and sisters, all children of Katherine Bartlett.[124] Other sibling groups were common in the Chiltern Hills: James, Richard, Ralph, and Marion Morden were all siblings; John Phips, William Phips, Sybil Afrike, alias Littlepage, and "Old Widemore's wife" were brothers and sisters; and David, Raynold, and William Sherwood were all brothers.[125] Groups of three siblings are found in other communities as well: in Coventry, Thomas Villers, Thomasina Bradeley, and the wife of Banbrooke were siblings;[126] Richard, John, and William Colins of Ginge and Burford were brothers;[127] in Essex, William, Antony, and Robert Beckwyth of

Braintree were brothers, as were Jenkin, John, and Richard Butler, and possibly Henry, John, and Richard Chapman.[128] There are also numerous examples of two siblings who were both involved in Lollard communities.[129]

Only rarely does information survive about relationships between siblings and how they came to be involved in the Lollard movement. Some children were taught by their parents: Christopher and John Grebill of Kent,[130] for instance, and at least two of the three children of the wife of Villers.[131] Several examples also indicate that siblings taught one another. Robert Bartlett taught his brother Richard and his sister Agnes Wells the Epistle of James and Lollard doctrines about images.[132] Their sister Isabel Morwyn tried unsuccessfully to instruct yet another sibling, Elizabeth Copland:

> In talk together, coming from their father being at the point of death, Isabel said to her sister Elizabeth, that all who die, either pass to hell or heaven: "Nay," said the other, "there is between them purgatory." Again; when Elizabeth came from the rood of rest, Isabel said, that if she knew so much as she had heard, she would go no more on pilgrimage while she lived; for all saints, said she, be in heaven. Then asked Elizabeth, wherefor pilgrimage was ordained by doctors and priests? The other said, for gain and profit. "Who hath taught you this?" quoth Elizabeth, "man or woman? Your curate, I dare say, never learned you so." "My curate," said she "will never know so much." And moreoever, Isabel said to Elizabeth her sister, that if she would keep counsel, and not tell her husband, she would say more. And when Elizabeth answered that she would not tell: "But," saith the other, "I will have you to swear:" and because she would not swear, the other would not proceed any further.[133]

John Ryburn of Risborough also tried to teach his sisters Elizabeth and Alice about the sacrament of the Eucharist, but they too were unreceptive.[134]

Other familial relationships outside the nuclear family or family of origin could occasionally prove important. John Phisicion, alias Blumstone, who was a leader of the Lollard community in Coventry, instructed his nephew John Bull (age seventeen in 1511), against the sacrament of the altar from the age of nine.[135] When Phisicion died, he committed his nephew into the care of Thomas Villers, and when Bull appeared before the court he was working as Villers's servant.[136] Relationships between first cousins could also be instrumental.

SERVANTS

Alongside blood relations, servants and apprentices were an integral part of many medieval households. About one-third of households in larger towns employed servants. Many of these servants were adolescents working as apprentices (these were usually men rather than women) and as domestic help. Even daughters of the mercantile elite went into service in households of status similar to their own to receive instruction on how to run a household. These servants, sometimes transient, sometimes permanent, were considered part of the family.[137]

Servants inevitably became involved to some extent in their employers' personal and spiritual lives, as is shown by the detailed testimony that some were able to give about their masters' and mistresses' Lollard activities. John Burrell, servant of Thomas Mone of Loddon, was a witness to both Thomas Mone's and Hawise Mone's heretical practices, including Thomas's preaching to his neighbors and Hawise's fast-breaking gathering in her "chesehous chambr." Rose Furnour, formerly the servant of Robert Hachet of Coventry, was able to provide the court with considerable detail about who came and went in her employer's house.[138]

Not surprisingly, Lollards often had Lollard servants, male and female, in their pay; it was in the interests of both Lollard employer and Lollard employee to avoid living at close quarters with people who would be unsympathetic to their beliefs. Thomas Hilles of Essex, for example, worked first for John Tyball of Steeple Bumpstead and later moved into the employ of Christopher Ravins of Witham, a tailor. Ravins also employed John and Richard Chapman and John Hilles, all Lollards.[139] Whether servants were Lollards before they were engaged or were converted subsequently by their employers is not always clear, but there are many cases in which servants were led into Lollardy by their masters or mistresses. Both John Burrell of Loddon and Rose Furnour of Coventry, who testified against their employers, were instructed in the doctrines of the sect by them.[140] Burrell's employer, Thomas Mone, had at least two other Lollard servants or apprentices: John Pert and Edmund Archer.[141] Katherine Gerton of Coventry was also reportedly instructed by her mistress, Alice Flexall (otherwise unknown), as was Joan Gest by her master, John Smyth.[142] John Edmunds sent his daughter Agnes into service in a Lollard household precisely so that she would become instructed in the faith.[143] Alice Cottismore of Brightwell tried unsuccessfully to teach her servant, Elizabeth Wighthill, who then deposed against her before the bishop.[144] Alice and Richard Saunders even withheld employment from a wavering adherent of the sect and held him up as a warning to others.[145] Occasionally employees could teach their employers: John Harding of Broughton Gifford said he had come into the Lollard faith through the instruction of his servant, John Newman.[146]

The influence that an employer was thought to exert was so great that some Coventry Lollards named men and women as suspects simply because they were the servants of Lollards or presumed Lollards. Robert Silkby said that "he considered the wife of Bluet to be suspect because she was the servant of the wife of Bentham and for no other reason."[147] Agnes de Bakehouse similarly said she thought that John Harris was a Lollard because he was the servant of a heretic.[148] Both Agnes de Bakehouse and Silkby suspected that Roger Bromley was a Lollard because he had been apprenticed to Master Forde.[149] Servants, as part of their employers' households, were perhaps as likely as blood relatives to be subjected to pressure or influence to become a Lollard.

Extended Families

The large number of family ties in the Lollard movement is also reflected in the extended families that can be traced in the older Lollard communities in Buckinghamshire and Berkshire. Women played various roles in these large kin groups. Some families consisted of a husband and wife, with their adult sons and their wives. In these cases, women may not have been particularly active. But other families, particularly the largest example, the Bartletts, provided an opportunity for women to act within the confines of the family.

In some families, we do not even know the names of the women. Witnesses reported that men of the family gathered, along with their wives; it was evidently the tie between the men that brought the group together, leaving the women (especially the sons' wives) as outsiders, probably with little power. Roger Dod, for instance, testified against "John Brabant and his wife; John Brabant his son, with his wife; John Brabant the younger son, with his wife; [and] Reginald Brabant of Stanlake," all for reading the Bible at John Brabant Sr.'s house at Stanlake.[150] Similarly, Robert Carver or Carder testified that he had seen "old Durdant of Iver-court [Robert Durdant of Staines], sitting at dinner with his children and their wives," reading from the Scriptures.[151] The Durdant children included Robert's heir Nicholas and Davy of Ankerwick as well as at least one daughter; the only reference to her is of her marriage, which occasioned a Lollard gathering.[152] Men dominated these families, at least as the depositions reported their activities.

Evidence for the role of women in other families is more substantial. The two Colins families of Oxfordshire, probably interrelated, included the active Richard and Alice Colins, whose household in Ginge was an important center of Lollard activity. Richard's father Thomas and his wife, his two brothers John of Burford and William, and two of his and Alice's children,

John and Joan, were involved in the sect, as were another extended family of Colinses located in Asthall.[153] They were clearly an important part of the Lollard community in Oxfordshire, and Alice Colins, at least, was active within the context of her family and even outside it.

Two large extended families in the Chiltern Hills can be traced in some detail: the Bartletts and the Ashford-Tredway-Morden family. Both families, especially the Bartletts, had a number of active women. Katherine Bartlett and her husband (who is not named in the sources, but was apparently an adherent of the sect) had six children who were involved to some extent in the Lollard community in Amersham: Robert Bartlett (and his wife Isabel), Richard Bartlett (and his wife Margaret), John Bartlett, Agnes Wells (and her husband John), Isabel Morwyn (and her husband John), and Elizabeth Copland (and her husband Thomas).[154] Not all members of the family were uniformly enthusiastic about Lollardy: Elizabeth Copland, despite the involvement of her mother and five siblings, apparently did not respond to her sister Isabel Morwyn's attempts to convert her to the creed. Nor is there any evidence of heresy for her husband, Thomas Copland, and both Elizabeth and Thomas acted as informants against various suspects, which may have affected their relationship with the rest of the family.[155] Other women of the Bartlett family, Isabel Bartlett (wife of Robert), Agnes Wells, and Isabel Morwyn, were more active, although their reported contacts were mostly with other members of their family. Membership in a large family of this type allowed women an arena in which to be active.

Another extended interrelated family in Amersham were the Ashfords, Tredways, and Mordens (see Figure 1). Agnes Ashford was the mother of two Lollards, Thomas Tredway and Richard Ashford, alias Tredway. Alice Tredway, who was an informant, may also have been related to this family.[156] Richard Ashford converted to Lollardy through his marriage to Alice Morden; her father, John Morden, passed his faith and his books to Richard as he lay dying from the plague about 1514. John Morden's wife (probably the Marion Morden [Sr.] who left a will in 1521) was also a Lollard, as were the children of his brother Harry Morden (James, Richard, Marion [Jr.], and Radulph). James Morden was burned for his heresy in 1522.[157]

The connections between the Ashford-Tredways and the Mordens extended beyond the marriage between Richard Ashford and Alice Morden. James Morden, Alice's cousin, was the servant of Richard Ashford. He learned heretical doctrines from Richard's mother Agnes Ashford and detected Richard's brother Thomas Tredway. Tredway knew and testified

FIGURE 1   Ashford-Tredway-Morden Family Tree (c. 1521).

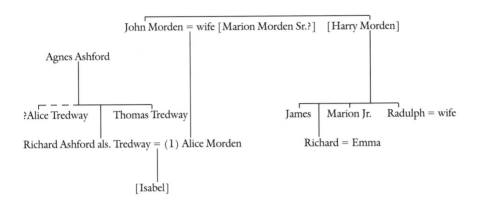

Sources: *A&M*, 4:124, 224–32, 242–45; 5:454; Reg. Fox, 4, fols. 18r–19v; *L&P*, vol. 3, pt. 2, no. 3062; *VCH Bucks.*, 3:143; *Bucks. Muster*, 236–37; *Bucks. Subsidy*, 15–16; BRO, MSS D/A/We/4/5, Will of Emps Morden of Chesham, 1540; D/A/We/1/8, Will of Marion Morden (Sr.) of Ashley-Green Chesham, 1521, edited in Elvey, *Courts of Buckingham*, 329–30. Marion Morden of Ashley-Green, Chesham, is conjecturally identified with the wife of John Morden of Ashley-Green, Chesham. She names Herry Morden as the father of Marion Morden (Jr.) in her will and leaves a bequest to Isabel Ashford, who may have been her granddaughter (daughter of Richard and Alice Ashford).

against his brother Richard's father-in-law, John Morden. A will shows there may have been a continued connection between the two families a generation later: the 1566 testament of Robert Tredway named Robert Morden as overseer.[158]

The Harding family may have been as important to the survival of Lollardy in Amersham as the Bartletts or the Ashford-Tredway-Mordens, but the relationships between the eleven Hardings named in the records are not clear. The Lollard pedigree of the Hardings may have reached back to 1414 when a rebel named William Hardynge of Little Missenden participated in Oldcastle's Revolt.[159] The most important of the sixteenth-century Hardings were Alice and Thomas Harding, who were active from at least 1506, when they first abjured. Thomas was eventually executed for his recalcitrance in 1532, when he was about 60;[160] Alice's fate is unknown. At the same time as Alice and Thomas abjured in 1506, three other men named Harding (Henry, Richard, and Robert) abjured, too,[161] although there is no further record of their heretical activities, and their relationship to Thomas and Alice and each other (if any) is not made clear. Several other Hardings were detected in later proceedings in the early 1520s, again with little information about their relationships to one another: Edmund Harding, William Harding, and Roger Harding and his wife and elder daughter.[162]

Another surname that recurs in the records touching on the Chiltern Hills Lollards is Littlepage, alias Africke.[163] As with the Hardings, there is little indication how the Lollard Littlepages were related to one another, if they were, but, like the Hardings, the Lollard tradition in their family may have been old. William Littlepage or Africke, who abjured about 1508 and was cited as a Lollard again in the 1520s, said that his grandmother had taught him the Creed in English. William was the brother of John Littlepage or Africke, and his wife was named Emma.[164] The relationship of William and John to the other Littlepages is not clear. John learned the Ten Commandments from Alice, the wife of Thurstan Littlepage, while Thurstan was said to have taught William, along with many others.[165] Henry Littlepage, Joan Littlepage, Thomas Littlepage or Africke, and his wife Sybil Littlepage or Africke were all named by other Lollards.[166]

The extended families of the Amersham area—the Bartletts, the Tredway-Ashford-Mordens, the Hardings, and the Littlepages—were connected to one another and to other Lollards in the town. The offspring of such families sometimes married into another Lollard clan. Margaret Bartlett (wife of Richard) and Emma Africke (wife of William Africke, alias Littlepage) may have been Hardings by birth.[167] Sybil Littlepage, wife of Thomas Littlepage, was the sister of John and William Phip.[168] John Wells (perhaps the son of Agnes and John Wells Sr.) was named as Henry Harding's son-in-law in 1558.[169] The Mordens were connected by familial ties or by friendship with the Wedons and the Hardings.[170] Robert Tredway's 1566 will connects him to the Hardings and the Morwyns.[171]

Lollard traditions in extended families naturally encouraged the participation of their female members. Alice Colins, Alice Harding, Isabel Morwyn, Agnes Wells, and Agnes Ashford were all active Lollards. But, at least in the cases of Isabel Morwyn, Agnes Wells, and Agnes Ashford, that activity most often took place within the family rather than in the larger Lollard community. In some of the families, particularly the Brabants and the Durdants, it is unclear whether women were given even that opportunity. Witnesses represented these Lollard families as male-dominated, consisting of a *paterfamilias* surrounded by adult sons, with their wives unnamed and without identity. While women's activities usually took place in the context of a family, and thus the family-oriented nature of Lollardy can be seen as the basis of women's limited power in the movement, it is still clear that the late medieval norm of the patriarchal family governed the roles that men and women played.

*   *   *

Family relationships provided a significant means by which people became involved in Lollardy. While men and women had significant numbers of family ties to the Lollard community, it is rarer to find women with no relations in the movement than men. Parents naturally taught their children, male and female, both as minors and as adults. Not all children were receptive to this instruction, but clearly many were. In Coventry, parent-child relationships particularly involved mothers and daughters, while in other communities, notably the large sixteenth-century Chiltern Hills group, male parents with sons were more common. Another avenue of recruitment was sibling ties—men and women were taught by their brothers and sisters.

Men's and women's social and heretical ties within the Lollard movement differed. Women had little contact with Lollards in other communities; their relationships in the movement tended to be limited to the local scene and particularly to their families. Men and women could be recruited to the sect through their families, but men's horizons were wider than women's, and they came to be involved in the movement because of the influence of others outside the family as well as within it. The most active woman in the movement, Alice Rowley, was a widow and was apparently not related to anyone in the movement; the unusual range of her activity may have been possible because she was not limited by family and particularly marital ties.

5. Gender and Social Status

Although women did not generally play leading roles in Lollardy, this chapter examines the exceptions: active and enthusiastic members of the sect who were recognized as such by other Lollards and by the authorities. One common factor among prominent women was high social position, which could allow a woman, interacting with a group of men below her in rank, to stretch the conventions governing the behavior of lower-status women. Gender was shaped partly by social position, at the same time as social position itself was gendered. This does not mean, however, that gender became an unimportant factor among the social elite—elite men and women still constituted their identities through sexually differentiated roles and activities.[1]

One woman of the wealthy merchant elite, Alice Rowley, acted as a leader of conventicles of male and female Lollards. Even if prescriptions generally militated against an active public role for women, an exceptional woman with an assertive personality and a high station could encompass within her individual gender identity acts not usually associated with feminine behavior. But even more striking than the extraordinary influence of Alice Rowley on the Coventry Lollard community are the limitations on the activity and authority of other women, even those of high social status: conventional gender boundaries were sufficiently narrow that they rarely expanded so far as to include public teaching and preaching.

Nonetheless, it is clear that elevated wealth and station brought greater influence to some female Lollards. The most influential men in the movement, on the other hand, came from varying social backgrounds, from the highest to the lowest. For relatively poor men to act as teachers in conventicles that included much wealthier men was not unusual. The authority of men in the movement depended less on social station than on charisma and learning, following a clerical model of leadership.[2]

Indeed, Lollardy appears to have been more attractive to men of the lower orders—artisans, rural laborers, and *petits bourgeois*—than to more substantial men. While women were only able to play significant roles in the movement when their social status demanded respect, leading men were sometimes undistinguished tradesmen whose authority in the movement was a reflection of their skill and charisma rather than their station. Lollardy thus provided new opportunities for two groups: a very small number of elite women and a much larger number of artisan men.

The status of members of Lollard communities has been a matter of debate for several decades now. Discussions of social position have traditionally followed the view laid out by K. B. McFarlane in his influential biography of John Wyclif: after the final failure of Oldcastle's Revolt in 1417, Lollardy was confined to the "new industrial groups" or artisans of town and village, people whom McFarlane characterized as "solemn, if well-meaning, bumpkins."[3] More recent historians have sought to revise this view, especially Derek Plumb, who notes that some Lollards in the Chiltern Hills in the early sixteenth century were substantial persons.[4] Scholars of Lollardy have not addressed, however, the interplay between gender and social position, and such an analysis will provide a reinterpretation of the importance of both these factors in the dynamic of Lollard communities.

Prominent Women in Lollardy

The activities of the exceptional women in Lollardy, those who were able to achieve some measure of prominence in the movement, reveal why they were able to become more active than other women and what the limitations on that activity were. Certainly a woman's character and intelligence were important factors in her relationships with other people; while the sources present only an incomplete picture of personalities, assertiveness was a common trait among these notable women. The environment was also important. Neither women nor men could achieve power within the community without recognition from others, without some measure of authority, an attribute most women lacked. A cohort of active women in a community made it more likely that one of their number could assume an influential position; if, as in Coventry, enough women participated, they could take roles in all-female groups normally played by men in mixed conventicles. Perhaps most important, women who were able to become prominent Lollards were almost always from higher socioeconomic backgrounds, which in itself gave them a loftier status in the community.

Still, in only one case, that of the exceptional Alice Rowley, was a

woman able to take advantage of a combination of all of these factors —
personality, social status, and support from other women — in order to play
a public role like that of the leading men in her community. Other women
may have possessed very assertive personalities, but the lack of a cohort of
other women or a higher social status kept them from breaking convention
and participating in their communities on the same level as men. Similarly,
some women of a social position equivalent to Alice Rowley's did not play
leading roles, perhaps because their personalities were unsuited or their
socialization did not predispose them to such a part in their sect. The social
norms that restricted women to the more informal aspect of Lollard activities were strong indeed.

Enthusiastic Women Lollards with Restricted Roles

Some women possessed great strength of character and dedication to their
faith, but, perhaps because they had neither wealth nor the support of an
active group of other women, they acted almost entirely within familial
confines. Two women conspicuous in the records of prosecution, Agnes
Grebill and Margery Baxter, provide interesting case studies. The courts
collected a substantial amount of material relating to their heretical activities, not because of their importance within their Lollard communities,
but because each obstinately refused to recant her beliefs. While neither
played a central role in her Lollard community, a closer examination of
these two women's heretical careers furnishes us with a valuable picture of
the restrictions of many Lollard women's activities.

Agnes Grebill of Tenterden was enthusiastic and certainly stubborn,
but her role in the Kentish Lollard group was limited to the sphere of home
and family. Agnes is the only woman in the Kentish community for whom
there is much detailed evidence. About sixty when brought before Archbishop Warham on 29 April 1511, she obstinately denied all charges against
her; as a result, William Riche of Benenden, her husband John Sr., and her
sons John Jr. and Christopher were all called as witnesses against her. Even
after the testimonies of her husband, sons, and Riche were read to her,
Agnes continued to deny everything, saying that the witnesses would lose
their souls by telling such falsehoods and "that she lamented that she had
ever borne her sons."[5] On May 2, she was excommunicated for her contumacy, was handed over to the secular arm, and was burned unrepentant.[6]

The depositions made against her reveal that she was burned not for
her position in the Lollard community (as has been alleged) but for her
stubborn, and unusual, refusal to admit and abjure her heresy. She had been

a Lollard for a long time: her husband deposed she had first learned her heresy from him and from John Ive[7] at the end of Edward IV's reign (in the early 1480s) and that she had continued in her beliefs until brought before the bishop in 1511. She was active in her family, evidently participating in her sons' education in heresy. But the reports of her proselytization given by her husband and sons illustrate that the perceptions others had of women's activities could limit their influence. Her husband testified that when their children were about seven years old,

> than this deponent [John Sr.] taught theym the said errour ayenst the sacrament of thaulter, in the presence of his said wif, divers tymes in his owne house. . . . She always withoute contradiccion affermed his teching and said the said opynion was goode and [was] well contentid that hir childern aforsaid wer of the said opynyons ayenst the sacrament of thaulter.[8]

Although John Sr.'s account of the instruction of their children presents Agnes's role as approving but essentially passive, her son Christopher's deposition shows that Agnes, too, took part in the teaching: "Examyned by whom he was first induced into those errours, he saith that his fader and moder Agnes aforsaid taught this deponent and comyned divers tymes with this deponent in the said errours."[9] John Jr.'s deposition similarly credits both his father and his mother.[10] Perhaps Agnes taught her sons when her husband was not present: a mother's influence could thus be substantial even if it customarily ceded to the greater authority of the father if he was present. Yet John Sr.'s account of his wife's activities relegated her to, at best, a supporting part alongside his primary role. Such perceptions indicate one of the handicaps faced by women in the movement. Women could not achieve power and influence without recognition of their importance by others.

Two glimpses of Agnes Grebill's interaction with Lollards outside her immediate family show that visitors understood her role to be even less active than did her own husband and sons. William Riche deposed he had been many times in the house of John Grebill and at these visits he communed with John, "Agnes beyng present and heryng and consentyng to the same,"[11] although apparently (in Riche's eyes) not contributing herself. Agnes seems similarly to have been on the periphery when William Carder came to visit. John Grebill Sr., when testifying against William Carder, took pains to insist that no one else had been present at their communications at Grebill's house, except once when his son Christopher had been there; as if "by the way," he adds that another time in the winter "when this deponent went owte of his house, he left the said Carder commenyng with this deponentis wife."[12] Christopher Grebill's testimony about his encounter with Carder at his parents' house does not mention his mother's presence, reinforcing the marginality of her participation.[13]

In discussions involving outsiders like Carder and Riche, Agnes did not play a participatory role, or at least one that was recognized as such by the men in her life. She was present (although even this was not always clear), she heard, but any contributions she might have made went unreported and perhaps even unheeded by her husband and her sons. Her burning has made her role in the Kentish group seem greater than it probably was. The limits on her participation may have been typical: she had some influence within her family, especially on her sons, but outside visitors to her house interacted with the male members of the household rather than with her. Whether Agnes wished a greater role than she had in the movement is unclear; if she did, her social status, the absence of a female community in Tenterden, and the attitude of her family may have hampered her.[14]

Margery Baxter of Martham and Norwich, like Agnes Grebill, showed great enthusiasm for her sect but was similarly unable to interact as her husband did with other members of the East Anglian Lollard community. She was handicapped by geographical isolation, living miles away from the center of the East Anglian group at Loddon, while her husband's travels kept him in touch with the leaders of the movement.

Margery Baxter is the Lollard most fully portrayed in the records of Bishop Alnwick's prosecution in the diocese of Norwich between 1428 and 1431, for, like Agnes Grebill, she was unwilling to give up her faith.[15] Although we cannot know how typical Margery was (and one suspects that she was not at all typical), she had a very interesting character. She was highly irreverent and seems to have taken delight in shocking. Her denial of the Real Presence in the eucharist, for instance, was earthy and direct:

> If any such sacrament is God and the true body of Christ, the gods are infinite, because a thousand priests and more every day make and then eat a thousand such gods and when they are eaten, they are passed through their posteriors into fetid stinking privies where you could find enough of such gods if you wanted to search carefully for them.[16]

Margery was not opposed to authority on principle—she showed great reverence for Lollard leaders, particularly William White—but she enjoyed attacking established authority. She appears especially to have derived satisfaction from feeling that she had deceived the clergy. For instance, she boasted to her neighbor of tricking her confessor in Norwich:

> And then the aforesaid Margery said to Joan that she had often confessed falsely to the dean of [the secular college of St. Mary in the Fields, Norwich], so that he would repute her to be of good life. And on this account he often gave her money. And then Joan asked whether Margery confessed to the priest all her sins. And Margery said that she had never sinned against a priest and therefore never wished to confess to a priest.[17]

Margery's rebelliousness against ecclesiastical and secular authority, rather than intellectual attraction, may have been a major factor in her fascination with Lollardy. She showed an imperfect understanding of Lollard teachings, often denying the validity of a sacrament or other orthodox practice without comprehending the principles behind the denial. Her objection to fasting, "that it is better for anyone on a fast day to eat meat leftover from Thursday than to go to the market and put oneself into debt by buying fish,"[18] may be practical, but it reveals an unsophisticated understanding of why other Lollards objected to the practice. Margery's views on the cult of saints also show that she did not grasp, or did not accept, the basic premises behind Lollard objections to it. Although Margery, along with other members of the East Anglian community, rejected the saints of the Catholic Church,[19] she retained her belief in the efficacy of invoking her own saints to intercede with God on her behalf, praying to her Lollard teacher, William White.[20]

Although Margery Baxter did not fully master Lollard teachings, she was nonetheless zealous enough to try to make converts to her creed, even if her seeds fell on unfertile ground. We have already seen her attempts to convert her neighbor, Joan Clyfland, and Clyfland's servants. Farther away from home, on a trip to Yarmouth with her husband to retrieve some books (possibly Wycliffite scriptures) for William White, Margery even tried to convert a Carmelite friar whom she described as "the most learned friar in the whole country."[21] She told him to stop begging and to take up the plow, for the life of the plowman was more pleasing to God than that of the friar. The Carmelite, apparently amused, asked her if she had anything more to teach him, but when she proceeded to show him the Gospels in English, he drew back from her and accused her of heresy. Margery, in turn, accused the friar of wanting to "know her carnally" and told the friar that her husband would kill him if he found out. The friar held his tongue and retreated from the scene with haste.[22] Margery must have had a great deal of confidence in herself and her creed, albeit rather poor judgment, to have attempted to convert a man of the cloth, although the utter contempt in which she and the leaders of her movement regarded the clergy, and friars in particular,[23] may have been a contributing factor.

Margery was clearly an active and enthusiastic Lollard, but her participation in East Anglian Lollardy was limited. She was geographically isolated: although she traveled to Great Yarmouth, there is no evidence that she ever visited Lollards in Loddon or other heretical centers when her husband did. Her main contacts seem to have been the men (William White and Nicholas Belward) who visited the Baxters' home in Martham and, after she and her husband moved to Norwich, her neighbors in that city, a bastion of orthodox piety where she was apparently unable to find others sympathetic to her ideas. Margery's personality, while certainly assertive, may also have made her leadership unlikely—her grasp of Lollard doctrine was evidently shaky, and she may even have been somewhat unstable. Lastly, there is no sign that her social position was elevated: William, her husband, was a carpenter. The limitations on the participation and activities of Agnes Grebill and Margery Baxter were shared by many other Lollard women, who also lacked an elevated social position and the support of others of their sex.

Elite Women Lollards with Little Influence

But even high socioeconomic status in itself did not suffice to give a woman a leading position in a community, as the case of Alice Cottismore, the only gentlewoman implicated in later Lollardy,[24] illustrates. Alice Cottismore, alias Mistress Dolly, widow of William Cottismore of Britwell, was brought to the attention of the authorities in 1521.[25] While left with six sons and a child *in utero* when her husband died in 1519, Widow Cottismore was by no means indigent, as, by the terms of her husband's will, she held the manors of Britwell Salome and Brightwell Baldwin as well as other lands and chattels for the term of her life.[26] Her husband William had come from an important county family; although he was not very active in local political life, perhaps due to his relatively early death,[27] he was closely related to two prominent Oxfordshire families, the Stonors and the Barentynes, who participated in county and even, to some extent, national political life.[28]

Two years after her husband's death, Alice Cottismore's servant, Elizabeth Wighthill, and the parson of the parish of Britwell, Sir John Booth, denounced her to the ecclesiastical authorities for heretical activities. Elizabeth Wighthill testified that her mistress knew and approved of the wandering heresiarch John Hacker and his teaching, and further that she had tried to convert her servant to these beliefs. To that end Alice had "caused" Sir John Booth to read from the *Legenda aurea* and from a saint's life, both of which Alice thought—perhaps mistakenly—spoke against pilgrimages. Another book that he read, "covered with boards and red covering," contained the articles of the Creed. Alice also used other opportunities to try to convince her servant of her views; while visiting the house of Sir William Barentyne, she ridiculed images that Lady Barentyne had had newly gilded. When Wighthill defended them, saying that "images do provoke devotion," Alice Cottismore said, "Ye should not worship that thing that hath ears and cannot hear, and hath eyes and cannot see, and hath mouth and cannot speak, and hath hands and cannot feel."[29]

Whether William Cottismore had shared his wife's interest in Lollardy is not clear. The parson, John Booth, denounced both Alice and William as heretics, but also charged Alice with refusing, after William's death, to fulfill her husband's promise, made while he was ill, to undertake a pilgrimage to Our Lady of Walsingham.[30] William Cottismore's own deathbed wishes cannot be discerned from his will, which was unremarkably orthodox, commending his soul in the preamble according to the usual Catholic formula (to almighty God, the Virgin, and the holy company of heaven) and making several bequests to various churches. He ambiguously bequeathed money to his wife, as sole executor, "to dispose for my Soule after hir discrecion." Although this was a usual testamentary formula, in this case the discretion of the executor—as a Lollard—would probably dictate that no such offerings could avail his soul. Booth may have felt a personal responsibility to see William's wishes fulfilled, at least as he interpreted them, since he acted as witness to the will.[31]

More than doctrinal differences may have been behind the quarrel between Booth and Alice Cottismore. Although Booth clearly objected to her activities and deposed against her before the bishop, he also evidently came to her house at her command and read books to her and her servant. A visitation of his parish, undated but probably after William Cottismore's death, even raises the possibility that they were sexually involved. It was recorded that "the rector does not sleep in the parish but in the home of Widow Cottismore, for what reason it is not known."[32]

Although Alice Cottismore could clearly use her social position to further her interest in Lollardy, her interaction with other Lollards, apart from her servant's reference to her approval of John Hacker, is not documented. She was relatively geographically isolated from other Lollards in Oxfordshire and Berkshire, so that participation in Lollard gatherings was probably difficult if not impossible. Although under different circumstances she might have been able to act as a gentle patron to a Lollard community, instead she apparently remained cut off and frustrated in her attempts to convert those who came into her world.

Another wealthy woman, Alice Saunders of Amersham, was not geographically isolated like Alice Cottismore but was also thwarted in her evangelizing efforts, perhaps by her unpleasant personality. She was the wife of a very wealthy man, Richard Saunders, and used her economic status to intimidate people in the Lollard community. Thomas Houre, for instance, who decided to eschew Lollardy after seeing many condemned for heresy, was warned by Alice that he would lose opportunities for employment if he left the Lollard group. As Alice predicted, Thomas had no more work from her husband and was soon after removed from the position of holy-water clerk in Amersham. She later used Houre's example to threaten Thomas Rowland: "Ye may see how Thomas Houre and others, who labored to have heretics detected before bishop Smith, are brought now to beggary; you may take example by them."[33] Her high-handed attitude may have provoked resentment; there is no evidence even for her participation in any of the Lollard conventicles in the Amersham area, much less leadership. Although Alice's wealth allowed her to wield some influence in the Lollard group in the Chiltern Hills, her manner failed to induce others to accord her the respect necessary for leadership.

The roles of other socially elevated women suspected of Lollardy are obscure, either because the evidence for their activities has not survived or because their participation in the sect, for various reasons, was peripheral. At least one woman from the highest echelons of London burgher society may have become involved in London Lollardy, but her role in that community is impossible to assess because only chance references to her activity survive. Lady Jane Yonge was the widow of Sir John Yonge (d. 1481), grocer, alderman, M.P. for London (1455–56), and mayor of London (1466–67). Jane was his second wife, whom he married sometime after the death of his first wife in 1466–67.[34] There is no evidence that Sir John was involved in heterodox activities, but Lady Yonge's mother, Joan Boughton, was burned in 1494 for obstinate heresy. Lady Yonge herself, some of the chronicles reported, "had a grete smell of an heretyk aftyr the modyr."[35] Lady Yonge may even have died as her mother had; Joan Baker of London, tried about 1510, said that Lady Yonge had "dyed a martir be for god,"[36] although no other reference to her execution survives (and it is possible that Joan Baker confused Lady Yonge with her mother). Jane Yonge's place in London Lollardy remains obscure; her social position may have allowed her to play an influential role in the local heretical community, but it is also possible that her adherence to Lollardy was no more than an unsubstantiated rumor.

Although more evidence survives for the participation of a group of moderately wealthy women, mostly widows, in the Lollard community in Colchester, their roles are also ultimately obscured by patchy records. Some hints survive that these women were prominent members of the Lollard community in their city, but there are as many indications that their role was peripheral. Widow Denby, probably the widow of John Denby (who had been assessed at the high level of £40 in 1523), was brought before the court as a Lollard suspect in July 1528 but was absolved absolutely without compurgation. Did her social position excuse her, or was the charge unfounded? On surviving evidence, the latter seems more likely. John Pykas, who was intimately involved in Lollard circles in Colchester, was questioned and said he knew nothing of her, and no other evidence for her involvement is recorded.[37]

Others who were permitted to clear their name by compurgation were not wealthy. Several damaging depositions implicated the widow Margaret Cowbridge, but nonetheless she was able to purge herself of the accusations against her. It seems unlikely, however, that her economic or social position swayed the court, since her valuation in the subsidy (£6) indicated that she possessed only moderate wealth.[38] Margaret Bowgas, wife of the Lollard Thomas Bowgas, was similarly able to clear her name with six compurgators, despite some evidence against her. Her socioeconomic status was not elevated either; her husband was a fuller and his wealth modest.[39]

There is evidence of heretical activity in the case of another widow, Katherine Swayn, whose goods were valued at a substantial £20 in 1523 and 1524. Both John Hacker and John Pykas testified against her, but Pykas may not have known her well; he said that he had taught in her presence and that she was reputed to be a "known woman," but when questioned about her specific beliefs he was unable to respond. Swayn was summoned to the court and did appear, although no record of an abjuration or penance survives.[40]

The only widow certainly involved in the Lollard community was Margaret Bowgas's mother, Alice Gardner, whose valuation in the 1524 subsidy (£3) indicates fairly humble status. She had close relationships with

John Pykas and John Tyball and, perhaps because of that, she was the first woman to be summoned before the court, appearing months before any other female suspect. But even her adherence to Lollardy may have been ambivalent. When John Tyball of Steeple Bumpstead, her godson, came to visit her, she proposed that he accompany her on pilgrimage to Ipswich; he chastised her for considering this activity, saying that she should give any extra money she had to the poor rather than to dead images. Tyball's report of her response is ambiguous: "To the whiche answere sche did not greatly speke ayenst, nor gretly holde withal, as he saythe."[41]

The roles played by wealthier widows like Widow Denby and Katherine Swayn in the Colchester Lollard community remain unclear to us. While they may have been prominent and influential members of conventicles and protected from prosecution by their status, the evidence that survives does not indicate they were central to the Lollard community.

INFLUENTIAL WOMEN: WITHIN THE BOUNDARIES

Women of higher social station in Colchester or in Oxfordshire and Berkshire were not necessarily prominent figures among Lollards in their area, but other, wealthier women had important positions in the community and personalities that evidently commanded respect. Yet in most groups there was a boundary beyond which women, even women of this sort, did not go. That boundary demarcated public or formal from casual or informal activities.

Such was apparently the case with the most influential woman in East Anglian Lollardy, Hawise Mone of Loddon. Although her personality and her relatively high social status allowed her to play a more prominent role than any other woman in the community, there is no evidence that she publicly contributed to discussions in the group's gatherings. Hawise was the wife of Thomas Mone, an apparently prosperous shoemaker who was also a prominent Lollard known for preaching to his neighbors on the evils of the Catholic Church and its clergy.[42] The Mone house may well have been the center of Lollard activity in East Anglia — it was the site of schools at which William White and others taught, as well as of activities such as the Easter Saturday fast-breaking ceremony.[43]

Hawise's abjuration shows her to have been an assertive woman, unafraid to declare her beliefs even in the bishop's court. Although most abjurations in the prosecution in the diocese of Norwich were similar, with the same formulaic renditions of articles repeated in each, Hawise's was less stereotyped.[44] Rather than simply admitting to a heretical belief, she launched several times into an invective against the orthodox clergy. For instance, after admitting that she held the often-repeated belief that "he oonly that is moost holy and moost perfit in lyvyng in erthe is verry pope," she added,

> and these singemesses that be cleped prestes ben no prestes, but thay be lecherous and covetouse men and fals deceyvours of the puple, and with thar sotel techyng and prechyng, syngyng and redyng piteously thay pile the puple of thar good, and tharwith thay susteyne here pride, here lechery, here slowthe and alle other vices, and alway thay makyn newe lawes and newe ordinances to curse and kille cruelly all other persones that holden ageyn thar vicious levyng.[45]

Hawise must have been a bold woman to make such a virulent condemnation of the clergy before so eminent a person as the bishop of Norwich.

Hawise also showed assertiveness within the Lollard community. Margery Baxter called her "the most uncommon and wise woman in the doctrine of William White."[46] She was a great receiver of heretics: the Easter Saturday fast-breaking took place when her husband was out of town, indicating he was not the prime mover behind the occasion. Hawise may in fact have been the motivating force behind the schools held in her house; William Baxter made no reference to Thomas when he noted that Hawise favored heretics and "receive[d] them often."[47] Hawise was quite willing to act independently from her husband in her heretical activities; there are few parallels for this in the evidence for other women in her community or elsewhere.

Hawise was also the only woman whose importance in the East Anglian Lollard group was recognized by the courts. Unlike the other women who were brought before the bishop, Hawise had been arrested and incarcerated before her trial.[48] Of all the women whose husbands were also charged with Lollardy, she was the only one who was tried before her husband, indicating that her trial was not a consequence of her husband's, as some of the others appear to have been.[49] Hawise was the only woman to make a point-by-point abjuration, as many of the men did; the other women made general abjurations.[50] Hawise was also charged with receiving all the most important Lollard teachers, but, significantly, she was charged with learning from them, not with teaching.[51]

Hawise was the most prominent female Lollard in East Anglia and perhaps the most important receiver of heretics in the community. One of the factors in Hawise's ability to take a prominent role in the group may have been the Mones' relative prosperity; higher social and economic status perhaps gave her more confidence and prestige. If any woman in the East Anglian group were to become a teacher, it is likely she would have been the one. Yet she was never charged with teaching, even privately. Perhaps she was held back by her illiteracy.[52] Her role in discussions in the Lollard schools held at her home is unclear, and there is no evidence that she attended conventicles elsewhere.

While Hawise was an enthusiastic and active Lollard, she did not play a public teaching role in the community in East Anglia (although her part as a facilitator should not be underestimated). Some Lollards in this group held the radical theory that women could act as priests equally with men, but the only evidence for a woman acting as a great teacher (the case of Joan White)[53] is inconclusive. The inability of Hawise or any other woman to move into such a role in the East Anglian community may be due partly to the relative isolation of women in different villages. Female Lollards in East Anglia were not numerous enough to be able to provide one another with support as women in Coventry, for example, were able to do.

Similarly, although the Lollard group in Amersham detected in the sixteenth century was large, and women often interacted (although not, as far as we know, in all-female conventicles), there is no clear evidence that women there taught publicly in gatherings. The most influential woman in Amersham Lollardy was Alice Harding, but the situations in which she was most active were informal ones.

Alice Harding and her husband, Thomas Harding, were comfortably well-off, according to Thomas's assessment in the 1524–25 subsidy.[54] They first did penance for heresy in 1506 under Bishop William Smith of Lincoln, and then in 1515 they appeared before Bishop Atwater, who released them from some of their penance, including the wearing of badges depicting faggots. According to Foxe, they observed the remainder of their penance until 1522.[55] Although Thomas continued to be active in Lollardy, Alice does not appear in the records again.

Alice's position in her community was important. Isabel Tracher sent her daughter to her to be taught, "saying, that she could better instruct her than many others,"[56] and Joan Norman accused Alice of dissuading her from pilgrimages, from the worship of images, and from vowing money to saints for the health of her child. Alice also gave advice to men, telling Robert Bartlet that having been "chosen to Almighty God," he must not forsake his faith. She went to the house of Richard Bennet to warn him that a priest was coming to his house to give him communion and counseled him about what he should do.[57]

Alice also participated in the conventicles of the Amersham area, although no deposition remarks on her role in such meetings. The Hardings' home was a gathering place for "known-men" after the abjurations before Bishop Smith in 1506–7. Alice and Thomas also used to meet with a group of other couples at the home of Thomas Man to speak about matters of religion. Alice may have been present without her husband at the wedding of Robert Durdant's daughter at Staines, Middlesex.[58] Alice appears to have been a respected and prominent member of the Lollard community in the Amersham area; while no evidence about the nature of her participation in the public arena of the conventicle survives, in the less formal aspects of Lollard activity she was evidently influential. Her personality and social station (which together evidently commanded respect from men and women) and the large number of female Lollards in the Amersham area allowed Alice an important role in the Lollard community there. Nonetheless, she did not breach the conventions that militated against public activity in a conventicle.

Although some women in the Lollard communities in London and Essex were evidently active, few have left more than isolated anecdotal evidence. But the activities of one Colchester woman, Marion Westden Mathew,[59] indicate an interesting Lollard career and a high level of commitment to the sect. She was the wife of Thomas Mathew, whose position in Colchester civic life and in the Lollard community there was prominent. Marion may have acted independently from her husband in business deals,[60] and she was certainly active in the Lollard group in Colchester. John Hacker testified that she was a member of the sect, and John Pykas also confessed that he had taught in her presence. When specifically asked about Marion's activities, Pykas said

> that the deponent hath herd speke of the epistoles and gospells, which hath she well by hert, in her owne house diverse and many tymes; and have herd the said Marion say to this deponent, diverse and many tymes within this iii yeris in her house, that men shuld not go on pilgremages, for they wer nowght and shuld not be used, and that she shuld say to this deponent that she had sett up as few candells to Imagis as any woman had, for it was not lefull.[61]

But her activities were not known throughout Essex and were not even necessarily remarked by Lollards who came to her house. John Tyball, who had stayed at the Mathews' house when he, Richard Fox, and John Smyth, all of Steeple Bumpstead, came to Colchester, said that he was not sure if she was of the sect (although he deposed against her husband).[62] Marion might have been more willing to speak freely in front of a frequent visitor to her house, such as John Pykas, than before strangers, even if they were of her belief. Again, women were constrained to activity among intimates rather than the wider sphere permitted to men.

Two Influential Coventry Women: Stretching the Boundaries

Women in the Lollard community in Coventry were able to circumvent some of the restrictions felt by women in other communities because they associated mostly with others of their sex. Two women of particular importance to the Coventry Lollard group, Joan Smyth and Alice Rowley, were members of the city's ruling elite. While Joan Smyth's activities were, like those of other prominent women in the movement, confined in the main to informal interaction, Alice Rowley was able to use her social station to achieve a position in the Lollard community unparalleled elsewhere in the movement. Men as well as women accorded her a measure of authority and respect no other Lollard woman was able to achieve.

Joan Smyth's sphere of activity was centered around other women, a common pattern even among the most active of Lollard women. In 1511 she was the wife of a wealthy merchant and important civic official, Richard Smyth;[63] she had been married to two other men, one of commensurate status and the other of lower status. Significantly, it was her first and least socially prominent husband, Richard Landesdale, who converted her to the Lollard creed about 1500.[64] Although there is no sign that either her second or third husband sympathized with her Lollard leanings, she remained active through these marriages, consorting with Alice Rowley and the women's circle and with Roger Landesdale, probably her brother-in-law. She exchanged books with several Lollards, although she herself could not read. She also proselytized: John Cropwell, the husband of one of her servants, said that she had often railed to him against priests and the church. Joan had two daughters (probably by Richard Landesdale), who were said to be of the sect, and one of them married Richard Northopp, also accused of heresy.[65]

Joan Smyth apparently continued her heresy after her abjuration before the bishop in November 1511. In 1520, by then again a widow, she was one of seven Lollards who were brought before the bishop as relapsed heretics.[66] The other six (Hachet, Archer, Hawkyns, Bowen, Wrixham, and

Landesdale[67]) were condemned to be burned, but, according to Foxe, "Mistress Smith" was initially dismissed, perhaps because of her sex or her social position. As Foxe tells it, however, when she was being accompanied home by Simon Mourton, the summoner, he

> heard the rattling of a scroll within her sleeve; "Yea," saith he, "what have ye here?" And so took it from her, and espied that it was the Lord's Prayer, the Articles of the Faith, and the Ten Commandments in English. When the wretched sumner understood this; "Ah sirrah!" said he, "Come, as good now as another time."[68]

Mourton brought her back to the bishop, and she was burned along with the six men.

Although Joan Smyth was active among the women in the community and traded books and presumably conversation with several men in the group,[69] it is not clear that this extended to any public role in their conventicles. One prominent Lollard man, Robert Hachet, appears not to have known her well. When asked about her, he reported only that he knew she was a heretic and that, according to rumor, she possessed heretical books.[70] Her sphere of activity, like that of other women, was mostly informal and centered around other women.

In contrast, Alice Rowley not only was prominent among the women in the group but was able to become one of the leading Lollards in the male conventicles as well. As we saw earlier, her social rank, as the widow of a prominent merchant of the Calais Staple and former Coventry mayor, was high.[71] Although she was already active in the sect by the early 1490s, Alice did not appear before the bishop for her beliefs until 1506. At that time she was able to clear her name with the help of sixteen compurgators,[72] but her continued activities caused her to be brought before Bishop Blyth again during his investigation of 1511–12. She appeared before the court several times between 31 October 1511 and 24 January 1512; at first she denied her heresy, but then reluctantly she admitted that her compurgation in 1506 had been false and proceeded to testify against her fellows. A preliminary penance of fasting on bread and water on vigils of the Assumption of the Virgin for seven years was superseded by another more in keeping with her activities: she was to walk in procession, carrying faggots of wood, as other Lollards had done, and then she was to stand by while her companion Joan Warde was burned, still carrying the faggots on her shoulder. After this she was to proceed to the shrine of St. Mary in the Tower and offer 12d. to the image of the Virgin there.[73] This is the last we see of her in the surviving records; we do not know if she continued to be involved in Lollardy or even when she died.

Alice was a powerful woman in the Lollard community in Coventry. She converted men and women to her faith, she taught many people, she read privately and publicly, and she was heavily involved in the Lollard book trade. Her power and confidence may have come to some extent from her social position and wealth, which she attributed to her creed:

> My beleve is bettr than thers save that we dar not speke it. And why shuld god geve us greate goodis more than other men hath but bicause of our good stedefaste beleve and good bookis?[74]

Alice was in a position of social superiority to most (if not all) men with whom she consorted in the conventicles, giving her the confidence to act as their equal. Her status also may have facilitated her contacts with other prominent people who were on the fringes of the movement, such as Dr. Preston and Mistress Coke.[75]

Alice Rowley was the only woman in the Lollard movement who was able to combine a forceful personality with a high social status in the unique context of the Coventry community. This milieu allowed women an autonomous role within all-female conventicles and perhaps gave Rowley the opportunity to extend her influence beyond the women's group. Other Lollard women were also powerful within the movement but were restricted by social norms from playing the formal teaching roles that men played in conventicles and other Lollard gatherings.

Parallels can be seen in other heterodox sects, in which women of higher social standing also took prominent roles. In Catharism, John Mundy found in his study of the Amnesty of 1279 that the women given pardons were on the average wealthier and from a higher social position than the men.[76] Similarly, among the Hussites and later among Reformers, noblewomen acted as patrons and suppporters.[77] On occasion, forceful and intelligent women could act in ways that stretched the usual expectations of the gender system of medieval society by using other conventions, those of wealth and social status.

Prominent Men and Elite Men in Lollardy

A number of variables, including gender roles, personality, and social status, defined a woman's position in a Lollard group; these same variables also governed a man's position, but they operated differently. Late medieval gender roles specified public activity as male, so that men were much more likely than women both to be predisposed to take leading parts in a conventicle and to be recognized as authoritative figures. But whereas higher socioeconomic status elevated the position of women in a community, the most important male Lollards were not necessarily the wealthiest or the highest in social status. Perhaps by analogy to the Roman Catholic clergy, Lollards may have demanded of their leaders qualities that depended little on economic status, such as charisma or intelligence. Although Lollardy did not furnish women of the artisanry with a possibility of playing a greater role than they did in orthodox religion, it may have given artisan men just that opportunity.

The participation of the social and economic elite in Lollardy, both male and female, varied from community to community. In Kent, for instance, little can be discovered about the social status of the Lollards, suggesting that it was probably low. A list of the mayors and bailiffs for the town of Tenterden, a Lollard center, contains no Lollard names. Even a list of the freemen of the town in 1529 contains the name of only one man, William Pellond, who was brought before the Archbishop in 1511–12.[78] Few of the Lollards in this diocese (Canterbury) even left wills, a sign that their wealth was not great.[79] Similarly, the social status of the Lollards in East Anglia in the 1420s (although less easily characterized due to the poor records of the pre-Tudor period) appears not to have reached beyond that of a master craftsman.[80] Records concerning the Lollards of the diocese of Salisbury (with the exception of Alice Cottismore, discussed earlier) are not sufficient to determine their social status, although those whose occupations are reported were laborers or craftsmen.[81]

Gentlemen in Later Lollardy

The Lollard movement was, however, by no means confined to the lower orders of society. As the example of Alice Cottismore shows, members of the gentry became involved in Lollardy, even after Oldcastle's Revolt. Although often their participation in or patronage of local Lollard communities is obscure, men of the gentry probably had more influence than did Alice Cottismore. In one fifteenth-century Lollard group, uncovered by Bishop Chedworth in the Chiltern Hills in the 1460s, the continued involvement of a family that had been active in the movement since before Oldcastle's Revolt may have been crucial to the community's survival.

The Cheynes of Drayton Beauchamp and later of Chesham Bois had a

long-standing association with Lollardy. Roger Cheyne of Drayton Beauchamp and his two sons, John and Thomas, were all implicated in Oldcastle's Revolt in 1414, and Charles Kightly sees them as the leaders of Lollard
activity in Buckinghamshire during that period.[82] Thomas, the younger
brother, acquired the manor of Chesham Bois sometime within ten years of
1423. He was succeeded there on his death (sometime after 1446) by his
son, John (I), and upon John I's death, by another John (II), who died in
1466, leaving a son, yet another John (III), age eight weeks. Before the
long minority of John III, there is evidence that John I and John II continued the Lollard family tradition (albeit more quietly than their forebears
Thomas and his brother Sir John) by appointing a Lollard to the local
parish church.[83] There was family precedent for using advowsons to protect
Lollard clergy: Roger Cheyne had appointed the Lollard priest Thomas
Drayton to the living of Drayton Beauchamp in 1410 and probably protected him as he preached Lollardy in Buckinghamshire and beyond between 1410 and 1414.[84]

No evidence of any attempt on the part of ecclesiastical or secular
officials to examine this case of gentle Lollardy survives, perhaps implying
that gentry who wished to follow Lollard beliefs may have been able to do
so with relative ease and virtual immunity from prosecution in the tu-
multuous years of the mid-fifteenth century. However, there is also no
evidence that the Cheynes participated directly in the Lollard community
that Chedworth uncovered in the 1460s; those who were examined by the
bishop were generally of lowly stature.[85] Perhaps the social gulf between the
gentle Cheynes and the artisans could not be bridged even by a common
faith.

Lollardy was still prevalent in the Chiltern Hills in the next century,
but the early sixteenth-century representatives of the Cheyne family were
no longer patrons of the movement. One tenuous clue connects Robert
Cheyne, son of John III, to the community in the Amersham area — the
1537 will of John Gardner of Chesham Bois, a Lollard, named Robert
Cheyne as supervisor.[86] But Gardner's will is orthodox, and it would not be
unusual to ask the local lord of the manor to supervise one's will.[87] Robert
Cheyne and his father, John Cheyne III (whose long minority marked a
break in family religious tradition) appear, unlike their ancestors, to have
been Catholic conservatives interested in the prosecution rather than support of local Lollards. Both Robert Cheyne and John Cheyne III were present, with other local dignitaries, at the condemnation of Thomas Harding,
formerly of Amersham, then of Chesham, before the vicar general in the

Chesham parish church in 1532.[88] In 1538, John Tracher, yeoman, who had been detected as a Lollard before the bishop in the early 1520s, complained to Thomas Cromwell because his landlord, Robert Cheyne, evicted him for reading the New Testament.[89] The sixteenth-century Lollard community in the Chiltern Hills thus did not have the patronage and possibly the protection that the early- and mid-fifteenth-century community had had from the local lords of the manor.

But another family of gentry stature was active in the Lollard communities in Buckinghamshire and in the other counties surrounding London. Robert Durdant, the patriarch of a Lollard family, was the lessee of the manor of Yeoveney, Middlesex (held in chief by the abbey of Westminster); the rent was the considerable sum of £25 per annum. Robert's heir, Nicholas, took over the lease of Yeoveney when his father died in 1524; even in 1522, before he had received this inheritance, Nicholas was assessed as possessing £13 6s. 8d. worth of goods, a sizable amount.[90] The Middlesex Durdants, stationed between the Amersham and London communities, played host to many Lollard gatherings.[91] Like the Cheynes of the 1460s, there is no evidence that the Durdants were ever examined by ecclesiastical officials, perhaps because of their status.[92] The Durdants were probably not as wealthy as the Cheynes (fifteenth- or sixteenth-century), but their status certainly exceeds what was usual for post-Oldcastle Lollards.

The Durdants also differed from the sixteenth-century Cheynes in another particular, which may provide a clue to the Durdants' religious proclivities, unusual for their time and station: the Cheynes were very politically active while the Durdants were not. John Cheyne III regularly acted on commissions of the peace and of gaol delivery between 1509 and 1532. He was sheriff of Buckinghamshire in 1520 and, perhaps in that capacity, was present at the Field of the Cloth of Gold in the same year. Both John and his son Robert were members of the commission to collect the 1524 subsidy.[93] The Durdants, on the other hand, cannot be found at all in the *Letters and Papers of Henry VIII*, suggesting that they were politically inactive; their religious beliefs were thus less likely to interfere with their political ambitions.

The participation in the sect of another gentleman, Balthasar Shugborow of Coventry and Napton, is certain, but how his status affected his place in the community is unclear. Balthasar, described in his examination as a gentleman ("generosus") of the parish of Napton, age fifty,[94] must have belonged to the Shukborowe family of Warwickshire which held the manors of Upper Shukburgh and Napton (and had done so since the thirteenth and early fifteenth centuries, respectively).[95] A Thomas Shukborowe, conceivably father, brother, or cousin to Balthasar, was justice of the peace for Warwickshire from 1502 to 1507 and in 1509, and he acted on commissions of gaol delivery in 1503, 1505, and 1509.[96] Balthasar (a black sheep of the Shukborowe family?) was held up as one of the leading heretics in the Lollard community in Coventry, although there is no sense that he acted as a patron or even that he hosted gatherings in his dwelling, as might be expected of a wealthier man.[97] Although a number of other prominent men (burghers rather than gentry) were named by the Lollards of Coventry as favoring their beliefs,[98] Balthasar Shugborow is the only one who actively participated in the community's gatherings, and he is the only one who was brought before the bishop on charges of heresy.

Thus men of the gentry occasionally participated in fifteenth- and sixteenth-century Lollardy; with the exception of the Durdants, who hosted many Lollard gatherings, it is unclear that gentry activity within the Lollard groups materially affected these groups' circumstances. It does seem clear, though, that the gentry of either sex was not much interested in Lollardy by 1500, perhaps because of its association with groups of lesser social status, or perhaps because adherence to heresy may have been damaging to anyone interested in politics on a county or national level.

URBAN ELITES

Another socially elevated group that may have found Lollardy attractive was the urban elite — merchants and wealthier craftsmen of the villages, towns, and cities where the heresy had taken hold. Evidence for the involvement of men of these stations does survive, but it by no means indicates they dominated the movement.

There are signs that prominent Londoners became involved in Lollard groups. Some of the evidence is hearsay: for instance, a deponent in the Richard Hunne case testified, "I could bring my lord of London to the doors of heretics in London, both of men and women, that be worth a thousand pounds."[99] A certain Payn, woolwinder, invited John Whitehorn, rector of Letcombe Basset and a Lollard, to his home in London where he would find "many rich heretical men."[100]

But some more concrete examples survive of substantial Londoners who were implicated in Lollardy. Besides Jane Yonge, a mayor's widow who may have participated in the community, men, too, were involved. For instance, John Barret, goldsmith of Cheapside and merchant of the Calais Staple, was, according to Robert Benet, a "bonus et perfectus homo and a prevy man" (the last being a usual designation for a Lollard).[101] He employed two apprentices who were Lollards, Robert Wigge and William Tylsworth, the latter with Amersham connections.[102] Although there is no record that he was brought before the authorities for his beliefs, Barret may in fact have suffered a loss of his goods as a result of Lollardy: he was recorded as a recipient of the Goldsmiths' Company's alms in 1516.[103] Richard Wryght of London, a master of an unknown trade, was said to be "grett with" Barret. He was the master of Alice Ray's son, and she boasted that he was "vir honestus dives et bonus ac perfectus homo . . . he is a prevy man . . . and he will deele with no poer folks."[104] This last "virtue" was rather un-Lollard but perhaps indicative that he was of a different social station from many others in the sect. The celebrated heresy case of merchant Richard Hunne — whether he was in fact a Lollard or was framed[105] — shows that officials could at least plausibly accuse members of the civic elite. The evidence for London indicates that the Lollard groups there included both men and women of some substance. Unfortunately, the patchy nature of the records for the city makes it impossible to know what their roles were in the community.

SOCIAL STATUS AND MEN'S LOLLARD ACTIVITIES: SOME CASE STUDIES

Substantial men were also involved in the Lollard community in the Chiltern Hills. The evidence is particularly full regarding wealth (and thus social status) for the community uncovered in the first and third decades of the sixteenth century by Bishops Smith and Longland. Derek Plumb has analyzed this material and finds that Lollards came from virtually all social levels below the very highest, and that there was a significant number of relatively wealthy people involved in the Buckinghamshire Lollard community.[106] Richard G. Davies's work on Buckinghamshire Lollards shows further that Lollards in Amersham included the most important men in the town and that they tended to do business with one another.[107] I employ here the records from the 1522 Muster and the 1524–25 Subsidy and other government documents along with the records of Lollard activity to investigate the relationship between wealth and level of activity in the group. Active male Lollards of the community came from all social strata, indicating there was no strict correlation between a man's prominence within the group and his wealth.

Foxe says that there were "four principal readers or instructors" of the Amersham community in about 1507: William Tylsworth, Thomas Chase, Thomas Man, and Robert Cosin.[108] The secular records contain no further information about their wealth or status; they all died or were executed for their heresies before 1522 and so do not appear in either the Muster or the Subsidy. Another William Tylsworth (perhaps the executed man's son) was a goldsmith and citizen of London, perhaps indicating a high status for the Tylsworth family.[109] Robert Cosin, a miller of Missenden according to Foxe,[110] was perhaps of less elevated status.

There is more complete evidence for those who survived after 1520. As Plumb and Davies note, government records for the 1510s and 1520s show that a number of affluent inhabitants of the town of Amersham were involved in the Lollard movement. Of twelve Amersham men from whom horses were bought by the king's commissioners in Buckinghamshire in 1513, seven had already been or later would be implicated in the sect.[111] Most remarkably, testimony was given in the 1520s against Amersham's wealthiest resident, Richard Saunders, a dyer. The extent of his involvement in the movement, however, is unclear. John Sawcoat said that Richard "ever defended them that were suspected to be 'known-men.'" Sawcoat further indicated that Saunders had abjured heresy in the first decade of the sixteenth century and that the court had given him penance for it, although he had been able to buy it out.[112] Saunders could well afford to purchase an exemption: in 1522 he was assessed at £6 13s. 4d. in land and the relatively immense sum of £300 in goods, while in 1524 he was valued at £200 in goods.[113] Although Richard Saunders was wealthier (at least in goods) than local gentry,[114] there is no evidence that he played a leading role in the local Lollard community or even that he attended conventicles or taught others his beliefs. Richard's wife, Alice Saunders, was more clearly involved in the community, and she used her husband's wealth (perhaps with his approval) to influence recalcitrant Lollards, but she was not a leader either.[115]

Other prominent men of Amersham were implicated in the Lollard community, but, like Richard Saunders, their role in the sect does not appear to have been central. Several men testified that Roger Harding of Amersham was involved in the sect, although there is no detailed evidence. He was well off by village standards, possessing £30 in goods.[116] John Milsent of Amersham, who abjured and did penance for heresy in 1506 and may have continued to be active after that, had comparable wealth,[117] but he was never cited as a teacher or a leader either. John Hill admitted in about 1521 that he had had contact with a number of Lollards, although again there is no sign that he instructed others or led conventicles. He died in 1523, soon after his appearance before the bishop; an inventory of the goods of Hill and his wife found that their belongings were worth the relatively large sum of £36 13s. 6d.[118] Thomas Wydmer of Hughenden, a wealthy man assessed as possessing £4 10s. in land and £35 in goods in 1522 and £30 in goods in 1524, was named by a Lollard as a member of the sect, and his wife was cited twice.[119] These men, leaders of their village community, apparently did not as a matter of course become leaders of the local heretical community.

But some of the more substantial inhabitants of Amersham were among the most vigorous members of the community. Thomas Harding of Amersham, for instance, whose goods were valued at £20 in 1524,[120] was demonstrably a committed and active Lollard. He first abjured and did penance for heresy in 1506, along with his wife Alice.[121] Although the penance he and Alice had been assigned was partially remitted in 1515,[122] both husband and wife apparently continued their Lollard activities. Several men testified against Thomas in 1521, and he apparently made a deposition against Robert and Richard Bartlett the same year.[123] Despite evidence at this time of his relapse into heresy, it was not until 1532, when Thomas was caught in possession of various heretical books, that he was burned.[124] Thus, Thomas and his wife Alice, who had moderate wealth, were active in the Lollard community over several decades.

The other notable Amersham Lollards who were comfortably well-off were the Bartletts, a large Lollard family consisting of a mother, Katherine, and her five Lollard offspring. Two of Katherine's sons, Robert and Richard, had sizable assessments of their worth in the 1522 Muster Rolls: Richard possessed 13s. 4d. in land and £24 in goods, while Robert was valued at 15s. in land and £40 in goods.[125] The brothers may indeed have been wealthier but for their Lollard activities. Both Robert and Richard abjured in 1506 during Bishop Smith's prosecution, and Robert may have lost his property. Foxe says that Robert, "a rich man, . . . was put out of his farm and goods, and was condemned to be kept in the monastery of Ashridge, where he wore on his right sleeve a square piece of cloth, the space of seven years together."[126] In 1521 the bishop prosecuted both brothers again, and they confessed that they had continued their activities despite their previous abjurations. Although they were relapsed, they apparently were not executed, although Robert's fate is uncertain.[127]

Although Robert and Richard Bartlett were clearly committed to Lollardy and risked their goods for their faith, adherence to the sect may have been tempered by worldly concerns for at least some members of the family. Richard, for instance, endangered his soul through excessive interest in commerce, according to Alice Harding, who said of him: "he hath so much mind of buying and selling, and taking of farms, that it putteth his mind from all goodness."[128] Isabel Bartlett, Robert's wife, may have been less willing than her husband to risk her property for her faith. When the bishop's officials came to arrest her husband in 1521 she cried out, Robert said, because of "a vehement fear for the loss of her goods."[129] More substantial men in Amersham society, such as the Bartletts and Thomas Harding, were enthusiastic Lollards who were able to take leading roles in the heretical community, but it is also clear that these men had more to lose than their poorer fellows if they were caught.

Wealthier men were not the only leading male Lollards; active men in the Chiltern Hills community came from all social strata. Some were of middling circumstances. Robert Andrew of Amersham, for instance, was worth 2s. in land and £6 in goods in 1522 and £11 in goods in 1524.[130] Andrew had apparently abjured in 1506–7 and was called to witness against the Bartletts in 1521; his connections to others in the community (including the Bartletts and the Saunders) are shown in their wills.[131] John Tracher of Chesham (who was detected as a teacher in 1521 and later evicted by Robert Cheyne for reading a New Testament) was valued as possessing £18 in goods in 1522 and £8 in goods in 1524.[132] David Sherwood of Great Marlow, implicated by John Gardiner in the Lollard community centered in Amersham, was assessed at £8 in goods in both 1522 and 1524,[133] and Henry Phip of Hughenden, reported to speak often against pilgrimage and idolatry, had £6 in goods in 1522 and £4 in goods in 1524.[134]

While these men were comfortable, a good number of men implicated in the proceedings, some prominently, were relatively poor.[135] Six men, including the active John Say of Little Missenden and John Phip of Hughenden (Henry's brother), a physician, were recorded as holding the equivalent of between £2 and £4 in goods.[136] Another seven were valued at £2 in goods. This group included Robert Carder of Iver, a weaver, who was a member of a group of men who gathered at the home of Robert Durdant to discuss Lollard doctrine, and John Morwyn of Amersham, who, as the husband of the former Isabel Bartlett, had married into an important Lollard family.[137] Three alleged Lollards were said to be worth £1 or less; of these, at least one, Benet Ward of Beaconsfield, was active in the community.[138]

The Buckinghamshire Lollard community included men (and women) from a wide range of social backgrounds. One very wealthy man, Richard Saunders, participated in the community at least peripherally, while several men of comfortable means, notably Thomas Harding, Robert Bartlett, and Richard Bartlett, took an active role in the community. Other men who were active in the Lollard group were by no means wealthy and perhaps fit the usual characterization of Lollards as poor artisans. There appears to have been no direct correlation between a man's wealth and social status and his position in the Lollard community.

Indeed, in the two Essex communities in Colchester and Steeple Bumpstead, there is even clearer evidence that wealthier men in the sect were taught and led by men of lesser means. The men who were leaders of the Colchester Lollard community were, with one or possibly two exceptions, not of high status. The wealthiest was Thomas Mathew, host of many Lollard gatherings, who was worth £30 in 1523. He was also active in civic affairs both before and after his abjuration in 1528: he was a member of the common council for the borough in 1523 and acted as a collector of the subsidy in the same year. Later, in 1524 and 1529, he was a member of the Second Council of the city.[139]

Another man involved in civic affairs may also have been involved in the Colchester Lollard community, but the evidence here is more ambiguous. In 1511 James Brewster testified that he had heard a certain Master Bardefield saying, "He that will not worship the Maozim in heart and thought, shall die in sight." Brewster was unsure what this meant, but another man explained later that Maozim signified "the masing God, to wit the sacrament of the altar,"[140] indicating that Master Bardefield spoke in favor of the eucharist (not against it, as would be expected of a Lollard). The Master Bardefield referred to by Brewster may have been either John Bardefield Sr. or his son, John Bardefield Jr. Although evidence that either of these men were Lollards is lacking (and indeed Brewster's testimony indicates the opposite), there were Lollard family connections: John Sr.'s daughter and John Jr.'s sister was Marion Westden Mathew, the wife of Thomas Mathew, and John Jr. was married to Katherine Cowbridge, the daughter or step-daughter of the possibly Lollard widow Margaret Cowbridge. The Bardefields, father and son, like Thomas Mathew, were both involved in the civic government of Colchester, but at least John Jr. was not Mathew's equal in wealth—his goods were valued at a middling £10 in 1523 and 1524. Although the Bardefields themselves may have been part of an extended Lollard family, their adherence to the sect cannot be firmly established.[141]

Other men who were more certainly part of the Lollard community were not abject, but they weren't of Mathew's stature. John Pykas, for instance, was valued at £1 in 1523 and £4 in 1524. Yet Pykas was clearly Mathew's teacher and probably the leader of the Colchester community: he said that he had taught many times in the presence of Mathew, Marion Westden Mathew, and their family, as well as John Thompson, Dorothy Lane, Robert Best, Katherine Swayn, John Girling, John Bradley, Thomas Parker, Margaret Bowgas, Margaret Cowbridge, John Hubbert, Robert Bate, Robert Collins alias Johnson, John Wyley, William Raylond, and Alice Gardiner.[142] Others who taught in Mathew's house were transient Lollard teachers of indeterminate status, such as John Hacker and Robert Necton.[143] Other Lollards with whom Pykas (and probably Mathew) had regular contact were also active but by no means wealthy. Pykas admitted to frequent communication with William Raylond and John Girling, valued at £1 and £2, respectively, in the subsidy.[144] John Thompson and his father-in-law Thomas Parker also communicated many times with Pykas and, like Mathew, hosted Lollard gatherings. Thompson and Parker were also worth between £1 and £2.[145] Thomas Mathew, although the wealthiest male Lollard, was by no means the leader of the group or even the most active. The men with whom he consorted were much poorer than he was, although some of the women were of his social station.

The subsidy assessments of a smaller Essex town, Steeple Bumpstead,[146] also indicate that the most prominent members of the heretical group in the town were not the wealthiest. John Tyball was the leader of the Steeple Bumpstead community and a very active Lollard, missionary, and traveler. But he was not wealthy; his tax assessment indicates that his goods were worth about £3. Gilbert Shipwright, who was dead by 1528, was less important to the group than Tyball, but he taught several people his beliefs. His tax assessment indicates that he was relatively poor, with goods worth £1 or less.

More substantial men in Steeple Bumpstead were not so active. John Craneford was said to have heard the teachings of Tyball, Richard Fox, and others; he also acted as a witness against three other suspects.[147] He appeared as a juror in views of frankpledge in Steeple Bumpstead fairly continuously between 1500 and 1537,[148] and his goods in 1523 were worth about £6. Edmund Tyball admitted that he had been taught by Richard Fox, and John Tyball (whose kin relationship to Edmund is unclear) said that he and Edmund had often discussed Lollard doctrine.[149] Although Edmund Tyball appears as a pupil and even a somewhat reluctant one who may have felt pressured to conform in a village where Lollardy had a firm hold — he said that he had "never believed nor consented to this [Fox's] teaching, but did not disclose it"[150] — he was one of the wealthiest men in the village. His tax assessment of 6s. 6d. indicates that his goods were worth between £8 and

£10. The leaders of the Lollard community in Steeple Bumpstead were not its wealthiest adherents; as in Colchester, wealthier men such as Edmund Tyball and John Craneford were the pupils of less substantial men like John Tyball.

The evidence for the socioeconomic status of men in the Coventry Lollard community — discussed fully in Chapter 2 — is both more complete and more ambiguous than is found in the records for other communities. As we have seen, women of the civic elite, Alice Rowley and Joan Smyth, participated vigorously in Lollard activities, but allegations that several important men of the same status were involved in the Lollard community are probably groundless.[151] The social position of the men with whom Alice Rowley and Joan Smyth consorted was modest: women of the elite were involved in the Coventry Lollard community, but men of similar social standing were not.

The men of the Coventry Lollard community who were brought before Bishop Blyth on charges of heresy were, for the most part, humble men. Balthasar Shugborow, gentleman, was an anomaly; besides him, only Richard Bradley, mercer, appears to have approached even moderate wealth.[152] The court book records the occupations of fourteen of the fifteen men who made up the core of the all-male gatherings; all but Shugborow worked in the crafts (one tailor, two shearmen, three shoemakers, two leatherdressers, one skinner, one tanner, and three painters).[153] The leaders of the community, according to depositions, were Roger Landesdale, a tailor; Robert Silkby, a shoemaker; Robert Hachet, a leatherdresser; and Shugborow.[154]

*   *   *

Evidence for the Lollard communities indicates that men of all social standings played leading roles in the sect, perhaps because leadership depended less on social status than on other, more personal factors. Moreover, men from the artisan trades may have found more in Lollardy to attract them than did wealthier men, and thus they may have been the movement's most enthusiastic supporters, while political penalties and social factors predisposed prominent men to orthodoxy. This is not to assert that men below the highest status had no political life: their involvement in juries, town councils, parish offices, and other local organizations was crucial to their position in their community and could, moreover, represent considerable power on the national scene.[155] Nonetheless, local power structures might more easily have tolerated involvement in a heretical movement than did national politics. In some cases (the town of Amersham being the clearest example), local political life may have been dominated by Lollards. On the other hand, in other towns there was little intersection between the Lollard communities and the political leadership, suggesting either that those ambitious in the public sphere chose not to risk their positions by involvement in a heterodox movement or that the Lollard movement attracted men who had been shut out of their towns' political processes.

The importance of social and economic position in the structure of Lollard communities remains somewhat enigmatic, its complexity compounded by patchy and ambiguous records. In some Lollard communities, there is little evidence that the social profile of their members extended beyond the artisanry, while in others there was occasional participation by members of the gentry and the urban merchant classes. Social position affected men and women Lollards differently. While prominent female Lollards were most often of higher economic and social status than was the norm for members of their sect, male leaders were both of humble and elite social positions. This suggests that women's importance in a community was at least partly a factor of their status in a village or a town, while men's influence was based on other variables, such as intelligence and charisma. Women were able to stretch their gender roles beyond normal prescriptions of female behavior only when another aspect of their identity, their social status, gave them some precedence over men of the sect.

6. Conclusion: Lollardy, Gender, and Late Medieval Religious Culture

Men and women did not respond to the lure of the Lollard movement in the same way. Men, both urban and rural, artisans and agricultural workers, joined the sect in much greater numbers than did women of similar socio-economic backgrounds. Men were, moreover, the movement's more enthusiastic and active adherents. Most Lollard women became involved as wives or other relatives of men of the sect, suggesting that their involvement was less an individual choice than a family decision.[1] Clearly, men of these social groups were more attracted to the sect than were their wives, sisters, mothers, and daughters.

How do we account for this gender disparity? The nature of a religious movement's appeal for different groups is a complex amalgamation of social and spiritual factors sometimes interrelating with one another in concert and sometimes in tension. Separating the different strands is neither simple nor desirable; both individual personality and the social construction of gender affect the way an individual responds psychologically to a creed or a religious movement's style of devotion. That all women and all men do not respond the same way to religion is obvious, yet the pattern of gender-differentiated participation in Lollardy is striking enough that it demands explanation. Concerns apparently rooted in this world, particularly social structures and family dynamics, go a long way to explaining the Lollard movement's greater attractions for men than for women. The sect offered men a greater role, and it was simply easier for men to participate. But the Lollard creed's spiritual appeal was also crucial.

Recent work on the subjects of gender and the nature of religious culture in late medieval and early modern Christianity by historians like Caroline Walker Bynum, Eamon Duffy, André Vauchez, Lyndal Roper, Natalie Zemon Davis, and Robert Scribner has greatly enhanced our understanding of the experience of religion in the premodern past. These studies show pre-Reformation religion to be fluid, responsive, and intricate, allowing for substantial lay creativity, which permitted women as well as men to participate in the shaping of religious culture. Some aspects of late medieval orthodoxy have even been identified as the particular province of women, generated by female piety and suited to the economic and social patterns of their lives.

The Lollard creed was substantially different from late medieval Catholicism, and indeed many of its tenets were formulated in direct opposition to orthodox practice. Lollards most virulently attacked precisely those aspects of late medieval Catholicism that most reflected popular creativity, and thus women's devotion. In their zeal to rid Christianity of nonscriptural medieval accretions, they removed many of the elements that were both attractive to, and to a large extent created by, women. Born in the thoroughly masculine and clerical university environment, the Lollard creed developed with little feminine influence; this ultimately affected its ability to appeal to ordinary laywomen.

Women and Late Medieval Religion

My thesis that Lollardy attracted men more than women runs counter to much that has been written by historians on the drawing powers of medieval heretical sects. The standard argument for the appeal of heresy for women, perhaps best articulated in Brenda Bolton's 1973 article "Mulieres Sanctae" and recently presented as axiomatic in the medieval volume of *The History of Women in the West*, rests on a syllogism: Catholicism after about 1100 did not provide opportunities for religious expression for women; heresies did provide women with such outlets; so women joined heretical movements in preponderant numbers.[2]

All three parts of this syllogism have been challenged. Caroline Walker Bynum has argued against the first premise, contending that orthodox spirituality of the high and late medieval periods was to a significant degree generated by women as well as by men and that many of the characteristics of late medieval Catholic piety appealed especially to women.[3] André Vauchez has called the fourteenth and fifteenth centuries the "golden age of the laity," especially for the female sex.[4] Recently, other historians have reopened the question of what alternatives were available to women wishing to live a formal or semiformal religious life. They, like Bynum, have emphasized the range of options and the vitality of late medieval religion.[5]

Eleanor McLaughlin has disputed the evidence for the conclusion to the syllogism: she warns against unquestioning acceptance by modern historians of hostile observers' characterization of heretical movements as preponderantly female. This was not necessarily a reflection of the actual makeup of the groups, she asserts, but a way of casting aspersions both on the "spiritual weakness" of women (always more open to diabolical temptations) and on the heresy itself, which exploited this frailty.[6] Work on the Cathar movement has also argued that women's involvement in the sect has been exaggerated and never matched that of men.[7] Peter Biller has suggested that the syllogism should indeed be turned on its head; women were underrepresented in Catharism because orthodoxy provided them with a creed better suited to them. The laywoman, in choosing Catholicism over Catharism, "was voting with her feet."[8]

An oft-made but problematic assumption is that all medieval heresies had the same spiritual appeal—the rebellion against orthodoxy, not the content of the creed, is seen as most significant. Discussions of the appeal of heterodoxy for women often group Lollardy with other heretical sects,[9] but it was a very different kind of movement from Catharism (the most frequently studied heresy). The Cathars' creed, their social and political context, and indeed even the orthodoxy against which they rebelled had little in common with the world of the Lollards.

More relevant here is the recent historiography of late medieval and early modern orthodox religious culture. This literature has focused on two areas, "popular religion" and the role of women, that have too rarely intersected.[10] Scholars in these two fields have not asked the same questions, but their findings complement an investigation into the gendered appeal of a sect like Lollardy.

Natalie Zemon Davis, John Van Engen, Robert W. Scribner, and others have challenged historians to examine the history of Christianity from the perspective of "religion as practiced and experienced," rather than through modern rational or denominational definitions of orthodoxy.[11] It is imperative to take religious beliefs seriously and on their own terms, whether they pertain to the lower orders or to the elite; Scribner's characterization of sixteenth-century German peasants' beliefs as "a complex body of observances"[12] is more useful than dismissing them as ignorant superstitions based on a "pagan" past.[13]

Scribner views religious culture as a complex interweaving of "official" ritual life (performed by and according to the prescriptions of the institutional church) with folklorized and "magical" ritual developed at the initiative of laypeople (such as processions on feast days of saints or using blessed objects as forms of protective magic). From the point of view of the institutional church, the latter category of ritual may have included "improper" activities, difficult to supervise or control, but from the point of view of the layperson who practiced all these forms, they made up a seamless whole and were equally legitimate and Christian. Scribner ascribes significant initiative and creativity in the practice of their religion to ordinary laypeople.[14] Eamon Duffy's recent *The Stripping of the Altars* goes some way toward applying Scribner's models to late medieval England. Duffy also insists that religious practices, such as the use of incantations, must be seen not as paganism but as legitimate "lay Christianity."[15]

Although neither Scribner nor Duffy considers the question of gender in an extended fashion,[16] their work intersects with much that has been written lately on gender (particularly on women) and late medieval and Reformation religion. This literature shares the view that medieval women's religious practices should be taken seriously and that we should regard these women as agents rather than as passive recipients of dogma from the ecclesiastical hierarchy. Historians of medieval women's religiosity have focused, however, on different subjects — the extraordinary religious women (mystics, nuns, and saints) rather than the ordinary lay believer. They see medieval women's spirituality as consistently different from that of medieval men.[17] Bynum, in her studies of medieval mystics, identifies a characteristically female spirituality of the later Middle Ages, an affective and ascetic piety that emphasized the humanity of Christ (especially in eucharistic devotions) and sought to bypass clerical authority in favor of direct communication with God.[18] But Bynum's work leaves unexplored the relationship between the style of devotion of atypical women who made religion their profession and that of women who remained in the world. As Peter Biller points out, laywomen's religious lives have been ignored both by historians of medieval women and by those who study popular religion.[19]

The religious life of the late medieval English laity had institutional forms (through the structures of the parish and the confraternity) and informal aspects (through private, unsupervised use of practices allied with sacramentals and the cult of saints). Both were to a great extent configured by lay concerns and lay piety. But while women were active in the institutions of parish and confraternity, in neither, as a rule, did they play a prominent role. As in Lollardy, laywomen's greatest role in late medieval religion was in the informal sphere, and particularly in the practices associated with the cult of saints.

By the late Middle Ages in England, the laity had clearly defined duties regarding the parish. Careful study of the means by which they organized the practice of their duties reveals to us a great deal about lay participation in the shaping of parish life.[20] But the parishioners were not a homogeneous group; churchwardens — those annually deputed as responsible for the administration of lay duties — were usually chosen from among the men of middling status in the parish. Women occasionally served the parish as churchwardens (most cases coming from the second and third decades of the sixteenth century), but more often their duties corresponded to those that characterized their work life inside and outside the home: washing and mending vestments and basic cleaning.[21]

Religious guilds, sometimes organized around parish structures and sometimes extra-parochial, were another lay-dominated institution of late medieval religion.[22] Women's roles in confraternities were often as subordinate as in the parish; although most guilds admitted women on terms equal with men, in practice men usually outnumbered women, often significantly. Some guilds, however, were organized and administered by and for women; although little is yet known about these "Maydens' Guilds" and "Women's Guilds," they hint at institutional forms of lay religious life that catered especially to lay female spirituality.[23]

But perhaps most important for late medieval laywomen's religiosity were those noninstitutional aspects of medieval Catholicism that were, in Scribner's terms, most open to lay appropriation and creativity: the cult of saints and allied sacramentals. Practices such as pilgrimages to shrines, devotions to images, and invocations of saints (often involving blessed objects) involved a good deal of independent lay action, even from those who were least powerful in medieval society.[24] While its adherents were of both sexes (and indeed the saints had a significant role in the male public world of politics and guilds), medieval as well as modern commentators have connected the cult of saints particularly with women. For example, Mechtild of Magdeburg, a thirteenth-century mystic, wrote that God sent women saints especially to teach and convey messages to other women.[25] Female saints were figures women could relate to, look to as models, and pray to in their particularly feminine hours of distress, such as during childbirth.[26]

Despite the association of medieval women with the cult of saints, there has been insufficient investigation of the question, and thus as yet little concrete evidence that pilgrimages, offerings to images, or invocation of saints were, as such, predominately female practices. Ronald Finucane's study of the shrines of several English saints in the thirteenth century found that upper-class men visited shrines much more often than women of the same station, but that among the lower classes, the numbers were about equal. The sex ratio of pilgrims, however, also differed greatly, depending on the type of shrine; men were more likely to visit shrines of male saints with political or military associations (such as Thomas of Canterbury or Simon de Montfort), while women made up two-thirds of the visitors to the shrines of the female saint Frideswide of Oxford and of the nonpolitical, nonmilitary Godric of Finchale. Finucane does not examine the clientele of shrines of the Virgin, which were the most popular pilgrimage destinations (and Lollard targets) in the fifteenth century. His study does suggest, though, that women enthusiastically practiced specific aspects of the cult of saints.[27]

Perhaps the cult of saints was associated with women less because of a primarily female clientele overall than because practices associated with it were more accessible to women, especially those of lower orders, than other aspects of religion. The cult represented an enormously flexible style of devotion, open to the development of particularized practices for separate groups in late medieval society. Every imaginable aspect of medieval life, at all stages and statuses, had its patron saint. The cult was able to encompass the lives of many people, men or women, humble or elite. Images could be venerated in the home, at roadsides, or on pilgrimages. The cult's elasticity made it more open to female appropriation, creation, and agency than other aspects of late medieval or early modern religion. A movement that attacked the cult of saints thus attacked aspects of medieval Christianity that had been most available to women.

Lollardy and Orthodoxy

The Lollards assailed orthodoxy on two levels, on the one hand resenting the control exercised by the Catholic clergy and on the other wishing to restrain the appropriation of religious practices by "foolish people." They attacked the emphasis on sacerdotalism in late medieval Catholicism, the specialness conferred on the priesthood in their association with the sacraments, and, while not all Lollards rejected it outright, they denigrated popular practices associated with the cult of saints. The Lollards' scriptural fundamentalism determined both targets. Ultimately the goal of the sect was to rid Christianity of nonbiblical accretions in order to return to a purer, scripturally based religion.

That Lollard ideas appealed to medieval men and women has often been assumed by historians, perhaps because the creed has elements attrac-

tive to modern men and women, especially academics.[28] Scriptural fundamentalism meant an emphasis on literacy, a subject of much current interest, and, according to some, a more intellectualized religion.[29] Lollard objections to late medieval practices associated with the cult of saints have
been admired for their rationalism.[30] And as the supposed precursors of
Protestantism or nonconformity, the "independent" Lollards have often
been praised as the harbingers of England's success in later centuries.[31]

But it is not clear that any of these elements would have been particularly alluring to fifteenth- or sixteenth-century women or men. How
attractive would a book-centered sect have been to an illiterate woman from
the artisan class? To what extent are rationalism and individualism modern
values outside the experience of laymen and laywomen of the fifteenth
century? Indeed, the surviving evidence for the Lollard movement indicates
late medieval English people did *not* find it very attractive; even if we were
to assume that a hundred Lollards went undetected for every one who was
caught, they could never have made up more than a tiny minority of the
English population.

But clearly, some found the sect appealing, artisans apparently more
than civic leaders, men more than women. The little evidence that survives
concerning the beliefs of individual Lollards does not indicate that male and
female adherents of the sect emphasized different teachings. Individual
women were active and committed to the sect, suggesting strong attraction
to its tenets. But I argue that among the social groups where Lollardy found
its constituency, women were less inclined than men to its creed.

Certain aspects of Lollardy may have been as attractive to women as
they were to men. Both sexes may have felt equally strongly the emphasis
on a direct relationship with God and objections to the abuses of the clergy.
Hawise Mone of Loddon's invective against the clergy, for instance, was
vitriolic:

> The pope of Roome is fadir Antichrist, and fals in all hys werkyng, and hath no
> poar of God more than ony other lewed man but if he be more holy in lyvyng,
> ne that pope hath no poar to make bisshops, prestes ne non other ordres, and
> he that the puple callen the pope of Roome is no pope but a fals extersioner
> and a deseyver of the puple.[32]

Mone also thought that the lower clergy were "lecherous and covetouse
men and fals deceyvours of the puple,"[33] and Margery Baxter held that
priests sinned more grievously than laypeople.[34]

But Lollards, in their zeal to knock down all "inventions" of the medieval clergy, attacked various aspects of medieval piety that have been associated particularly with female religiosity: eucharistic devotions, ascetic practices, and veneration of the saints. Whether such aspects of medieval Catholic religion can indeed be identified as specifically female is still an open question. Nonetheless, Lollard opposition to nonscriptural Catholic practices, particularly the cult of saints, took away from women one of the only spheres of religious activity over which they had a significant measure of control.

The sacrament of the altar was perhaps at the center of Wyclif's theology and was the focus of much attention from his followers.[35] The views of the Lollards in the communities studied in this book were marked by a disbelief in the real presence, rising apparently from an anticlerical denial that priests could "make" a miracle as well as from a commonsense, skeptical refusal to believe that substance could be present without accidents.[36] John Burrell, for example, argued that if the host did not walk or talk like Christ, it could not be Christ:

> the sacrament which so many priests assert is the true body of Christ does not have eyes to see, ears to hear, a mouth to speak, hands to touch, nor feet to walk, but is a cake of bread made from wheat flour.[37]

At most, Lollards saw the eucharist as a memorial of Christ's passion,[38] but often because of its association with Catholic practice it was given no reverence at all.[39] Less common than attacks on the sacrament of the eucharist were objections to fasting, a tenet confined to the East Anglian community in the 1420s and in a few isolated cases later.[40] Opposition to fasting and to another sort of abstinence, celibacy, were based on lack of clear scriptural precedent and a feeling that such practices were unnatural.

Eucharistic devotions and ascetic practices have been identified by Bynum as central to, and to a large extent generated by, the piety of women. The eucharist symbolized and celebrated the central doctrine of Christianity, the word made flesh. The flesh, and food that supports it, was associated with women in the Western tradition, Bynum argues, and thus medieval devotion to the humanity or fleshliness of Christ was characteristically female. Eucharistic miracles were an almost entirely female genre in medieval saints' lives, and in male and female writers the sacrament of the altar was associated with women. Fasting and virginity, two means of manipulating the flesh, were also particularly linked with female religiosity.[41] Thus, Lollard assaults on these aspects of medieval Catholicism may have affected women more negatively than men.

But whether Bynum's findings regarding the religious lives of female mystics or saints can be directly related to the devotion of ordinary lay-women is unclear. Ordinary women, who communicated but once a year, did not have the access to the host that the holy women Bynum studies did. Moreover, eucharistic piety was appropriated from the clergy by groups other than mystical women: Corpus Christi festivals, for instance, were an important means of expressing civic pride and confirming the social order.[42] These celebrations were organized by and for men; women's place in Corpus Christi processions was distinctly secondary, as befitted their roles in other public aspects of society.[43] Lollardy's rejection of the eucharist and related ascetic practices may have been less important to women than the sect's attack on the sorts of practices over which they had more control — those associated with sacramentals and devotions to the saints.

Denial of the efficacy of pilgrimages, offerings to images, and invocations of saints were central to the beliefs of the later Lollards.[44] While some early Lollard writers (such as William Thorpe and the authors of the Wycliffite sermons) continued to regard the Virgin as worthy of respect,[45] later Lollards were indiscriminate in their rejection of the saints. Lollard opposition to the practices associated with Catholic saints was based on the insistence that Christian doctrine and practice must be based on the scriptures; neither the existence of saints (as the Catholic Church defined them[46]) nor the devotion to them or their invocation was based on biblical precedents, and thus they must be deplored. Some explicitly recalled the Decalogue, as John Burrell of Loddon testified was taught to him by his brother Thomas:

> In the first commandment it is preserved that no honor is to be shown to any images sculpted in churches by the hands of men, [the text continues in English] ne likened after hem in hevene above ne after hem that be in water benethe erthe, to lowte thaym ne worsshipe thaym.[47]

Allied to scriptural fundamentalism in the attack on the cult of saints was a rationalist critique of popular beliefs identifying the saint with the image. A common Lollard saying was that images were not to be worshipped because they were nothing but "stokkis and stonys."[48] Lollards made puns on the names of popular shrines of the Virgin and St. Thomas: "no pilgrimage shuld be do to the Lefdy [Lady] of Falsyngham [Walsingham], the Lefdy of Foulpette [Woolpit] and to Thomme of Cankerbury."[49] Such images or relics were promoted simply to enrich the clergy[50] and, as Hawise Mone said, those who worked at inns that profited from the pilgrims' trade: "all pilgrimage goyng servyth of nothyng but oonly to yeve

prestes good that be to riche and to make gay tap[s]ters and proude os-
telers."[51] Ridicule of those foolish enough to offer to images sometimes
turned to violent hostility, some Lollards going so far as to attack images
physically and destroy them, although this was relatively unusual.[52] Several
East Anglian Lollards were associated with iconoclastic activities. John
Burrell pierced an old cross lying near Loddon Hall with a "fagothook."[53]
Some burned crucifixes, including William Wardon and John Skilly, who
forcefully entered the cemetery at the church of St. Andrew at Trowse (near
Norwich) and stole and then burned an image worth 2s.[54]

In their attacks Lollards, both male and female, sought to distance
themselves from the sorts of credulous and "simple pepul" who practiced
devotions to the saints. Lollards were thereby "self-fashioning," in Stephen
Greenblatt's sense, forging a new identity for themselves as they left behind
the old, creating their new identity in relation to an Other that represented everything they rejected.[55] For Lollards, the Other had two aspects:
the greedy, immoral cleric who hid the message of the Scriptures from
good Christians,[56] and the gullible layperson—often enough specifically a
woman—who believed that the saints could save him or her.

When Lollards and other critics of images ridiculed those who offered
to them or went on pilgrimages, they sometimes specifically targeted the
credulity of the female sex.[57] Wyclif himself thought that women were
particularly susceptible to images painted with silver, gold, and various
colors.[58] The Wycliffite sermons portray women as frail, witless, and particularly prone to draw men "to worshipe here false goddis."[59] Michael
Gamare, priest of the parish of Wynbourn St. Giles, spoke to his parishioners against the worship of images, which he associated with women: "it is
a lewde thyng and a madde condition or use occupyed in this contree or
paryshe þt wemen will cumme and sette their candles afore a tree, þe Image
of Saynte Gylys."[60] The femaleness of the Virgin, a primary symbol of
medieval Catholic Christianity, was vilified as the very opposite of godli-
ness, as it was to be later by some Protestants.[61] Henry Knighton reported
that Lollards called the shrines of Mary at Lincoln and Walsingham the
"wyche of Lincolne and wyche of Walsyngham."[62] Lollards not only accused the Virgin of being a witch, but also of being a diseased whore.
Elizabeth Sampson of London[63] ridiculed those who held reverence for the
shrine of Mary at Willesden (Middlesex):

> Our Lady of Willesdon was a brent ars Elfe and a brent ars Stocke; and yf she
> myght have holpen men and women which go to hyre of pilgrimage she wolde

not have sufferd hyr tayle to have byn brent; and what shold folke wurshippe our lady of Willesdon or our lady of Crome for, the tone is but a brent ars stoke and tother is but a popet.[64]

A "brent arse" or "brent tayle" signified the venereal disease that attacked prostitutes and others of loose life;[65] to defame Mary in this way was both to allege her to be the very opposite of what the Catholics claimed her to be and to invoke the most potent means of insulting a woman.[66]

In their attacks of popular devotions to the saints, Lollards also explicitly rejected religious rituals associated with women's life cycle. Childbirth, for instance, was customarily accompanied by a host of practices to aid the woman in labor and to ensure a safe delivery. The Virgin Mary and St. Margaret of Antioch were invoked in the pain of labor.[67] Candles blessed by the clergy for devotional purposes on the feast of the Purification of the Virgin Mary — Candlemas — were used as a form of protective magic at childbirth. Later, when a birth mother was "churched," she offered another candle, often at the altar of the Virgin in her parish church.[68]

These practices were given special attention in attempts to convert women to Lollardy. Richard Belward of Earsham "counselled divers women, that they should not offer in the church for the dead, nor with women that were purified."[69] Joan Norman of Amersham testified that Robert Cosin and Thomas Man "had instructed and persuaded [her] . . . not to go on pilgrimage, nor to worship any images of saints. Also when she had vowed a piece of silver to a saint for the health of her child, they dissuaded her from the same."[70] The customary blessing of candles on the Feast of the Purification was disowned by John Pasmer of Bray: "A candell blessed is no better than a candell not blessed, for our lady went on Candlemas day on procession with no candell blessed."[71] Elizabeth Sampson objected to the invocation of the Virgin to aid a woman in childbed; at one woman's labor she confronted those who were asking the aid of the Virgin and "contumeliously spake against the invocators."[72] When she herself was in labor and her mother-in-law, "after the manner then of women, called much upon the help of the Virgin Mary, she, spitting thereat, was in such sort aggrieved, that the other party was compelled to forsake the house."[73] But few women apparently felt the hostility Elizabeth did. The renunciation of supernatural aid at such a dangerous time in a woman's life would have served to wrest from her a powerful psychological support.

Not all Lollard women were ready to surrender the aid the saints provided: at least one retained her belief in the efficacy of invoking saints to intercede with God on her behalf. Margery Baxter, who denied the power of saints made by the Catholic Church,[74] nonetheless prayed to a Lollard saint, her own teacher William White:

> William White, who was falsely condemned as a heretic, is a great saint in heaven and the most holy doctor ordained and sent by God; and . . . every day she prayed to this saint William White, and every day of her life she will pray to him so that he will deign to intercede for her to God in heaven.[75]

The followers of Joan Boughton (their sex is not specified) similarly acted contrary to the usual behavior of Lollards when they gathered up her ashes after she was burned in 1494 and kept them in a pot "ffor a precious Relyk."[76] Anticlericalism or anticatholicism may have led Lollards such as Margery Baxter to reject the saints of the Catholic Church, but some of them may not have wished to dispense completely with the functions these saints performed.

The rejection of popular Catholic practices, especially those associated with the cult of saints, rendered Lollardy less attractive to women than to men. Women were not more likely to use the saints as a crutch than were men (who arguably invoked the saints as often), but devotional practices associated with the saints had been the one area of religious practice that women could control and make their own. Lollardy did not offer women the same autonomy.

Gender and Religion

Lollardy did not compensate for the elements of late medieval devotion — especially practices associated with the cult of saints — that gave women a creative and active role in their religion. Lollardy's emphasis on and interpretation of Scripture reinforced patriarchal norms and male control over religion that the affective female piety of late medieval Catholicism had been able to circumvent, at least to some extent. Men also lost when they turned away from the religious culture of late medieval orthodoxy, but for them Lollardy offered in return new opportunities not matched in Catholicism. If they were literate (and they were much more likely to be than women), the Lollard book exchange could open up vast new horizons. Artisan men who acted as teachers and leaders of Lollard conventicles played roles other laymen of their station were unlikely to find in the established church. These constituted important aspects of the sect's attraction for these men, who made up much of its membership. The circumstances of Lollardy's development as a sect and a creed may have oriented it in a masculine rather than feminine direction.

Religious cultures and notions of appropriate masculine and feminine behavior work together dialectically, one influencing the other. In the creation of a new religious culture — at the birth of the Lollard sect, or of Protestantism, or of reformed Catholicism[77] — less powerful or influential social groups, particularly women, were unlikely to have much leverage to negotiate their own place. The context out of which Lollardy grew — the clerical male world of Oxford, the martial and political ethos of the Lollard knights[78] — did not allow for much, if any, female influence. Insistence on scriptural fundamentalism eschewed Christian practices that accommodated specifically female experiences. The later Lollard communities continued to be dominated by men, and the social construction of those communities made it very difficult for women to get their foot in the door except under the influence of male relatives. Lollardy was made by, and in a sense for, men.

The influence of women in the patriarchal culture of the late Middle Ages was a process of subtle interchange, one that took time to make itself felt. Although the Lollard sect may have begun to feel the dialectical process of redefining religious culture and gender norms through the influence of women like Alice Rowley, women had not made much headway in the Lollard movement by the time we come to the end of our records in about 1530. Heresy did not offer an alternative to patriarchy: even when Lollards rejected orthodoxy, they continued to assign gender roles to men and women in conformity with the old patriarchal models.

Appendix: The Lollard Communities

Legend: Underlined name = woman
Italicized name = related to another Lollard
* = woman married to another Lollard
(2) = appears in two different prosecutions
⊗ = literate (includes all clerics)

ALNWICK'S PROSECUTIONS IN EAST ANGLIA, 1428–31

John Abraham of Colchester
Edmund Archer of Loddon
John Ayltr of Earsham
John Baker als. Ussher of Tunstall
William Bate of Seething
⊗ *Son of William Bate of Seething*
* *Wife of William Bate of Seething*
* *Margery Baxter als. Wright of Martham*
⊗ *William Baxter als. Wright of Martham*
John Bayser
John Belward Jr. of Earsham
John Belward Sr. of Earsham
⊗ *Nicholas Belward of Earsham*
⊗ *Richard Belward*
John Bungay of Beighton
* *Batild Burrell of Loddon*
John Burrell of Loddon
Thomas Burrell of Loddon
⊗ William Caleys
⊗ Robert Cavell of Bungay
Isabella Chapleyn of Martham
Thomas Chatrys of Nayland or Needham Market
John Clerk of Loddon
John Clerk Jr. of Bergh
⊗ Bartholomew Cornmonger

Baldwin Cowper of Beccles
Isabella Davy of Toft
John Eldon of Beccles
⊗ *Thomas Everden*
William Everden
* *Matilda Fleccher of Beccles*
⊗ *Richard Fleccher of Beccles*
John Florence of Shelton
⊗ John Fowlyn
John Godesell of Ditchingham
* *Sybil Godesell of Ditchingham*
Henry Goode of Earsham
John Goodwyn of Earsham
Richard Grace of Beccles
Thomas Gremner of Ditchingham
John Grey
Robert Gryggys of Martham
William Hardy of Mundham
* *Katherine Hobbes*
Richard Horn of Earsham
John Josse of Loddon
Richard Knobbyng of Beccles
⊗ John Kynget of Nayland
Henry Lachecold of Earsham
Simon Mansthorpe of Ilketshall
William Masse of Earsham
John Mendham of Aldborough
⊗ John Midelton of Halvergate

* *Hawise Mone of Loddon*
   Thomas Mone of Loddon
⊗ *Daughter of Hawise and Thomas*
       Mone of Loddon
   Bartholomew Monk
⊗ William Northampton
   William Osbourn of Seething
   Thomas Pell of Neatishead
   John Perker of near Ipswich
⊗ John Pert of Loddon
⊗ *Thomas Pert*
⊗ Hugo Pye of Loddon
   Thomas Pye of Aldborough
   John Pyry of Martham
   John Reve of Beccles
   William Skirving of Seething

   John Skylan of Bergh Apton
   John Skylly of Flixton
   John Spyr of Bungay
   William Taylor of Loddon
   John Terry of Earsham
   John Tucke
* *Joan Waddon*
⊗ *John Waddon*
   John Wade of Earsham
   John Wardon of Loddon
   Joan Webbe of Dawne Hill
   John Werkwood of Colchester
* *Joan White*
⊗ *William White*
   John Wroxham of Loddon

Numbers: 83 suspected Lollards; 13 women
        17 men, 10 women related to another Lollard
        18 literate men, 1 literate woman

Sources: HT; A&M, 3:584–96; FZ, 417–32; *Reg. Chichele*, 3:85, 4:297–301; Amundesham, *Annales*, 1:29; *Records of the City of Norwich*, 2:66.

CHEDWORTH'S PROSECUTIONS IN THE CHILTERN HILLS, 1462–64

⊗ William Ayleward of Henley
   John Baron of Amersham
   John Baydyn of Wycombe
   William Belgrave of Stokenchurch
   Richard Benell of Wycombe
   William Bennett of Princes
       Risborough
   Robert Body of Amersham
   John Brewer of Wycombe
* *Isabella Browne of Wycombe*
   John Browne of Wycombe
   John Brykhill of Marlow
   George Carpenter
   Henry Chowne of Turville
   William Clerk of Marlow
   William Cok of West Wycombe
   John Colverhouse of Amersham
   John Cowper
   John Crane of Amersham

   Robert Delle
   John Gose of Amersham
   Thomas Grenelane of Hambleden
   John Hamond of Wycombe
   Margaret Huester of Wycombe
   William Hunt of Turville
   Hugh Leche
   John Myncent of Henley
   Nundmas of Godstow
   Patryk
   John Paytever of Wycombe
   John Phippis of Hughenden
   John Polley of Henley
⊗ Pope
   John Pymme of Wycombe
   John Qwyrk
   John Redhade of Henley
⊗ Thomas Scryvener of Amersham
   Henry Smyth of Chinnor

Robert Spycer of Wycombe
William Stevyns of Chinnor
Geoffrey Symeon of Amersham
John Thrassher of Amersham
William Tylby of Great Marlow
William Webster of London
Wheler of Staunton

Wife of John Wheler of Wycombe
John White of Chesham
Thomas White als. Gateley of
    Amersham
⊗ James Wyllys of Bristol
⊗ Rector of Chesham Boys

Numbers: 49 suspected Lollards; 3 women
          1 man, 1 woman related to another Lollard
          5 literate men

Source: Reg. Chedworth, fols. 57r–63r.

LANGTON'S PROSECUTIONS IN THE DIOCESE OF SALISBURY, 1485–91

Harry Benette of Spene
William Brigger of Thatcham
Philip Browne of Hinton
William Carpenter, als. Herford,
    als. Daniell of Newbury (2)
George Carpenter of Woodstock
Isabell Dorte of East Hendred
John Edwards of Newbury
Robert Elton of Newbury
Joan Farlingham of Hinton
Richard Goddard of Newbury
Alice Hignell of Newbury

⊗ Richard Hyllyng of Newbury
    Richard Lyllyngston of Castle-
      combe
    Richard Nores of Baldesdon
    William Priour of Newbury
    Richard Sawyer of Newbury
⊗ Austin Stere of Newbury
    John Sterengare of Hinton
⊗ Thomas Tailour of Newbury
    John Tanner of Steventon
    Richard Whithed of Newbury

Numbers: 21 suspected Lollards; 3 women
          No men, no women related to another Lollard
          3 literate men

Source: Salisbury Reg. Langton, vol. 2, fols. 35r–42v.

J. BLYTHE'S PROSECUTIONS IN THE DIOCESE OF SALISBURY, 1499

William Berford als. Carpenter of
    Cokesbell (Coxwell?) (2)
* *Alice Bishop of Reading*
    John Bishop of Reading
Thomas Boughton of Hungerford
John Clerk of Buscot
John Edwards of Wantage
John Godson of Buscot

John Gray of West Hendred
Richard Herford of Letcombe
    Basset
Richard Hughlott of Hanney
Cecily Letcomb of Reading
Thomas Loryng of Chipping
    Faringdon
Joan Martyn of Wantage

Roger Parker of Letcombe Basset
(2)
Agnes Redhood of Reading
John Reye of Reading
* *Agnes Scochyn of Reading*
Thomas Scochyn of Reading

* *Elizabeth Seward of Chipping*
Faringdon
Thomas Seward of Chipping
Faringdon
John Stanwey of Reading
⊗ John Whitehorn of Letcombe
Basset (2)

Numbers: 22 suspected Lollards; 6 women
3 men, 3 women related to another Lollard
1 literate man

Sources: Reg. J. Blythe, fols. 70r–79v; Reg. Morton, vol. 1, fols. 194rv.

AUDLEY'S PROSECUTIONS IN THE DIOCESE OF SALISBURY, 1502–21

John Acome
⊗ John Barly of Newbury
John Benet of Maidenhead
John Bent of Chirton
Joan Burges of Pulton
Robert Carpetmaker
* *Alice Colyns of Locking* (2)
John Colyns Sr. of Locking (2)
Richard Colyns of Locking (2)
Henry Cowrtman of Bisham
Katherine Cucklewe of Reading
John Drake of Ockborn
⊗ Thomas Duke
Walter Erle of Clyffe Pypard
John Est Sr. of Buscot
⊗ Michael Gamare of Wynbourn St.
Giles
John Godwyn of Fyfield
John Goodson Jr. of Highworth
John Goodson Sr.
Katherine Goodson of Highworth
Thomas Goodson of Highworth
John Hardyng of Broughton
Gyfford
Richard Hempton
William Hynton of Chirton
John Isbery
Lewis John of Reading
⊗ Richard John

John Kymbre of Hanney (2)
Walter Kymbre of Hanney (2)
* *Wife of John Kymbre of Hanney*
Robert Makam als. Bragge of Kevill
⊗ Richard Mower als. Warmar of
Newbury
John Newman
* *Christian Nicols of Chirton*
John Nicols of Chirton
John Okeford of Bishopston
John Page als. Bage of Marl-
borough
Edward Parker of Reading
John Parker Jr. of Letcombe Regis
Richard Parker of Reading
Roger Parker of Letcombe Regis
(2)
John Pasmer of Bray
Payn, woolwinder
John Polle of Salisbury
Eleanor Prat als. Flory of Pewsey
William Priour als. Kenser of
Devizes
John Rabettis of Chalvey (2)
Richard Raundyll of New Salisbury
Henry Shercot of Devizes
William Smart of Milton
Alice Smyth of Mardon
* *Alison Smyth of Chirton*

John Smyth
* *Margaret Smyth of Chirton*
  Richard Smyth of Chirton
  Thomas Smyth of Chirton
⊗ Geoffrey Spenser
⊗ John Stilman of Reading (2)
  John Swayne als. Barnard of
    Willesford
* *Margery Swayne als. Barnard of*
    Willesford
  Margaret Symson of Reading
  Alice Tailour of Bisham

John Tropnell of Bradford
Simon Waiver of Windsor
⊗ John Whithorn of Letcombe Basset
  (2)
John Whityng of East Hendred
* *Wife of John Whityng of East*
    Hendred
  Henry Wylshyre of Turleigh
  Joan Wylshyre of Turleigh
  Thomas Wylshyre of Turleigh
  Henry Wyrdrawer

Numbers: 71 suspected Lollards; 15 women
          14 men, 9 women related to another Lollard
          8 literate men

Source: Reg. Audley, fols. 107v–108v, 130v–131r, 142v–149v, 155v–163v, 168v–169v, 183v.

PROSECUTIONS AND DETECTIONS IN THE DIOCESES OF SALISBURY AND
WINCHESTER BEFORE BISHOP LONGLAND, C. 1521

Father Amershaw of Steventon
John Baker of Witney
Thomas Baker of Wheatley
John Boyes
Brother of John Boyes
Mother of John Boyes of Sudbury
John Brabant I of Stanlake
* *Wife of John Brabant I of Stanlake*
  John Brabant II of Stanlake
* *Wife of John Brabant II of Stanlake*
  John Brabant III of Stanlake
* *Wife of John Brabant III of Stanlake*
  Philip Brabant of Ginge
⊗ Reginald Brabant of Stanlake
* *Joan Burges of Burford*
  Mother of Joan Burges
  Robert Burges of Burford
  John Clemson of Burford
  John Clerk of Claufield
* *Alice Colins of Ginge* (2)
  Joan Colins of Asthall
  Joan Colins of Ginge
  John Colins of Asthall

* *Wife of John Colins of Asthall*
  John Colins of Betterton or Ginge
    (2)
  John Colins of Burford
⊗ *Richard Colins of Ginge* (2)
⊗ *Robert Colins of Asthall or Hertford-*
    Wallis
  Father of Robert Colins
* *Wife of Robert Colins of Asthall or*
    Hertford-Wallis
  Thomas Colins of Asthall
  Thomas Colins of Ginge
* *Wife of Thomas Colins of Ginge*
  William Collins of Ginge
* *Alice Cottismore als. Dolly of Bright-*
    well
  William Cottismore of Brightwell
⊗ Roger Dodd of Burford
⊗ John Drury of Windrish
⊗ John Eden als. Ledishall of
    Hungerford
  Agnes Edmunds of Burford and
    Ginge

James Edmunds of Burford
⊗ *John Edmunds als. Ogins of Burford*
* *Elizabeth Fitton of Newbury*
  Robert Fitton of Newbury
⊗ Robert Freeman of Orton
  John French of Long Wittenham
  Robert Geydon of Newbury
* *Wife of Robert Geydon of Newbury*
  Laurence Ghest of Salisbury
  Edward Gray of East Hendred
* *Wife of Edward Gray of East Hendred*
  Thomas Gray of West Hendred
  William Gray of East Hendred
* *Alice Gun of Witney*
  William Gun of Witney
  Roger Hachman of North Stoke
  William Haliday of East Hendred
  Thomas Hall of Hungerford
  John Harris of Upton or Burford
* *Wife of John Harris of Upton or*
    Burford
  Robert Hickman of Lechlade
  Elenor Higges of Burford
  Margaret House of East Ginge
  John Kember of Hennybarkes (2)
  Walter Kember of Hennybarkes (2)
  Robert Livord of Steventon
  William Livord of Steventon
  John Ludlow of Hungerford
  Isabel or Elizabeth More of East
    Hendred

  Thomas New of Wantage
  Richard Nobis of East Hendred
* *Wife of Richard Nobis of East Hendred*
⊗ *Robert Pope of Amersham and West*
    Hendred (2)
  Thomas Quicke of Reading
  William Ramsey of Newbury
⊗ Edward Red of Burford
  Thomas Reiley of Burford
  John Semand of Newbury
  Humfrey Shoemaker of Newbury
⊗ Richard Smart of Steventon
  William Squire of Shaw
  Brother of William Squire of Shaw
* *Matild Stephenton of Charney*
  Thomas Stephenton of Charney
  Joan Steventon of Ginge
⊗ John Stilman of Salisbury (2)
  John Sympson of Steventon
  Joan Taylor of Bisham
  Mother of Joan Taylor of Bisham
  John Taylor of Burford
  John Through of Burford
  Simon Wisdom of Burford
  Margery Young of East Hendred

⊗ A monk of Burford
  The bailiff of Witney
  Father Joan of Hungerford
  Mother Joan
  John of Reading

Numbers: 98 suspected Lollards; 29 women
           33 men, 25 women related to another Lollard
           13 literate men

Source: *A&M*, 4:126–27, 234–45, 582–83.

SMITH'S AND LONGLAND'S PROSECUTIONS IN THE DIOCESE OF LINCOLN
(CHILTERN HILLS, EASTERN BERKSHIRE, AND MIDDLESEX), 1500–1530

  William Ameriden of Amersham
  Robert Andrew of Amersham
  Agnes Ashford of Chesham
* *Joan Ashford of Walton-on-Thames*

⊗ *Richard Ashford, als. Tredway, als.*
    Nash of Chesham and Walton-on-
    Thames
  Alice Atkins

Isabella Atkin of Missenden
William Atkins of Great Missenden
John Austy of Henley
Thomas Austy of Henley
John Baker of Uxbridge
John Barbar of Amersham
Joan Barnard
Richard Barnard
⊗ *Thomas Barnard of Amersham*
Father Bartlett of Amersham
* *Isabel Bartlett of Amersham*
John Bartlett of Amersham
* *Katherine Bartlett of Amersham*
* *Margaret Bartlett of Amersham*
Richard Bartlett of Amersham
⊗ *Robert Bartlett of Amersham*
⊗ Richard Bennet of Amersham
Roger Bennet of Amersham
Alice Brown of Chesham
Jenkin Butler of Uxbridge
⊗ *John Butler of Uxbridge*
⊗ *Richard Butler of Uxbridge*
Robert Butterfield
Richard Carder of Iver
Robert Carder of Iver
Thomas Carder
William Carder of Amersham
⊗ Thomas Chase of Amersham
William Chedwell of Amersham
Thomas Clement of Chesham
* *Joan Clerk of Little Missenden*
John Clerk of Amersham and
    Denham
Thomas Clerk Jr. of Chesham
Thomas Clerk Sr. of Hughenden
Widmore Clerk Sr. of Hughenden
Joan Cocks of Staines
Joan Collingborne/Collingworth
    of Amersham
Robert Copland
⊗ Robert Cosin of Missenden
Thomas Cowper of Amersham
* *Elizabeth Dean of West Wycombe*
Richard Dean of West Wycombe and
    Chesham
Wife of William Dean

Henry Dein
Richard Dell of Missenden
Thomas Dorman als. Yomand of
    Amersham
Edmund Dormer of Amersham
William Dorset of King's Langley
John Dosset of Amersham
Daughter of Robert Durdant (Jehn
    Cobham?)
Davy Durdant of Ankerwick
* *Wife of Nicholas (Eleanor?) Durdant*
    of Staines
* *Wife of Robert (Felicia?) Durdant of*
    Iver Court
Nicholas Durdant of Staines
⊗ *Robert Durdant of Iver Court*
* *Cecily Eaton of Speen*
John Eaton als. Taylor of Speen
Henry Etkin of Little Missenden
Mother of Henry Etkin of Little Mis-
    senden
* *Agnes Frank of Amersham*
Joan Frank
William Frank Jr. of Amersham
William Frank Sr. of Amersham
John Frier of Amersham
Andrew Fuller of Uxbridge
* *Alice Funge*
Francis Funge
John Funge
* *Isabel Gardiner*
John Gardiner
⊗ *Thomas Geffrey of Uxbridge and*
    Ipswich and London
* *Wife of Thomas Geffrey of Uxbridge*
J. George
Joan Glasbroke of Harrow-on-the-
    Hill
William Glasbroke of Harrow-on-the-
    Hill
John Grace
Richard Grace
John Gray of Marlow
Thomas Gray of Amersham
William Grinder
* *Wife of William Grinder*

*   *Joan Grove of Amersham and London*
    (2)
    Thomas Grove of Amersham and
      London (2)
*   *Joan Gudgame*
    William Gudgame
    Joan Gun of Chesham
    Thomas Halfeaker of Amersham
    Elizabeth Hamon
*   *Alice Harding of Amersham*
    Edmund Harding
    Henry Harding of Amersham
    Richard Harding of Amersham
    Robert Harding of Amersham
    Roger Harding of Amersham
    Daughter of Roger Harding of
      Amersham
*   *Wife of Roger Harding of Amersham*
⊗   *Thomas Harding of Amersham*
    William Harding of Amersham
    Hartop of Windsor
    Robert Hawes of West Wycombe
    John Hawks of Coblers Hill
    Thomas Hawks of Hughenden
    William Hawks of Chesham
    John Heron of Hambleden
    Laurence Herne of Hughenden
    Roger Herne of Little Missenden
    Thomas Herne of Coblers Hill
    Widow Herne
*   *Wife of Herne*
    Edmund Hill of Penn
    John Hill of Amersham
    Henry Hobbes of Hughenden
    Radulph Hobbes
    Richard Hobbes of Hughenden
    William Hobbes
    Thomas Holmes
    Alice Holting
    Thomas Houre of Amersham
    Elizabeth Hover of Little Missenden
    Joan Jenings
    John Jennings
    Thomas King
    Mother of William King of Uxbridge
⊗   *William King of Uxbridge*

    John a Lee of Henley
    Agnes Lenall of Amersham
    David Lewis of Henley
*   *Wife of David Lewis of Henley*
    Father of Wife of David Lewis of
      Henley
*   *Alice Littlepage of Amersham*
*   *Emma Littlepage, als. Africke, als.*
      Harding of Amersham
    Henry Littlepage of Amersham
    Joan Littlepage of Amersham
    John Littlepage als. Africke of
      Amersham
*   *Sybil Littlepage als. Africke of*
      Amersham
    Thomas Littlepage als. Africke of
      Amersham
    Thurstan Littlepage of Amersham
    William Littlepage als. Africke of
      Amersham
⊗   *Thomas Man I of Amersham*
    Thomas Man II of Amersham
*   *Wife of Thomas Man I of Amersham*
*   *Wife of Thomas Man II of Amersham*
    Alexander Mastal
    John Mastal
    Thomas Mastal
    Andrew Maysey of Burton
    John Merrywether
    Son of John Merrywether
*   *Wife of John Merrywether*
    John Merston
⊗   Henry Miller of Kent, Amersham,
    Chelmsford, and Tucke-by-Ware
    John Milsent of Amersham
*   *Wife of John Milsent of Amersham*
    John Monk of Amersham
*   *Emma Morden of Chesham*
    James Morden of Amersham,
      Chesham, and Walton-on-Thames
⊗   *John Morden of Chesham*
*   *Wife of John (Marion?) Morden of*
      Chesham
    Marion Morden
    Radulph Morden of Chesham
*   *Wife of Radulph Morden of Chesham*

Richard Morden of Chesham
* *Isabel Morwin of Amersham*
John Morwin of Amersham
John Mucklyf
John Mumbe of Amersham
* *Wife of John Mumbe of Amersham*
Alice Nash als. Chapman of Missenden
Nash Sr.
* *Wife of Nash Sr.*
John Nash of Little Missenden
Joan Norman of Amersham
William Norton of Chesham
John Okenden
William Page of Amersham
Roger Parker of Hughenden
Matild Philby of Chalvey
Henry Phips of Hughenden
⊗ *John Phips of Hughenden*
William Phips of Hughenden
Daughter of John Phips
Daughter of William Phips
Edward Pope Jr.
Edward Pope Sr. of Little Missenden
⊗ *Robert Pope of Amersham and West Hendred* (2)
* *Wife of Robert Pope of Amersham and West Hendred*
Thomas Pope
Wife of Thomas Potter of Hughenden
John Rabettes of Chalvey (2)
⊗ *Andrew Randal of Rickmansworth*
Father of Andrew Randal
?⊗* *Wife of Andrew (Marian?) Randal of Rickmansworth*
Robert Rave of Dorney
Thomas Rave or Rever of Great Marlow
William Rogers
* *Wife of William Rogers*
Robert Rowland
Thomas Rowland of Amersham
John Ryburn of Risborough
⊗ John Samme
* *Alice Saunders of Amersham*

Richard Saunders of Amersham
John Sawcoat
John Say of Little Missenden
William Say of Little Missenden
John Scrivener Sr.
* *Wife of John Scrivener Sr.*
Thomas Scrivener
William Scrivener
John Shepard of Dorney
* *Wife of John Shepard of Dorney*
Davy Shirwood of Great Marlow
Raynold Shirwood of Great Marlow
William Shirwood of Great Marlow
⊗ Christopher Shoemaker of Great Missenden
Oliver Smith of Newline
* *Wife of Oliver Smith of Newline*
William Smith
John Sparke of Chesham
Agnes Squire
Roger Squire
* *Joan Stamp of Amersham*
John Stamp of Amersham
Robert Stamp of Amersham
Richard Stephens
Thomas Stilman
Nicholas Stokeley of Henley
* *Wife of Nicholas Stokeley of Henley*
William Stokeley of Henley
Thomas Susan
⊗ *John Symonds of Great Marlow*
* *Matild Symonds of Great Marlow*
Thomas Tailor of Uxbridge
* *Wife of Thomas Tailor of Uxbridge*
* *Isabel Tracher*
⊗ *John Tracher of Chesham*
William Tracher of Amersham
Daughter of Isabel Tracher
Alice Tredway
Thomas Tredway
* *Emma Tylsworth of Amersham and London*
⊗ *William Tylsworth of Amersham and London* (2)
Richard Vulford of Ruislip
* *Wife of Richard Vulford of Ruislip*

Henry Vulman of Uxbridge
* *Wife of Henry Vulman of Uxbridge*
Agnes Ward of Marlow
Bennet Ward of Beaconsfield
* *Wife of Bennet Ward of Beaconsfield*
Daughter of Wife of Ward of
  Beaconsfield
John a Weedon
Agnes Wells of Amersham
Richard White of Beaconsfield
Thomas White
William White
Thomas Widmore of Hughenden

* *Wife of Thomas Widmore of*
  Hughenden
Wife of Old Widmore of Hughenden
Wigmer of Hughenden
Thomas Wilbey of Henley
Wilie Jr.
Wilie Sr.
William Wingrave of Hughenden
John Wood of Henley
William Wood
Christopher, tinker of Wycombe
⊗ A canon of Missenden
⊗ The vicar of Little Missenden
⊗ The vicar of Rickmansworth

Numbers: 275 suspected Lollards; 86 women
87 men, 67 women related to another Lollard
26 literate men, 1 possibly literate woman

Sources: Reg. Fox, 4, fols. 18r–19v; Reg. Longland, fols. 180v, 201v, 228r–228v; TCD, MS 775, fol. 128v; *A&M*, 4:123–26, 208–36, 580–81, 583–85; Bowker, *Episcopal Court Book*, 15–16; *Bucks. Subsidy*; *Bucks. Muster*.

Prosecutions in London and Environs and Hertfordshire, 1500–1530

John Acome
John Anstead of London
* *Joan Austy of London*
⊗ *Thomas Austy of London*
Joan Baker of London
* *Joan Barret of London*
⊗ *John Barret of London*
?⊗ *Robert Benet of London*
Joan Blackbury of London
Elizabeth Blake of London
Thomas Blake of London
Thomas Blissed of London
Joan Boughton of London
Joan Brede of Southwark
Mother Bristow of London
Wife of Bulley of London
John Calverton of London
⊗ Thomas Capon of London
Rafe Carpenter of London
* *Wife of Rafe Carpenter of London*

⊗ *Cony of London*
* *Wife of Cony of London*
Robert Cook of London
⊗ Nicholas Field of London
* *Alice Forge of London*
John Forge of London
Thomas Forge of London
Christopher Glasbroke of London
Hugh Glover of London
Thomas Goodred of Stratford-at-
  Bow
John Goter of London
⊗ Simon Grene of London
John Grosar of London
* *Joan Grove of Amersham and London*
  (2)
Thomas Grove of Amersham and
  London (2)
⊗ *John Hacker of London*
Son of John Hacker of London

Henry Hert of Westminster
Roger Hilliar of London
John Houshold of London
⊗   Jessop of London
John Knight of London
⊗   Thomas Maryet of Southwark
⊗   *William Mason of London*
*   *Wife of William Mason of London*
Elizabeth Mathew of London
Laurence Maxwell of London
Richard Mildenhall of London
John Newman of London
⊗   Thomas Philip of London
Robert Quicke of London
⊗   Robert Raskell of London
Thomas Rawlyn of London
Alice Ray of London
John Redman of London
William Russell of London
⊗   Elizabeth Sampson of London
John Sercot of London
⊗   John Southwick or Southake of
London
⊗   *Thomas Spencer of London*
?⊗*   *Wife of Thomas Spencer of London*
John Stacy of London

Stere of London
James Sturdy of London
Wife of Styes of London
⊗   Laurence Swaffer of Shoreditch
⊗   John Tewksbury of London
Henry Tuck of London
⊗   Thomas Tykhill of London
Robert Tylsworth of London
*   *Wife of Robert Tylsworth*
Thomas Tylsworth of London
*   *Wife of Thomas Tylsworth, als. Wife of
Nicholas Saunder, of London*
*William Tylsworth of Amersham/
London* (2)
⊗   *Thomas Vincent of London*
Thomas Walker als. Talbot of
London
Thomas Wassyngborn of London
⊗   *John Woodrof of London*
*   *Wife of John Woodrof of London*
⊗   Henry Woolman of London
⊗   Richard Woolman of London
⊗   Richard Wryght of London
Lady Jane Yonge of London

Alice of London

Numbers: 84 suspected Lollards; 24 women
20 men, 15 women related to another Lollard
22 literate men, 1 literate woman, 1 possibly literate man, and 1 possibly
literate woman

Sources: Reg. Fitzjames, fols. 4r–4v, 25r–27r; Reg. Fox, 2, fols. 86v–88r; Winchester Reg.
Langton, fol. 66r; TCD, MS 775, fols. 122v–125r; Lichfield Court Book, fols. 16r–16v; Reg.
Audley, fol. 144r; Hale, *A Series of Precedents*, 8–9, 54–55; *A&M*, 4:7–8, 172–246, 688–94;
5:29–30; *L&P*, vol. 4, pt. 2, nos. 4029, 4175, 4545, 4850; *EM*, vol. 1, pt 1:113–34; vol. 1, pt.
2:50–65; vol. 2, pt. 1:334–35; *Chronicle of London*, 208, 261; *Great Chronicle of London*, 252,
262; Fabian, *Chronicle*, 685.

PROSECUTIONS IN ESSEX AND HERTFORDSHIRE, 1500–1530

Joan Agnes als. Smyth of Steeple
Bumpstead
John Barbitonsore
Master Bardfield of Colchester
Robert Bate of East Donyland

*   *Rose Bate of East Donyland*
Anthony Beckwyth of Braintree
Mother Beckwyth of Braintree
Robert Beckwyth of Braintree
William Beckwyth of Braintree

Robert Berkeway
⊗ Robert Best of Colchester
Joan Bocher of Steeple Bumpstead
William Bocher of Steeple Bump-
    stead
* *Margaret Bowgas of Colchester*
Thomas Bowgas of Colchester
John Bradley of Colchester
* *Wife of John Bradley of Colchester*
⊗ James Brewster of Colchester
George Browne
William Browne of Steeple Bump-
    stead
Stephen Carde of Ware
Henry Chapman
John Chapman of Colchester and
    Witham
Richard Chapman of Colchester and
    Witham
Mother Charte
Old Christmas of Bocking
John Clerk
Thomas Clerk of Ware
* *Wife of Thomas Clerk of Ware*
Margaret Cowbridge of Colchester
Alice Cowper
William Cowper
John Craneford of Steeple Bump-
    stead
Mother Denby of Colchester
Thomas Eglestone
Robert Faire of Steeple Bumpstead
⊗ Richard Fox of Steeple Bumpstead
Alice Gardiner of Colchester
⊗ William Gardiner of Clare
John Garter
Geldener of Hertford
Daughter I of Geldener of Hertford
Daughter II of Geldener of Hertford
* *Joan Girling of Colchester*
John Girling of Colchester
Thomas Grant
* *Joan Hemsted of Steeple Bumpstead*
Son of Joan Hemsted of Steeple
    Bumpstead
Robert Hemsted of Steeple Bumpstead

Thomas Hemsted of Steeple
    Bumpstead
John Higgins
John Hilles of Witham
⊗ Thomas Hilles of Witham
Isabel Holden
John Hubbert of East Donyland
* *Wife of John Hubbert of East*
    Donyland
* *Joan John*
Lewis John
* *Alice Johnson of Boxted*
Richard Johnson als. Collins of Boxted
⊗ George Laund of St. Osithe's
Dorothy Long of Colchester
William Man of Boxted
Thomas Mathew of Colchester
* *Marion Westden Mathew of Colchester*
⊗ *Friar Medow of Colchester and*
    Amersham
* *Margery Parker of Colchester*
Thomas Parker of Colchester
Wife of George Preston of Steeple
    Bumpstead
Agnes Pykas of Bury St. Edmunds
    and Colchester
⊗ *John Pykas of Colchester*
William Pykas or Dykes of Colchester
Christopher Ravins of Witham
Dyonise Ravins of Witham
Henry Raylond of Colchester
* *Wife of Henry Raylond of Colchester*
⊗ *William Raylond of Colchester*
* *Wife of William Raylond of Colchester*
Gilbert Shipwright of Steeple
    Bumpstead
* *Agnes Smyth of Ridgewell*
John Smyth of Ridgewell
⊗ John Smyth of Steeple Bumpstead
⊗ Edmund Spilman
Elizabeth Stamford
Katharine Swayn of Colchester
⊗ William Sweeting of Essex and
    London
John Thompson of Colchester
* *Wife of John Thompson of Colchester*

⊗ Thomas Topley of Clare
   Alice Tyball of Steeple Bumpstead
   Edmund Tyball of Steeple Bumpstead
* *Wife of Edmund Tyball of Steeple*
     Bumpstead
   Elene Tyball of Steeple Bumpstead

⊗ *John Tyball of Steeple Bumpstead*
   John Webb
   Marion Westden of Colchester
⊗ John Wiggen of Clare
   John Wikes
   John Wyley of Great Horkesley

Numbers: 99 suspected Lollards; 36 women
          30 men, 26 women related to another Lollard
          15 literate men

Sources: TCD, MS 775, fols. 123r, 123v, 124v; BM, Harl. MS 421, fols. 11r–35v; *A&M*, 4:7–8, 172–216; *L&P*, vol. 4, pt. 2, nos. 4029, 4175, 4545, 4850; *EM*, vol. 1, pt. 1:113–34, vol. 1, pt. 2:50–65; vol. 2, pt. 1:334–35.

WARHAM'S PROSECUTIONS IN THE DIOCESE OF CANTERBURY, 1511–12

* *Margaret Baker of Cranbrook*
⊗ *William Baker of Cranbrook*
   John Bampton of Otham and
     Bearsted
* *Joyce Bampton of Bearsted*
   Richard Bampton of Boxley
   John Bans of Boxley
   John Benett of Staplehurst
* *Rabage Benett of Staplehurst*
   Robert Bright of Maidstone
* *Elizabeth Browne of Ashford*
   John Browne of Ashford
   Thomas Browne of Cranbrook
   James Bukherst
   John Bukherst of Staplehurst
   William Bukherst
   Katherine Carder of Tenterden
⊗ William Carder of Tenterden
⊗ Stephen Castelyn of Tenterden
   Agnes Chetynden of Canterbury
   Thomas Churche of Great Charte
   Joan Colyn of Tenterden
   Joan Dodde
   Thomas Felde of Boxley
   John Franke of Tenterden
   Robert Franke of Tenterden
* *Agnes Grebill of Tenterden*
⊗ *Christopher Grebill of Cranbrook*

   John Grebill Jr. of Tenterden
   John Grebill Sr. of Tenterden
   Robert Harryson of Canterbury
* *Joan Harwode of Rolvenden*
   Philip Harwode of Rolvenden
   Thomas Harwode of Rolvenden
   Alice Hilles of Tenterden
* *Julian Hilles of Tenterden*
   Robert Hilles of Tenterden
* *Agnes Ive of Canterbury*
⊗ *John Ive of Canterbury*
   William Lorkyn of East Farley
   Joan Lowes of Cranbrook
   John Lynche of Tenterden
   Vincent Lynche of Halden
   Thomas Mannyng of Benenden
* *Joan Olberde of Godmersham*
   William Olberde Jr. of Godmersham
   William Olberde Sr. of Godmersham
   William Pelland of Tenterden
   Alice Raynold of Tenterden
   Agnes Reignold of Cranbrook
⊗ Robert Reignold of Cranbrook
   Joan Riche of Wittisham
   John Riche
   William Riche of Benenden
   Agnes Roche of Tenterden
   Edward Walker of Maidstone

*   *Wife of Edward Walker of Maidstone*
     Elizabeth White of Canterbury

Numbers: 57 suspected Lollards; 21 women
            15 men, 10 women related to another Lollard
            6 literate men

Sources: Reg. Warham, vol. 1, fols. 159r–175v; Wood-Legh, *Kentish Visitations*, 207–11; *A&M*, 4:181–82; 5:647–52.

HALES'S AND G. BLYTH'S PROSECUTIONS IN COVENTRY, 1485–1512

Thomas Abel
*   *Alice Acton*
     Thomas Acton
⊗   John Alcock of Ibstock
     William Alen
     John Archer
     Thomas Archer
*   *Wife of Thomas Archer*
     John Atkynson als. Peintour Jr.
     Agnes de Bakehouse
     Thomas Banbrooke
*   *Wife of Thomas Banbrooke*
     Robert Bastell
     Wife of Bentham
     Wife of Bluet
⊗   Thomas Bowen
⊗   *Richard Bradley*
⊗* *Thomasina Bradley*
     Roger Bromley
*   *Wife of Roger Bromley*
     Agnes Brown
     Daughter of Agnes Brown
     Richard Brown
⊗   Roger Brown
     John Bull
     Thomas Butler
*   *Constance or Cristina Clerk*
     David Clerk
     John Clerk
⊗   *Thomas Clerk*
     Agnes Corby
     John Cropwell

     Robert Crowther
     Roger Cutler
     John Davy als. Peintour Sr.
     Lawrence Dawson
⊗   Richard Dowcheman
     Katherine Edmund
     John Falkys
⊗   Thomas Flesshour
     Alice Flexall
     Stephen Frayne
     Rose Furnour
     Katherine Gerton
     Elizabeth Gest
*   *Joan Gest of Birmingham*
     John Gest Jr. of Birmingham
     Richard Gest of Birmingham
     Margaret Grey
     Richard Gylmyn
*   *Katherine Hachet*
⊗   *Robert Hachet*
     Robert Haghmond
     John Harris
     William Hawkyns
     John Hebbis
     Richard Hegham
     William Heywod
     John Holbache
*   *Wife of John Holbache*
⊗   John Holywod
⊗   *Agnes Jonson*
⊗   John Jonson als. Cutler
⊗   *Ralph Kent of Leicestershire*

⊗ *William Kent of Staunton*
  Thomas Kylyngworth
* *Margaret Landesdale*
  Richard Landesdale
⊗ *Roger Landesdale*
  Thomas Lieff
  <u>Margery Locock</u>
  William Lodge
  John Longhald
  Master Longland
* *Alice Lye*
  Ralph Lye
  Robert Lye
  Matthew Markland
  Richard Northopp
* *Wife of Richard Northopp*
  Hugh Parret
  Robert Pegge
  John Phisicion als. Blumstone
* *Katherine Revis*
  William Revis
⊗ <u>Alice Rowley</u>
  Richard Ryse
⊗ Ralph Shor

⊗ Balthasar Shugborough
⊗ Robert Silkby
* *Joan Smyth*
  Daughter of Joan Smyth
  John Smyth
  Thomas Spenser
  John Spon
  John Tarkour
  Roger Tofft
  <u>Isabella Trussell</u>
  Tuke
⊗ *Mother Villers*
⊗ *Thomas Villers*
* *Joan Warde als. Wasshingbury*
  Thomas Warde
  Richard Weston
  <u>Agnes or Margaret White</u>
  Thomas Wrixham
  Agnes Yong
⊗ *Juliana Yong*

  Christopher, a shoemaker
  Mother Margaret

Numbers: 110 suspected Lollards; 37 women
       21 men, 25 women related to another Lollard
       17 literate men, 5 literate women

Sources: Reg. Hales, fols. 166r–166v; Reg. G. Blyth, fols. 98r–100r; Lich. Ct. Bk.

TOTALS

Note: Adjusted for those who appear in two different lists: Fourteen appear twice (2 women and 12 men), 2 women and 6 men who were related to other Lollards, 2 married couples, and 4 literate men.

955 suspected Lollards
271 women, 28% of total
684 men, 72% of total

189 women related to another Lollard = 70% of women
173 women related to male Lollard(s) = 92% of those with family connections

16 women related only to female Lollard(s) = 8% of those with family connections

235 men related to another Lollard = 34% of men

136 married couples (50% of women, 20% of men)

130 literate men (19% of men) and 1 possibly literate man
9 literate or possibly literate women (3% of women)

Notes

Chapter 1

1. Natalie Zemon Davis, "'Women's History' in Transition: The European Case," *Feminist Studies* 3 (1976): 83–103, esp. 89–92; see also Clare A. Lees, ed., *Medieval Masculinities: Regarding Men in the Middle Ages* (Minneapolis: University of Minnesota Press, 1994), esp. Thelma Fenster's preface, ix–xiii; and Lyndal Roper, *Oedipus and the Devil: Witchcraft, Sexuality and Religion in Early Modern Europe* (London: Routledge, 1994), 38, 47.

2. The work of Max Weber, which associates women especially with prophetic and "emotional or hysterical" elements of religion, has been very influential. Max Weber, *The Sociology of Religion*, trans. Ephraim Fischoff (Boston: Beacon, 1964), 104–6. Also influential: Herbert Grundmann, *Religiöse Bewegungen im Mittelalter*, 2nd ed. (Hildesheim: Olms, 1961); Gottfried Koch, *Frauenfrage und Ketzertum im Mittelalter* (Berlin: Akademie-Verlag, 1962); Keith Thomas, "Women and the Civil War Sects," *Past and Present* 13 (1958): 42–62; Brenda Bolton, "Mulieres Sanctae," *SCH* 10 (1973): 77–95. Among recent proponents: Patricia Crawford, *Women and Religion in England, 1500–1720* (London and New York: Routledge, 1993), esp. 4–5 (using elements of Weber's theory); Gerda Lerner, *The Creation of Feminist Consciousness: From the Middle Ages to Eighteen-Seventy*, vol. 2 of *Women and History* (New York: Oxford University Press, 1993), 3–6, 74, 99.

3. See Richard Abels and Ellen Harrison, "The Participation of Women in Languedocian Catharism," *Mediaeval Studies* 41 (1979): 215–51; John Hine Mundy, "Le mariage et les femmes à Toulouse au temps des cathares," *Annales: Economies, Sociétés, Civilisations* 42 (1987): 117–34; Eleanor McLaughlin, "Les femmes et l'hérésie médiévale: Un problème dans l'histoire de la spiritualité," *Concilium (Nijmegen)* 111 (1976): 73–90; Shannon McSheffrey, "Women and Lollardy: A Reassessment," *Canadian Journal of History* 26 (1991): 199–223. Joy Wiltenburg's recent book suggests that depictions of women as disorderly or deviant in popular literature tell us more about male anxiety than about female behavior. *Disorderly Women and Female Power in the Street Literature of Early Modern England and Germany* (Charlottesville: University Press of Virginia, 1992), esp. 7–25, 253–66.

4. Christiane Klapisch-Zuber, ed., *Silences of the Middle Ages*, vol. 2 of *A History of Women in the West* (Cambridge, Mass.: Belknap Press of Harvard University Press, 1992), 30, 204, 313, 484; Susan Stuard, "The Dominion of Gender: Women's Fortunes in the High Middle Ages," in *Becoming Visible: Women in European History*, 2d ed., ed. Renate Bridenthal, Claudia Koonz, and Susan Stuard (Boston: Houghton Mifflin, 1987), 168; Bonnie S. Anderson and Judith P. Zinsser, *A*

History of Their Own: Women in Europe from Prehistory to the Present, vol. 1 (New York: Harper & Row, 1989), 224–27; see also Shulamith Shahar, *The Fourth Estate: A History of Women in the Middle Ages*, trans. Chaya Galai (London: Methuen, 1983), 251–80.

5. See Denise Riley, *"Am I That Name?": Feminism and the Category of "Women" in History* (Minneapolis: University of Minnesota, 1988).

6. Caroline Walker Bynum, *Holy Feast and Holy Fast: The Religious Significance of Food to Medieval Women* (Berkeley: University of California Press, 1987), and *Fragmentation and Redemption: Essays on Gender and the Human Body in Medieval Religion* (New York: Zone, 1991). See also Roberta Gilchrist and Marilyn Oliva, *Religious Women in Medieval East Anglia*, Studies in East Anglian History, 1 (Norwich: Centre of East Anglian Studies, 1993), 9–11, 21–22, 81–82.

7. R.W. Scribner, *Popular Culture and Popular Movements in Reformation Germany* (London: Hambledon, 1987), esp. 17–47.

8. Even as sensitive a historian as Bynum has done this: see, for instance, *Holy Feast*, 17.

9. In *American Historical Review* 91 (1986): 1053–75; reprinted in her *Gender and the Politics of History* (New York: Columbia University Press, 1988), 28–50.

10. Scott, *Gender and the Politics of History*, 2.

11. Roper, *Oedipus and the Devil*, quotation at 4, 13–18; Judith Butler, *Gender Trouble: Feminism and the Subversion of Identity* (New York: Routledge, 1990), 6–7, 35–78. See also Gisela Bock, "Challenging Dichotomies: Perspectives on Women's History," in *Writing Women's History: International Perspectives*, ed. Karen Offen, Ruth Roach Pierson, and Jane Rendall (Bloomington: Indiana University Press, 1991), 1–23, esp. 7–9; and, from a psychoanalytic perspective, Nancy F. Partner, "No Sex, No Gender," *Speculum* 68 (1993): 419–44.

12. Judith Butler, *Bodies that Matter: On the Discursive Limits of "Sex"* (New York: Routledge, 1993); Butler, *Gender Trouble*; Elizabeth Grosz, *Volatile Bodies: Toward a Corporeal Feminism* (Bloomington: Indiana University Press, 1994).

13. Riley, *"Am I That Name?"*, passim.

14. Ibid., 1–2, 6, 8, 16.

15. Butler, *Gender Trouble*, 3.

16. Ibid., 24–25, 139–40; Stanley Chojnacki, "Subaltern Patriarchs: Patrician Bachelors in Renaissance Venice," in *Medieval Masculinities: Regarding Men in the Middle Ages*, ed. Clare A. Lees (Minneapolis: University of Minnesota Press, 1994), 74. For discussions of the self and identity in the early modern period, see also Natalie Zemon Davis, "Boundaries and the Sense of Self in Sixteenth-Century France," in *Reconstructing Individualism: Autonomy, Individuality, and the Self in Western Thought*, ed. Thomas C. Heller et al. (Stanford: Stanford University Press, 1986), 53–63; and Roper, *Oedipus and the Devil*, passim, esp. 4–9.

17. Butler, *Gender Trouble*, 140.

18. Judith M. Bennett, "Medieval Women, Modern Women: Across the Great Divide," in *Culture and History, 1350–1600: Essays on English Communities, Identities and Writing*, ed. David Aers (London: Harvester Wheatsheaf, 1992), 147–75.

19. Among the many contributions to these questions: Bolton, "Mulieres Sanctae"; Bynum, *Holy Feast* and *Fragmentation and Redemption*; Gilchrist and

Oliva, *Religious Women*; Penelope D. Johnson, *Equal in Monastic Profession: Religious Women in Medieval France* (Chicago: University of Chicago Press, 1991); André Vauchez, *The Laity in the Middle Ages: Religious Beliefs and Devotional Practices*, ed. Daniel J. Bornstein, trans. Margery J. Schneider (Notre Dame: University of Notre Dame Press, 1993).

20. Peter Biller has made this point; "The Common Woman in the Western Church in the Thirteenth and Fourteenth Centuries," *SCH* 27 (1990): 127–57.

21. See Merry E. Wiesner's historiographical article, "Beyond Women and the Family: Towards a Gender Analysis of the Reformation," *Sixteenth Century Journal* 18 (1987): 311–21; Wiesner, "Women's Response to the Reformation," in *The German People and the Reformation*, ed. R. Po-Chia Hsia (Ithaca, N.Y.: Cornell University Press, 1988), 148–71; E. William Monter, "Protestant Wives, Catholic Saints, and the Devil's Handmaid: Women in the Age of the Reformations," in *Becoming Visible: Women in European History*, 2d ed., ed. Renate Bridenthal, Claudia Koonz, and Susan Stuard (Boston: Houghton Mifflin, 1987), 203–19; Lyndal Roper, *The Holy Household: Women and Morals in Reformation Augsburg* (Oxford: Clarendon, 1989); Roper, *Oedipus and the Devil*; Sherrin Marshall [Wyntjes], *Women in Reformation and Counter-Reformation Europe* (Bloomington: Indiana University Press, 1989); and Crawford, *Women and Religion in England*.

22. Roper, *Holy Household*, 2; see also 1–5.

23. The literature on Lollardy is large. See Anne Hudson's recent survey, *The Premature Reformation: Wycliffite Texts and Lollard History* (Oxford: Clarendon Press, 1988) and works published since: Margaret Aston, "Iconoclasm at Rickmansworth, 1522: Troubles of Churchwardens," *JEH* 40 (1989): 524–52; Richard G. Davies, "Lollardy and Locality," *TRHS*, 6th ser., 1 (1991): 191–212; Patrick J. Horner, " 'The King Taught Us the Lesson': Benedictine Support for Henry V's Suppression of the Lollards," *Mediaeval Studies* 52 (1990): 190–220; Peter McNiven, *Heresy and Politics in the Reign of Henry IV: The Burning of John Badby* (Woodbridge, Suffolk: Boydell, 1987); John A.F. Thomson, "Orthodox Religion and the Origins of Lollardy," *History* 74 (1989): 39–55.

24. For Lollard beliefs, see Hudson, *Premature Reformation*, passim, but esp. 278–389; John A. F. Thomson, *The Later Lollards, 1414–1520* (Oxford: Oxford University Press, 1965), 239–53; Charles Kightly, "The Early Lollards: A Survey of Popular Lollard Activity in England, 1382–1428" (D.Phil. diss., University of York, 1975), 576–81; Helmar Härtel, "Lollardische Lehrelemente im 14. und 15. Jahrhundert" (Ph.D. diss., Universität Göttingen, 1969). Apocalypticism has been studied by Curtis V. Bostick, "The Apocalypse and the 'ABC's': Lollard Strategies for Success in Late Medieval and Early Modern England," paper presented at the Sixteenth Century Studies Conference, Toronto, 28 October 1994. My thanks to Dr. Bostick for allowing me to cite his paper; I regret that his thesis, "The Antichrist and the 'Trewe Men': Lollard Apocalypticism in Late Medieval and Early Modern England" (Ph.D. diss., University of Arizona, 1993), came to my notice too late to be taken into consideration here.

25. The standard earlier works were K. B. McFarlane, *John Wycliffe and the Beginnings of English Nonconformity* (London: English Universities Press, 1952), 89–159; McFarlane, *Lancastrian Kings and Lollard Knights* (Oxford: Clarendon,

1972), 140–225; Kightly, "The Early Lollards"; and Thomson, *Later Lollards*. Margaret Aston has also written extensively on the Lollard movement; see especially *Lollards and Reformers: Images and Literacy in Late Medieval Religion* (London: Hambledon, 1984).

26. See n. 27 below.

27. J. J. Scarisbrick, *The Reformation and the English People* (Oxford: Blackwell, 1984), 46; R. N. Swanson, *Church and Society in Late Medieval England* (Oxford: Blackwell, 1989), 335, 343.

28. Davies, "Lollardy and Locality."

29. See especially Derek Plumb, "The Social and Economic Spread of Rural Lollardy: A Reappraisal," *SCH* 23 (1986): 111–30; Imogen Luxton, "The Lichfield Court Book: A Postscript," *BIHR* 44 (1971): 120–25; Susan Brigden, *London and the Reformation* (Oxford: Clarendon Press, 1989), 89–98.

30. In addition to the works cited in notes 2 and 3 above, see Janet L. Nelson, "Society, Theodicy and the Origins of Heresy: Towards a Reassessment of the Medieval Evidence," *SCH* 9 (1972): 65–77, esp. 74–75; Lucienne Julien, "Le catharisme et la femme," *Cahiers d'études cathares* 27 (1976): 29–37; Shulamith Shahar, "De quelques aspects de la femme dans la pensée et la communauté religieuses aux XIIe et XIIIe siècles," *Revue de l'histoire des religions* 185 (1974): 29–77; John Klassen, "Women and Religious Reform in Late Medieval Bohemia," *Renaissance and Reformation* 17 (1981): 203–21, esp. 203, 205.

31. Margaret Aston, "Lollard Women Priests?" in her *Lollards and Reformers*, 49–70 (previously appearing in *JEH* 31 [1980]: 441–61); John F. Davis, "Joan of Kent, Lollardy and the English Reformation," *JEH* 33 (1982): 225–33.

32. Claire Cross, "'Great Reasoners in Scripture': The Activities of Women Lollards 1380–1530," in *Medieval Women*, ed. Derek Baker, *SCH* Subsidia 1 (Oxford: Blackwell, 1978), 359–80; see also McSheffrey, "Women and Lollardy."

33. Cross, "Great Reasoners," 360, 378.

34. See Hudson, *Premature Reformation*, 32–42, for an evaluation of these sources.

35. See ibid., 9–32.

36. See Natalie Zemon Davis, *Fiction in the Archives: Pardon Tales and Their Tellers in Sixteenth-Century France* (Stanford: Stanford University Press, 1987), esp. 1–6; Laura Gowing, "Women, Sex and Honour: The London Church Courts, 1572–1640" (Ph.D. diss., University of London, 1993), 172–80; and Roper, *Oedipus and the Devil*, 19–20, 55.

37. Cross, "Great Reasoners," 379; Aston, *Lollards and Reformers*, 50.

38. See N. Z. Davis, *Fiction in the Archives*, 8; and Roper, *Oedipus and the Devil*, 55.

39. One exception is the testimony of Margery Baxter's neighbors in Norwich. *HT*, 43–51.

40. "Juliana filia Agnetis Yong, etatis xx^{ti} annorum, nata Coven', jurata et examinata. Interrogata an scivit legere, negat. Tandem affirmante Silkeby in facie sua quod perfecte novit legere, fatebatur. Et dixit quod audivit Aliciam Rowley communicantem contra peregrinaciones, ymaginum veneraciones, et sacramentis altaris, dicendo quod illud quod oblatum erat, erat nil aliud nisi panis et vinum. Quibus

dictis credidit ista ut asserit. Interrogata de libro quem ab Alicia Rowley habuit, negat se huiusmodi librum habere, affirmando eum librum traditum fuisse dicte Alicie Rowley. Et dicit quod apportavit dictum librum in domum prenominate Alicie et eundum unacum libro de mandatis posuit in lecto sub culcitra infra *the chapell chambre*, que ut asserit intimavit dicte Alicie. Dicit insuper quod hoc ideo fecit quia Silkeby agressus est iuramentum suam, eam admonendo ut si quos libros haberet eosdem occultaret, h<ii> [?] fortassis in custodia sua deprendantur." Lich. Ct. Bk., fol. 14r. The examination is undated in the court book, but Bishop Blyth's register dates her appearance at 3 December 1511 (Reg. G. Blyth, fol. 99r).

41. Lich. Ct. Bk., fols. 3v, 8v.

42. Ibid., fols. 2r, 3v, 8v.

43. See, for instance, *HT*, 51–52, 139, 211; Lich. Ct. Bk., fols. 1r, 5r.

44. Lich. Ct. Bk., fol. 24r.

45. One court book, from the proceedings against heretics in the diocese of Norwich by Bishop William Alnwick, has been edited by Norman P. Tanner (*HT*). It includes both depositions and abjurations. Another survives from Bishop Geoffrey Blyth's prosecution of Coventry heretics in 1511–12 (Lich. Ct. Bk.), but it is in poor condition and has not been edited. Fragments from the court book, since lost, of Richard Fitzjames of London, also about 1511, were transcribed by Archbishop Ussher in the seventeenth century (TCD, MS 775). For the first two books, see Aston, *Lollards and Reformers*, 71–100, and John Fines, "Heresy Trials in the Diocese of Coventry and Lichfield, 1511–1512," *JEH* 14 (1963): 160–74.

46. *A&M*, 3:584–96; 4:7–8, 123–27, 172–246, 557–58, 580–85, 688–94; 5:647–52.

47. Foxe's accuracy is considered by John A. F. Thomson, "John Foxe and Some Sources for Lollard History: Notes for a Critical Appraisal," *SCH* 2 (1965): 251–57; Patrick Collinson, "Truth and Legend: The Veracity of John Foxe's *Book of Martyrs*," in *Clio's Mirror: Historiography in Britain and the Netherlands*, ed. A. C. Duke and C. A. Tamse, Britain and the Netherlands, 8 (Zutphen: de Walburg, 1985), 31–54; Stefan J. Smart, "John Foxe and 'The Story of Richard Hun, Martyr,'" *JEH* 37 (1986): 1–14. See also Carole Levin, "Women in *The Book of Martyrs* as Models of Behavior in Tudor England," *International Journal of Women's Studies* 4 (1981): 196–207; and Ellen Macek, "The Emergence of a Feminine Spirituality in *The Book of Martyrs*," *Sixteenth Century Journal* 19 (1988): 63–80.

48. Elizabeth Sampson of London, for instance, is called Joan by Foxe (see Reg. Fitzjames, fols. 4rv; TCD, MS 775, fol. 122v; *A&M*, 4:206), and James Morden (also called John by Foxe) and Thomas Barnard are variously said to have been burned in 1509, 1521, and 1541 (see *L&P*, vol. 4, pt. 2, no. 3062, which fixes the date at 1522, and *A&M*, 4:124, 245; 5:545).

49. For instance, a comparison of his account of the fifteenth-century East Anglian Lollards with the records he used shows that he manipulated the use of the name Margery Baxter, alias Wright, in order to produce a pristine portrait of "Margery Baxter." Any of Margery's actions or beliefs that were inconsistent with Foxe's view of a proto-Anglican Lollard were either omitted or ascribed to the less heroic "Margaret Wright" (*A&M*, 3:591, 594–96; *HT*, 39–51).

50. See the bibliography for information about the bishops' registers used.

51. "Penultimo die mensis Novembris anno domini millesimo cccclx tercio, Johannes Qwyrk, laicus, super crimine heretice pravitatis denunciatus et detectus, de et super articulis infrascriptis per reverendos viros magistros Johannem Botuler decretorum, Thomam Edmunde in phisica ac rectorem ecclesie Sancti Andree in Holbourne London et priorem domus predicatorum Oxon' in theologia, doctores, examinatus. Eosdem articulos coram eosdem doctores reverendi in Christo patris ac domini, domini Johannis Dei gracia Lincoln episcopi, commissarios in hac parte iudicialiter sedentes fatebatur.

"In primis fatebatur quod habuit familiaritatem cum Jacobo Wylly pro crimine heresis crematum qui ipsum Johannem Epistolas Sancti Pauli in anglicis verbis docuit. Item fatebatur quod docuit et predicavit quod sacramentum altaris erat tantum in memoria Christi et quod non ibidem remaneret nisi substancia panis. Item fatebatur quod docuit et predicavit quod iudex ecclesiasticus nulla de causa potest separare hominem et mulierem inter quod matrimonium extitit solempniza-tum, quia quod Deus coniunxit homo non separet. Item fatebatur et recognovit quod docuit et predicavit quod oblaciones non sunt vicariis aut presbiteris quibus-cumque faciende nec sanctis et piis locis offerende sed pocius inter pauperes erog-ande. Et quod ymagines in ecclesia non sunt venerande sed quod sufficit homini tantum dicere Pater Noster, Ave, et Credo tantum Deo et Beate Marie. Item fateba-tur quod tenuit et predicavit quod Petrus et apostoli submiserunt se paupertati voluntarie et sic pervenerunt ad regnum Dei. Sed episcopi moderni habent exces-simas possessiones. Item fatebatur quod docuit et predicavit quod non est locus purgatorii, sed aut ad celum vel infernum quisquis post eius mortem perveniat. [Passage in English] . . . et fecit tale signum +." Reg. Chedworth, fols. 59v–60r.

52. See Anne Hudson, *Lollards and Their Books* (London: Hambledon, 1985), 125–40, where such a list, probably circulated to bishops around 1428, is discussed.

53. *FZ*, 417–32. See James Crompton, "*Fasciculi Zizaniorum*," *JEH* 12 (1961): 35–45, 155–66.

54. BL, Harl. MS 421; *EM*, vol. 1, pt. 1:113–34, vol. 1, pt. 2:50–65; vol. 2, pt. 1:334–35; *L&P*, vol. 4, pt. 2, nos. 4029, 4175, 4545, 4850. *Ecclesiastical Memorials* and the *Letters and Papers* have been cited in this study in preference to the manu-script when the material is identical.

55. I have not, however, comprehensively examined the voluminous corpus of Wyclif's work and later Lollard texts. Wyclif was little interested in issues concerning women; see Simon Forde, "The 'Strong Woman' and 'The Woman Who Surrounds a Man': Perceptions of Woman in Wyclif's Theological Writings," *Révue d'histoire ecclésiastique* 88 (1993): 54–87, esp. 59; my thanks to Dr. Forde for allowing me to have a copy of his paper prior to publication.

56. Edited by Anne Hudson and Pamela Gradon in *EWS*.

57. For the definition used here and on the concept of community in general, see C. J. Calhoun, "Community: Toward a Variable Conceptualization for Com-parative Research," *Social History* 5 (1980): 105–29. Recent examinations of the concept of community by late medieval historians include a special issue of *Journal of British Studies* 33/4 (October 1994), entitled *Vill, Guild, and Gentry: Forces of Com-munity in Later Medieval England*, ed. Maryanne Kowaleski; and David Gary Shaw, *The Creation of a Community: The City of Wells in the Middle Ages* (Oxford: Claren-don, 1993), esp. 2–8.

A relatively loose definition was used here to determine who were members of these Lollard communities. A person is considered a Lollard if he or she was brought before a court and admitted heresy, if he or she was able to resort to compurgation but there was reasonably reliable evidence that he or she did participate in Lollard activities, or if he or she is cited as a member of the sect by a deponent, unless there is evidence to the contrary. See Appendix.

58. See, for instance, A. P. Cohen, *The Symbolic Construction of Community* (Chichester: Horwood, 1985); Mark S. Granovetter, "The Strength of Weak Ties," *American Journal of Sociology* 78 (1973): 1360–80; and Granovetter, "The Strength of Weak Ties: A Network Theory Revisited," in *Social Structure and Network Analysis*, ed. Peter V. Marsden and Nan Lin (Beverly Hills: Sage, 1982), 105–30.

59. Nor have I considered isolated cases of Lollard activity in the period after 1420, as it was precisely the relationship *between* Lollards on which I wished to focus.

60. See *HT*; Margaret Aston, "William White's Lollard Followers," in her *Lollards and Reformers*, 71–100; Edwin Welch, "Some Suffolk Lollards," *Suffolk Institute of Archaeology Proceedings* 29 (1962): 154–65; Thomson, *Later Lollards*, 120–32; Kightly, "Early Lollards," 410–20; Hudson, *Premature Reformation*, esp. 137–40; McSheffrey, "Women and Lollardy."

61. *Reg. Chichele*, 3:85; 4:297–301.

62. Aston, *Lollards and Reformers*, 71–100.

63. *Johannis Amundesham annales monasterii Sancti Albani*, ed. H. T. Riley, R. S. (London: Public Record Office, 1871), 1:29; *Records of the City of Norwich*, ed. J. C. Tingley (Norwich: Jarrold, 1910), 2:66.

64. Kightly, "Early Lollards," 354, 369–70, 405, 421–25; Thomson, *Later Lollards*, 53–54.

65. Reg. Chedworth, fols. 57r–63r.

66. See Chapter 5, "Gentlemen in Later Lollardy."

67. Two men named in the first group, John Fip and Pope (no forename was recorded), may have been related to or perhaps even identified with men of the same names cited half a century later. See Reg. Chedworth, fols. 61r, 62rv; *A&M*, 4:217, 225–42; Hudson, *Premature Reformation*, 459–60. On the sixteenth-century Lollards of Buckinghamshire, see Plumb, "Social and Economic Spread"; Aston, "Iconoclasm at Rickmansworth"; Thomson, *Later Lollards*, 87–94; W. H. Summers, *The Lollards of the Chiltern Hills* (London: Griffiths, 1906).

68. *A&M*, 4:213. Plumb has estimated that about 25 percent of those named in the subsidy in the Amersham area were involved to some degree in the Lollard community. "Social and Economic Spread," 113–16. This estimate assumes that the sex ratio of the Lollard group was even.

69. *Significavits* date the burning of several ringleaders to 1510 rather than Foxe's date of 1506. PRO, C.85/115/10; *A&M*, 4:123–26; Thomson, *Later Lollards*, 87; Thomson, "John Foxe," 255.

70. *A&M*, 4:123–26, 217–19.

71. Ibid., 219–46.

72. The area around Wantage, known as the Vale of the White Horse, was in Berkshire until the 1974 reorganization of counties, when it was transferred to Oxfordshire.

73. Salisbury Reg. Langton, fols. 35r–42v. (I did not notice the edition of this register until after the completion of my research: *The Register of Thomas Langton, Bishop of Salisbury, 1485–93*, ed. D. P. Wright [Canterbury and York Society 74 (1985)]; the above material appears at 70–83.) Reg. J. Blythe, fols. 70r–79v; Reg. Morton, vol. 1, fols. 194rv; Reg. Audley, fols. 107v–108v, 130v–131r, 142v–149v, 155v–163v, 168v–169v, 183v.

74. *A&M*, 4:126–27, 234–45, 582–83.

75. See Reg. Fitzjames, fols. 4rv, 25r–27r; Reg. Fox, vol. 2, fols. 86v–88r; Winchester Reg. Langton, fol. 66r; TCD, MS 775, fols. 122v–125r; Lich. Ct. Bk., fols. 16rv; Reg. Audley, fol. 144r; William Hale, *A Series of Precedents and Proceedings in Criminal Causes, 1475–1640* (London: Rivington, 1847), 8–9, 54–55; *A&M*, 4:7–8, 172–246, 688–94; 5:29–30; *L&P*, vol. 4, pt. 2, nos. 4029, 4175, 4545, 4850; *EM*, vol. 1, pt. 1:113–34; vol. 1, pt. 2:50–65; vol. 2, pt. 1:334–35; *Chronicles of London*, ed. Charles Lethbridge Kingsford (Oxford: Clarendon, 1905), 208, 211, 226, 229, 232, 261; *The Great Chronicle of London*, ed. A. H. Thomas and I. D. Thornley (London: George W. Jones, 1938), 252, 264, 290, 294, 331; Robert Fabyan, *The New Chronicles of England and France*, ed. Henry Ellis (London: Rivington, 1811), 686, 687, 689. London Lollardy is discussed by Brigden, *London and the Reformation*, 86–106; and Thomson, *Later Lollards*, 138–71.

76. See, for instance, Lich. Ct. Bk., fol. 16r; Reg. G. Blyth, fol. 100r; *EM*, vol. 1, pt. 2:54–55; *L&P*, vol. 4, pt. 2, no. 4545.

77. See Brigden, *London and the Reformation*, 86–106.

78. BL, Harl. MS 421, fols. 11r–35v; *EM*, vol. 1, pt. 1:113–34, vol. 1, pt. 2:50–65; vol. 2, pt. 1:334–35; *L&P*, vol. 4, pt. 2, nos. 4029, 4175, 4545, 4850. This evidence as it touches Colchester is also discussed in Laquita Mae Alexander Higgs, "Lay Piety in the Borough of Colchester, 1485–1558" (Ph.D. diss., University of Michigan, 1983); and L. R. Poos, *A Rural Society After the Black Death: Essex, 1350–1525* (Cambridge: Cambridge University Press, 1991), 229–30, 263–75.

79. Reg. Warham, fols. 159r–175v; Kightly, "Early Lollards," 371–78, 406–12; Thomson, *Later Lollards*, 184–91; John F. Davis, "Lollard Survival and the Textile Industry in the South-East of England," *SCH* 3 (1966): 191–201; and Davis, *Heresy and Reformation in the South-East of England, 1520–1559* (London: Royal Historical Society, 1983).

Chapter 2

1. Charles Phythian-Adams, *Desolation of a City: Coventry and the Urban Crisis of the Late Middle Ages* (Cambridge: Cambridge University Press, 1979), 19–22.

2. Ibid., 26–67.

3. Thomson, *Later Lollards*, 102–4. John Fines and Imogen Luxton have each written articles describing the Lollards of early sixteenth-century Coventry, so there is no need here to give more than a brief history of the group. My interpretation of the social status of Lollardy diverges from theirs, so it will be given greater attention. Fines, "Heresy Trials," 160–74; Luxton, "Lichfield Court Book," 120–25.

4. The other men were Richard Hegham, Robert Crowther, Thomas Butler, Richard Gilmyn, and John Falkis. Reg. Hales, fols. 166r–167v; *A&M*, 4:133–35. See also the entry in the city annals for 1486: "In his yeare came ye bishopp of Chester [*sic*] to Coventry. Before him was brought divers persons suspect of heresy, whome [the bishop] appoynted to beare faggotts about ye Citty one ye markett day." Bodl. MS 31431, fol. 12v; see also BCRL MS 273978, fol. 5r. The diocese of Chester (carved out of the dioceses of Coventry and Lichfield and York) was not created until 1541.

5. Matthew Markland said that he had been of the sect with Landesdale during the time of Bishop Hales, but that he (Matthew) had renounced the sect at the time that Smyth and others abjured. Lich. Ct. Bk., fols. 1v, 10r, 13r, 14v–15r, 16r, 20v.

6. Although no evidence survives for a major process against Lollards in Coventry between 1486 and 1511, we do know that Alice Rowley found it necessary to purge herself of charges of heresy about 1506. Lich. Ct. Bk., fols. 6r, 17r.

7. Blyth's prosecutions are recorded in Reg. G. Blyth, fols. 98r–100r, and in a more extensive court book from which the material in the register was abstracted (Lich. Ct. Bk.). The first recorded date in the court book is 28 October, but the two cases heard that day were resumptions of proceedings begun earlier. Lich. Ct. Bk., fols. 2v, 10r.

8. Bodl. MS 31431, fol. 15r; BCRL MS 273978, fol. 5v. The annalists do not name the others burned and there is no other evidence for this mass execution; it is possible that the annalists confused this occasion with the later burning of seven Lollards in 1520. Joan Warde is also called by her married name, Joan Wasshingbury, in the court book and the register; here she will be referred to as Joan Warde to avoid confusion.

9. E.g., Alice Rowley and Thomas Villers. Lich. Ct. Bk., fols. 6v, 21v.

10. E.g., Thomasina Bradeley (despite damning evidence) and Alice Acton. Ibid., fols. 11v, 17r.

11. Ibid., fols. 14r, 21v.

12. Foxe's date is 1519; one annal dates it 1519–20, another 1520. Fines, although he apparently did not see the annals, believes the date of 1520 to be more accurate. See *A&M*, 4:557–58; Bodl. MS 31431, fol. 16r; BCRL MS 273978, fol. 6r; Fines, "Heresy Trials," 173. A 1530 printing of the testimony of the early fifteenth-century Lollard William Thorpe also refers to seven burnt at Coventry "not many yeres paste." *Two Wycliffite Texts*, ed. Anne Hudson, EETS, 301 (1993), 142.

13. In 1512 the court had in fact determined that Archer had not been a heretic; he was counted among a group of men who had attended Lollard meetings but had not believed the Lollards' opinions, although they vacillated on the questions of pilgrimage and the veneration of images. Reg. G. Blyth, fol. 99v; Lich. Ct. Bk., fol. 26v.

14. Bodl. MS 31431, fol. 16r; Lich. Ct. Bk., fols. 4r, 5v.

15. Lich. Ct. Bk., fol. 9r; Bodl. MS 31431, fol. 16r; BCRL MS 273978, fol. 6r; *A&M*, 4:558.

16. Lich. Ct. Bk. fols. 2r, 5v–6r, 7r, 8v, 24r; Reg. G. Blyth, fol. 99v. Thomson found no evidence of Lollard activity in Leicester apart from what was included in the Lichfield Court Book; there must have been some prosecution in that city in the

years preceding 1511, however, according to two references to abjurations made there. Lich. Ct. Bk., fols. 7r, 8v.

17. Lich. Ct. Bk., fols. 2rv, 6v, 14v, 16rv. See Hudson, *Premature Reformation*, 143, for use of the term "knowen man."

18. Fines, "Heresy Trials," 162, and 162 n.5. See below, Chapter 5, "Social Status and Men's Lollard Activities: Some Case Studies," where this is discussed further.

19. West Country parish accounts often mention "Bachelors," "Young Mens," "Maydens," and "Wyves." See Eamon Duffy, *The Stripping of the Altars: Traditional Religion in England, 1400–1580* (New Haven: Yale University Press, 1992), 150; and Katherine French, "Local Identity and the Late Medieval Parish: The Communities of Bath and Wells" (Ph.D. diss., University of Minnesota, 1993), 207–8, 215–16.

20. Lich. Ct. Bk., fols. 6r, 12r, 14v, 17v, 18v, 20v; Reg. G. Blyth, fol. 99v. Holbache's examination does not survive in the court book.

21. The only information on their conversion is Banbrooke's statement that Master John Phisicion taught him. Lich. Ct. Bk., fol. 10r. Although Fines says that Thomasina brought her husband Richard to Roger Landesdale for instruction, I interpret the passage (from the deposition of Roger's wife, Margaret Landesdale) differently: "Et ad quinque annos elapsos uxor Bradeley predicta accessit ad domum istius et cum viro suo communicavit, effectum tamen huiusmodi communicationis non novit." I have taken "viro suo" to mean Margaret's husband, not Thomasina's; an earlier reference in Margaret's deposition to Robert Silkby's visits with "viro suo" can only mean Roger. Ibid., fol. 11v; Fines, "Heresy Trials," 165. See also n. 23 below.

22. Lich. Ct. Bk., fols. 11v, 21v. Their mother's abjuration in Leicester is referred to at fols. 7r, 8v.

23. "Dicit quod circiter viii vel ix[nem] annos preteritos mater Thome Villers, unacum filia sua nunc uxor Bradeley, intraverunt in domi istius et manserunt ibidem a meridie usque ad vi[ta]. Et dicta mater (iacente marito istius valitudinario in lecto suo) legit in quodam magno libro presente dicta filia sua et eam audiente." Lich. Ct. Bk., fol. 11v. Whether the ill husband referred to was Margaret's or Mother Villers's is not absolutely clear — "istius" and "suo/sua" are used indiscriminately by the scribe to refer to Margaret or to those about whom Margaret deposed. As Mother Villers is called here and elsewhere "mater Thome Villers" rather than "uxor Villers," she was probably then a widow. It is possible that her husband had been the Charles Villers of Bristol who was mentioned by John Jonson. Ibid., fol. 14v. The family had another Bristol connection: Thomas Villers apprenticed his trade (of spicer) at Bristol. Ibid., fol. 21v.

24. Ibid., fols. 11rv.

25. Ibid., fols. 3r, 8v, 10r, 11r, 18v, 21v.

26. Ibid., fols. 3r, 6rv, 10r, 11r. Richard Northopp also denied charges on behalf of his wife. Ibid., fol. 10v.

27. Ibid., fols. 3r, 6r, 7r, 10r, 11rv; Reg. G. Blyth, fol. 99r. Banbrooke was also reported to own a copy of the Gospels.

28. See Lich. Ct. Bk., fols. 2r, 5rv, 7r, 8r, 13r, 19v–20r. Shugborow was a gentleman ("generosus"), although there is no sign he was particularly wealthy.

29. Lich. Ct. Bk., fols. 2r, 8r, 14v.

30. Ibid., fols. 2r, 3r, 4r, 5r–6v, 7v–8r, 11v, 20v.

31. Ibid., fol. 5v; other versions fols. 2v, 7r, 13r.

32. "A quodam vocato." Ibid., fol. 18v.

33. Ibid., fols. 4r, 6r, 11r, see also fols. 18v–19r. Records indicate that a Roger Landeseal rented a house near the park in Littlepark Street from the Guild of the Holy Trinity in 1485–86. *Register of the Holy Trinity Guild, Coventry*, 2 vols., ed. M. D. Harris and G. Templeman, Dugdale Society, 13, 19 (1935, 1944), 2:56. The nearby park is called Cheylesmore Park. *The Victoria History of the County of Warwick*, 8 vols., ed. H. Arthur Doubleday and William Page (London: Constable, 1904–69), 8:9.

34. Lich. Ct. Bk., fol. 7r.

35. Ibid., fol. 24r.

36. Ibid., fols. 2r, 3v, 8v, 14r, 21v; for panic, 21r.

37. Ibid., fols. 1v–2r, 3r, 5r, 6v, 7v, 10rv, 11v, 13r, 14v, 15v, 16v, 18v, 20r, 21r; Reg. G. Blyth, fols. 98r, 100r.

38. Silkby's second trial is recorded in the court book on a folio (now numbered 9) probably added to the book later. The folio is of a different size from the others, and the hand is distinct. Two annals date his burning to the Monday before Christmas, 1521 (December 23). Foxe dates the trial 13 January 1521 (Old Style). Lich. Ct. Bk., fol. 9r; Bodl. MS 31431, fol. 16r; BCRL MS 273978, fol. 6r; *A&M*, 4:558.

39. Phyllis Mack, "Women as Prophets during the English Civil War," *Feminist Studies* 8 (1982): 19–47.

40. Gail Malmgreen, "Domestic Discords: Women and the Family in East Cheshire Methodism, 1750–1830," in *Disciplines of Faith: Religion, Patriarchy, and Politics*, ed. James Obelkevich, Lyndal Roper, and Raphael Samuel (London: Routledge and Kegan Paul, 1986), 59–60.

41. Cross, " 'Great Reasoners.' "

42. *CPR 1494–1509*, 230, 288, 449; *Cal. Inq. Hen. VII*, vol. 3, 580; M. D. Harris, ed., *Coventry Leet Book, 1420–1555*, 4 pts. consecutively paginated, EETS, o.s., 134, 135, 138, 146 (1907–13), 343, 424, 528, 542, 553, 579; Will of William Rowley, PRO, PCC Prob. 11/15 (5 Adeane), 1505.

43. Fines, "Heresy Trials," 166, and Phythian-Adams, *Desolation*, 278n., both suggest this.

44. Lich. Ct. Bk., fol. 16r.

45. Joan Smyth's Lollard career and the question of gender, social status, and position within the Lollard community will be discussed in detail in Chapter 5.

46. See Chapter 5.

47. It is assumed they were single or widowed if no husband is mentioned.

48. Lich. Ct. Bk., fols. 3v, 5r, 8r.

49. Ibid., fols. 4r, 20v.

50. "Et postea metu Willelmi Rowley recessit a Coven' ad Northampton." Ibid., fol. 16r.

51. Possibly the same as the Thomas Wassyngborn of All Saints, Stanyng, who abjured heresy in the Commissary Court of London in 1482. William Hale, *A Series of Precedents and Proceedings in Criminal Causes, 1475–1640* (London: Rivington, 1847), 8–9.

52. Lich. Ct. Bk., fol. 16r; Reg. G. Blyth, fol. 100r.

53. If he was Thomas Wassyngborn, he would have relapsed in 1495.

54. Lich. Ct. Bk., fols. 14v, 16r, 17v, 20v–21r; Reg. G. Blyth, fol. 100r.

55. Lich. Ct. Bk., fol. 21r; Reg. G. Blyth, fol. 100r.

56. Bodl. MS 31431, fol. 15r; see also "City Annal" recorded in *Records of Early English Drama: Coventry*, ed. R.W. Ingram (Toronto: University of Toronto Press, 1981), 107.

57. Bodl. MS 31431, fol. 15r; see also BCRL MS 273978, fol. 5v.

58. Although "little moder Agnes" is never specifically identified with Agnes Jonson, it has been assumed here that they are the same person, based on the evidence of Rose Furnour's conversion. Joan Ward said that Agnes Jonson instructed Rose, while Rose herself said that "little moder Agnes" and Joan Ward taught her. Lich. Ct. Bk., fols. 14v, 21r.

59. "Optime novit legere." Ibid., fol. 14v, see also fol. 21r.

60. Ibid., fols. 5r, 14v, 16v–17r, 21r. She traded a book to Joan Blackbury of London (fol. 16v).

61. Ibid., fols. 14v, 21r.

62. Ibid., fols. 3v, 5r, 6v, 14r, 16v, 17v.

63. Reg. G. Blyth, fol. 99v. Some of the other examinations, abjurations, and penances of the accused were arranged in Blyth's register or court book in a way that may indicate that they were grouped together: Joan Gest and her husband abjured together, and Juliana Yong (age twenty) abjured along with another young offender, John Bull (age seventeen). Lich. Ct. Bk., fols. 13r, 14r, 23v; Reg. G. Blyth, fol. 99r.

64. Lich. Ct. Bk., fol. 17r; Reg. G. Blyth, fol. 99v; Bodl. MS 31431, fol. 15r; *REED: Coventry*, 107.

65. Lich. Ct. Bk., fols. 3v, 5r, 6v, 8r, 14v, 20r, 21r.

66. Ibid., fols. 5r, 7v, 14rv, 16r, 17v, 20r, 21r.

67. Ibid., fols. 3v, 6v–7r, 11rv, 18v, 20v, 21v.

68. Ibid., fols. 4r, 5r, 13r, 20v–21r.

69. See Chapter 4.

70. Lich. Ct. Bk., fols. 5r, 7r, 8v, 14v, 20v–21r; *Coventry Leet Book*, 421, 485.

71. Lich. Ct. Bk., fols. 2r, 3v, 7r, 8rv, 11rv, 14rv, 21r.

72. See Shannon McSheffrey, "Literacy and the Gender Gap in the Late Middle Ages: Women and Reading in Lollard Communities," in *Women, The Book and the Word*, ed. Jane H. M. Taylor and Lesley Smith (Woodbridge, Suffolk: Boydell and Brewer, 1995), 157–70.

73. Lich. Ct. Bk., fol. 21r.

74. Ibid., quotation at fol. 7r; 20r; a Lawrence Dawson is mentioned fol. 21r.

75. "Alium librum de tota vetere lege anglice confectum ad modum portiferii per manus." Ibid., quotation at fol. 5v; see also 7v.

76. "Fatetur etiam quod infra trimestre emensum Alicia Rowley accessit ad domum istius deponentis [Roger Landesdale] afferens secum librum super epistolas Pauli anglice scriptum et auduit istum deponentem legere super eodem libro in presentia uxoris sue, et librum ipsum denuo ad domum suam propriam dicta Alicia reportavit." Ibid., fol. 15v. Fines has interpreted this passage as saying that Alice

Rowley's husband read to her from the Epistles (Fines, "Heresy Trials," 166), but Alice's husband was dead by 1505 (his will, PRO, PCC Prob. 11/15 [5 Adeane], was proved that year) and the deponent is clearly Landesdale.

77. Lich. Ct. Bk., fol. 14r.

78. Ibid., fols. 4r, 5v, 11v. The text says she brought them to Roger about three months "a tempore obitus eiusdem Johannis"; I assume here that the "Johannis" of the text is a scribal error for "Ricardi."

79. Ibid., fol. 6v.

80. "Quemdam librum de passione Christi et Ade." Ibid., fol. 4r.

81. Ibid., fols. 4r, 6v.

82. Ibid., fol. 21r. Perhaps the first book was a devotional work on the art of dying (as Thomson suggests in *Later Lollards*, 113), with no specific connections to Lollardy.

83. Lich. Ct. Bk., fols. 14v, 16v; see also 17r.

84. Ibid., fols. 7r, 26v.

85. In contrast to the interest the bishop and his officials showed in books, however, the depositions record relatively little about matters of doctrine.

86. Lich. Ct. Bk., fols. 15r, 16v, 21r.

87. Ibid., fol. 17v.

88. Ibid., fol. 6v; cf. fol. 14r. Alice Rowley may be the person whom Joan Smyth heard saying "May a preiste make god to daie and ete hym and doo likewise to morowe?" Ibid., fol. 4r.

89. Ibid., fol. 17v, cf. fols. 2r, 20r; *The Holy Bible . . . Made from the Latin Vulgate by John Wycliffe and his Followers*, 4 vols., ed. Josiah Forshall and Frederic Madden (Oxford: Oxford University Press, 1850), 4:190 (Luke 12:33).

90. Lich. Ct. Bk., fol. 14v.

91. Luxton, "Lichfield Court Book."

92. On the question of oligarchy in late medieval English towns, see Stephen Rigby, "Urban 'Oligarchy' in Late Medieval England," in *Towns and Townspeople in the Fifteenth Century*, ed. John A. F. Thomson (Gloucester: Sutton, 1988), 62–86; Maryanne Kowaleski, "The Commercial Dominance of a Medieval Provincial Oligarchy: Exeter in the Late Fourteenth Century," *Mediaeval Studies* 46 (1984): 355–84, esp. 355–56.

93. *BRUO to 1500*, 1517–18. There were two Doctor Prestons to whom deponents in the court book referred: one the vicar of St. Michael's (Lich. Ct. Bk., fol. 7r), the other a friar. Thomas Acton said he always used to confess to Dr. Preston, Friar Minor (ibid., fol. 20r), while Rose Furnour said she had confessed to a certain Friar Preston during the Lent just past, that is, 1511 (ibid., fol. 14v). As James Preston was apparently not a friar and was dead by 1507, they cannot have been the same man.

94. Lich. Ct. Bk., fol. 7r.

95. Ibid., fols. 18v–19r; *Coventry Leet Book*, 601–706.

96. Lich. Ct. Bk., fols. 3v, 5r, 7r; *Coventry Leet Book*, 313–629 passim; on W. Forde's mayoralty, 582–88.

97. Lich. Ct. Bk., fols. 6r, 7r (three others mention him as well: fols. 14v, 19r); *Coventry Leet Book*, 516–629.

98. Lich. Ct. Bk., fols. 5v–6v, 18v, 20v; *Coventry Leet Book*, 481, 532, 553–628.

99. Lich. Ct. Bk., fols. 2r, 8r; *Coventry Leet Book*, 528–605, 609. There may also be confusion in the court book between this man and Thomas Bowen. Foxe, for instance, alters Thomas Bowen's name to Bonde in his account of the 1520 burnings. *A&M*, 4:557.

100. Lich. Ct. Bk., fols. 7r, 19r; Josiah Clement Wedgwood, *Biographies*, vol. 2 of *History of Parliament, 1439–1509* (London: His Majesty's Stationery Office, 1936), 216.

101. *Coventry Leet Book*, 431, 528, 601; Wedgwood, *Biographies*, 216; *CPR 1494–1509*, 230, 288, 474, 488.

102. Both families were wealthy and politically powerful. William Pysford the Elder was active in Coventry civic politics from 1486 to 1518 and held the position of mayor in 1501. His son Henry Pysford was evaluated as possessing £400 in the 1524 subsidy. The Wigstons made their chief home in Leicester, but John Wigston held prominent civic offices in Coventry, including the mayoralty and the Mastership of the Holy Trinity Guild (1497). A William Wigston (either John's son or nephew) was also referred to in the *Coventry Leet Book* from 1491 to 1509. In Leicester, William Wigston the Younger was by far the wealthiest man in the city by 1523, and he and his brothers and cousins held a number of important political positions. *Coventry Leet Book*, 528–653; PRO, E.179/192/125; W. G. Hoskins, "English Provincial Towns in the Early Sixteenth Century," *TRHS*, 5th ser., 6 (1956): 6–9; *CPR 1494–1509*, 194, 286, 503; *Cal. Inq. Hen. VII*, 2:374–75; 3:245; *L&P*, vol. 1, nos. 1015, 3209, 4742, 5186; Wedgwood, *Hist. of Parl., Biographies*, 948–49.

103. "Et audivit Bowen dicentem quod Magistri Wiggeston et Pysford habeunt pulcherrimos libros de heresi." Lich. Ct. Bk., quotation at fol. 18v; see also 5r.

104. Ibid., fol. 15v.

105. PRO, PCC Prob. 11/15 (22 Adeane), Will of James Preston of Coventry, 1506.

106. PRO, PCC Prob. 11/19 (9 Ayloffe), Will of William Pysford of Coventry, 1518. Thomas Forde apparently had no sons.

107. PRO, PCC Prob. 11/19 (22 Ayloffe), Will of William Pysford of Coventry, 1518.

108. Luxton, "Lichfield Court Book," 123; *CPR 1494–1509*, 230, 288, 567.

109. William Dugdale, *The Antiquities of Warwickshire Illustrated from Records, Leiger-Books, Manuscripts, Charters, Evidences, Tombes and Armes* . . . (London: Thomas Warren, 1656), 117.

110. *Cal. Inq. Hen. VII*, 2:393.

111. PRO, PCC Prob. 11/15 (29 Adeane), Will of Richard Coke of Coventry, 1507.

112. Thomas Bayly and James Preston were the witnesses to William Rowley's will (PRO, PCC Prob. 11/15 [5 Adeane], 1505). William Forde and William Pysford were executors of Thomas Bonde's will (Prob. 11/15 [22 Adeane], 1507). William Wigston was overseer and Roger Wigston and John Bonde (son of Thomas) were witnesses to William Pysford Sr.'s will (Prob. 11/19 [9 Ayloffe], 1518). William Wigston was also executor of William Pysford Jr.'s will, while Wigston's chaplain, Sir William Fissher, and John Bonde acted as overseers (Prob.

11/19 [22 Ayloffe], 1518). William Wigston again acted as executor for his other brother-in-law Henry's will, and Richard Rice, probably the same as Richard Ryse, acted as witness (Prob. 11/21 [37 Bodfelde], 1525). William Forde and William Pysford acted as overseers for Richard Coke's will, while Richard Smyth and William Banwell acted as witnesses (Prob. 11/15 [29 Adeane], 1507). William Pysford acted as executor for William Forde's will (Prob. 11/15 [35 Adeane], 1508).

113. Luxton, "Lichfield Court Book," 123–24.

114. The identification of "Lollard" or "Protestant" wills by K. B. McFarlane and A. G. Dickens has been questioned by more recent scholars. McFarlane (in *Lancastrian Kings and Lollard Knights*, 207–20) determined three characteristics that he thought defined a "Lollard" will: excessive humility, loathing of the body, and dislike of funereal pomp. He found these sentiments in the wills of several late fourteenth- and early fifteenth-century men whom he identified as "Lollard Knights." The preambles to sixteenth-century wills have also been used as a barometer of religious belief (Catholic, Protestant, and later Calvinist) by A. G. Dickens, Margaret Spufford, and J. J. Scarisbrick (Dickens, *Lollards and Protestants in the Diocese of York, 1509–1538* [1959; London: Hambledon, 1982], 171–73, 215–18; Spufford, *Contrasting Communities: English Villagers in the Sixteenth and Seventeenth Centuries* [Cambridge: Cambridge University Press, 1974], 320–35; and Scarisbrick, *Reformation*, 2–6). But use of wills and preambles as a means of identifying religious belief has been criticized. John A. F. Thomson, M. G. A. Vale, and R. N. Swanson have challenged McFarlane's characterization of the three "Lollard" elements found in wills, contending that these sentiments were not restricted to Lollards but were part of a much wider movement in fifteenth-century piety (Thomson, "Orthodox Religion," 46–47; Vale, *Piety, Charity and Literacy among the Yorkshire Gentry, 1370–1480*, Borthwick Papers, 50 [York, 1976], 6, 11; Swanson, *Church and Society*, 266, 336). Michael L. Zell has also suggested caution in the use of religious preambles of sixteenth-century wills to determine the religious leanings of the testator during the murky period of the Reformation, noting that so-called "Protestant" preambles are often coupled with bequests that strongly suggest adherence to Catholicism. Zell, "The Use of Religious Preambles as a Measure of Religious Belief in the Sixteenth Century," *BIHR* 50 (1977): 246–49; see also R. Po-Chia Hsia, "Civic Wills as Sources for the Study of Piety in Muenster, 1530–1618," *Sixteenth Century Journal* 14 (1983): 321–48, esp. 327; and Duffy, *Stripping of the Altars*, 502–23.

115. PRO, PCC Prob. 11/15 (22 and 35 Adeane), Prob. 11/19 (9 and 22 Ayloffe), Prob. 11/21 (37 Bodfelde), and Prob. 11/25 (F. 39 Hogen).

116. Duffy, for instance, cites a number of preambles from elsewhere that are similar to the Coventry wills. *Stripping of the Altars*, 323–27.

117. PRO, PCC Prob. 11/15 (35 Adeane), Will of William Forde of Coventry, 1508.

118. PRO, PCC Prob. 11/19 (9 Ayloffe), Will of William Pysford Sr., 1518; Prob. 11/19 (22 Ayloffe), Will of William Pysford Jr., 1518; Prob. 11/21 (37 Bodfelde), Will of Henry Pysford, 1525; Prob. 11/15 (22 Adeane), Will of Thomas Bonde, 1507.

119. PRO, PCC Prob. 11/25 (F. 39 Hogen), Will of William Wigston, 1536.

120. Ibid.

121. PRO, PCC Prob. 11/15 (29 Adeane), Will of Richard Coke of Coventry, 1507; see also Lich. Ct. Bk., fol. 19r; Luxton, "Lichfield Court Book," 120–21.

122. PRO, PCC Prob. 11/15 (29 Adeane), Will of Richard Coke of Coventry, 1507.

123. McFarlane, *Lancastrian Kings and Lollard Knights*, 207–20. Vale has found this to be a relatively common element of late fifteenth-century wills of the orthodox Yorkshire gentry. *Piety, Charity and Literacy*, 11–14; see also Gail McMurray Gibson, *The Theater of Devotion: East Anglian Drama and Society in the Late Middle Ages* (Chicago: University of Chicago Press, 1989), 28–29.

124. For instance, Imogen Luxton writes: "The vast majority of laymen who showed knowledge of the Bible in the vernacular after 1408 . . . were Lollards"; thus, Richard Coke's "possession of two English Bibles would appear to suggest Lollard inclinations on his part." Luxton, "Lichfield Court Book," 121.

125. Hudson, *Premature Reformation*, 231–34; Gibson, *Theater of Devotion*, 29–30.

126. Dugdale, *Antiquities of Warwickshire*, 109.

127. *L&P*, vol. 1, no. 1672.

128. The Thomas Wigston above-named was the nonresident rector of Houghton-on-the-Hill and canon of Newark college in Leicester (the same church at which the chantry was founded). John Pysford, brother of Agnes and William Pysford the Younger, was the rector of Baginton in Warwickshire, while Master Roger Pysford was the nonresident rector of Medbourne. *Visitations in the Diocese of Lincoln, 1517–1531*, 3 vols., ed. A. Hamilton Thompson, Lincoln Record Society, 33, 35, 37 (1940–47), 1:xxx, 12.

129. *Coventry Leet Book*, 587. On late medieval religious guilds, sober orthodox piety, and civic governments, see Barbara A. Hanawalt and Ben R. McRee, "The Guilds of *Homo Prudens* in Late Medieval England," *Continuity and Change* 7 (1992): 163–79, esp. 169–71; and McRee, "Religious Gilds and Civic Order: The Case of Norwich in the Later Middle Ages," *Speculum* 67 (1992): 69–97.

130. *REED: Coventry*, 112–13.

131. *CPR 1494–1509*, 567; Dugdale, *Antiquities of Warwickshire*, 124.

132. Bodl. MS 31431, fol. 12v; BCRL MS 273978, fol. 5r.

133. Luxton, "Lichfield Court Book," 122–23; Cross, "Great Reasoners," 367–68.

134. Lich. Ct. Bk., fol. 15v.

135. *Lincoln Diocese Documents, 1450–1544*, ed. Andrew Clark, EETS, o.s., 149 (1914): 209–10. On vowesses, see Gilchrist and Oliva, *Religious Women*, 78–79.

136. "Idem Rogerus, interrogatus preterea quare credit Johannem Spon fuisse hereticum, dicit ob eam causam quod idem Johannes attulit sibi quemdam librum de et super veteri iure in anglicis traductum." Lich. Ct. Bk., fol. 6r.

137. Ibid., fol. 7r.

138. Ibid., fol. 18v. See two other cases where Lollards may have mistaken orthodox books of devotion for heretical works: Joan Warde's book on the art of dying and Alice Cottismore's *Legenda aurea*. Ibid., fol. 21r; *A&M*, 4:582.

139. See Chapter 3, "The Trade in Lollard Books"; and Hudson, *Lollards and Their Books*, 141–63.

140. This distinction on the basis of social status differs with the argument recently made by Duffy in *Stripping of the Altars*, passim, esp. 122. Duffy pays too little attention to two factors: first, the rarity of lay literacy, its heavy correlation with social station and the male gender, and the consequent limitation of written religious materials to the upper echelons of society; and, second, fears regarding the Lollard sect (which he dismisses as irrelevant) and their influence on the elites' view of access to vernacular devotional literature by the lower orders. See also Ann M. Hutchison, "Devotional Reading in the Monastery and in the Late Medieval Household," in *De Cella in Seculum: Religious and Secular Life and Devotion in Late Medieval England*, ed. Michael G. Sargent (Woodbridge, Suffolk: Boydell and Brewer, 1989), 215–28.

141. "An Acte for thadvauncement of true Religion," 34 and 35 Henry VIII, ch. 1, *Statutes of the Realm*, vol. 3 (1817; reprint London: Dawson of Pall Mall, 1963), 896; Duffy, *Stripping of the Altars*, 433.

142. Thomas More, *A Dialogue Concerning Heresies*, ed. Thomas M. C. Lawler, Germain Marc'hadour, and Richard C. Marius, vol. 6, pts. 1–2 of *The Complete Works of St. Thomas More* (New Haven: Yale University Press, 1981), vol. 6, pt. 1:316.

143. Ibid., vol. 6, pt. 1:317.

144. Margaret Deanesly, *The Lollard Bible and Other Medieval Biblical Versions* (Cambridge: Cambridge University Press, 1920; reprint 1966), 1–17.

145. Luxton hypothesizes that Cook bequeathed his Bibles to parish churches "to spare his family and friends the risk involved in inheriting" them. "Lichfield Court Book," 125.

146. Lich. Ct. Bk., fols. 2r, 17v, 20r; Hudson, *Premature Reformation*, 304; Margaret Aston, "'Caim's Castles': Poverty, Politics and Disendowment," in *The Church, Politics and Patronage in the Fifteenth Century*, ed. Barrie Dobson (Gloucester: Sutton, 1984), 61–62; J. Gilchrist, "The Social Doctrine of John Wycliffe," *Canadian Historical Association Historical Papers* (1969), 164.

147. Dugdale, *Antiquities of Warwickshire*, 109, 117; CPR *1494–1509*, 567; *L&P*, vol. 1, nos. 4345, 5578. Cf. similar interests later among sixteenth-century Catholics in Lyons: Natalie Zemon Davis, "Poor Relief, Humanism, and Heresy," in *Society and Culture in Early Modern France* (Stanford: Stanford University Press, 1975), 17–64.

148. *Coventry Leet Book*, 600. He also referred to it in his will, PRO, PCC Prob. 11/19 (9 Ayloffe), 1518.

149. See Charles Phythian-Adams, "Ceremony and the Citizen: The Communal Year at Coventry, 1450–1550," in *Crisis and Order in English Towns, 1500–1700*, ed. Peter Clark and Paul Slack (London: Routledge and Kegan Paul, 1972), 78–79; Mervyn James, "Ritual, Drama and Social Body in the Late Medieval English Town," *Past and Present* 98 (1983): 4, 21–24; Scarisbrick, *Reformation*, 22–23; Sylvia Thrupp, *The Merchant Class of Medieval London* (Ann Arbor: University of Michigan Press, 1948), esp. 15–16; Hanawalt and McRee, "The Guilds of *Homo Prudens*," 169–71; McRee, "Religious Gilds and Civic Order."

150. *Coventry Leet Book*, 662.

151. *Register of the Holy Trinity Guild*, 1:xviii. See also McRee, "Religious Gilds and Civic Order."

152. As suggested by Hudson, *Premature Reformation*, 132; Luxton, "Lichfield Court Book."

153. See Chapter 5, "Gentlemen in Later Lollardy."

154. *EM*, vol. 1, pt. 1:120–21; vol. 1, pt. 2:53, 64; *L&P*, vol. 4, pt. 2, no. 4029; *Red Paper Book of Colchester*, ed. W. Gurney Benham (Colchester: Essex County Standard Office, 1903), 29, 30–31.

155. See L. R. Poos's remark that "an activist stance towards management of parochial affairs" typified both Lollardy and orthodox lay piety in the late Middle Ages. Poos, *A Rural Society*, 273.

156. See Bryan Wilson, *Religion in Sociological Perspective* (Oxford: Oxford University Press, 1982), 118.

Chapter 3

1. Clive D. Field, "Adam and Eve: Gender in the English Free Church Constituency," *JEH* 44 (1993): 63–79.

2. Granovetter, "The Strength of Weak Ties," 1360–80; "The Strength of Weak Ties: A Network Theory Revisited," 105–30.

3. E.g., Judith M. Bennett, *Women in the Medieval English Countryside: Gender and Household in Brigstock Before the Plague* (New York: Oxford University Press, 1987), 6, 37–38, 136–38; Martha C. Howell, *Women, Production and Patriarchy in Late Medieval Cities* (Chicago: University of Chicago Press, 1986), 90.

4. Linda E. Mitchell, "The Lady Is a Lord: Noble Widows and Land in Thirteenth-Century Britain," *Historical Reflections/Réflexions historiques* 18 (1992): 71–97.

5. See Leonore Davidoff and Catherine Hall, *Family Fortunes: Men and Women of the English Middle Class, 1780–1850* (London: Hutchinson, 1987); Judith M. Bennett, "Public Power and Authority in the Medieval English Countryside," in *Women and Power in the Middle Ages*, ed. Mary Erler and Maryanne Kowaleski (Athens: University of Georgia Press, 1988), 18–36; Diane Willen, "Women in the Public Sphere in Early Modern England: The Case of the Urban Working Poor," *Sixteenth Century Journal* 19 (1988): 559–75; Mitchell, "The Lady Is a Lord."

6. See Hudson, *Premature Reformation*, 180–86; J.W. Martin, "Tudor Popular Religion: The Rise of the Conventicle," in *Religious Radicals in Tudor England* (London: Hambledon, 1989), 13–39.

7. Reg. Warham, fol. 174v. For other examples, see Reg. P. Courtenay, fols. 26r–27r; *A&M*, 4:238; *EM*, vol. 1, pt. 1:116; *L&P*, vol. 4, pt. 2, no. 4029; *HT*, 60, 140, 146, 179.

8. *A&M*, 4:215–16; for other examples, see *EM*, vol. 1, pt. 2:60; Lich. Ct. Bk., fols. 5r, 6r, 11r, 14v, 18v–19r; Reg. Warham, fols. 172r, 173v.

9. Reg. Chedworth, fol. 60r.

10. Ibid., fols. 57v, 59v–60r, 62rv.

11. Reg. Warham, fols. 173rv. Although Baker did not know whose garden it was, it may have belonged to Thomas Church of Great Charte, who also abjured Lollardy. Ibid., fols. 163v–164r.

12. Ibid., fols. 174rv.

13. Ibid., fols. 174v–175r. The public jail for the western division of the county of Kent was in the middle of the town of Maidstone. Edward Hasted, *The History and Topographical Survey of the County of Kent*, 12 vols. (Canterbury: Bristow, 1797–1801; reprint, Wakefield: E.P. Publishing, 1972), 4:265. Other examples of all-male conventicles: Reg. Warham, fols. 169rv, 172rv, 173v, 174v.

14. Reg. Warham, fols. 166r–167r.

15. Ibid., fols. 174v–175r.

16. Ibid., fols. 173rv.

17. Ibid., fols. 173rv.

18. *HT*, 63–64, 66, 68, 85–86, 130–33, 217–19; *A&M*, 3:586, 597. Hawise Mone was cited in William Baxter's, Margery Baxter's, and John Burrell's trials. *HT*, 47, 75–76.

19. At the beginning of many abjurations of those brought before Alnwick's court, the suspects admitted something similar to "Y have be right familier, conversant and homly with many notorie and famous heretikes—that is to say . . . ," followed by a list of names (sometimes one or two, often as many as fifteen). See *HT*, 85–86, 126, 140, 146, 156; quotation at 165.

20. Cited by Hawise Mone and John Skylan. Ibid., 140, 146.

21. See the case of Joan and Thomas Harwode of Rolvenden visiting John and Elizabeth Browne of Ashford. Reg. Warham, fols. 173rv.

22. This aspect of medieval life has been little investigated. See Howell, *Women, Production and Patriarchy*, 156–57. To say that women's unescorted travel was difficult is not, however, to deny that young adults of both sexes often migrated to find work. P. J. P. Goldberg, "Marriage, Migration, Servanthood, and Life-Cycle in Yorkshire Towns of the Later Middle Ages: Some York Cause Paper Evidence," *Continuity and Change* 1 (1986): 141–69.

23. *The Book of Margery Kempe*, ed. S. B. Meech and H. E. Allen, EETS, o.s., 212 (1940); modern translation by B. A. Windeatt (London: Penguin, 1985); passim, especially ch. 26–33, 42–43, 52 (references to Margery Kempe's *Book* will be made by chapter number to facilitate reference to either edition). See also the hardships endured by Dorothy of Montau and her husband on pilgrimage in the late fourteenth century. Richard Kieckhefer, *Unquiet Souls: Fourteenth-Century Saints and Their Religious Milieu* (Chicago: University of Chicago, 1984), 24.

24. Reg. P. Courtenay, fol. 26v.

25. *EM*, vol. 1, pt. 1:115, 116; *L&P* vol. 4, pt. 2, no. 4029.

26. *A&M*, 4:228.

27. Ibid., 222.

28. Ibid., 234.

29. *EWS*, 1:355.

30. *A&M*, 4:224 (my emphasis).

31. Carol Lois Haywood notes that women become authority figures in modern-day spiritualist religious movements only when leadership of the movement is of a nonclerical kind. "The Authority and Empowerment of Women among Spiritualist Groups," *Journal for the Scientific Study of Religion* 22 (1983): 157–66.

32. For authority there must exist "a collectivity or socio-cultural matrix

where the individual's attributes are either institutionalized and/or proved and acknowledged collectively by others in the setting as legitimate." Jackson W. Carroll, "Some Issues in Clergy Authority," *Review of Religious Research* 23 (1981): 99–117, quotation at 100.

33. *L&P*, vol. 4, pt. 2, no. 4254; *EM*, vol. 1, pt. 2:53–54, 60.

34. *Reg. Chichele*, 3:85; 4:297–301; *A&M*, 3:586.

35. Reg. Chedworth, fols. 62rv.

36. TCD, MS 775, fol. 124v; *A&M*, 4:208–40, 582; *L&P*, vol. 4, pt. 2, nos. 4029, 4175, 4545; *EM*, vol. 1, pt. 1:114–32; vol. 1, pt. 2:50–64.

37. This question has been considered in detail by Aston, *Lollards and Reformers*, 49–70; see also Hudson, *Premature Reformation*, 326–27.

38. *HT*, 142; cf. 49, 57, 61, 67, 147.

39. See Aston, *Lollards and Reformers*, 49–70.

40. *HT*, passim, e.g., 108, 115, 119.

41. Suggested by Aston, *Lollards and Reformers*, 60. See also the example of the Czech Andrew of Brod (d. 1427), who opposed Hussite utraquism on the grounds that the priestly office might be diminished to the extent that even women might make claims to administer the sacrament. Miri Rubin, *Corpus Christi: The Eucharist in Late Medieval Culture* (Cambridge: Cambridge University Press, 1991), 35.

42. Aston, *Lollards and Reformers*, 49–51, 62–66.

43. Although William White (a priest) was said to have led the layman John Scutte to perform the sacrament of the eucharist in White's home. *FZ*, 423–24.

44. Lich. Ct. Bk., fols. 5r, 14r–15r, 16rv, 17v, 21r.

45. Ibid., fols. 3v, 5r.

46. *A&M*, 3:591.

47. It should be noted that Foxe's veracity is less reliable when he does not quote directly from a register; his vagueness here may indicate exaggeration.

48. *A&M*, 3:597; *FZ*, 420. See also Netter, *Doctrinale*, vol. 3, cols. 412, 415.

49. *A&M*, 4:208–11, 213–14, 226, 228, 230, 234.

50. Although she may have been the Sabine Manne whom Foxe specified as having abjured. Ibid., 206–7.

51. Ibid., 234.

52. TCD, MS 775, fol. 124v. See also Foxe's version, *A&M*, 4:211.

53. Thomas was said to have taught at Amersham, London, Billericay (Essex), Chelmsford, Stratford Langthorn (Essex), Suffolk and Norfolk, Uxbridge, Burnham, Henley-on-Thames, and Newbury. Only at Amersham was his wife mentioned. Andrew Randal of Rickmansworth and his wife were said to have received him as he fled from prosecution, and William King of Uxbridge also received him; neither mentioned his wife. *A&M*, 4:213, 226, 230.

54. Lich. Ct. Bk., fols. 6v–7r, 8r.

55. Ibid., fols. 7r, 8r.

56. Ibid., fols. 7v, 20r.

57. Brian Stock, *The Implications of Literacy: Written Language and Models of Interpretation in the Eleventh and Twelfth Centuries* (Princeton, N.J.: Princeton University Press, 1983), esp. 3–12, 88–150, 522–23.

58. Ibid., 6–8. See also Franz H. Bäuml, "Varieties and Consequences of

Medieval Literacy and Illiteracy," *Speculum* 55 (1980): 237–65; Scribner, "Oral Culture and the Diffusion of Reformation Ideas," in *Popular Culture*, 49–69.

59. Aston, *Lollards and Reformers*, 206; see also Hudson, *Premature Reformation*, 185–87.

60. E.g., *A&M*, 4:214.

61. See, for instance, on the optimistic side, M. T. Clanchy, *From Memory to Written Record: England 1066–1307* (London: Arnold, 1979), 175–201; Jo Ann Hoeppner Moran, *The Growth of English Schooling, 1340–1548: Learning, Literacy, and Laicization in Pre-Reformation York Diocese* (Princeton, N.J.: Princeton University Press, 1985), 17–20, 177–79; Duffy, *Stripping of the Altars*, 68, 212, 281–82. On the pessimistic side: David Cressy, *Literacy and the Social Order: Reading and Writing in Tudor and Stuart England* (Cambridge: Cambridge University Press, 1980), 128, 144, 158, 177; and Poos, *A Rural Society*, 286–87.

62. See McSheffrey, "Literacy and the Gender Gap."

63. Some attempted to conceal their literacy, as did Juliana Yong of Coventry, who only admitted her literacy when confronted with Robert Silkby's accusation. Lich. Ct. Bk., fols. 3v, 8v, 14r, and Chapter 1, "Sources." John Pert and Richard Fleccher of Norfolk also claimed they could not read, although other evidence indicated that they could. *HT*, 85, 169; *A&M*, 3:596–97. See also John Martin, "Popular Culture and the Shaping of Popular Heresy in Renaissance Venice," in *Inquisition and Society in Early Modern Europe*, ed. Stephen Haliczer (Totawa: Barnes and Noble, 1987), 122.

64. The seven (of 270 women identified in the communities) are: the daughter of Hawise and Thomas Mone of Loddon, Norfolk; Elizabeth Sampson of London; and Thomasina Bradeley, Agnes Jonson, Alice Rowley, Juliana Yong, and the wife of Villers, all of Coventry. *A&M*, 3:597; TCD, MS 775, fol. 122v; Lich. Ct. Bk., fols. 2r, 3v, 7r, 8rv, 11rv, 14rv, 21r. Two other women, Andrew Randall's wife of Rickmansworth and Thomas Spencer's wife of London, may also have been literate, although the evidence is ambiguous. *A&M*, 4:226, 233.

65. Overall, 113 men in the communities studied here were positively identified as able to read, a literacy rate of about 17 percent (113 of 684). When members of the clergy not explicitly described as reading are added, the rate climbs to 19 percent (130 of 684). See Appendix. These numbers do not include ambiguous implications of literacy to large groups; for instance, Roger Dodds noted that Thomas Baker, Robert Livord, John Sympson, Thomas Reiley, John Clemson, James Edmunds, William Gun, and John Harris used to gather together to read (*A&M*, 4:237). The only man in this group who is described elsewhere as literate is Roger Dodds himself. All may have been literate, or none but Dodds; for the sake of this calculation, the latter is assumed in order not to unduly inflate male literacy figures.

66. See McSheffrey, "Literacy and the Gender Gap."

67. Cross, "Great Reasoners," 370–71.

68. *Plumpton Correspondence*, ed. T. Stapleton, Camden Society, 4 (1839), 8; Nicholas Orme, *English Schools in the Middle Ages* (London: Methuen, 1973), 55.

69. BL, Harl. MS 421, fols. 22v–23r.

70. TCD, MS 775, fol. 122v. Other examples: *A&M*, 4:222, 224–25, 227, 229, 238.

71. *A&M*, 4:222.

72. Ibid., 238 (my emphasis).

73. TCD, MS 775, fol. 124r.

74. *A&M*, 5:42–43.

75. *EM*, vol. 1, pt. 1:126; vol. 1, pt. 2:53; Lich. Ct. Bk., fols. 14v, 25v; see also *L&P* vol. 4, pt. 2, no. 4175.

76. *A&M*, 4:228.

77. Mary Potter, "Gender Equality and Gender Hierarchy in Calvin's Theology," *Signs* 11 (1986): 725–39; Wiesner, "Women's Response," 153; Allison P. Coudert, "The Myth of the Improved Status of Protestant Women: The Case of the Witchcraze," in *The Politics of Gender in Early Modern Europe*, ed. Jean R. Brink, Allison P. Coudert, and Maryanne C. Horowitz, Sixteenth Century Essays and Studies, 12 (Kirksville, Mo.: Sixteenth Century Journal, 1989), 75–76; D. Colin Dews, "Ann Carr and the Female Revivalists of Leeds," in *Religion in the Lives of English Women, 1760–1930*, ed. Gail Malmgreen (London: Croom Helm, 1986), 68–87; Crawford, *Women and Religion*, 140; Wilson, *Religion in Sociological Perspective*, 105–6.

78. Priscilla J. Brewer, "'Tho' of the Weaker Sex': A Reassessment of Gender Equality among the Shakers," *Signs* 17 (1992): 609–35.

79. *HT*, 140, 176, 179; *A&M*, 3:596–97.

80. Apparently, Lollards often wore russet gowns, which were the simplest and least expensive of garments; see Hudson, *Premature Reformation*, 145.

81. *HT*, 75–76; other examples of fast-breaking in East Anglia: ibid., 49–51, 104–5.

82. *EM*, vol. 1, pt. 1:121; *L&P*, vol. 4, pt. 2, no. 4029. It is unclear whether Pykas actually taught in all these women's homes; although he includes Katherine Swayn in his list, he also later said that he did not know anything about her except that she was reputed to be a "known woman." *EM*, vol. 1, pt. 1:129; *L&P*, vol. 4, pt. 2, no. 4175.

83. *L&P*, vol. 4, pt. 2, no. 4545.

84. *EM*, vol. 1, pt. 1:133; *L&P*, vol. 4, pt. 2, no. 4545; Philip Morant, *The History and Antiquities of the County of Essex, Compiled from the Best and Most Ancient Historians* (London: Osborne, 1768; reprint, Chelmsford: Meggy and Chalk, 1816), 2:348. See also Chapter 5, n.24. Other examples of women hosting conventicles include: Reg. J. Blythe, fols. 70r, 71r, 72r; Reg. Audley, fol. 156r.

85. See BL, Harl. MS 421, fols. 11r–35v; *EM*, vol. 1, pt. 1:114, 118–31; vol. 1, pt. 2:50, 56, 59–61; *L&P*, vol. 4, pt. 2, nos. 4029, 4175, 4218, 4242, 4254, 4545.

86. A Lollard named Thomas Vincent (the father of Joan Austy) was active in the London area around 1511. (See *A&M*, 4:175–76; *EM*, vol. 1, pt. 1:115; *L&P*, vol. 4, pt. 2, no. 4029; TCD MS 775, fol. 123r.) It is possible that Joan Girling's previous husband, John Vincent, was related in some way to this Lollard family.

87. BL, Harl. MS 421, fol. 30v; *EM*, vol. 1, pt. 1:118–20, 126–31; *L&P*, vol. 4, pt. 2, nos. 4029, 4175.

88. This possibility has been suggested by Aston, *Lollards and Reformers*, 50; and Cross, "'Great Reasoners,'" 379.

89. Of 294 Lollards appearing before ecclesiastical courts (in communities for

which registers or court books survive), 67, or 23 percent, were women. In these same communities, 411 people were implicated altogether (either appearing in court or named in depositions); of these, 98, or 24 percent, were women. See references in the Appendix.

90. Cited by Hawise Mone and John Skylan. *HT*, 140, 146.

91. Ibid., 33, 60, 73–74, 79, 81, 85–86, 93–94, 140–41, 146, 165, 176; *A&M*, 3:596–97.

92. The literature on this subject is considerable. See, most recently, Bennett, "Medieval Women, Modern Women," 151–62; P. J. P. Goldberg, *Women, Work and Life Cycle in a Medieval Economy: Women in York and Yorkshire, c. 1300–1520* (Oxford: Clarendon, 1992); David Herlihy, *Opera Muliebria: Women and Work in Medieval Europe* (New York: McGraw-Hill, 1990), esp. xi, 154–90. Some historians (Herlihy and Goldberg, for instance) have linked economic downturn with even greater restriction on women's labor and social lives; at least two cities examined here, Colchester and Coventry, were in particularly serious economic decline during the first quarter of the sixteenth century, a period central to this study. See R. H. Britnell, *Growth and Decline in Colchester, 1300–1525* (Cambridge: Cambridge University Press, 1986), 2–3, 193–205, 262–68; and Phythian-Adams, *Desolation*, esp. 37–38, 45–60.

93. Bennett, *Women in the Medieval English Countryside*, 6, 36–42, 129–41; Howell, *Women, Production, and Patriarchy*, 90.

94. Mitchell, "The Lady Is a Lord."

95. See Gowing, "Women, Sex and Honour," 70–88, regarding women's speech and chastity around 1600.

96. See *Memoriale presbiterorum*, a fourteenth-century English pastoral text, cited in P. P. A. Biller, "Marriage Patterns and Women's Lives: A Sketch of a Pastoral Geography," *Woman Is a Worthy Wight: Women in English Society, c. 1200–1500*, ed. P.J.P. Goldberg (Gloucester: Sutton, 1992), 66, 99.

97. *Coventry Leet Book*, 544–45, 568. See also Ben R. McRee, "Religious Gilds and Regulation of Behavior in Late Medieval Towns," in *People, Politics and Community in the Later Middle Ages*, ed. Joel T. Rosenthal and Colin Richmond (New York: St. Martin, 1987), 108–22; Margaret L. King, *Women of the Renaissance* (Chicago: University of Chicago Press, 1991), 29–30; Guido Ruggiero, " 'Più che la vita caro': Onore, matrimonio e reputazione femminile nel tardo Rinascimento," *Quaderni Storici*, n.s., 66 (1987): 753–75.

98. "Mulier, quamvis docta et sancta, viros in conventu docere non presumat." Gratian, *Decretum*, D.23 c.29, vol. 1 of *Corpus iuris canonici*, 2 vols., ed. Aemilius Friedberg (Leipzig: Tauchnitz, 1879–81), 1, col. 86. He goes on to exclude laymen as well. See also Jacques Dalarun, "The Clerical Gaze," in *Silences of the Middle Ages*, vol. 2 of *A History of Women in the West*, ed. Christiane Klapisch-Zuber (Cambridge, Mass.: Belknap Press of Harvard University Press, 1992), 40–41.

99. "Mulieri non permittitur publice docere in ecclesia, permittitur autem ei privatim aliquos domestica admonitione instruere." Thomas Aquinas, *Summa theologiae*, 5 vols. (Ottawa: Collège Dominicain d'Ottawa, 1941), vol. 3, quest. 55, art. 1; see also vol. 2, pt. 2, quest. 177, art. 2. Joan Ferrante, "The Education of Women in the Middle Ages in Theory, Fact, and Fantasy," in *Beyond Their Sex: Learned Women of the European Past*, ed. Patricia H. Labalme (New York: New York Univer-

sity Press, 1980), 12; Herlihy, *Opera Muliebria*, 118; Kari Elisabeth Børresen, *Subordination and Equivalence: The Nature and Role of Woman in Augustine and Thomas Aquinas*, trans. Charles H. Talbot (Washington, D.C.: University Press of America, 1981), 239.

100. Crawford, *Women and Religion*, 135, 143–47.

101. Mary Elizabeth Perry, "Beatas and the Inquisition in Early Modern Seville," in *Inquisition and Society in Early Modern Europe*, ed. Stephen Haliczer (Totowa, N.J.: Barnes and Noble, 1987), 148, 154, 157; Mack, "Women as Prophets," 19–47, esp. 27–28.

102. Wiesner, "Women's Response," 160–70.

103. "Margeria dixit, 'vide,' et tunc extendebat brachia sua in longum, dicens isti iurate, 'hec est vera crux Christi, et istam crucem tu debes et potes videre et adorare omni die hic in domo tua propria, et adeo tu in vanum laboras quando vadis ad ecclesias ad adorandas sive orandas aliquas ymagines vel cruces mortuas.'" *HT*, 44.

104. "Legem Christi." Ibid., 47.

105. "Dixit quod maritus suus est optimus doctor Christianitatis." Ibid., 48.

106. *A&M*, 4:232. Joan Collingborne may be the same as the J. Collingworth who hosted Lollard gatherings. Ibid., 224.

107. Ibid., 229; see also 225.

108. Ibid., 227–28. Hudson interprets this to mean that Alice Harding functioned equally with men in Lollard schools. *Premature Reformation*, 183.

109. *A&M*, 4:238.

110. Ibid., 235, 239.

111. Ibid., 582.

112. Ibid., 206.

113. Reg. Audley, fol. 162v.

114. *A&M*, 4:224–25; Reg. Fox, 4, fol. 18r.

115. *A&M*, 4:231.

116. *HT*, 74–75.

117. *EM*, vol. 1, pt. 1:130–31; *L&P*, vol. 4, pt. 2, no. 4175.

118. *A&M*, 4:224.

119. Ibid., 233.

120. TCD, MS 775, fol. 124v.

121. Reg. Warham, fols. 169v–170v.

122. Ibid., fol. 172v.

123. *A&M*, 4:214, 222–23, 225–26, 228–29.

124. Ibid., 222, 225, 227–28; Reg. Fox, 4, fols. 18rv.

125. *EM*, vol. 1, pt. 1:114–17; *L&P*, vol. 4, pt. 2, no. 4029.

126. *EM*, vol. 1, pt. 1:121–23, 126–29; *L&P*, vol. 4, pt. 2, nos. 4029, 4175.

127. See Hudson, *Premature Reformation*, 166–68, 200–225.

128. See, for discussion of similar points, French, "Local Identity and the Late Medieval Parish," 24–27.

129. Reg. J. Blythe, fol. 74v.

130. These works are discussed in Duffy, *Stripping of the Altars*, 68–87, 210–98.

131. The association of the vernacular with heresy is discussed by Hudson, *Lollards and Their Books*, 141–63.

132. *A&M*, 4:582; Duffy, *Stripping of the Altars*, 79.

133. Lich. Ct. Bk., fols. 19v, 21r; Thomson, *Later Lollards*, 113; *A&M*, 4:230, 236. Duffy discusses primers at length, *Stripping of the Altars*, 207–98. It is noteworthy that printed primers before 1530 were in Latin; English primers were not produced after the middle of the fifteenth century due to their association with Lollardy. Ibid., 213. Rowley's primer was probably either copied for Lollard use or dated from the early fifteenth century.

134. *A&M*, 4:582. Cf. Martin, "Popular Culture," 122.

135. Lich. Ct. Bk., fol. 21r.

136. Ibid., fols. 4r, 6v.

137. TCD, MS 775, fol. 123v. Note that Thomas Walker testified (fols. 123v–124r) that Benet could indeed read. This may be a matter of proficiency: Benet's reading ability may not have been sufficient to understand this book.

138. *EM*, vol. 1, pt. 1:116; *L&P*, vol. 4, pt. 2, no. 4029; *A&M*, 4:228.

139. *A&M*, 4:230.

140. Ibid., 231.

141. Lich. Ct. Bk., fols. 4r, 5v, 11v.

142. TCD, MS 775, fol. 124v.

143. *EM*, vol. 1, pt. 1:121; *L&P*, vol. 4, pt. 2, no. 4029.

144. TCD, MS 775, fols. 122v–123r.

145. *A&M*, 4:234–36, 238.

146. *HT*, 47–48.

147. Hudson, *Premature Reformation*, 190–92.

148. Susan Brigden, "Religion and Social Obligation in Early Sixteenth-Century London," *Past and Present* 103 (1984): 82.

149. *The Book of Margery Kempe*, ch. 12–13, 46, 52–55.

150. Reg. Audley, fol. 155v.

151. See, for instance, *HT*, 78; Reg. G. Blyth, fols. 98r–100r; Reg. Chedworth, fol. 14r; Salisbury Reg. Langton, 2, fols. 5rv, 35v, 37r–38r; Reg. J. Blythe, fols. 71rv; Hudson, *Premature Reformation*, 164. These penances were similar to those handed out for other grave or public offences against the community, such as adultery or fornication (see, for instance, Reg. Morton, 2, fols. 75r, 78v), except for the faggot, which had special symbolism for heresy.

152. For instance, *Chronicle of London*, 226; *Great Chronicle of London*, 290; *A&M*, 4:123–24, 180, 208–9, 215–16; *An Episcopal Court Book for the Diocese of Lincoln, 1514–1520*, ed. Margaret Bowker, Lincoln Record Society, 61 (1967), 15–16.

153. *Chronicle of London*, 226; *Great Chronicle of London*, 290; Lich. Ct. Bk., fol. 16r; Reg. Fox, 2, fol. 87v; *A&M*, 4:123–24.

154. *L&P*, vol. 4, pt. 2, no. 4038. Two other men, at the urging of their employers, left off their badges without the court's permission. James Brewster was hired by the comptroller of the earl of Oxford, who "would not suffer him, working there, to wear that counterfeit cognizance any longer." William Sweeting gained the position of holy-water clerk in a Colchester parish two years after abjuration; the parson of the parish "plucked" the badge from his sleeve. *A&M*, 4:180, 215–16 (note that Foxe calls James Brewster both John and James).

155. See *HT*; Norman P. Tanner, *The Church in Late Medieval Norwich 1370–1532*

(Toronto: Pontifical Institute of Mediaeval Studies, 1984); and Gilchrist and Oliva, *Religious Women*, 73–75. But compare the attitude of Tenterden parishioners, who, when their parish was visited in September and October 1511, complained that two women who had been named as heretics had not been examined along with the others, and that another woman who had been a notorious heretic was buried in consecrated ground. *Kentish Visitations of Archbishop William Warham and His Deputies, 1511–12*, ed. K. L. Wood-Legh, Kent Records, 24 (1984), 207–10.

156. Thomson, *Later Lollards*, 223–26; Aston, *Lollards and Reformers*, 76–81.

157. Fines, "Heresy Trials," 160.

158. Forty-six certainly lived there and seventy-nine people whose place of residence was not recorded had strong connections there. (See Appendix.) Plumb, "Social and Economic Spread," estimates that 25 percent of the population of Amersham was Lollard (although this assumes an equal sex ratio among Lollards).

159. See the case of Alice Saunders and Thomas Houre. *A&M*, 4:231.

160. *L&P*, vol. 4, pt. 2, nos. 4254, 4545; *EM*, vol. 1, pt. 2:50–53, 60–62.

161. *L&P*, vol. 4, pt. 2, no. 4254; *EM*, vol. 1, pt. 2:60; see also *EM*, vol. 1, pt. 2:53–54.

162. See Annette P. Hampshire and James A. Beckford, "Religious Sects and the Concept of Deviance: The Mormons and the Moonies," *British Journal of Sociology* 34 (1983): 208–29, esp. 224–25.

163. *HT*, 41–51.

164. *A&M*, 4:227.

165. William Grant, vicar of Helions Bumpstead (near Steeple Bumpstead), was censured in the manor court of Helions Bumpstead in 1506 for frequenting the house of Joan Wolwarde and for keeping 10d. of the goods of John Hemsted in Joan's house. According to a will, Grant was still curate of Helions Bumpstead in 1533; his continued tenure of the position may have been a source of frustration and hostility for the Hemsteds. ERO, D/DB M2, Manor court roll for Helions Bumpstead; D/ABW 13/4; T/G 107, Index of Clergy.

166. *A&M*, 4:231, 242.

167. See Rodney Stark and William Sims Bainbridge, "Networks of Faith: Interpersonal Bonds and Recruitment to Cults and Sects," *American Journal of Sociology* 85 (1980): 1376–95; David A. Snow, Louis A. Zurcher, and Sheldon Ekland-Olson, "Social Networks and Social Movements: A Microstructural Approach to Differential Recruitment," *American Sociological Review* 45 (1980): 787–801.

168. " . . . diversis vicinis suis." *HT*, 73.

169. Ibid., 41–51.

170. *A&M*, 3:585.

171. Michael M. Sheehan, *The Will in Medieval England from the Conversion of the Anglo-Saxons to the End of the Thirteenth Century* (Toronto: Pontifical Institute of Mediaeval Studies, 1963), 178–85; Michael L. Zell, "Fifteenth- and Sixteenth-Century Wills as Historical Sources," *Archives* 14 (1979): 67–68.

172. Bowker, *Episcopal Court Book*, 139; *The Courts of the Archdeaconry of Buckingham, 1483–1523*, ed. E. M. Elvey, Buckinghamshire Record Society, 19 (1975), 289; *A&M*, 4:220–21.

173. BRO, D/A/We/2/52, Will of Katherine Bartlett of Amersham, 1525; PRO, PCC Prob. 11/29 (F.29 Spert), Will of Alice Saunders of Amersham, 1539.

174. BRO, D/A/We/2, fols. 5v–6r, Inventory of Goods of John and Florence Hill, 1524; *A&M*, 4:220–21.

175. BRO, D/A/We/2/5, Will of John Hill of Amersham, 1523; and D/A/We/2/6, Will of Florence Hill of Amersham, 1523; BRO, D/A/We/2/107, Will of Robert Flemmyng of Amersham, 1526. There is no sign that Fleming sympathized with the Lollard community in his parish.

176. PRO, PCC Prob. 11/21 (F.28 Bodfelde), Will of Richard Saunders of Amersham, 1524; PRO, PCC Prob. 11/29 (F.29 Spert), Will of Alice Saunders of Amersham, 1543; BRO, D/A/We/4/186, Will of Roger Bennett of Amersham, 1544. Godparents, as a rule, gave their names to godchildren. Michael Bennett, "Spiritual Kinship and the Baptismal Name in Traditional European Society," in *Principalities, Powers and Estates: Studies in Medieval and Early Modern Government and Society*, ed. L.O. Frappell (Adelaide: Adelaide University Union Press, 1979), 1–13; Philip Niles, "Baptism and the Naming of Children in Late Medieval England," *Medieval Prosopography* 3 (1982): 95–108; Louis Haas, "Social Connections Between Parents and Godparents in Late Medieval Yorkshire," *Medieval Prosopography* 10 (1989): 1–21.

177. PRO, PCC Prob. 11/21 (F.34 Bodfelde), Will of John Denby Sr. of Colchester, 1525. The charges against Widow Denby were dismissed in default of proof. *L&P*, vol. 4, pt. 2, no. 4545.

178. ERO, D/ABW 25/35, Will of Thomas Mathew of Colchester, 1534.

179. ERO, D/ACR 4/70, Will of Alice Garner of Colchester, 1539.

180. Thomson, *Later Lollards*, passim; Hudson, *Premature Reformation*, 456–83.

181. See the debate on the so-called "Christian Brethren" in E. G. Rupp, *Studies in the Making of the English Protestant Tradition* (Cambridge: Cambridge University Press, 1947), 6–14; John F. Davis, "Lollardy and the Reformation in England," *Archiv für Reformationsgeschichte* 73 (1982): 227–32; A. G. Dickens, *The English Reformation* (London: Batsford, 1964), 28–29, 70–71; Hudson, *Premature Reformation*, 482–83; Davies, "Lollardy and Locality," 200.

182. *Reg. Chichele*, 3:85; 4:297–301; *FZ*, 417–32; Aston, *Lollards and Reformers*, 71–100.

183. See *A&M*, 4:205, 207, 213–14; *EM*, vol. 1, pt. 2:56; TCD, MS 775, fols. 123r–124r.

184. Lich. Ct. Bk., fols. 2rv, 14v, 16rv.

185. The 1538 will of Nicholas Durdant of Staines, Middlesex, indicates that by his death he had probably become a Protestant — his prologue commends his soul to God "trusting undoubtedly that by the merites of his onlie sonne Jhesus Criste to be one of his electe," and his bequests do not include any offerings for his soul — but some of his closest associations were still with men who had also been implicated in Lollardy in the early 1520s. William Grinder was to act as supervisor, and Henry Hobbes and Thomas Holmes witnessed the will. PRO, PCC Prob. 11/27 (F.22 Dyngeley), Will of Nicholas Durdaunt of Staines, 1538. The Thomas

Holmes who acted as witness may not be the same as the one implicated in the early 1520s, since Foxe says he was condemned as a relapsed heretic at that time. Foxe seems doubtful, however, that he was actually executed: he notes that his name appears in the register with others who were relapsed, and that "most likely he was also adjudged and executed with the others." *A&M*, 4:245. Holmes probably knew Henry Hobbes — he detected "Hobs, with his sons, of Hichenden." Ibid., 226. The 1541 will of Christopher Ravin of Witham, Essex, was similar; two old Lollard friends (John Chapman and Lawrence Swaffer or Swarther) witnessed the will and received legacies. ERO, D/ACR 4/185, Will of Christopher Ravin of Witham, 1541. Chapman had been his servant in 1528. Swaffer, who shared Ravin's occupation of tailor, had lived in Shoreditch in the 1520s and was active in London and Essex Lollard activities. *EM*, vol. 1, pt. 1:114, 116; *L&P*, vol. 4, pt. 2, no. 4029.

186. Reg. Warham, fols. 173rv.

187. *EM*, vol. 1, pt. 2:53–54.

188. *EM*, vol. 1, pt. 2:54–55; *L&P*, vol. 4, pt. 2, no. 4850.

189. TCD, MS 775, fol. 124v; *A&M*, 4:208–14, 234.

190. *EM*, vol. 1, pt. 1:114–26, 132; vol. 1, pt. 2:52, 64; *L&P*, vol. 4, pt. 2, no. 4029; *A&M*, 4:226, 234, 236–37, 239–40, 242, 582.

191. *A&M*, 4:681.

192. He was with her on this or another trip to Yarmouth. *HT*, 48.

193. Ibid., 41.

194. Ibid., 39, 86, 140, 179; *A&M*, 3:596–97.

195. Lich. Ct. Bk., fol. 16r; Reg. G. Blyth, fol. 100r.

196. J. F. Davis, "Joan of Kent," 227–29.

197. Reg. Warham, fol. 172r.

198. Richard Belward of Earsham was accused in 1424 of keeping a Lollard school in Ditchingham for which "a certain parchment-maker" (probably Godesell) brought Lollard books from London. *A&M*, 3:585–86.

199. Ibid., 597.

200. Loddon: *HT*, 163, 168, 175, 189, 217; Martham: ibid., 71, 195, *A&M*, 3:596–97; Beccles: *HT*, 107, 119, 133.

201. J. F. Davis has suggested that Lollards made connections with one another through a particular kind of occupation, the cloth trade. Textile workers, he argues, were characterized by mobility, and he proposes that Lollardy spread from one region to another through these workers. In some cases, Davis stretches the evidence: he posits, for instance, that William White fled from Tenterden in the 1420s to Norfolk because of trade connections in the cloth industry. However, none of the Lollards in East Anglia were directly involved in the production of cloth (although several were tailors), and White himself had no known connection to the cloth business. The one case Davis cites as a link between the cloth industries in these two areas is by no means clear. He assumes that William Everden of Kent and later of Norfolk was a tailor because Foxe said that he lived and "wrought" with a man named William Taylor for one month. Fifteenth-century surnames cannot be assumed to identify a person's trade, and the verb form "wrought" (a past tense of "to work") was used by Foxe in the same passage in the sense of working as a wright or

carpenter. In any case, tailors cannot be put in the same category as migratory cloth production workers. J. F. Davis, "Lollard Survival," 191–201; *A&M*, 3:596–97; *Oxford English Dictionary*, 2nd ed., 20 vols. (Oxford: Clarendon Press, 1989), s.v. "wright" and "wrought." See also A. P. Evans, "Social Aspects of Medieval Heresy," in *Persecution and Liberty: Essays in Honor of George Lincoln Burr* (New York: Century, 1931), 93–116. Poos notes that laborers were, at least in late medieval Essex, more mobile than craftsmen and retailers. Poos, *A Rural Society*, 280–81.

202. Master Robert Bert of Bury St. Edmunds, chaplain (*HT*, 99–102); William Caleys, chaplain (*HT*, 140, 146, 152–53, 165; Amundesham, *Annales*, 1:151); Robert Cavell, parish chaplain of Bungay (*HT*, 93–96, 105); John Cupper, vicar of Tunstall (*HT*, 39, 70); John Midelton, vicar of Halvergate (*HT*, 38–39); Thomas Pert, chaplain (*HT*, 64, 140, 146, 165, 195; *A&M*, 3:586–87); Hugh Pye, chaplain of Loddon (*A&M*, 3:586, 596–97; *HT*, 33, 60, 66, 81, 85, 93, 126, 134, 140, 165; Amundesham, *Annales*, 1:29; *Records of the City of Norwich*, 2:66); William White (*A&M*, 3:591, 596–97; *Reg. Chichele*, 3:85; 4:297–301; *FZ*, 417–32; Amundesham, *Annales*, 1:29; *Records of the City of Norwich*, 2:66).

203. See *HT*, passim.

204. See Hudson, *Premature Reformation*, 449–50, 467.

205. Lich. Ct. Bk., fols. 8v, 24r (quotation at 24r); Fines, "Heresy Trials," 172. Stoney Stanton, as Thomson notices, lies on the road between Coventry and Leicester and could conceivably have served as a resting place between the two centers. Thomson, *Later Lollards*, 115.

206. Lich. Ct. Bk., fol. 8v.

207. Ibid., fols. 2r, 7r; A. B. Emden, *Biographical Register of the University of Cambridge to 1500* (Cambridge: Cambridge University Press, 1963), 6.

208. Lich. Ct. Bk., fol. 7r.

209. *EM*, vol. 1, pt. 2:52–53.

210. Ibid., 61. Churchwardens were probably usually chosen (exactly how is not clear) by their fellow lay parishioners. Charles Drew, *Early Parochial Organisation in England: The Origins of the Office of Churchwarden* (London: St. Anthony, 1954), 24–25; French, "Local Identity and the Late Medieval Parish," 42–79. Sylvia L. Thrupp notes that in London churchwardens were elected in a parish meeting every year or two, chosen from the "more sufficient" citizens. Thrupp, *Merchant Class*, 25; see also Richard Wunderli, *London Church Courts and Society on the Eve of the Reformation* (Cambridge, Mass.: Medieval Academy of America, 1981), 29.

211. Only one anecdote describes Fox instructing a woman: when at the house of Johnson of Boxted, Fox read from "Wycliffe's Wicket," Johnson's wife being present and "sometyme gyving hering to yt." Either Johnson or his wife, as John Tyball remembers, then asked Fox a question about the Trinity, but Tyball did not remember Fox's answer. *EM*, vol. 1, pt. 2:53–54. Among a list of persons known to have been taught by Fox, John Tyball, and others, three women (Joan Bocher, widow; the wife of George Preston; and Joan Hemsted, wife of Thomas Hemsted) were named, but no details are known about their relationship with Fox. Three Augustinian friars, probably from the Austin friary in nearby Clare, Suffolk (the source that names their house ambiguously calls them "fratres Augustinensis de

Clara London'" [ibid., 62]), also taught in the Steeple Bumpstead Lollard community, but there is no direct evidence of their contact with women in the group. Ibid.,
60, 62.

212. Alice Gardiner, his godmother; Elene Tyball, his mother; and Alice Tyball, his wife. Ibid., 54–56.

Chapter 4

1. For literature on family, see Michael M. Sheehan and Jacqueline Murray,
Domestic Society in Medieval Europe: A Select Bibliography (Toronto: Pontifical In-
stitute of Mediaeval Studies, 1990; updated electronic version forthcoming). On
peasant families in England, see Bennett, *Women in the Medieval English Countryside*;
Barbara A. Hanawalt, *The Ties That Bound: Peasant Families in Medieval England*
(New York: Oxford University Press, 1986). On gentle and noble families of the fifteenth century, see Joel T. Rosenthal, *Patriarchy and Families of Privilege in Fifteenth-
Century England* (Philadelphia: University of Pennsylvania Press, 1991). On English urban families, see Nancy Lee Adamson, "Urban Families: The Social Context
of the London Elite, 1500–1603" (Ph.D. diss., University of Toronto, 1983); Maryanne Kowaleski, "The History of Urban Families in Medieval England," *Journal of
Medieval History* 14 (1988): 47–64.

2. Koch, *Frauenfrage*, followed by Shahar, *The Fourth Estate*, 267; Abels and
Harrison, "The Participation of Women"; Mundy, "Le mariage et les femmes";
Mundy, *Men and Women at Toulouse in the Age of the Cathars* (Toronto: Pontifical
Institute of Mediaeval Studies, 1990), 43–44; Emmanuel Le Roy Ladurie, *Mon-
taillou: The Promised Land of Error*, trans. Barbara Bray (New York: Vintage, 1979),
24–30; Lambert, *Medieval Heresy*, 112–13.

3. Monter, "Protestant Wives," 207; Wiesner, "Women's Response," 151–52;
Wiesner, "Beyond Women and the Family"; Miriam Usher Chrisman, "Women and
the Reformation in Strasbourg, 1490–1530," *Archiv für Reformationsgeschichte* 63
(1972): 143–68; N. Z. Davis, *Society and Culture*, 88–89; Sherrin Marshall [Wynt-
jes], "Women in the Reformation Era," in *Becoming Visible: Women in European
History*, 1st ed., ed. Renate Bridenthal and Claudia Koonz (New York: Houghton
Mifflin, 1977), 186; Merry E. Wiesner, "Luther and Women: The Death of Two
Marys," in *Disciplines of Faith: Religion, Patriachy and Politics*, ed. James Obelkevich,
Raphael Samuel, and Lyndal Roper, 295–308; Amanda Porterfield, "Women's At-
traction to Puritanism," *Church History* 60 (1991): 196–209, esp. 205–6; the essays
in Marshall, ed., *Women in Reformation and Counter-Reformation Europe*; Crawford,
Women and Religion, 38–52.

4. Aston, *Lollards and Reformers*, 203; Fines, "Heresy Trials in Coventry,"
165; Hudson, *Premature Reformation*, 134–37.

5. "Patriarchal" and "patriarchy" are used here in the sense that the model of
the father-ruled household was considered ideal and that this ideal extended out of
the family into society as a whole, so that men, rather than women, and particularly
older men, were seen as the natural rulers. Patriarchy within late medieval elite

families is discussed in Rosenthal, *Patriarchy and Families of Privilege*, 14–19 and passim; see Roper, *Oedipus and the Devil*, 37–52, 55–56 for the Reformation era. Gerda Lerner, *The Creation of Patriarchy* (New York: Oxford University Press, 1988), 238–39, defines patriarchy in a more universal sense, but here the emphasis is on its historical specificity in late medieval England rather than its universality.

6. Cross, "Great Reasoners," 360.

7. Lollards' attitudes to never-married women (that is, lifelong spinsters rather than young women who might yet marry) are not clear, but there are no Lollard women who can be positively identified as such. Protestants generally viewed unmarried women with disfavor and sometimes even antagonism. Luther thought that women who chose not to marry were unnaturally suppressing their sexual urges and were implicitly challenging the divine order by which a wife came under the protection and authority of her husband. Roper, *Oedipus and the Devil*, 42; Wiesner, "Luther and Women," 299–303; Wiesner, "Women's Response," 151; Crawford, *Women and Religion*, 47.

8. Some Lollards (and others whose adherence to mainstream Lollardy is doubtful) held unusual views on marriage, which are not taken into account here precisely because of their eccentricity. Early Lollards William Ramsbury and John Becket, for instance, advocated free love. See the edited process against William Ramsbury in Hudson, *Lollards and Their Books*, 120–23, and the articles charged against John Becket in Kightly, "Early Lollards," 366–67. Another heretic and possible Lollard, William Colyn of South Creake, Norfolk, was brought before Bishop Alnwick of Norwich in 1429 and 1430. He believed, among other things, that women should be held in common. Colyn cannot be linked to the Lollard group that centered itself around Loddon, and there is some doubt that his beliefs derived from Lollardy at all. See *HT*, 91; Aston, *Lollards and Reformers*, 88; Keith Thomas, *Religion and the Decline of Magic* (London: Weidenfeld and Nicholson, 1971), 168. Later Lollard suspects also held eccentric beliefs about marriage and male-female relationships; see Reg. Fitzjames, fols. 26r–27r; *A&M*, 4:240. Despite the views of Colyn, Ramsbury, and Becket, it is worth noting that although continental heretics were assumed to be sexual deviants (see Vern L. Bullough, "Postscript: Heresy, Witchcraft, and Sexuality," in *Sexual Practices and the Medieval Church*, ed. Vern L. Bullough and James Brundage [Buffalo: Prometheus, 1982], 206–10), Lollards were rarely accused of this.

9. John Wyclif, *Trialogus*, ed. Gotthard Lechler (Oxford: Clarendon, 1869), 315–25; *Opus evangelicum*, 2 vols., ed. Johann Loserth (London: Wyclif Society, 1895), vol. 1, 169, 171; vol. 2, 40, 42; *Opera minora*, ed. Johann Loserth (London: Wyclif Society, 1913; reprint, New York: Johnson Reprint Co., 1966), 191; *De officio pastorali*, ed. Gotthard Lechler (Leipzig: Edelmann, 1863), 11, 46.

10. Anne Hudson, ed., *Selections from English Wycliffite Writings* (Cambridge: Cambridge University Press, 1978), 24–29; Roger Dymmok, *Liber contra XII errores et hereses Lollardorum*, ed. H. S. Cronin (London: Wyclif Society, 1922). Sir John Oldcastle and his followers advocated clerical marriage, but whether as a remedy or as a positive good is not clear. Henry Hargreaves, "Sir John Oldcastle and Wycliffite Views on Clerical Marriage," *Medium Aevum* 42 (1973): 141–46.

11. *EWS*, 1:317, see also 360. In other passages, the sermons endorse virginity and celibacy. Ibid., 3:184; for Mary's virginity spoken of approvingly, see also 1:390–91, 445; 2:200–201, 210, 248, 256–58.

12. *HT*, 166.

13. *EWS*, 3:317.

14. Thomas Netter, *Doctrinale antiquitatum fidei Catholicae Ecclesiae*, 3 vols., ed. F. Bonaventura Blanciotti (Venice: Antonio Bassanesi, 1759), vol. 3, cols. 412, 415–20; *FZ*, 420–21, 426; *Reg. Chichele*, 4:298; *HT*, 195.

15. Salisbury Reg. Langton, 2, fol. 35r.

16. "Ex antiquo tempore." Reg. P. Courtenay, fol. 26r.

17. *EM*, vol. 1, pt. 2:51. See also the case of John Symonds of Great Marlow in 1530 (who had Lutheran as well as Lollard contacts). *A&M*, 4:584.

18. Wyclif, *Trialogus*, 322–23; see also Hudson, *Lollards and Their Books*, 121.

19. James A. Brundage, *Law, Sex, and Christian Society in Medieval Europe* (Chicago: University of Chicago Press, 1987), 239, 276, 336, 361–64, 415, 441–43, 500; Charles Donahue Jr., "The Canon Law on the Formation of Marriage and Social Practice in the Later Middle Ages," *Journal of Family History* 8 (1983): 144–58.

20. Reg. Audley, fol. 160r.

21. "Item quod solus consensus inter virum et mulierem facit matrimoniam, et quod sufficit absque aliqua alia solempnitate, ad effectum quod tanquam vir et uxor cohabitare possint. Et quod solempnitas per ecclesiam ordinata propter avariciam sacerdotum erat constituta." Reg. Chedworth, fol. 13r.

22. *HT*, 153.

23. Ibid., 126; see also 46, 57, 61, 67, 71, 81, 86, 95, 107–8, 115, 121, 131, 135, 141, 147, 153, 158, 165, 170, 177, 182–83, 189, 194, 196, 199, 205.

24. "Solus consensus mutui amoris inter virum et mulierem sufficit pro sacramento matrimonii, absque expressione aliorum verborum." Ibid., 46.

25. Ibid., 147.

26. Ibid., 86.

27. In marital litigation in fifteenth-century ecclesiastical courts, the deponents and the courts placed a good deal of emphasis on the actual words stated in a contract of marriage. There was clearly popular knowledge of exactly which words would make a marriage; see, for instance, London, Guildhall Library MS 9065, fols. 23r–24r, where witnesses to a 1469 contract fear that "verba matrimonialia" of present consent were not properly spoken.

28. While some influential historians of the early modern period have characterized "traditional" or premodern marriages as devoid of emotional content—see, for instance, Lawrence Stone, *The Family, Sex and Marriage in England, 1500–1800* (London: Weidenfeld and Nicolson, 1977), 70–71, 81, 128, and Edward Shorter, *The Making of the Modern Family* (New York: Basic Books, 1975), 54–65—recent work on the subject has almost unanimously rejected this conclusion. See Bennett, *Women in the Medieval English Countryside*, 101–3; Hanawalt, *The Ties That Bound*, 8–10, 188–219; Alan Macfarlane, *Marriage and Love in England: Modes of Reproduction, 1300–1840* (Oxford: Blackwell, 1986), 182–90; Kathleen M. Davies, "Continuity and Change in Literary Advice on Marriage," in *Marriage and Society: Studies in the Social History of Marriage*, ed. R. B. Outhwaite (London: Europa, 1981), 60–61,

78; Martin Ingram, "Spousals Litigation in the English Ecclesiastical Courts, c. 1350–1640," in ibid., 50; Ralph A. Houlbrooke, *The English Family, 1450–1700* (London: Longman, 1984), 76–78.

29. Compare the importance the Lollard sermon for the wedding mass placed on love. *EWS*, 3:317–18.

30. *HT*, 56, 60, 66, 111, 115, 126, 134, 157, 165, 196, 198; Reg. Chedworth, fol. 12v; see also Hudson, *Premature Reformation*, 291.

31. Clarissa W. Atkinson, " 'Precious Balsam in a Fragile Glass': The Ideology of Virginity in the Later Middle Ages," *Journal of Family History* 8 (1983): 131–43; Shahar, *Fourth Estate*, 22–27, 65–68.

32. Gratian, *Decretum*, C.33 q.5 cc.12–19; Shahar, *Fourth Estate*, 11–14, 22–27, 66, 89–90; Biller, "Marriage Patterns," 83.

33. "Uxor debet honorare virum diligentius quam e contra, in cujus signum mulier facta est ex viro, non vir ex femina, ut patet Gen. iii; debet tamen inter ipsos esse mutua dilectio socialis, in cujus signum non ex capite vel pede viri facta est mulier sed ex costa, ad denotandum quod non debet esse viro ancilla nec domina sed socia lateralis." Wyclif, *Trialogus*, 318. Cf. Hugh of St. Victor (d. 1141): " 'Hoc autem quid esse dicendum est, nisi societas illa quam Deus Creator a principio inter masculum et feminam instituit quando mulierem de latere viri formatam eidem sociavit?' Quia enim socia data est, non ancilla, aut domina; idcirco nec de imo sed de medio fuerat producenda. Si enim de capite fieret, de summo fieret, et videretur ad dominationem creata. Si autem de pedibus fieret, de imo fieret; et videretur ad servitutem subjicienda. Propterea de medio facta est, ut ad aequalitatem societatis facta probaretur." *De sacramentis*, lib. 2, pars 11, in *Patrologia cursus completus . . . series latina*, vol. 176, ed. J. P. Migne (Paris: Garnier, 1880), col. 485. See also Peter Lombard, *Sententiae in iv libris distinctae*, 2 vols., ed. Patres Collegii S. Bonaventurae ad Claras Aquas, Spicilegium Bonaventurianum, 4–5 (Grottaferrata: Editiones Collegii S. Bonaventurae ad Claras Aquas, 1971–81), 2:435 (lib. 4, dist. 28, cap. 4, §1); Raymond of Pennaforte, *Summa de matrimonio*, ed. Xavierus Ochoa and Aloisius Diez, Universa Bibliotheca Iuris, I/C (Rome: Commentarium Pro Religiosis, 1978), col. 913 (tit. 2, §3).

34. *Lanterne of Liʒt*, ed. Lilian M. Swinburne, EETS, o.s. 151 (London, 1917), 31.

35. "The Testimony of William Thorpe," in *Two Wycliffite Texts*, 49.

36. *EWS*, 1:493; 3:213.

37. Ibid., 1:223–26, 236–37, 253–54, 273, 284, 301, 361–62, 439, 444–45, 470–71, 552, 592, 620, 627, 687; 2:106; 3:41–42, 102–5, 211. See also ibid., 2:346–47, where God is said to have divided mankind into two genders, men to signify rulers and women to signify the ruled. Crawford, *Women and Religion*, 10–17, discusses the various uses of gender metaphors in religious debate in early modern England.

38. Roper, *Holy Household*, 2–3, 54.

39. Bennett, *Women in the Medieval English Countryside*, 103.

40. Kowaleski, "Urban families," 54–55; Phythian-Adams, *Desolation*, 80–81, 96.

41. 189 of 271 female Lollards (or 70 percent) and 235 of 684 male Lollards (34 percent). For this and following figures, see Appendix.

42. Ninety-two percent (173 of 189, or 64 percent of all women) had male family members in the sect, while only 8 percent (16 of 189, or 6 percent of all women) had only female Lollard relatives.

43. Monter, "Protestant Wives," 207.

44. These proportions are minimums: only those whose marital status is certainly or almost certainly known are counted. Others whose surnames were identical but whose relationship is not clear may also have been married to one another.

45. *A&M*, 4:214.

46. *HT*, 75–76.

47. *A&M*, 4:234–36, 238–39.

48. Ibid., 227–28, 232. The first name of Isabel's husband is not certain. She was married to John Tracher according to one source (ibid., 227) and to William Tracher according to another (ibid., 232). Both John and William were detected as Lollards (ibid., 225, 228–29). William's will names his widow as Isabel (BRO, D/A/We/2/f. 95v, Probate of Will of William Tracher of Amersham, 1525), while John's will does not survive. It does not seem likely that there were two Isabels, since the same story is told both about the wife of John and about the wife of William.

49. Lich. Ct. Bk., fols. 2v, 4v, 20v, 23v, 25v; Reg. G. Blyth, fol. 99r. The only other married couple in the Coventry community where both partners were given penance — Roger and Margaret Landesdale — received it at different times. Lich. Ct. Bk., fol. 23v; Reg. G. Blyth, fol. 99r.

50. Isabel: *A&M*, 4:223, 225–29, 242; John: ibid., 226. See below regarding the Bartletts.

51. Lich. Ct. Bk., fols. 17r, 19r, 20v. She is called Cristina in Thomas's deposition, but Constance in her own examination (fol. 19r).

52. Ibid., fols. 5v, 7r, 14v, 15v.

53. Ibid., fols. 11v, 22r; Reg. G. Blyth, fol. 99r. See also the case of Alice Walker, wife of Thomas Walker, alias Talbot. TCD, MS 775, fol. 124r.

54. Lich. Ct. Bk., fols. 3r, 4v, 6r, 20v, 25v.

55. Nancy Lyman Roelker notes that widows were particularly powerful in Calvinism. "The Appeal of Calvinism to French Noblewomen in the Sixteenth Century," *Journal of Interdisciplinary History* 2 (1971–72): 397–98.

56. No husband is mentioned in her trial, and she was apparently an old woman — her sentence was reduced "propter senectutem, miseriam, et impotenciam." *HT*, 198–200.

57. Reg. Warham, fols. 160r–161r, 169v, 172v.

58. Joan Martyn of Wantage, who abjured before Bishop John Blythe in 1499; Margaret Symson of Reading, who appeared before Bishop Audley in 1511; and Margery Young of East Hendred. Reg. J. Blythe, fol. 78v–79r; Reg. Audley, fol. 162v; *A&M*, 4:234.

59. "Herne widow of Amersham" was reported as a Lollard by Isabel Bartlett. Nothing more is known about her. *A&M*, 4:224.

60. Ibid., 224–25, 230–31.

61. *Great Chronicle of London*, 252; *Chronicles of London*, 261; Fabyan, *Chronicles*, 685; "Chronicle from the Register of the Grey Friars of London," ed. Richard

Howlett, in *Monumenta Franciscana*, vol. 2, R.S. (London: Longman, 1882), 181; Wedgwood, *Biographies*, 980; PRO, PCC Prob. 11/7 (4 Logge), Will of Sir John Yonge of London, 1481; Reg. Fitzjames, fol. 24v; TCD MS 775, fol. 122v.

62. *EM*, vol. 1, pt. 1:121, 129, 132; vol. 1, pt. 2:54; *L&P*, vol. 4, pt. 2, nos. 4029, 4175, 4545.

63. Mother Beckwyth: *EM*, vol. 1, pt. 1:117; vol. 1, pt. 2:52; *L&P*, vol. 4, pt. 2, no. 4029; ERO T/A 427/1/1, 427/1/2. Joan Bocher: *EM*, vol. 1, pt. 2:62; *L&P*, vol. 4, pt. 2, no. 4850; J. F. Davis, "Joan of Kent". Mother Charte: *L&P*, vol. 4, pt. 2, no. 4850. Joan Agnes alias Smyth: *L&P*, vol. 4, pt. 2, nos. 4545, 4850; *EM*, vol. 1, pt. 1:133.

64. Her husband William's will survives: PRO, PCC Prob. 11/15 (5 Adeane), Will of William Rowley of Coventry, 1505.

65. She had married Thomas Wasshingbury in London, but she returned to Coventry without him, presumably because he had died, perhaps as a relapse. Lich. Ct. Bk., fol. 16r.

66. Lich. Ct. Bk., fol. 20v. "Worst" here means most heretical.

67. Lich. Ct. Bk., 3v, 6v; Reg. G. Blyth, fol. 99v.

68. Lich. Ct. Bk., fols. 6v, 20v, 26r.

69. Ibid., fols. 5r, 14v, 16r–17r, 21r; Reg. G. Blyth, fol. 99v.

70. Lich. Ct. Bk., fols. 5r, 16v; Reg. G. Blyth, fol. 99v.

71. Reg. Warham, fols. 162rv, 164v, 173rv, 174r–175r.

72. Ibid., fols. 166r–167r, 174v–175r.

73. Ibid., fols. 169v–171v.

74. Wiesner, "Women's Response," 166.

75. Sharon Farmer, "Persuasive Voices: Clerical Images of Medieval Wives," *Speculum* 61 (1986): 517–43.

76. This parallels earlier medieval writers' interest in men's rather than women's conversions. Farmer, "Persuasive Voices," 533.

77. *EM*, vol. 1, pt. 2:55.

78. Ibid., 61; *L&P*, vol. 4, pt. 2, no. 4850; Lich. Ct. Bk., fols. 2v, 4v, 6r, 20v, 25v.

79. TCD, MS 775, fol. 123v.

80. Lich. Ct. Bk., fols. 5v, 7r, 15v.

81. *A&M*, 4:215.

82. Ibid., 238.

83. *Kentish Visitations*, 211.

84. *A&M*, 4:210.

85. Reg. Warham, fols. 167r–168r.

86. "Quod exnunc bene et honeste tractabit uxorem suam." Ibid., fols. 167v–168r, quotation at 168r.

87. Marie B. Rowlands, "Recusant Women, 1560-1640," in *Women in English Society, 1500–1800*, ed. Mary Prior (London: Methuen, 1985), 149–56. Cf. Roper, *Holy Household*, 186, where similar responsibilities were accorded to husbands and wives regarding prevention of adultery.

88. "Sed dominus, propterea quod timetur de repudiacione a viro suo facienda, distulit abiuracionem solempnam eidem iniungere faciendam. Et eam ad

perimplendam penitentiam sibi iniungendam iuramento corporali oneratam ad cautelam absoluit etc." Lich. Ct. Bk., fol. 6v.

89. Ibid., fol. 16r.

90. Le Roy Ladurie, *Montaillou*, 79, 184; Shahar, *Fourth Estate*, 264; Euan Cameron, *The Reformation of the Heretics: The Waldenses of the Alps, 1480–1580* (Oxford: Clarendon, 1984), 104–6.

91. *A&M*, 4:223.

92. Lich. Ct. Bk., fol. 16r. A John Brian of the parish of St. Stephen was named by Foxe as one of those specified to abjure in the early sixteenth century. *A&M*, 4:206.

93. *A&M*, 4:226.

94. Ibid., 175–76; *EM*, vol. 1, pt. 1:115; *L&P*, vol. 4, pt. 2, no. 4029; TCD MS 775, fol. 124v.

95. *EM*, vol. 1, pt. 1:129, 132; *L&P*, vol. 4, pt. 2, nos. 4175, 4545.

96. *A&M*, 4:228. It is not stated which of Paul's Epistles was read; two appropriate passages for weddings (1 Cor. 11:3–12, Ephesians 5:22–33) stress the submission of wives to husbands. The Epistles of Peter, also read and memorized by Lollards such as Alice Colins of Ginge (*A&M*, 4:238), speak similarly of the relative positions of husbands and wives (e.g., 1 Peter 3:1).

97. *A&M*, 4:237; see also 235.

98. This differs from the interpretation of Claire Cross, who sees the relationship of female children to their parents as more important than that of male children. "The way in which the daughters, rather than the sons, of lollard missioners tried to continue their fathers' work merits a special mention." Cross, "'Great Reasoners,'" 378.

99. *A&M*, 4:123.

100. Ibid., 245; PRO C.85/115/13.

101. *A&M*, 4:126–27.

102. Ibid., 182.

103. Ibid., 181–82.

104. Reg. Warham, fol. 169v.

105. "Iste oritur ex stirpe vitiata: quia avus patris sui erat ob heresim concrematus, ut dicitur." *EM*, vol. 1, pt. 2:60; *L&P*, vol. 4, pt. 2, no. 4254.

106. Cf. the late medieval Waldensians, who were not inducted into the faith until they were fifteen or twenty years old for fear they would give the sect away. Cameron, *Reformation of the Heretics*, 103.

107. TCD, MS 775, fol. 123r.

108. *HT*, 104–5.

109. "Idem Edwardus, puer undecimo annorum vel circa, publice aliis presentis secum ludentibus, dixit corpus Cristi non esse in sacramento altaris sed tantum panis, ac eciam quod imagines sanctorum non essent adorande eo quod sunt lapides et ligna." Reg. Audley, fol. 148v.

110. Ibid., fol. 148v.

111. TCD, MS 775, fol. 124r.

112. *A&M*, 4:238.

113. Ibid., 238.

114. Ibid., vol. 3, 597.

115. Reg. Warham, fols. 170v–171r. A third Grebill child, a daughter, is mentioned only once and by an outsider to the family: William Riche records that John Grebill Sr., Agnes Grebill, and a "distrawght yong woman, doughter to the said John and Agnes Grebill," were present when he visited. Reg. Warham, fol. 171r–171v. It is likely that "distrawght" was being used in the sense of "mentally deranged" rather than "agitated" (see *OED*, s.v.), which would explain why apparently no attempt was made to educate her in the Lollard faith along with her brothers.

116. *A&M*, 4:236.

117. *EM*, vol. 1, pt. 1:121; *L&P*, vol. 4, pt. 2, no. 4029.

118. *EM*, vol. 1, pt. 2:55, 54.

119. No one from the diocese is known to have taken part in Oldcastle's Revolt in 1414 except two men who were personally connected with Oldcastle. There are no cases of heresy in the surviving registers of Bishops Richard Courtenay (1413–15) or Wakering (1415–25), although Foxe apparently had access to records of proceedings against three Lollards from the diocese who were brought before Wakering in July 1424. Kightly, "Early Lollards," 364 n. 4; Thomson, *Later Lollards*, 117; *A&M*, 3:585–86. These 1424 prosecutions provide the first evidence for the existence of the community studied here; the group may have antedated 1424 but probably not by many years.

120. *A&M*, 3:597; *HT*, 104–5.

121. The examples are too numerous to cite here: see *A&M*, 4:123, 222–35, 245.

122. Lich. Ct. Bk., fols. 3v, 6v–7r, 11rv, 18v, 20v–21v.

123. Katherine Bartlett, Agnes Ashford, the mother of Henry Etkin, the mother of William King, and Alice Saunders; Thomas Barnard, Edmund Dormer, Robert Durdant, William Phip, John Phip, Edward Pope Sr., Andrew Randal's father, John Say, William Tylsworth, Geldener the Elder, Roger Harding, Richard White, John Scrivener, Hobbes, and Wilie. *A&M*, 4:123, 177–78, 222, 225–28, 230–32, 234–35.

124. Ibid., 221–22; BRO D/A/We/2/52, Will of Katherine Bartlett of Amersham, 1525.

125. Mordens: *A&M*, 4:225, 227; Phips: ibid., 227, 229–30, 235, and 237; Sherwoods: ibid., 229; PRO, PCC Prob. 11/21 (F.19 Bodfelde), Will of David Sherewode of Great Marlow, 1524.

126. Lich. Ct. Bk., fol. 21v.

127. See this chapter, "Extended Families."

128. Beckwyths: *EM*, vol. 1, pt. 1:117; *L&P*, vol. 4, pt. 2, no. 4029. Butlers: *A&M*, 4:227. John and Richard Chapman were certainly brothers, but Henry's relationship to them is uncertain. *EM*, vol. 1, pt. 1:114; *L&P*, vol. 4, pt. 2, no. 4545.

129. For a list, see Shannon McSheffrey, "Women in Lollardy, 1420–1530: Gender and Class in Heretical Communities" (Ph.D. diss., University of Toronto, 1992), 196, n.144.

130. Reg. Warham, fols. 170v–171r.

131. Thomas Villers admitted that he had been converted by his mother, but

his sister Thomasina Bradeley denied it, as she denied everything. Thomasina was, however, apparently taught by her mother; Margaret Landesdale deposed that Thomasina had been brought to the Landesdale house by her mother and that she listened while her mother read a large book of heresy. Mother Villers had previously abjured heresy at Leicester. Lich. Ct. Bk., fols. 8v, 11v, 21v.

132. *A&M*, 4:221–22.

133. Ibid., 229.

134. Ibid., 582.

135. Reg. Hales, fols. 166r, 167r; Lich. Ct. Bk., fols. 5r, 10r, 11r, 13r, 14v–15r.

136. Lich. Ct. Bk., fols. 11r, 13r.

137. P. J. P. Goldberg, "Women in Fifteenth-Century Town Life," in *Towns and Townspeople in the Fifteenth Century*, ed. John A. F. Thomson (Gloucester: Sutton, 1988), 112–13; Goldberg, *Women and Work*, passim; Shahar, *Fourth Estate*, 203–5; Adamson, "Urban Families," 88.

138. *HT*, 72–76; Lich. Ct. Bk., fols. 14v, 21r.

139. *L&P*, vol. 4, pt. 2, nos. 4029, 4850; *EM*, vol. 1, pt. 1:114; vol. 1, pt. 2:53.

140. *HT*, 72–74; Lich. Ct. Bk., fol. 14v.

141. *HT*, 165; *A&M*, 3:597.

142. Lich. Ct. Bk., fols. 8v, 20v.

143. *A&M*, 4:238.

144. Ibid., 582.

145. Ibid., 231–32.

146. Reg. Audley, fol. 161v.

147. "Uxorem Bluet suspectam opinatur propterea quod famula erat uxoris Bentham et nulla alia de causa." Lich. Ct. Bk., fol. 3v.

148. Ibid., fol. 5r.

149. Ibid., fols. 3v, 5r.

150. *A&M*, 4:237. John Sr.'s brother Philip, the servant of the well-known heretic Richard Colins of Ginge, was also involved in Lollardy. Ibid., 235–42.

151. Ibid., 226.

152. Ibid., 177–78, 226–30; *The Victoria History of the County of Middlesex*, 3 vols., ed. J. S. Cockburn (London: Institute for Historical Research, 1970), 3:19; London, Guildhall Library, MSS 9171/10, fol. 56r, Will of Robert Durdant of Staines, 1524 (which names Jehn Cobham as a daughter), and 9168/8, fol. 38r, notice of probate (which names his wife as Felicia); PRO, PCC Prob. 11/27 (F.22 Dyngeley), Will of Nicholas Durdant of Staines, 1538.

153. William Colins of West Ginge left a will in 1544; two of his children are named Richard and Alice, perhaps after William's brother and sister-in-law. Reading, Berkshire Record Office, D/A1/1, fol. 223v. John and Joan Collins: *A&M*, 4:234–39; Reg. Audley, fol. 163v. A John Colins Sr. of Betterton or Locking (the parish in which Ginge and Burford were located) was probably also related to this family. *The Victoria History of the County of Berkshire*, 5 vols., ed. William Page and P. H. Ditchfield (London: Institute for Historical Research, 1972), 4:307. Asthall Colinses: *A&M*, 4:235–42. A John Colins of Asthall left a will in 1533 in which a Robert Colins was named as a son. ORO, MSS Wills, 178.95. The two extended families knew one another: John Colins of Burford (the son of Thomas Colins of

Ginge) detected Robert Colins of Asthall, saying that Robert read to him from the Scriptures. Robert Colins testified against Thomas Colins and his wife of Ginge, Richard and Alice Colins of Ginge and their children Joan and John, and William Colins, brother of Richard and son of Thomas. *A&M*, 4:235–36.

154. *A&M*, 4:123–24, 220–29, 424; BRO, MSS D/A/We/2/52, Will of Katherine Bartlett of Amersham, 1525; D/A/We/7/117, Will of Isabel Bartlett of Amersham, written 1547, proved c. 1553; D/A/We/12/150, Will of Margaret Bartlett of Woburn, dated 1558 (not certainly the same Margaret); D/A/We/8/165, Will of John Welles Sr. of Amersham, 1555 (not certainly the same John Wells); *Bucks. Muster*, 233–34; *Bucks. Subsidy*, 12, 92. There is some confusion in Foxe's *Acts and Monuments* between Margaret and Isabel Bartlett, who were married to brothers Richard and Robert. Foxe calls Isabel both the wife of Richard and the wife of Robert; since she is more often called the latter, it has been assumed that Foxe confused the names Robert and Richard at *A&M*, 4:221.

Wills show that the Bartletts maintained connections with their siblings' families into the next generation. Isabel Bartlett, wife of Robert, made a bequest to a Thomas Morwin in 1548, and John Bartlett, nephew to Richard Bartlett, named both his uncle and a John Morwin in his 1545 will. BRO, D/A/We/7/117, Will of Isabell Bartlett of Amersham, 1548; D/A/We/6/40, Will of John Bartlett of Amersham, 1545.

155. *A&M*, 4:225, 227, 229. Thomas Copland was churchwarden for Amersham in 1520 (Bowker, *Episcopal Court Book*, 139), although this was not a sure mark of orthodoxy. Robert Andrew, named as a Lollard and a witness against the Bartletts (*A&M*, 4:220–21), was also a churchwarden at the same time as Copland. Nonetheless, Isabel Morwyn's deposition indicates he opposed the movement. Ibid., 229. Katherine Bartlett, Elizabeth Copland's mother, named her other sons-in-law, John Wells and John Morwyn, as executors of her will, but not Elizabeth's husband (although Katherine did leave a bequest to the Coplands). BRO, D/A/We/2/52, Will of Katherine Bartlett of Amersham, 1525.

156. *A&M*, 4:232. As is discussed in Aston, "Iconoclasm at Rickmansworth," 547–48, the Tredways may have been related to a family of the same name living in Rickmansworth. Richard Tredway of Rickmansworth left a will in 1527. Hertford, Hertfordshire Record Office, ASA 2AR, fol. 201r. It is possible that the testator is the same man as Richard Ashford, alias Tredway (who had contacts in the Uxbridge area), although the will does not indicate any connection with the Lollard by that name. Reg. Fox, fol. 18v.

157. Reg. Fox, 4, fols. 18r–19v; *A&M*, 4:124, 224–25, 227, 230–31, 245. BRO, D/A/We/1/8, Will of Marion Morden of Ashley-Green, Chesham, 1521; also edited in *Courts of the Archdeaconry of Buckingham*, 329–30; *L&P*, vol. 3, pt. 2, no. 3062; Bowker, *Henrician Reformation*, 60.

158. Reg. Fox, 4, fol. 18r; *A&M*, 4:224, 230–31; BRO, D/A/We/16/28, Will of Robert Tredway of Amersham, 1566.

159. Kightly, "Early Lollards," 391.

160. *A&M*, 4:123–24, 126, 220–21, 224–25, 227–28, 234, 580–81; Bowker, *Episcopal Court Book*, 15–16, 58–59; Reg. Longland, fols. 201v, 228rv; *Bucks. Subsidy*, 16.

161. *A&M*, 4:123–24.

162. The latter may be Emma Harding, alias Africke, probably identifiable with Emma, the wife of William Africke or Littlepage. Ibid., 224–28; *Bucks. Muster*, 233.

163. Härtel, "Lollardische Lehrelemente," 151, notes the importance of this family.

164. *A&M*, 4:124, 225–29, 242. John's will may survive: BRO, D/A/We/3/44, Will of John Lyttyllpage of Little Marlow, 1532.

165. *A&M*, 4:222–23, 228.

166. Ibid., 220–21, 225, 227, 229, 234, 242; *Bucks. Muster*, 232; *Bucks. Subsidy*, 24.

167. A will for a Margaret Bartlett of Woburn, dated 1558 (BRO, D/A/We/12/150), bequeathed her goods to two men, both named Richard Harding, one of whom was the son of a Harding of Amersham. Emma Africke was also known as Harding and may have been the daughter of Roger Harding. John Littlepage of Penn, perhaps the son of Emma and William Littlepage, named a Thomas Harding as a cousin in 1561. *A&M*, 4:225–26, 228; BRO, D/A/We/14/171, Will of John Littlepage of Penn, 1561.

168. *A&M*, 4:225–28, 237.

169. BRO, D/A/We/12/267, Will of Henry Harding of Amersham, 1558; see also D/A/We/9/3, Will of John Harding of Amersham (son of Henry), 1556. D/A/We/8/165, Will of John Welles Sr. of Amersham, 1555, names a John as his son.

170. Marion Morden (Sr.) left bequests in 1521 to Marion, Thomas, Henry, John Jr., and Isabel Wedon, while Robert Wedon was an executor. BRO, D/A/We/1/8; *Courts of Archdeaconry of Buckingham*, 329–30. The will of Emma Morden, wife of Richard, named John Wedon as executor in 1540. D/A/We/4/5. A John Wedon was named as a Lollard in the early 1520s. *A&M*, 4:239. Thomas Harding acted as overseer to Marion Morden (Sr.)'s will in 1521. BRO, D/A/We/1/8; *Courts of Archdeaconry of Buckingham*, 329–30.

171. BRO, D/A/We/16/28, Will of Robert Tredway of Amersham, 1566.

Chapter 5

1. Cf. Mitchell, "The Lady Is a Lord," esp. 79, and Jo Ann McNamara, "The *Herrenfrage*: The Restructuring of the Gender System, 1050–1150," in *Medieval Masculinities: Regarding Men in the Middle Ages*, ed. Clare A. Lees (Minneapolis: University of Minnesota Press, 1994), 3–29, esp. 4. Both Mitchell and McNamara see gender and social status as, in a sense, competing aspects of identity, differing from my more elastic view of gender identity as encompassing social position.

2. See Carroll, "Some Issues in Clergy Authority," 102–5.

3. McFarlane, *John Wycliffe*, 180, 184. See also Dickens, *Lollards and Protestants*, 8.

4. Plumb, "Social and Economic Spread." Imogen Luxton also suggests that Lollardy penetrated the apex of Coventry civic society, including some of the wealthiest merchant families in England; I disagree with her conclusions. Luxton,

"Lichfield Court Book," and above, Chapter 2, "Coventry's Civic Oligarchy and the Lollard Community." See Hudson, *Premature Reformation*, 128–32, 466, for a review of this literature.

5. "Quod penitet eam ipsos filios suos umquam peperisse." Reg. Warham, fols. 170rv.

6. Ibid., fols. 171v, 172v–173r; PRO, C.85/24/24.

7. Note that Cross (" 'Great Reasoners,' " 364) says that Agnes, having learned heresy from John Ive, proceeded to teach her husband and her sons. The register reads: "at the same tyme whan John Ive and he [i.e., John Grebill Sr.] taught hir of the said errour ayenst the sacrament of thaulter, they taught hir also of the said opynions of pilgremagis and worshipping of seyntis ymagis and offeryngis that they were not in any wise to be kept nor profitable for manys soule." Reg. Warham, fol. 170v.

8. Reg. Warham, fol. 170v.

9. Ibid., fol. 171r.

10. Ibid., fol. 171r.

11. Ibid., fol. 171v.

12. Ibid., fol. 169v.

13. "He [Christopher] was present in wynter last past whan the said Carder came to the house of this deponentis faders in Benynden and there taught and commyned with his said fader and with this deponent yn the said hous ayenst the sacrament of thaulter, that it was not Cristis body but oonly brede. . . . And the said William Carder, John Grebill his fader, and he hymself togider aggreed, held, and affermed all the same opinions and errours." Ibid., fol. 170r.

14. Cross has seen Agnes Grebill as a very prominent member of the Kentish Lollard group, having "almost equal influence" with the community's leader, William Carder. Hudson concurs: "To judge from the fact that they were burned early in the proceedings, Agnes Grevill and William Carder, along with Robert Harrison, were the ringleaders in the area." Cross, " 'Great Reasoners,' " 364; Hudson, *Premature Reformation*, 136. Davies, on the other hand, notes that some of those burned for heresy were "small-fry," marginal to their communities, and regards neither Agnes Grebill nor Carder as a leader. Davies, "Lollardy and Locality," 203, 209.

15. She was first tried for heresy in September 1428, after which she and her husband, William Baxter, moved to Norwich. In January 1429 her neighbors, Joan Clyfland and Clyfland's servants, Joan Grymle and Agnes Bethom, testified at length about her continued Lollardy. What happened after this is unclear; Margery could have been burned as a relapsed heretic, although there is no record of this. *HT*, 41–51.

16. "Si quodlibet tale sacramentum esset Deus et verum corpus Christi, infiniti sunt dii, quia mille sacerdotes et plures omni die conficiunt mille tales deos et postea tales deos comedunt et commestos emittunt per posteriora in sepibus turpiter fetentibus, ubi potestis tales deos sufficientes invenire si volueritis perscrutari." Ibid., 44–45. This may echo Wyclif's horror of the real body of Christ being subjected to the human digestive process: Wyclif, *De eucharistia tractatus maior*, ed. Johann Loserth (London: Wyclif Society, 1892; reprint, New York: Johnson Reprint Co., 1966), 16–18, 22–24, 308–9.

17. "Dixit eciam dicta Margeria isti iurate quod ipsa fuit sepius ficte confessa

decano de Campis ad finem quod ipse decanus reputaret eam esse bone vite. Et propterea ipse sepius dedit eidem Margerie pecuniam. Et tunc ista iurata dixit sibi nunquid est confessa sacerdoti de omnibus peccatis suis. Et ipsa Margeria dixit quod ipsa nunquam egit malum alicui sacerdoti, et ideo ipsa nunquam voluit confiteri sacerdoti." *HT*, 48–49. It is not clear why the dean gave Margery Baxter money, although another priest gave her near-contemporary Margery Kempe money to pray for him. *The Book of Margery Kempe*, chap. 12.

18. "Quod melius esset cuilibet comedere carnes remanentes die Jovis de fragmentis in diebus ieiunalibus quam ire in mercatum et indebitare se emendo pisces." *HT*, 46.

19. Ibid., 42, 44–45, 47, 49; see also 64, 69, 71, 73, 78, 86, 122, 127, 131, 142, 154, 166, 170, 192, 194.

20. Ibid., 47.

21. "Doctissimus frater tocius patrie." Ibid., 48.

22. Ibid., 48.

23. Aston, "Caim's Castles"; Hudson, *Premature Reformation*, 75, 91, 299, 348–51.

24. A tantalizing but ultimately unlikely possibility of a gentlewoman Lollard in Steeple Bumpstead is the case of Joan Agnes, alias Smyth. Thomas Hilles said that Richard Fox, John Tyball, John Smyth, Friar Topley, and Friar Gardyner used to meet at Bower Hall, the home of Joan Agnes, alias Smyth. Bower Hall was a manor house just outside Steeple Bumpstead; however, during the sixteenth century it was in the hands of the Bendish family, who used it as their seat and residence. *EM*, vol. 1, pt. 1:133; *L&P*, vol. 4, pt. 2, nos. 4545, 4850; Morant, *Essex*, 2:348. Other people named Agnes, alias Smyth, lived in the village of Steeple Bumpstead, suggesting that Joan was a servant in the house rather than a relation. See ERO, D/ABR 4/102, Will of Christopher Agnes, alias Smyth, 1568; D/ABW 1/66, Will of Joan Annis, widow of Christopher Agnes, alias Smyth, 1569; Steeple Bumpstead manor court roll D/DB M3; subsidy roll T/A 427/1/1.

25. *A&M*, 4:239, 582.

26. PRO, PCC Prob. 11/19 (18 Ayloffe), Will of William Cottusmore of Brightwell Baldwin, 1519; *The Victoria History of the County of Oxford*, 12 vols., ed. L.F. Salzman (London: Institute for Historical Research, 1907–90), 5:103; 7:11, 13, 125; 8:46, 50.

27. He participated in only one commission, in 1513, and was about thirty-six when he died in 1519. *L&P*, vol. 1, no. 4254.

28. William's father was John Cottismore and his mother Joan Stonor, and he may be the "nevue Cottysmore," born in about 1473, referred to in the Stonor Letters. *Stonor Letters and Papers, 1290–1483*, 2 vols., ed. Charles Lethbridge Kingsford, Camden Society, 3rd ser., 29–30 (1919), 1:112; 2:113–14, 133, 140. Cottismore's cousins, Sir Walter Stonor and Sir William Barentyne, were active as sheriffs, justices of the peace, and so forth, and Sir Walter Stonor was present at the Field of the Cloth of Gold in 1520. Stonor: *L&P*, vol. 1, no. 4809, p. 905; vol. 2, pt. 1, nos. 674, 2735; vol. 3, pt. 1:240, 245; vol. 3, pt. 2, nos. 2415, 3282, 3504; vol. 4, pt. 1, p. 234, nos. 137(12), 1049(24), 2002(11). Barentyne: *Stonor Letters*, 1:vi; 2:13–14, 128–29, 142–43; *Calendar of Inquisitions Post Mortem . . . Henry VII*, 3 vols. (London: Public Record Office, 1898–1955), 2:6; *L&P*, vol. 1, nos. 1316, 1949,

4259, 4307; vol. 2, pt. 1, no. 2735; vol. 3, pt. 1, no. 906, p. 243; vol. 3, pt. 2, nos. 2415, 3282; vol. 4, pt. 1, p. 234, nos. 137(12), 1049(24), 1795, 2002(11); vol. 4, pt. 2, nos. 2427, 4199; vol. 4, pt. 3, nos. 6043(2), 6116, 6490(20), 6516(1). Sir Walter Stonor was named in William Cottismore's will, and Alice Cottismore visited Sir William Barentyne and his wife. PRO, PCC Prob. 11/19 (18 Ayloffe), Will of William Cottismore; *A&M*, 4:582.

29. *A&M*, 4:582. This echoes the words of John Burell of Loddon, Norfolk, who abjured in 1429, suggesting that it was a Lollard commonplace (although Burrell spoke against the eucharist rather than a saint's image). *HT*, 73.

30. *A&M*, 4:239.

31. PRO, PCC Prob. 11/19 (18 Ayloffe), Will of William Cottismore.

32. "Rector non cubat infra parochiam sed in domo matrone Cotismore, qua de causa nescitur." *Visitations in the Diocese of Lincoln*, 1:119, 121. The editor, A. Hamilton Thompson, reads the passage as "in domo Matild' Cotismore," but he provides also the alternative reading made by Salter in 1925, "in domo matrone Cotismore." The latter is preferred here, as there is no known Matilda Cottismore.

33. *A&M*, 4:231–32.

34. Wedgwood, *History of Parliament, Biographies*, 980; *Calendar of Letter Books . . . of the City of London, Letter Book L*, ed. Reginald R. Sharpe (London: Corporation of London, 1912), 55, 60, 68, 71, 98, 161; PRO, PCC Prob. 11/7 (4 Logge), Will of Sir John Yonge of London, 1481; "William Gregory's Chronicle of London," in *The Historical Collections of a Citizen of London in the Fifteenth Century*, ed. James Gairdner, Camden Society, n.s., 17 (1876), 233; *Great Chronicle of London*, 188, 203, 440.

35. *Great Chronicle of London*, 252; Fabyan, *Chronicles*, 685; *A&M*, 4:7.

36. Reg. Fitzjames, fol. 25v; TCD, MS 775, fol. 122v; *A&M*, 4:175.

37. ERO, T/A 427/1/1; *EM*, vol. 1, pt. 1:129; *L&P*, vol. 4, pt. 2, nos. 4175, 4545. Possession of goods worth £10 or more was considered "notable" wealth. R. H. Britnell, writing on Colchester, has estimated that those assessed taxes on such wealth in 1524 were from the top 16 percent of the population. Britnell, *Growth and Decline in Colchester*, 232; Margaret Bowker, *The Secular Clergy in the Diocese of Lincoln, 1495–1520* (Cambridge: Cambridge University Press, 1968), 8–11.

38. ERO, T/A 427/1/1, 427/1/5; *EM*, vol. 1, pt. 1:121; *L&P*, vol. 4, pt. 2, nos. 4029, 4175.

39. *EM* vol. 1, pt. 1:121; *L&P* vol. 4, pt. 2, no. 4029. There were two Thomas Bowgases residing in Colchester in the 1520s, but neither was well-off. One was valued at 20s. in 1523 and the second was valued at £3 in 1523 and 10 marks (£6 13s. 4d.) in 1524. ERO, T/A 427/1/1, 427/1/5.

40. ERO, T/A 427/1/1, 427/1/5; *EM*, vol. 1, pt. 1:121, 129; *L&P*, vol. 4, pt. 2, nos. 4029, 4175, 4545.

41. ERO, T/A 427/1/5; *EM*, vol. 1, pt. 1:129, vol. 1, pt. 2:54; *L&P*, vol. 4, pt. 2, no. 4175; ERO, D/ACR 4/70, Will of Alice Garner of Colchester, 1539.

42. The Mones' home is referred to as a "mansio" by their servant John Burrell (*HT*, 75), and the Mones seem to have employed a number of servants/apprentices, including Lollards John Pert, Edmund Archer, and Burrell. Ibid., 72, 165; *A&M*, 3:597. Concerning Thomas's proselytization, see *HT*, 140.

43. *HT*, 75–76, 140, 176, 179; *A&M*, 3:596–97.

44. Although we cannot be altogether sure what procedure was followed in court, it seems likely that Lollards were asked to affirm or deny a list of Lollard heresies. The heretical beliefs to which the defendant admitted were then abjured. See Hudson, *Lollards and Their Books*, 125–40.

45. *HT*, 141.

46. "Dixit eciam eadem Margeria quod uxor Thome Mone est secretissima et sapientissima mulier in doctrina W. White." Ibid., 47.

47. *A&M*, 3:596–97.

48. If an accused was "led" or "led in chains" into the court ("adductus" or "adductus in vinculis"), it is assumed that they had been incarcerated before their trial; if a Lollard's trial record stated that they "appeared" or "appeared in person" ("apparuit/comparuit" or "apparuit personaliter"), it is assumed that they had been summoned to the court and had not been imprisoned before their trials. See Aston, *Lollards and Reformers*, 73. Hawise Mone had been arrested and kept in prison ("arestata et sub carcerali custodia servata") before her trial (*HT*, 139); all other women "appeared" or "appeared in person," except for Matilda Fleccher. In Fleccher's case, the scribe mistakenly omitted the predicate in the sentence and Tanner has supplied "[ad iudicium fuit adducta]" rather than "[apparuit]." Ibid., 131; London, Westminster Diocesan Archives, MS B.2, fol. 92r. The latter emendation would seem more likely to have been the intention of the scribe: the court does not seem to have seen Matilda Fleccher as a particularly important Lollard, and there is no reason to think that she would have been arrested and imprisoned before her trial when others were not. *HT*, 41, 64, 66, 193–94, 198.

49. The dates of the trials were: Hawise Mone, 4 August 1430, Thomas Mone, 19–21 August 1430; Margery Baxter, 7 October 1428, William Baxter, sometime prior to 5 October 1428, when he is described as "de heresi convictus"; Sybil Godesell, 22 March 1429, John Godesell, 18–21 March 1429; Matilda Fleccher, 18 March 1430, Richard Fleccher, 27 August 1429. *HT*, iv–v, 39.

50. Ibid., 139–44; cf. 41–43, 64–65, 66–68, 131–33, 193–94, 198–200. The form of Hawise's abjuration was different from those of the other women and resembled those of the more important male Lollards. It is also remarkably like that of John Skylan of Loddon, who abjured the same day as Hawise. Ibid., 138–51.

51. Ibid., 140.

52. Ibid., 139. Hudson (*Premature Reformation*, 182) suggests that Hawise taught Margery Baxter since Margery called her "sapientissima."

53. See Chapter 3, "Leadership of Lollard Conventicles: Women Priests?"

54. He was valued as possessing £20 in goods. *Bucks. Subsidy*, 16.

55. *A&M*, 4:123, 580; *Episcopal Court Book for the Diocese of Lincoln*, 15–16.

56. *A&M*, 4:228.

57. Ibid., 221, 224, 228.

58. Ibid., 227–28, 234. Foxe says that Isabel, wife of Thomas Harding, was present at the wedding of Durdant's daughter; no Isabel Harding is named in the records, and Alice's husband was clearly Thomas. There may, of course, have been another Thomas Harding. Ibid., 228.

59. There were, apparently, two women named Marion Westden, mother and daughter. The mother, Marion Westden Mathew, was probably the daughter of

John Bardefeld Sr., who named her (as Marion Westden) along with his other children in his 1506 will. At this date, she was married to Thomas Westden and had children. PRO, PCC Prob. 11/15 (18 Adeane). At some point between 1506 and 1528 Thomas Westden died, and Marion married Thomas Mathew, bringing with her into her second marriage her children from her first husband, among whom was a daughter named Marion Westden. In 1528 Hacker referred to her (the mother), saying that "Maryon Westden wif to Thomas Mathew of Colchestre is of the same sect." BL, Harl. MS 421, fol. 12v. John Pykas testified against the whole Mathew family, admitting that he had taught "in the house of Thomas Mathew in the presence of the said Mathews wif, William Pykas, and Marion Westden dowghter to Mathewes wif. . . ." Ibid., fol. 17r. Marion Westden Mathew died before her husband, whose 1534 will (ERO, D/ABW 25/35) bequeaths her clothes and other belongings to her daughters Jane Westden, Agnes Sayer, Marion Alen (probably the daughter referred to above, by then married), and Joan Motte.

60. The Colchester Oath Book records that in 1529–30 Marion Westden and William Aleyn, mariner, of Colchester, were the recipients of a deed from Robert Flyngaunt of Colchester, bachelor. The Marion Westden named here may have been Marion Westden Mathew, operating under her previous married name, or it may have been her daughter, also called Marion Westden. The latter may have married William Aleyn, as Thomas Mathew named Marion Alen as his wife's daughter in 1534. *The Oath Book or Red Parchment Book of Colchester*, ed. W. Gurney Benham (Colchester: Essex County Standard Office, 1907), 155; ERO, D/ABW 25/35, Will of Thomas Mathew of Colchester, 1534.

61. BL, Harl. MS 421, fols. 22v–23r.

62. *EM*, vol. 1, pt. 2:53–54.

63. Richard Smyth was warden of Coventry in 1481, sheriff in 1483, mayor in 1508, and member of the electoral and leet juries from 1486 until January 1519. He seems to have died soon after his last appearance in the Leet Book, as Joan is described as a widow in April 1520. Interestingly enough, Smyth's career suffered no visible interruptions due to his wife's misdemeanors in 1511–12; he remained a member of the electoral and leet juries through this period. *Coventry Leet Book*, 474, 516, 586–665, esp. 619; *A&M*, 4:557.

64. Lich. Ct. Bk., fol. 4r. Richard Landesdale died about 1503. He is probably the same as the Richard Lansdale who was warden of the city in 1495, member of the mayor's council in 1496, member of the electoral jury in 1500 and 1501, and bailiff in 1502 — a civic career that did not go beyond the junior level, perhaps because of premature death (for the structure of civic life in Coventry, see Phythian-Adams, *Desolation*, passim, esp. 118–21, and *Coventry Leet Book*, 563, 579, 599–601). There is some confusion as to the identity of Joan's second husband. The name of her second husband is recorded in the court book as John Padland, capper. A John Padland is very prominent in the *Coventry Leet Book*, but as his will was dated 1 January 1516, Joan cannot have been his widow in 1511. Thomas Padland, capper, John's brother, also appears in the Leet Book; it is possible that a scribal error was made in calling her former husband John instead of Thomas. Thomas was chamberlain in 1488, bailiff in 1492, and member of the electoral and leet juries from 1494 to 1503. His will was dated 1 July 1505; he did not, however, name a wife in his will. *Coventry Leet*

Book, 533, 543, 557–602, esp. 563; PRO, PCC Prob. 11/18 (15 Holder), Will of John Padland of Coventry, 1516; Prob. 11/14 (41 Holgrave), Will of Thomas Padland of Coventry, 1505.

65. Lich. Ct. Bk., fols. 6v–7r, 10v, 15v, 18v.

66. Ibid., fol. 4r; *A&M*, 4:557; Bodl. MS 31431, fol. 16r; BCRL, MS 273978, fol. 6r.

67. The Landesdale named in the Bodleian Annal is the hitherto unknown Thomas Landesdale, brother-in-law to Joan Smyth (the other sources for the 1520 burnings give only the surnames). This may be an error for Roger Landesdale. Bodl. MS 31431, fol. 16r.

68. *A&M*, 4:557.

69. Lich. Ct. Bk., fols. 4r, 5v–7r, 11v.

70. "Publica vox se habet eadem Johanna libros continentes heresim habuit." Ibid., fol. 7r.

71. See Chapter 2, "Women's Conventicles."

72. This appearance before the bishop was not recorded in surviving registers, but Rowley referred to it during her examinations in October and November 1511. Lich. Ct. Bk., fol. 6v. The three compurgators whom she was able to name in 1511, the wives of Duddlebury, Haddon, and Butler, were probably the wives of prominent men on the civic scene, commensurate with her own status as widow of a former mayor. The wife of Duddlebury could have been the wife of John Duddesbury, active in civic affairs from 1477 until 1523, chamberlain in 1484, sheriff in 1487, mayor in 1505, and Master of the Holy Trinity Guild in 1508. *Coventry Leet Book*, 422–684, esp. 518, 532, 603, 621. The wife of Haddon may have been the wife of John Haddon, active in civic affairs from 1480 until 1519, warden in 1488, sheriff in 1492, bailiff in 1493, and mayor in 1500. *Coventry Leet Book*, 432–665, esp. 533, 544, 547, 599. The wife of Butler may have been the wife of John Butler, steward and town clerk from 1481 until at least 1504 and coroner from 1509 to 1521. *Coventry Leet Book*, 474–603, 624–76. See Phythian-Adams, *Desolation*, 90–91, about the role of the mayoress and other women of the oligarchy.

73. Lich. Ct. Bk., fol. 17r; Reg. G. Blyth, fol. 99v; Bodl. MS. 31431, fol. 15r; BCRL, MS. 273978, fol. 5v; *REED Coventry*, 107.

74. Lich. Ct. Bk., fol. 1r. This may echo the words (although it reverses the sentiment) of a Wycliffite sermon: "And if þow seye þat þese rychessus [belonging to priests] ben goode, and Cristus preestus ben more worþi, why schulde þey not haue þese goodus passyng byfore oþre men? Manye such blynde resonys ben made by anticristus clerkys. . . ." *EWS*, 2:204.

75. Lich. Ct. Bk., fol. 7r. See Chapter 2, "Coventry's Civic Oligarchy and the Lollard Community."

76. Mundy, "Le mariage et les femmes," 133; *Men and Women*, 36.

77. Klassen, "Women and Religious Reform in Bohemia," 212–16; Roelker, "The Appeal of Calvinism"; Roelker, "The Role of Noblewomen in the French Reformation," *Archiv für Reformationsgeschichte* 63 (1972): 168–95; David P. Daniel, "Piety, Politics and Perversion: Noblewomen in Reformation Hungary," in *Women in Reformation and Counter-Reformation Europe*, ed. Sherrin Marshall (Bloomington: Indiana University Press, 1989), 68–88.

78. KAO, MS Te/C1, fols. 116r, 136r–139r; A.H. Taylor, "The Municipal Records of Tenterden, Part I," *Archaeologia Cantiana* 32 (1917): 283–302.

79. Possible wills: KAO, PRC, 17/19, fol. 152r, Will of William Bakar of Cranbrook, 1530; and KAO, PRC, 17/17, fol. 294r, Will of Vincent Lynche of Halden, 1527. Neither of these testators can be positively identified with the Lollards of the same name brought before Warham in 1511–12 (Reg. Warham, fols. 162rv, 164v–165r, 173r–175v).

80. Master shoemaker Thomas Mone of Loddon. *HT*, 72, 165; *A&M*, 3:597.

81. Salisbury Reg. Langton, 2, fol. 35r; Reg. J. Blythe, fols. 70r–79r; Reg. Audley, fols. 134rv, 144r, 147rv, 155v–169v; *A&M*, 4:235–38.

82. Kightly, "Early Lollards," 370, 388–93, 425–28; McFarlane, *Lancastrian Kings*, 163, 168–71; Aston, *Lollards and Reformers*, 1–47.

83. Thomas, John I, and John II, as successive lords of the manor of Chesham Bois, held the advowson of the rectory there. *The Victoria History of the County of Buckingham*, 5 vols., ed. William Page (London: Institute for Historical Research, 1905–27; reprint, 1969), 3:219–20. In 1464, two Lollards from Amersham, John Gose and John Crane, testified that the rector of the nearby parish of Chesham Bois had taught them certain Lollard beliefs. Reg. Chedworth, fols. 62rv.

84. Kightly, "Early Lollardy," 388–89.

85. Two men brought before Chedworth, William Ayleward and John Redhade, were burgesses of Henley but were probably not part of the Lollard community centered in Amersham and Chesham. Redhade purged himself of the charge of heresy, and Ayleward was likely not a Lollard. Reg. Chedworth, fols. 61r–62r; *Henley Borough Records: Assembly Books i–iv, 1395–1543*, ed. P. M. Briers, Oxfordshire Record Society (1960), 61–63, 65, 69–71; Davies, "Lollardy and Locality," 211.

86. BRO D/A/We/3/242, Will of John Gardner of Chesham Bois, 1537; *A&M*, 4:224, 229, 232. Another possible Lollard connection appears to be false: *Victoria History . . . Bucks.*, 3:220, states that Robert Cheyne was suspected of Lollard beliefs in 1520; however, the cited source (*L&P*, vol. 3, pt. 2, no. 1928[i]) makes no reference to Lollardy. The original (PRO, C.82/511/1) is a record that Robert Cheyny of Chesham Bois, Bucks.; Humfrey Stafford of Codered, Herts.; Walter Devereux; and Lord Ferrers of Chertely, Staffs. are quit of a payment due in 1521.

87. Zell, "Fifteenth- and Sixteenth-Century Wills," 67.

88. Reg. Longland, fols. 228rv.

89. *A&M*, 4:123, 225, 229; *L&P*, vol. 13, pt. 2, no. 253.

90. *Victoria History . . . Middlesex*, 3:19; *Bucks. Muster*, 214; Plumb, "Social and Economic Spread," 120–21.

91. *A&M*, 4:177–78, 226, 228, 230.

92. Another branch of the Durdant family (the relationship, if any, is unclear) may also have been involved in heresy. A Thomas Durdant, gentleman, of Denham Durdants, Buckinghamshire, was sued in Star Chamber in 1514 or 1522 by a local husbandman, Thomas Nell, for stealing his beasts. Nell said that Durdant had done this

> of his malicius mynde whiche he hadde of long tyme bourne ayenst the seid Thomas Nell and yet doith be cause your seid pore subiect [Nell] went with all

his neghbours to testifie and recorde ayens the seid Durdant for taken away of the goodis of the church. (PRO, STAC.2/32/106)

Plumb associates the manor of Denham Durdants with the Lollard Durdants of Middlesex, and thus Thomas Durdant and Robert Durdant may have been related, by blood and by heresy. But Thomas Durdant's activities described in the Star Chamber suit may have been more criminal than heretical; in 1511 Thomas Durdant Sr. and Thomas Durdant Jr. were forced to flee their lands when charged with a murder. Plumb, "Social and Economic Spread," 120–21; *Victoria History . . . Bucks.*, 3:259; *L&P*, vol. 1, no. 1759; vol. 2, pt. 1, no. 2511.

93. *L&P*, vol. 1, nos. 454, 943, 1379, 2045, 3219, 3310, 3522, 5506; vol. 3, pt. 1, nos. 703, 1036, 1042; vol. 3, pt. 2, nos. 1364, 3282; vol. 4, pt. 1, nos. 547, 1136, 1377; vol. 4, pt. 3, nos. 6490, 6751; vol. 5, nos. 457, 838, 1694; *Bucks. Subsidy*, 11.

94. Lich. Ct. Bk., fol. 19v.

95. *Victoria History . . . Warws.*, 4:183, 216.

96. *CPR, 1494–1509*, 359, 456, 663; *L&P*, vol. 1, nos. 282, 554.

97. Reg. G. Blyth, fol. 98r; see also Lich. Ct. Bk., fols. 2r, 8r, 19v, 24v.

98. See Chapter 2, "Coventry's Civic Oligarchy and the Lollard Community."

99. *A&M*, 4:193.

100. "Nonnullos viros locupletes hereticos." Reg. Audley, fol. 144r. Thomson has translated "locupletes" as "trusty," "because most Lollards appear to have been from the working class," while Brigden and I prefer "rich." Thomson, *Later Lollards*, 85–86; Brigden, *London and the Reformation*, 97.

101. TCD, MS 775, fol. 124r; Hudson, *Premature Reformation*, 143.

102. *A&M*, 4:228; Brigden, *London and the Reformation*, 97–98, 104; PRO, PCC Prob. 11.39 (F.19 Wrastley), Will of William Tyllesworth, citizen and goldsmith of London, 1557.

103. Brigden, *London and the Reformation*, 125, n. 214.

104. TCD, MS 775, fol. 124r.

105. The literature on this vexed question is vast: Thomas More, *A Dialogue Concerning Heresies*, vol. 1, 328; Polydore Vergil, *The Anglica Historia of Polydore Vergil A.D. 1485–1537*, ed. Denys Hay, Camden Society, 3rd ser., 74 (1950), 229; Simon Fish, "A Supplicacyon for the Beggers," in *Four Supplications*, ed. Frederick J. Furnivall, EETS e.s., 13 (1871); Thomson, *Later Lollards*, 164–70; J. Duncan M. Derrett, "The Affairs of Richard Hunne and Friar Standish," in *The Complete Works of St. Thomas More* (New Haven, Conn.: Yale Univerity Press, 1979), vol. 9, 215–46; Smart, "John Foxe"; Richard Wunderli, "Pre-Reformation London Summoners and the Murder of Richard Hunne," *JEH* 33 (1982): 209–24; John Fines, "The Post-Mortem Condemnation for Heresy of Richard Hunne," *English Historical Review* 78 (1963): 528–31; S. F. C. Milsom, "Richard Hunne's 'Praemunire,'" *English Historical Review* 76 (1961): 80–82; E. Jeffries Davis, "Authorities for the Case of Richard Hunne," *English Historical Review* 30 (1915): 477–88; Scarisbrick, *Reformation*, 47; Hudson, *Premature Reformation*, 485–86.

106. Plumb, "Social and Economic Spread."

107. Davies, "Lollardy and Locality," 204; PRO, C.1/100/38–46 and E.101/107/27; *Catalogue of Ancient Deeds*, 6 vols. (London: Public Record Office, 1890–1915), 4:330, 338, 422.

108. *A&M*, 4:214. Robert Cosyn of Little Missenden, William Tylsworth and William Scrivener of Amersham, Nicholas Colyns, and Thomas Man were all excommunicated for heresy in 1510. All except Man confessed and were relaxed to the secular arm and burned. Man was not captured until 1518. PRO, C.85/115/10; *A&M*, 4:208.

109. There were two William Tylsworths, perhaps father and son. One William Tylsworth of Amersham was burned in 1510 (Foxe erroneously gives 1506 as the date) along with William Scrivener, Robert Cosyn, and Nicholas Colyns. Another man by the same name, of Amersham and London, was cited by several Lollards in the 1521 investigation, in one case explicitly recalling events before 1506 but in other cases probably but not certainly referring to events after that date. A William Tylsworth was an apprentice to John Barret, goldsmith, and may be the same William Tylsworth, citizen of London and goldsmith, who left a will in 1557. The testator was apparently a Protestant, as he stated in the will that he was "a parisheoner in a couvenant plan" in the church of St. Peter Westcheap. PRO, C.85/115/10; *A&M*, 4:123, 214, 221–22, 226, 228; Brigden, *London and the Reformation*, 98, 104; PRO, PCC Prob. 11.39 (F.19 Wrastley).

110. *A&M*, 4:124.

111. Richard Saunders, Robert Bartlett, John Hill, John Mylsent, Robert Harding, William Tracher, and Thomas Barnard. PRO, E.101/107/27; Davies, "Lollardy and Locality," 204, n. 59.

112. *A&M*, 4:227.

113. *Bucks. Muster*, 231, 234; *Bucks. Subsidy*, 12, 92.

114. For instance, John Cheyne of Chesham Bois was assessed as holding £10 in land in 1522 and £100 in goods in 1524–25. *Bucks. Muster*, 235, 241; *Bucks. Subsidy*, 16, 48.

115. *A&M*, 4:231–32.

116. *A&M*, 4:224–25, 227; *Bucks. Muster*, 233.

117. *A&M*, 4:123–24, 220–21, 225; *Bucks. Muster*, 233; PRO, E.101/107/27.

118. BRO, D/A/We/2, fols. 5v–6r, Inventory of goods of John and Florence Hill of Amersham, 1524; PRO, E.101/107/27.

119. *Bucks. Muster*, 282; *Bucks. Subsidy*, 21; *A&M*, 4:226, 235, 237, 240.

120. *Bucks. Subsidy*, 16.

121. *A&M*, 4:123–24.

122. *Episcopal Court Book for the Diocese of Lincoln*, 15–16.

123. *A&M*, 4:220–21, 225, 227, 234.

124. Reg. Longland, fols. 201v, 228rv; *A&M*, 4:580–81.

125. *Bucks. Muster*, 233–34.

126. *A&M*, 4:124. Ashridge was in Buckinghamshire and is now in the modern county of Hertfordshire. David Knowles and R. Neville Hadcock, *Medieval Religious Houses, England and Wales* (London: Longmans, Green, 1953), 179.

127. Robert appeared as a resident of Amersham in the 1522 Muster, but the 1522 anticipation of the 1524 subsidy noted that he "remained outside the county" ("manet extra comitatum"). *Bucks. Subsidy*, 92; *Bucks. Muster*, 233, 234. His name did not appear at all in the 1524 subsidy rolls, and he was not named in his mother's 1525 will, indicating perhaps that he was dead by then, possibly even burned for heresy. He was certainly dead by 1547, when his widow Isabel made her will. His

brother Richard more clearly escaped execution; although, like Robert, he was not listed in the 1524 Subsidy Rolls, he was named in his mother's will in 1525 and was still alive and resident in Amersham in 1545, when his nephew John Bartlett made his will. *Bucks. Subsidy*, 92; BRO, D/A/We/2/52, Will of Katherine Bartlett of Amersham, 1525; D/A/We/7/117, Will of Isabel Bartlett of Amersham, 1547; D/A/We/6/40, Will of John Bartlett of Amersham, 1545.

128. *A&M*, 4:221.

129. Ibid., 224.

130. *Bucks. Muster*, 232; *Bucks. Subsidy*, 12.

131. *A&M*, 4:220–21; BRO, D/A/We/2/52, Will of Katherine Bartlett; PRO, PCC Prob. 11/29 (F.29 Spert), Will of Alice Saunders of Amersham, 1538.

132. *A&M*, 4:225, 229; *L&P*, vol. 13, pt. 2, no. 253; *Bucks. Subsidy*, 16; *Bucks. Muster*, 241.

133. *A&M*, 4:229; *Bucks. Muster*, 277; *Bucks. Subsidy*, 23.

134. *A&M*, 4:237–38; *Bucks. Muster*, 282; *Bucks. Subsidy*, 21.

135. See *Bucks. Muster*, 82–83, 216, 231–37, 249, 264, 277, 283; *Bucks. Subsidy*, 12, 15–16, 23–24, 29–30.

136. *A&M*, 4:123–24, 217, 225–27, 229–30, 235, 237, 242. The other four were Raynold Sherwood of Great Marlow, Robert Stampe of Amersham, John Monke of Amersham, and Ralph Morden of Amersham.

137. Ibid., 178, 226–27, 230; BRO, D/A/We/2/52, Will of Katherine Bartlett; see Chapter 4, "Extended Families," for the Bartletts. The other five were Richard Dean of West Wycombe, Francis Funge of Penne, John Funge of Penne, Thomas Halfeaker of Amersham, and Edmund Hill of Penne.

138. *A&M*, 4:226–27, 234, 242. The other two were Laurence Heron of Hughenden and William Say of Little Missenden.

139. ERO, T/A 427/1/1; *EM*, vol. 1, pt. 1:120–21; vol. 1, pt. 2:53, 64; *L&P*, vol. 4, pt. 2, no. 4029; *Red Paper Book of Colchester*, 29–31. For Colchester civic government, see Britnell, *Growth and Decline in Colchester*, 218–35.

140. *A&M*, 4:216.

141. Ibid., 216; PRO, PCC Prob. 11/15 (18 Adeane), Will of John Bardefield Sr. of Colchester, 1506; PCC Prob. 11/17 (22 Fetiplace), Will of Robert Cowbridge of Colchester, 1513; ERO, T/A 427/1/1, 427/1/5; *Red Paper Book of Colchester*, 65, 104, 111; *The Oath Book of Colchester*, 133–34, 139–40, 144, 152.

142. ERO, T/A 427/1/1, 427/1/5; *EM*, vol. 1, pt. 1:121–23, 126–29; *L&P*, vol. 4, pt. 2, nos. 4029, 4175.

143. *EM*, vol. 1, pt. 2:64.

144. Ibid., vol. 1, pt. 1:118–19, 129–31; *L&P*, vol. 4, pt. 2, nos. 4029, 4175; ERO, T/A 427/1/1, 427/1/5.

145. *EM*, vol. 1, pt. 1:121, 129–30; vol. 1, pt. 2:54; *L&P*, vol. 4, pt. 2, nos. 4029, 4175; ERO, T/A 427/1/1, 427/1/5. There are two men of each name resident in Colchester in 1532; both Thomas Parkers were worth 40s.; one John Thompson was valued at 20s., the other at 40s.

146. The evidence regarding assessments for Steeple Bumpstead all comes from ERO, T/A 427/1/1. The subsidy rolls for Steeple Bumpstead do not record the worth of taxpayers' goods or land but only the tax assessments they were re-

quired to pay. The wealth of Steeple Bumpstead residents has been estimated by comparing these assessments with those in other parts of the subsidy rolls where both the value of people's goods or land and their tax assessment is recorded. This is not foolproof, as people whose goods were recorded to have been worth the same amount did not always pay the same tax (for instance, the assessment for John Bardefield of Colchester, who was worth £10, was 10s., while Robert Bate of East Donyland, also worth £10, was required to pay 8s.). However, the assessments do roughly indicate the approximate wealth of an individual, which is sufficient for the purposes of this discussion. ERO, T/A 427/1/1, 427/1/2, 427/1/5.

147. *EM*, vol. 1, pt. 2:62; *L&P*, vol. 4, pt. 2, no. 4545.

148. ERO, D/DB M2 and D/DB M3, Manor Court Rolls for Steeple Bumpstead.

149. *EM*, vol. 1, pt. 2:56; *L&P*, vol. 4, pt. 2, no. 4545.

150. *L&P*, vol. 4, pt. 2, no. 4545.

151. See Luxton, "Lichfield Court Book"; and Chapter 2, "Coventry's Civic Oligarchy and the Lollard Community."

152. Bradley was assessed thirteen years after the Lollard trials as possessing goods worth £10. PRO, E.179/192/125, E.179/192/130. Only a few of those named in the court book in 1511–12 were recorded in the subsidies of 1524–25, perhaps because many had died or left Coventry. Margery Locock, widow, was assessed at £5; John Longhald was assessed at 40s.; Hugh Parret was assessed at 40s.; and John Atkyns, painter (perhaps the same as John Atkynson, painter) was also assessed at 40s. PRO, E.179/192/125, E.179/192/130.

153. Roger Landesdale, tailor; Robert Silkby, shoemaker; Robert Hachet, leatherdresser; Balthasar Shugborow, gentleman; Thomas Ward, barker (tanner); Thomas Bowen, shoemaker; Robert Peg, painter; John Atkynson, alias John Peintour Jr., painter; John Davy, alias John Peintour Sr., painter; Thomas Flesshour (no trade given); Thomas Lieff, shearman; John Longhald, shearman; William Hawkyns, skinner; David Clerc, currier (leatherdresser); Thomas Abell, shoemaker. Lich. Ct. Bk., passim.

154. Ibid., passim; Reg G. Blyth, fols. 98r–100r.

155. See R. B. Goheen, "Peasant Politics? Village Community and the Crown in Fifteenth-Century England," *American Historical Review* 96 (1991): 42–62; and, regarding the office of churchwarden, French, "Local Identity," 42–79.

Chapter 6

1. See Sherrin Marshall [Wyntjes]'s distinction between women's religious choices made from an active individual commitment as opposed to others' (especially family members') determinations. "Women and Religious Choices in the Sixteenth-Century Netherlands," *Archiv für Reformationsgeschichte* 75 (1984): 276–89. Cf. Crawford, *Women and Religion*, 209.

2. Bolton, "Mulieres Sanctae," 77–95; *A History of Women in the West*, vol. 2, *Silences of the Middle Ages*, ed. Klapisch-Zuber, 30, 204, 313, 484. See also Grundmann, *Religiöse Bewegungen*, 36, 94, 170–98, 356–59; Koch, *Frauenfrage und Ketzer-*

tum; Shahar, *Fourth Estate*, 251–80, esp. 267; David Herlihy, *Women in Medieval Society*, Smith History Lecture (Houston, Tex.: University of St. Thomas, 1971), 11–12; R. I. Moore, *The Origins of European Dissent* (London: Allen Lane, 1977), 272–73; Klassen, "Women and Religious Reform," 203, 205; Aston, *Lollards and Reformers*, 49; Cross, "Great Reasoners," 360; Marshall [Wyntjes], "Women in the Reformation Era," 168–69.

3. This argument runs throughout Bynum's works, *Jesus as Mother: Studies in the Spirituality of the High Middle Ages* (Berkeley: University of California Press, 1982), *Holy Feast*, and *Fragmentation and Redemption*; see particularly *Fragmentation*, 59–60. Nonetheless, she agrees with the second premise and the conclusion: heresies did draw women because they offered the same things as orthodoxy, not because they provided alternatives. While she clearly has in mind the continental heretical and quasiheretical movements in her characterization of the appeal of heterodoxy, she includes Lollardy as an example. See *Holy Feast*, 17.

4. Vauchez, *Laity in the Middle Ages*, xix and passim.

5. See Gilchrist and Oliva, *Religious Women*.

6. McLaughlin, "Les femmes et l'hérésie médiévale," 77.

7. Abels and Harrison, "Participation of Women"; Mundy, "Le mariage et les femmes"; Mundy, *Men and Women*, 43–44. While Bynum cites the work of Abels and Harrison, she does not integrate their findings into her argument. *Holy Feast*, 17.

8. Biller, "Common Woman in the Western Church," 156–57.

9. See, for instance, Stuard, "Dominion of Gender," 168; Bynum, *Holy Feast*, 17.

10. See Biller, "The Common Woman in the Western Church."

11. N. Z. Davis, "Some Tasks and Themes in the Study of Popular Religion," in *The Pursuit of Holiness in Late Medieval and Renaissance Religion*, ed. Charles Trinkhaus and Heiko A. Oberman (Leiden: Brill, 1974), 307–36; N. Z. Davis, "From 'Popular Religion' to Religious Cultures," in *Reformation Europe: A Guide to Research*, ed. Steven Ozment (St. Louis, Mo.: Center for Reformation Research, 1982), 321–41, quotation at 322; John Van Engen, "The Christian Middle Ages as an Historiographical Problem," *American Historical Review* 91 (1986): 519–52; Scribner, *Popular Culture*; Vauchez, *Laity*, 141–68, 265–66; Peter Brown, *The Cult of the Saints: Its Rise and Function in Latin Christianity* (Chicago: University of Chicago Press, 1981), 12–22. Roger Chartier and Eamon Duffy have pointed out the conceptual vagueness of the word "popular" in the study of popular religion. Roger Chartier, *Cultural History: Between Practices and Representations* (Ithaca, N.Y.: Cornell University Press, 1988), 38–45; Duffy, *Stripping of the Altars*, 3.

12. Scribner, *Popular Culture*, 23.

13. English historians have not always heeded the warnings of Davis and Scribner. J. J. Scarisbrick, writing from the perspective of modern English Catholicism, for instance, describes the religion of the late medieval peasantry as "shot through with semi-pagan survivals, sub-Christian folklore and magic"; English men and women were "profoundly addicted" to the "semi-Pelagian" emphasis on works in late medieval Catholicism. Ironically, he puts Lollards squarely within the same "semi-pagan" tradition as popular Catholicism. *The Reformation and the English*

People, 41, 46, 54–55. Imogen Luxton, from a different denominational perspective than that of Scarisbrick, similarly describes the popular religious culture of pre-Reformation England as reflecting "limited mental horizons," but Lollards, in her view, "fostered a devotion to biblical learning which contrasts with the religious ignorance of many of the laity." "The Reformation and Popular Culture," in *Church and Society in England: Henry VIII to James I*, ed. Felicity Heal and Rosemary O'Day (London: Macmillan, 1977), 65, 68.

14. Scribner, *Popular Culture*, esp. 17–47; see also N. Z. Davis, "Some Tasks and Themes," 309. Along these lines, Margery Baxter's attitude toward Lollard leader William White—that he was a saint who would intercede for her—might be interpreted as her shaping of Lollard beliefs to her own needs.

15. Duffy, *Stripping of the Altars*, 283 and passim.

16. Scribner's emphasis on the flexibility of late medieval religious culture implies that women were able to create forms of religiosity that particularly suited them. *Popular Culture*, 25, 32, 34. Duffy, on the other hand, does not treat women separately from men and apparently does not see gender as an important aspect of religious difference.

17. See Bynum, *Holy Feast*, 24–26; *Fragmentation*, 60; Donald Weinstein and Rudolph M. Bell, *Saints and Society: The Two Worlds of Western Christendom, 1000–1700* (Chicago: University of Chicago Press, 1982), 220. Gilchrist and Oliva, in *Religious Women*, esp. 9–11, 21–22, 68–82, emphasize a wide range of options open to the woman seeking a religious life in late medieval East Anglia, including living in an informal community with other women wishing to follow a pious life and working as a hospital sister.

18. Bynum, *Holy Feast*, 26

19. Biller, "The Common Woman in the Western Church," 127–57. See also Vauchez, who is skeptical about the accessibility of late medieval mysticism to the ordinary lay believer. *Laity*, 234–35.

20. See French, "Local Identity," esp. 1–9.

21. Ibid., 52, 60–61, 76, 193–227.

22. Caroline M. Barron, "The Parish Fraternities of Medieval London," in *The Church in Pre-Reformation Society: Essays in Honour of F.R.H. DuBoulay*, ed. Caroline M. Barron and Christopher Harper-Bill (Woodbridge, Suffolk: Boydell, 1985), 13–37; Gervase Rosser, "Going to the Fraternity Feast: Commensality and Social Relations in Late Medieval England," *Journal of British Studies* 33 (1994): 430–46; McRee, "Religious Gilds and Civic Order"; Hanawalt and McRee, "The Guilds of *Homo Prudens*."

23. French, "Local Identity," 27–28, 215–16; Hanawalt and McRee, "The Guilds of *Homo Prudens*," 166 (more optimistic about the participation of women).

24. See Eamon Duffy, "Holy Maydens, Holy Wyfes: The Cult of Women Saints in Fifteenth- and Sixteenth-Century England," *SCH* 27 (1990): 175–96; Duffy, *Stripping of the Altars*, 155–205; Scribner, *Popular Culture*, 7–8, 32, 39–41; Vauchez, *Laity*, 141–52.

25. Cited in Bynum, *Jesus as Mother*, 242.

26. Gilchrist and Oliva, *Religious Women*, 82; Eleanor McLaughlin, "Equality of Souls, Inequality of Sexes: Woman in Medieval Theology," in *Religion and Sex-*

ism: Images of Woman in the Jewish and Christian Traditions, ed. Rosemary Radford Ruether (New York: Simon and Shuster, 1974), 248–49; McLaughlin, "Les femmes et l'hérésie," 87; N. Z. Davis, *Society and Culture*, 68, 88; Caroline S. Andre, "Some Selected Aspects of the Role of Women in 16th Century England," *International Journal of Women's Studies* 4 (1981): 86; Susan C. Karant-Nunn, "Continuity and Change: Some Effects of the Reformation on the Women of Zwickau," *Sixteenth Century Journal* 12 (1982): 28; Roper, *Holy Household*, 261; Coudert, "Myth," 85; Monter, "Protestant Wives," 207; Wiesner, "Women's Response," 155–56.

27. Ronald Finucane, *Miracles and Pilgrims: Popular Belief in Medieval England* (London: Dent, 1977), 121–47.

28. See, for instance, Cross, "'Great Reasoners,'" 359: "The attractions of lollardy for lay people in general and women in particular are not hard to understand."

29. See, for example, Aston, *Lollards and Reformers*, 51–53, 101–33, 193–217; Luxton, "The Reformation and Popular Culture," 68.

30. See, for instance, Maurice Keen, "Wyclif, the Bible, and Transubstantiation," in *Wyclif in His Times*, ed. Anthony Kenny (Oxford: Oxford University Press, 1986), 11–13; Jeremy I. Catto, "John Wyclif and the Cult of the Eucharist," in *The Bible in the Medieval World*, ed. Katherine Walsh and Diana Wood, SCH, Subsidia, 4 (Oxford: Blackwell, 1985), 274.

31. For instance, Lambert, *Medieval Heresy*, 256–59; Summers, *Lollards of the Chiltern Hills*, esp. 136, 184–86.

32. *HT*, 141.

33. Ibid.

34. Ibid., 49.

35. Hudson, *Premature Reformation*, 281–90; Kightly, "Early Lollards," 577–78; Heather Phillips, "John Wyclif and the Optics of the Eucharist," in *From Ockham to Wyclif*, 245–58; Keen, "Wyclif, the Bible, and Transubstantiation," 1–16; Catto, "John Wyclif and the Cult of the Eucharist," 269–86.

36. See, for instance, *HT*, 64, 86, 95, 106, 126, 158, 165; Reg. Chedworth, fols. 61r–62r; Lich. Ct. Bk., fols. 4rv; *A&M*, 4:234.

37. "Illud sacramentum quod tales sacerdotes asserunt esse verum corpus Christi nec habet oculos ad videndum, aures ad audiendum, os ad loquendum, manus ad palpandum nec pedes ad ambulandum sed est torta panis facta de farina frumenti." *HT*, 73.

38. *FZ*, 124; Reg. Chedworth, fol. 57v; Lich. Ct. Bk., fol. 17v; *A&M*, 4:234.

39. See, for instance, the attitude of Margery Baxter, *HT*, 44–45; and the Amersham Lollards, *A&M*, 4:222, 225, 229–30, 232.

40. Wyclif does not seem to have written or preached about fasting; Aston suggests that the objection to it may have originated in William White, although she notes that there were two questions concerning the observation of fast days on the interrogation list used in the diocese of Worcester in 1428. See Aston, *Lollards and Reformers*, 93n.; Hudson, *Lollards and Their Books*, 134. For East Anglian cases, see *HT*, 64, 72–74, 76, 165; *FZ*, 427. For other cases, see for instance Reg. Chedworth, fol. 12v; *A&M*, 4:228.

41. Bynum, *Holy Feast*, passim, esp. 3–4, 20, 75–93, 208–18; *Fragmentation*, 119–50. See also Weinstein and Bell, *Saints and Society*, 73–99, 233–35; André Vauchez, *La Sainteté en occident aux derniers siècles du moyen âge*, Bibliothèque des études françaises d'Athènes et de Rome, 241 (Rome: Ecole Française de Rome, 1981), 405–7, 431–33; Vauchez, *Laity*, 237–42 (where he differs with Bynum's interpretation); Gibson, *Theater of Devotion*, 6–7.

42. James, "Ritual, Drama and Social Body," 3–29; Charles Zika, "Hosts, Processions and Pilgrimages: Controlling the Sacred in Fifteenth-Century Germany," *Past and Present* 118 (1988): 25–64; Rubin, *Corpus Christi*; French, "Local Identity," 155–60.

43. Zika, "Hosts," 42, 44–46.

44. See, for instance, *HT*, 42, 44, 64, 69, 73, 78, 122, 127, 142, 170, 192; Margaret Aston, *Laws against Images*, vol. 1 of *England's Iconoclasts* (Oxford: Clarendon Press, 1988), 97, 105; Hudson, *Premature Reformation*, 301–8; W. R. Jones, "Lollards and Images: The Defense of Religious Art in Later Medieval England," *Journal of the History of Ideas* 34 (1973): 27–50; Kightly, "Early Lollards," 577.

45. *EWS*, 1:390–91, 445; 2:200–201, 210, 248, 256–58; "The Testimony of William Thorpe," in *Two Wycliffite Texts*, 30.

46. As Christina von Nolcken has pointed out, mainstream Lollard opinion did not deny the existence of saints altogether—Wyclif himself was often referred to as a saint by his followers (for instance, by William White, *FZ*, 429). Instead, saints were redefined. They were thought of no longer as extraordinary Christians who occupied a median position between God and ordinary believers, but as those who would be saved, the predestined of the true Church. Von Nolcken, "Another Kind of Saint: A Lollard Perception of John Wyclif," in *From Ockham to Wyclif*, 432–40; Hudson, *Premature Reformation*, 171.

47. "In primo mandato continetur quod nullus honor est exhibendus aliquibus ymaginibus sculptis in ecclesiis per manus hominum, ne likened . . . " *HT*, 73.

48. See, for instance, Reg. Chedworth, fols. 57rv, 60r; Reg. Fitzjames, fol. 4r; Reg. Audley, fol. 148v; *A&M*, 4:134.

49. *HT*, 148; see also 47, 74.

50. See, for example, ibid., 34, 57, 61, 64, 67, 207–8; *A&M*, 3:584, 586.

51. *HT*, 142.

52. Aston, *Lollards and Reformers*, 137, 167; Aston, "Iconoclasm at Rickmansworth."

53. *HT*, 76.

54. Ibid., 218–19 (see also 76, 86); *A&M*, 3:586.

55. Stephen Greenblatt, *Renaissance Self-Fashioning: From More to Shakespeare* (Chicago: University of Chicago Press, 1980), 9.

56. See *EWS*, passim, e.g. 1:223–35, where clerical pride is the focus. See also Roper, *Oedipus and the Devil*, 43–44, regarding Reformation polemic and evil priests.

57. Aston, *England's Iconoclasts*, 1:13, 32, 107–9.

58. *Wyclifs Bibelkommentar*, ed. Gustav Adolf Benrath (Berlin: de Gruyter, 1966), 35–36, 338.

59. *EWS*, 1:661; 3:199, 210.

60. Reg. Audley, fol. 158v. See also Reg. Audley, fol. 169v; *A&M*, 4:215, 582; *Kentish Visitations*, 211.

61. Coudert, "Myth," 83–84.

62. Henry Knighton, *Chronicon*, 2 vols., ed. Joseph Rawson Lumby, R.S. (London: Public Record Office, 1889–95), 2:183.

63. She is called Elizabeth in Fitzjames's register and Ussher's transcript of Fitzjames's court book, and Joan by Foxe. Reg. Fitzjames, fol. 4r; TCD, MS 775, fol. 122v; *A&M*, 4:206.

64. Reg. Fitzjames, fol. 4r; see also Alice Hignell of Newbury, Salisbury Reg. Langton, vol. 2, fol. 39v.

65. Gowing, "Women, Sex and Honour," 51.

66. L. R. Poos, "Sex, Lies, and the Church Courts of Pre-Reformation England," *Journal of Interdisciplinary History*, forthcoming (my thanks to Dr. Poos for allowing me to read this essay in advance); Laura Gowing, "Gender and the Language of Insult," *History Workshop* 35 (1993), 1–21; Coudert, "Myth," 83–84. See also *EWS*, 2:175, where virgins and whores are contrasted.

67. Duffy, "Holy Maydens, Holy Wyfes," 196; *Stripping of the Altars*, 15–22.

68. Scribner, *Popular Culture*, 3, 6–7, 32; French, "Local Identity," 199–204.

69. *A&M*, 3:585; cf., however, *EWS*, 2:244–45, where churching is spoken of approvingly.

70. *A&M*, 4:214; see also 228.

71. Reg. Audley, fol. 147v.

72. *A&M*, 4:206.

73. Ibid., 206.

74. *HT*, 42, 44–45, 47, 49.

75. "Willelmus Whyte, qui fuit condempnatus falso pro heretico, est magnus sanctus in celo et sanctissimus doctor ordinatus et missus a Deo; quodque omni die ipsa oravit ad eundem sanctum Willelmum Whyte, et omni die vite sue orabit ad eum ut ipse dignetur intercedere pro ipsa ad Deum celi." Ibid., 47.

76. *Great Chronicle of London*, 252; cf. Duffy, *Stripping of the Altars*, 197.

77. For Protestantism, see Roper, *Holy Household*, passim; Coudert, "Myth"; Diane Willen, "Godly Women in Early Modern England: Puritanism and Gender," *JEH* 43 (1992): 561–80. Many historians see a circumscription of women's roles in Counter-Reformation Catholicism, similar in spirit to that in Protestantism. See Monter, "Protestant Wives," 209–11; Wiesner, "Women's Response," 159–60.

78. McFarlane, *Lancastrian Kings and Lollard Knights*, 140–225; Hudson, *Premature Reformation*, 60–119; Hudson, "Wycliffism in Oxford, 1381–1411," in *Wyclif in His Times*, ed. Anthony Kenny (Oxford: Clarendon Press, 1986), 67–84; Kightly, "The Early Lollards."

Works Cited

MANUSCRIPT SOURCES

Aylesbury, Buckinghamshire Record Office
   Wills: MSS D/A/We/1/8, D/A/We/1/32, D/A/We/1/77, D/A/We/2, fols.
   5v–6r, D/A/We/2/5, D/A/We/2/6, D/A/We/2/52, D/A/We/2/64,
   D/A/We/2, fol. 95v, D/A/We/2/107, D/A/We/2, fol. 115r,
   D/A/We/2/135, D/A/We/3/44, D/A/We/3/242, D/A/We/3/318,
   D/A/We/4/5, D/A/We/4/186, D/A/We/6/40, D/A/We/6/55,
   D/A/We/6/197, D/A/We/6/398, D/A/We/7/117, D/A/We/8/3,
   D/A/We/8/16, D/A/We/8/80, D/A/We/8/165, D/A/We/8/201,
   D/A/We/9/3, D/A/We/9/49, D/A/We/9/85, D/A/We/11/133,
   D/A/We/12/150, D/A/We/12/267, D/A/We/12/315, D/A/We/14/144,
   D/A/We/14/171, D/A/We/15/72, D/A/We/16/28, D/A/We/16/29,
   D/A/We/154/14, D/A/We/154/69, D/A/We/154/175, D/A/Wf/1/89,
   D/A/Wf/1/268, D/A/Wf/4/248, D/A/Wf/6/163
Birmingham, City Reference Library
   MS 273978 (Coventry City Annal)
Chelmsford, Essex Record Office
   Wills: MSS D/ABR 2/53, D/ABR 4/102, D/ABW 1/66, D/ABW 3/36,
   D/ABW 3/171, D/ABW 4/96, D/ABW 4/140, D/ABW 4/315, D/ABW
   8/106, D/ABW 13/4, D/ABW 14/55, D/ABW 25/35, D/ABW 33/69,
   D/ACR 3/159, D/ACR 4/70, D/ACR 4/81, D/ACR 4/185
   D/DB M2 (Manor Court Roll, Steeple Bumpstead)
   D/DB M3 (Manor Court Roll, Steeple Bumpstead)
   T/A 427/1/1 (Calendar of Lay Subsidy Roll, 1523)
   T/A 427/1/2 (Calendar of Lay Subsidy Roll, 1523)
   T/A 427/1/5 (Calendar of Lay Subsidy Roll, 1524)
   T/A 427/1/7 (Calendar of Lay Subsidy Roll, 1524)
   T/G 107 (Index of Clergy)
Dublin, Trinity College
   MS 775 (Ussher's Notebook)
Hertford, Hertfordshire Record Office
   ASA 2AR (Will Register)
Lichfield, Lichfield Joint Record Office
   MS B/A/1/12 (Reg. Hales)
   MS B/A/1/14i (Reg. G. Blyth)
   MS B/C/13 (Lich. Ct. Bk.)
   Inventory of Margery Locock of Coventry, 6 Feb. 1542/3

Lincoln, Lincolnshire Archives Office
  Episcopal Register XX (Reg. Chedworth)
  Episcopal Register XXVI (Reg. Longland)
London, British Library
  Harl. MS 421 (Foxe's papers)
London, Corporation of London Record Office
  Court of Husting, Roll 241 (13) (Will)
London, Greater London Record Office
  MS DL/C/205 (Consistory Court of London Deposition Book, 1467–76)
London, Guildhall Library
  MS 9065 (Commissary Court of London Deposition Book, 1489–97)
  Will registers MSS 9168/6, 9168/7, 9168/8, 9168/9, 9171/9, 9171/10, 9171/11
  MS 9531/9 (Reg. Fitzjames)
London, Lambeth Palace Library
  Reg. W. Courtenay
  Reg. Morton, vol. 1
  Reg. Warham, vol. 1
London, Public Record Office
  C.1 (Chancery Proceedings)
  C.85 (Signicavits)
  E.101 (Exchequer document, Horses bought at Amersham)
  E.150 (Inquisition post mortem)
  E.179 (Subsidy rolls)
  Prerogative Court of Canterbury Wills, Prob. 11/7 (4 Logge), Prob. 11/14 (41
  Holgrave), Prob. 11/15 (5 Adeane, 18 Adeane, 22 Adeane, 24 Adeane, 29 Ade-
  ane, 35 Adeane), Prob. 11/16 (9 Bennett, 19 Bennett, 24 Bennett), Prob. 11/17
  (10 and 20 Fetiplace, 22 Fetiplace, 24 Fetiplace, 30 Fetiplace, 31 Fetiplace), Prob.
  11/18 (15 Holder), Prob. 11/19 (9 Ayloffe, 14 Ayloffe, 18 Ayloffe, 22 Ayloffe, 28
  Ayloffe), Prob. 11/21 (F.19 Bodfelde, 23 Bodfelde, F.28 Bodfelde, F.32 Bodfelde,
  F.34 Bodfelde, 37 Bodfelde), Prob. 11/22 (37 Porch), Prob. 11/23 (20 Jankyn),
  Prob. 11/25 (14 Hogen, 25 Hogen, F.39 Hogen), Prob. 11/27 (F.22 Dyngeley),
  Prob. 11/29 (F.29 Spert), Prob. 11/31 (23 Alen, F.33 Alen), Prob. 11/32 (16
  Populwell), Prob. 11/39 (9 Wrastley)
  STAC 2 (Star Chamber)
London, Westminster Diocesan Archives
  MS B.2.8 (Alnwick's Court Book)
Maidstone, Kent Archives Office
  Wills, MSS PRC 3/7, 3/10, 3/11, 3/12, 17/11, 17/13, 17/16, 17/17, 17/19,
  32/11
  MS Te/C1 (Civic Records of Tenterden)
Oxford, Bodleian Library
  MS 31431 (Coventry City Annal)
Oxford, Oxfordshire Record Office
  MSS Wills Oxon. 178.95, 179.97, 180.14, 182.194
Reading, Berkshire Record Office
  D/A1 (Will Register)

Trowbridge, Wiltshire Record Office
  Reg. Audley
  Reg. J. Blythe
  Salisbury Reg. Langton
Winchester, Hampshire Record Office
  MS A1/15, Reg. P. Courtenay
  MS A1/16, Winchester Reg. Langton
  MSS A1/18, A1/20, Reg. Fox, vols. 2, 4

PUBLISHED PRIMARY SOURCES

Amundesham, John. *Johannis Amundesham annales monasterii Sancti Albani.* 2 vols. Edited by H. T. Riley. Rolls Series. London: Public Record Office, 1870–71.

Aquinas, Thomas. *Summa theologiae.* 5 vols. Ottawa: Collège Dominicain d'Ottawa, 1941.

Calendar of Inquisitions Post Mortem . . . Henry VII. 3 vols. London: Public Record Office, 1898–1955.

Calendar of Letter-Books . . . of the City of London. Letter Book L. Edited by Reginald R. Sharpe. London: Corporation of London, 1912.

Calendar of Patent Rolls, 1494–1509. London: Public Record Office, 1916.

Catalogue of Ancient Deeds. 6 vols. London: Public Record Office, 1890–1915.

The Certificate of Musters for Buckinghamshire in 1522. Edited by A. C. Chibnall. Royal Commission on Historical Manuscripts, Joint Publication 18. 1973.

"Chronicle from the Register of the Grey Friars of London," edited by Richard Howlett. In *Monumenta Franciscana.* Vol. 2. Rolls Series. London: Longman, 1882.

Chronicles of London. Edited by Charles Lethbridge Kingsford. Oxford: Clarendon, 1905.

The Courts of the Archdeaconry of Buckingham, 1483–1523. Edited by E. M. Elvey. Buckinghamshire Record Society, 19. 1975.

Coventry Leet Book, 1420–1555. 4 pts. Edited by M. D. Harris. Early English Text Society, Original Series, 134, 135, 138, 146. 1907–13.

Dymmok, Roger. *Liber contra XII errores et hereses Lollardorum.* Edited by H. S. Cronin. London: Wyclif Society, 1922.

English Wycliffite Sermons. 3 vols. Vols. 1 and 3 edited by Anne Hudson. Vol. 2 edited by Pamela Gradon. Oxford: Clarendon, 1983–90.

An Episcopal Court Book for the Diocese of Lincoln, 1514–1520. Edited by Margaret Bowker. Lincoln Record Society, 61. 1967.

Fabyan, Robert. *The New Chronicles of England and France.* Edited by Henry Ellis. London: Rivington, 1811.

Fasciculi zizaniorum Magistri Johannis Wyclif cum tritico. Edited by W. W. Shirley. Rolls Series. London: Public Record Office, 1858.

Fish, Simon. "A Supplicacyon for the Beggers." In *Four Supplications*, edited by Frederick J. Furnivall. Early English Text Society, Extra Series, 13. 1871.

Foxe, John. *Acts and Monuments.* 8 vols. Edited by George Townsend. London: Seeley, Burnside and Seeley, 1843.

Gratian. *Decretum*. Vol. 1 of *Corpus iuris canonici*. 2 vols. Edited by Aemilius Friedberg. Leipzig: Tauchnitz, 1879–81.

The Great Chronicle of London. Edited by A. H. Thomas and I. D. Thornley. London:
George W. Jones, 1938.

Hale, William. *A Series of Precedents and Proceedings in Criminal Causes, 1475–1640*.
London: Rivington, 1847.

Henley Borough Records: Assembly Books i–iv, 1395–1543. Edited by P. M. Briers. Oxfordshire Record Society, 1960.

Heresy Trials in the Diocese of Norwich, 1428–31. Edited by Norman P. Tanner. Camden
Society, 4th ser., 20. 1977.

The Holy Bible . . . Made from the Latin Vulgate by John Wycliffe and his Followers. 4
vols. Edited by Josiah Forshall and Frederic Madden. Oxford: Oxford University Press, 1850.

Hugh of St. Victor. *De sacramentis*. In *Patrologia cursus completus . . . series latina*,
176:479–520. Edited by J.P. Migne. Paris: Garnier, 1880.

Kempe, Margery. *The Book of Margery Kempe*. Edited by S. B. Meech and H. E.
Allen. Early English Text Society, Original Series, 212. 1940.

Kentish Visitations of Archbishop William Warham and His Deputies, 1511–12. Edited by
K. L. Wood-Legh. Kent Records, 24. 1984.

Knighton, Henry. *Chronicon*. 2 vols. Edited by Joseph Rawson Lumby. Rolls Series.
London: Public Record Office, 1889–95.

Lanterne of Liȝt. Edited by Lilian M. Swinburn. Early English Text Society, Original
Series, 151. 1917.

Letters and Papers, Foreign and Domestic, of the Reign of Henry VIII. 21 vols. and
addenda. Edited by J. S. Brewer et al. London: Public Record Office, 1862–
1932.

Lincoln Diocese Documents 1450–1544. Edited by Andrew Clark. Early English Text
Society, Original Series, 149. 1914.

Lombard, Peter. *Sententiae in iv libris distinctae*. 2 vols. Edited by Patres Collegii S.
Bonaventurae ad Claras Aquas. Spicilegium Bonaventurianum, 4–5. Grottaferrata: Editiones Collegii S. Bonaventurae ad Claras Aquas, 1971–81.

More, Thomas. *A Dialogue Concerning Heresies*. 2 vols. Edited by Thomas M. C.
Lawler, Germain Marc'hadour, and Richard C. Marius. Vol. 6, pts. 1–2, of *The
Complete Works of St. Thomas More*. New Haven, Conn.: Yale University Press,
1981.

Netter, Thomas. *Doctrinale antiquitatum fidei Catholicae Ecclesiae*. 3 vols. Edited by
F. Bonaventura Blanciotti. Venice: Antonio Bassanesi, 1759.

The Oath Book or Red Parchment Book of Colchester. Edited by W. Gurney Benham.
Colchester: Essex County Standard Office, 1907.

Plumpton Correspondence. Edited by T. Stapleton. Camden Society, 4. 1839.

Raymond of Pennaforte. *Summa de matrimonio*. Edited by Xavierus Ochoa and
Aloisius Diez. Universa Bibliotheca Iuris, I/C. Rome: Commentarium Pro
Religiosis, 1978.

Records of Early English Drama: Coventry. Edited by R. W. Ingram. Toronto: University of Toronto Press, 1981.

Records of the City of Norwich. 2 vols. Edited by J. C. Tingley. Norwich: Jarrold, 1906–
10.

Red Paper Book of Colchester. Edited by W. Gurney Benham. Colchester: Essex County Standard Office, 1903.

Register of Henry Chichele. 4 vols. Edited by E. F. Jacob. Canterbury and York Society, 42, 45–47. 1938–47.

Register of the Holy Trinity Guild, Coventry. 2 vols. Vol. 1 edited by M. D. Harris. Vol. 2 edited by G. Templeman. Dugdale Society, 13, 19. 1935, 1944.

The Register of Thomas Langton, Bishop of Salisbury, 1485–93. Edited by D. P. Wright. Canterbury and York Society, 74. 1985.

Selections from English Wycliffite Writings. Edited by Anne Hudson. Cambridge: Cambridge University Press, 1978.

Statutes of the Realm. 11 vols. in 12. London: Eyre and Strahan, 1810–28. Reprint, London: Dawson of Pall Mall, 1963.

Stonor Letters and Papers, 1290–1483. 2 vols. Edited by Charles Lethbridge Kingsford. Camden Society, 3rd ser., 29–30. 1919.

Strype, John. *Ecclesiastical Memorials . . . under King Henry VIII, King Edward VI, and Queen Mary I*. 3 vols. Oxford: Clarendon, 1822.

The Subsidy Roll for the County of Buckingham Anno 1524. Edited by A. C. Chibnall and A. Vere Woodman. Buckinghamshire Record Society, 8. 1950.

Taylor, A. H. "The Municipal Records of Tenterden, Part I." *Archaeologia Cantiana* 32 (1917): 283–302.

Two Wycliffite Texts. Edited by Anne Hudson. Early English Text Society, 301. 1993.

Vergil, Polydore. *The Anglica Historia of Polydore Vergil, A.D. 1485–1531*. Edited by Denys Hay. Camden Society, 3rd ser., 74. 1950.

Visitations in the Diocese of Lincoln, 1517–1531. 3 vols. Edited by A. Hamilton Thompson. Lincoln Record Society, 33, 35, 37. 1940–47.

"William Gregory's Chronicle of London." In *The Historical Collections of a Citizen of London in the Fifteenth Century*, edited by James Gairdner. Camden Society, 17. 1876.

Wyclif, John. *De eucharistia tractatus maior*. Edited by Johann Loserth. London: Wyclif Society, 1892. Reprint, New York: Johnson Reprint Co., 1966.

———. *De officio pastorali*. Edited by Gotthard Lechler. Leipzig: Edelmann, 1863.

———. *Opera minora*. Edited by Johann Loserth. London: Wyclif Society, 1913. Reprint, New York: Johnson Reprint Co., 1966.

———. *Opus evangelicum*. 2 vols. Edited by Johann Loserth. London: Wyclif Society, 1895.

———. *Trialogus*. Edited by Gotthard Lechler. Oxford: Clarendon, 1869.

———. *Wyclifs Bibelkommentar*. Edited by Gustav Adolf Benrath. Berlin: de Gruyter, 1966.

SECONDARY SOURCES

Abels, Richard, and Ellen Harrison. "The Participation of Women in Languedocian Catharism." *Mediaeval Studies* 41 (1979): 215–51.

Adamson, Nancy Lee. "Urban Families: The Social Context of the London Elite, 1500–1603." Ph.D. diss., University of Toronto, 1983.

Anderson, Bonnie S., and Judith P. Zinsser. *A History of Their Own: Women in Europe from Prehistory to the Present.* Vol. 1. New York: Harper and Row, 1989.

Andre, Caroline S. "Some Selected Aspects of the Role of Women in 16th Century England." *International Journal of Women's Studies* 4 (1981): 76–88.

Aston, Margaret. "'Caim's Castles': Poverty, Politics and Disendowment." In *The Church, Politics and Patronage in the Fifteenth Century*, edited by Barrie Dobson, 45–81. Gloucester: Sutton, 1984.

——. *England's Iconoclasts.* Vol. 1, *Laws Against Images.* Oxford: Clarendon, 1988.

——. "Iconoclasm at Rickmansworth, 1522: Troubles of Churchwardens." *Journal of Ecclesiastical History* 40 (1989): 524–52.

——. *Lollards and Reformers: Images and Literacy in Late Medieval Religion.* London: Hambledon, 1984.

Atkinson, Clarissa W. "'Precious Balsam in a Fragile Glass': The Ideology of Virginity in the Later Middle Ages." *Journal of Family History* 8 (1983): 131–43.

Barron, Caroline M. "The Parish Fraternities of Medieval London." In *The Church in Pre-Reformation Society. Essays in Honour of F.R.H. DuBoulay*, edited by Caroline M. Barron and Christopher Harper-Bill, 13–37. Woodbridge, Suffolk: Boydell, 1985.

Bäuml, Franz H. "Varieties and Consequences of Medieval Literacy and Illiteracy." *Speculum* 55 (1980): 237–65.

Bennett, Judith M. "Medieval Women, Modern Women: Across the Great Divide." In *Culture and History, 1350–1600: Essays on English Communities, Identities and Writing*, edited by David Aers, 147–75. London: Harvester Wheatsheaf, 1992.

——. "Public Power and Authority in the Medieval English Countryside." In *Women and Power in the Middle Ages*, edited by Mary Erler and Maryanne Kowaleski, 18–36. Athens: University of Georgia Press, 1988.

——. *Women in the Medieval English Countryside: Gender and Household in Brigstock Before the Plague.* New York: Oxford University Press, 1987.

Bennett, Michael. "Spiritual Kinship and the Baptismal Name in Traditional European Societies." In *Principalities, Powers and Estates: Studies in Medieval and Early Modern Government and Society*, edited by L. O. Frappell, 1–13. Adelaide: Adelaide University Union Press, 1979.

Biller, Peter. "The Common Woman in the Western Church in the Thirteenth and Fourteenth Centuries." *Studies in Church History* 27 (1990): 127–57.

——. "Marriage Patterns and Women's Lives: A Sketch of a Pastoral Geography." In *Woman Is a Worthy Wight: Women in English Society, c. 1200–1500*, edited by P. J. P. Goldberg, 60–107. Gloucester: Sutton, 1992.

Bock, Gisela. "Challenging Dichotomies: Perspectives on Women's History." In *Writing Women's History: International Perspectives*, edited by Karen Offen, Ruth Roach Pierson, and Jane Rendall, 1–23. Bloomington: Indiana University Press, 1991.

Bolton, Brenda. "Mulieres Sanctae." *Studies in Church History* 10 (1973): 77–95.

Børresen, Kari Elisabeth. *Subordination and Equivalence: The Nature and Role of Women in Augustine and Thomas Aquinas.* Translated by Charles H. Talbot. Washington: University Press of America, 1981.

Bostick, Curtis V. "The Apocalypse and the 'ABC's': Lollard Strategies for Success in

Late Medieval and Early Modern England." Paper presented at the Sixteenth Century Studies Conference, Toronto, 28 October 1994.

Bowker, Margaret. *The Henrician Reformation: The Diocese of Lincoln under John Longland, 1521–1547*. Cambridge: Cambridge University Press, 1981.

———. *The Secular Clergy in the Diocese of Lincoln, 1495–1520*. Cambridge: Cambridge University Press, 1968.

Brewer, Priscilla J. "'Tho' of the Weaker Sex': A Reassessment of Gender Equality among the Shakers." *Signs* 17 (1992): 609–35.

Brigden, Susan. *London and the Reformation*. Oxford: Clarendon Press, 1989.

———. "Religion and Social Obligation in Early Sixteenth-Century London." *Past and Present* 103 (1984): 67–112.

Britnell, R. H. *Growth and Decline in Colchester, 1300–1525*. Cambridge: Cambridge University Press, 1986.

Brown, Peter. *The Cult of the Saints: Its Rise and Function in Latin Christianity*. Chicago: University of Chicago Press, 1981.

Brundage, James A. *Law, Sex, and Christian Society in Medieval Europe*. Chicago: University of Chicago Press, 1987.

Bullough, Vern L. "Postscript: Heresy, Witchcraft and Sexuality." In *Sexual Practices and the Medieval Church*, edited by Vern L. Bullough and James Brundage, 206–17. Buffalo, N.Y.: Prometheus, 1982.

Butler, Judith. *Bodies That Matter: On the Discursive Limits of "Sex."* New York: Routledge, 1993.

———. *Gender Trouble: Feminism and the Subversion of Identity*. New York: Routledge, 1990.

Bynum, Caroline Walker. *Fragmentation and Redemption: Essays on Gender and the Human Body in Medieval Religion*. New York: Zone, 1991.

———. *Holy Feast and Holy Fast: The Religious Significance of Food to Medieval Women*. Berkeley: University of California Press, 1987.

———. *Jesus as Mother: Studies in the Spirituality of the High Middle Ages*. Berkeley: University of California Press, 1982.

Calhoun, C. J. "Community: Toward a Variable Conceptualization for Comparative Research." *Social History* 5 (1980): 105–29.

Cameron, Euan. *The Reformation of the Heretics: The Waldenses of the Alps, 1480–1580*. Oxford: Clarendon, 1984.

Camp, Anthony J. *Wills and Their Whereabouts*. Bridge Place: Phillimore, 1963.

Carroll, Jackson W. "Some Issues in Clergy Authority." *Review of Religious Research* 23 (1981): 99–117.

Catto, Jeremy I. "John Wyclif and the Cult of the Eucharist." In *The Bible in the Medieval World*, edited by Katherine Walsh and Diana Wood, 269–86. Studies in Church History, Subsidia, 4. Oxford: Blackwell, 1985.

Chartier, Roger. *Cultural History: Between Practices and Representations*. Ithaca, N.Y.: Cornell University Press, 1988.

Chojnacki, Stanley. "Subaltern Patriarchs: Patrician Bachelors in Renaissance Venice." In *Medieval Masculinities: Regarding Men in the Middle Ages*, edited by Clare A. Lees, 73–90. Minneapolis: University of Minnesota Press, 1994.

Chrisman, Miriam Usher. "Women and the Reformation in Strasbourg, 1490–1530." *Archiv für Reformationsgeschichte* 63 (1972): 143–68.

Clanchy, M. T. *From Memory to Written Record: England, 1066–1307*. London: Arnold, 1979.

Cohen, A. P. *The Symbolic Construction of Community*. Chichester: Horwood, 1985.

Collinson, Patrick. "Truth and Legend: The Veracity of John Foxe's *Book of Martyrs*." In *Clio's Mirror: Historiography in Britain and the Netherlands*, edited by A. C. Duke and C. A. Tamse, 31–54. Britain and the Netherlands, 8. Zutphen: de Walburg, 1985.

Coudert, Allison P. "The Myth of the Improved Status of Protestant Women: The Case of the Witchcraze." In *The Politics of Gender in Early Modern Europe*, edited by Jean R. Brink, Allison P. Coudert, and Maryanne C. Horowitz, 65–86. Sixteenth Century Essays and Studies, 12. Kirksville: Sixteenth Century Journal Publishers, 1989.

Crawford, Patricia. *Women and Religion in England, 1500–1720*. London and New York: Routledge, 1993.

Cressy, David. *Literacy and the Social Order: Reading and Writing in Tudor and Stuart England*. Cambridge: Cambridge University Press, 1980.

Crompton, James. "*Fasciculi Zizaniorum*." *Journal of Ecclesiastical History* 12 (1961): 35–45, 155–66.

Cross, Claire. "'Great Reasoners in Scripture': The Activities of Women Lollards, 1380–1530." In *Medieval Women*, edited by Derek Baker, 359–80. Studies in Church History, Subsidia, 1. Oxford: Blackwell, 1978.

Dalarun, Jacques. "The Clerical Gaze." In *A History of Women in the West*. Vol. 2, *Silences of the Middle Ages*, edited by Christiane Klapisch-Zuber, 15–42. Cambridge, Mass.: Belknap Press of Harvard University Press, 1992.

Daniel, David P. "Piety, Politics and Perversion: Noblewomen in Reformation Hungary." In *Women in Reformation and Counter-Reformation Europe*, edited by Sherrin Marshall, 68–88. Bloomington: Indiana University Press, 1989.

Davidoff, Leonore, and Catherine Hall. *Family Fortunes: Men and Women of the English Middle Class, 1780–1850*. London: Hutchinson, 1987.

Davies, Kathleen M. "Continuity and Change in Literary Advice on Marriage." In *Marriage and Society: Studies in the Social History of Marriage*, edited by R. B. Outhwaite, 58–80. London: Europa, 1981.

Davies, Richard G. "Lollardy and Locality." *Transactions of the Royal Historical Society*. 6th ser., 1 (1991): 191–212.

Davis, E. Jeffries. "Authorities for the Case of Richard Hunne." *English Historical Review* 30 (1915): 477–88.

Davis, John F. *Heresy and Reformation in the South-East of England, 1520–1559*. London: Royal Historical Society, 1983.

———. "Joan of Kent, Lollardy and the English Reformation." *Journal of Ecclesiastical History* 33 (1982): 225–33.

———. "Lollard Survival and the Textile Industry in the South-East of England." *Studies in Church History* 3 (1966): 191–201.

———. "Lollardy and the Reformation in England." *Archiv für Reformationsgeschichte* 73 (1982): 227–32.

Davis, Natalie Zemon. "Boundaries and the Sense of Self in Sixteenth-Century

France." In *Reconstructing Individualism: Autonomy, Individuality, and the Self in Western Thought*, edited by Thomas C. Heller et al., 53–63. Stanford, Calif.: Stanford University Press, 1986.

———. *Fiction in the Archives: Pardon Tales and Their Tellers in Sixteenth-Century France*. Stanford, Calif.: Stanford University Press, 1987.

———. "From 'Popular Religion' to Religious Cultures." In *Reformation Europe: A Guide to Research*, edited by Steven Ozment, 321–41. St. Louis, Mo.: Center for Reformation Research, 1982.

———. *Society and Culture in Early Modern France*. Stanford, Calif.: Stanford University Press, 1975.

———. "Some Tasks and Themes in the Study of Popular Religion." In *The Pursuit of Holiness in Late Medieval and Renaissance Religion*, edited by Charles Trinkhaus and Heiko A. Oberman, 307–36. Leiden: Brill, 1974.

———. "'Women's History' in Transition: The European Case." *Feminist Studies* 3 (1976): 83–103.

Deanesly, Margaret. *The Lollard Bible and Other Medieval Biblical Versions*. Cambridge: Cambridge University Press, 1920.

Derrett, J. Duncan M. "The Affairs of Richard Hunne and Friar Standish." In *The Complete Works of St. Thomas More*. Vol. 9, 215–46. New Haven, Conn.: Yale University Press, 1979.

Dews, D. Colin. "Ann Carr and the Female Revivalists of Leeds." In *Religion in the Lives of English Women, 1760–1930*, edited by Gail Malmgreen, 68–87. London: Croom Helm, 1986.

Dickens, A. G. *The English Reformation*. London: Batsford, 1964.

———. *Lollards and Protestants in the Diocese of York, 1509–1538*. London: Hambledon, 1982.

Donahue, Charles Jr. "The Canon Law on the Formation of Marriage and Social Practice in the Later Middle Ages." *Journal of Family History* 8 (1983): 144–58.

Drew, Charles. *Early Parochial Organisation in England: The Origins of the Office of Churchwarden*. London: St. Anthony, 1954.

Duffy, Eamon. "Holy Maydens, Holy Wyfes: The Cult of Women Saints in Fifteenth- and Sixteenth-Century England." *Studies in Church History* 27 (1990): 175–96.

———. *The Stripping of the Altars: Traditional Religion in England, 1400–1580*. New Haven, Conn.: Yale University Press, 1992.

Dugdale, William. *The Antiquities of Warwickshire Illustrated from Records, Leiger-Books, Manuscripts, Charters, Evidences, Tombes and Armes . . . .* London: Thomas Warren, 1656.

Emden, A. B. *Biographical Register of the University of Cambridge to 1500*. Cambridge: Cambridge University Press, 1963.

———. *Biographical Register of the University of Oxford to 1500*. 3 vols. Oxford: Oxford University Press, 1957–59.

———. *Biographical Register of the University of Oxford, A.D. 1501 to 1540*. Oxford: Clarendon, 1974.

Emmison, F. G. *Guide to the Essex Record Office*. 2nd ed. Chelmsford: Essex Record Office Publication 51. 1969.

———, ed. *Wills at Chelmsford*. Vol. 1 (1400–1619). Index Library, 78. London: British Record Society, 1958.

Evans, A. P. "Social Aspects of Medieval Heresy." In *Persecution and Liberty: Essays in Honor of George Lincoln Burr*, 93–116. New York: Century, 1931.

Farmer, Sharon. "Persuasive Voices: Clerical Images of Medieval Wives." *Speculum* 61 (1986): 517–43.

Ferrante, Joan. "The Education of Women in the Middle Ages in Theory, Fact, and Fantasy." In *Beyond Their Sex: Learned Women of the European Past*, edited by Patricia H. Labalme, 9–42. New York: New York University Press, 1980.

Field, Clive D. "Adam and Eve: Gender in the English Free Church Constituency." *Journal of Ecclesiastical History* 44 (1993): 63–79.

Fines, John. "Heresy Trials in the Diocese of Coventry and Lichfield, 1511–1512." *Journal of Ecclesiastical History* 14 (1963): 160–74.

———. "The Post-Mortem Condemnation for Heresy of Richard Hunne." *English Historical Review* 78 (1963): 528–31.

Finucane, Ronald. *Miracles and Pilgrims: Popular Belief in Medieval England*. London: Dent, 1977.

Fitch, Marc, ed. *Index to Testamentary Records in the Commissary Court of London (London Division)*. Vol. 2 (1489–1570). Historical Manuscripts Commission, Joint Publication 13. London: Her Majesty's Stationery Office, 1974.

Forde, Simon. "The 'Strong Woman' and 'The Woman Who Surrounds a Man': Perceptions of Woman in Wyclif's Theological Writings." *Révue d'histoire ecclésiastique* 88 (1993): 54–87.

French, Katherine. "Local Identity and the Late Medieval Parish: The Communities of Bath and Wells." Ph.D. diss., University of Minnesota, 1993.

Gibson, Gail McMurray. *The Theater of Devotion: East Anglian Drama and Society in the Late Middle Ages*. Chicago: University of Chicago Press, 1989.

Gilchrist, J. "The Social Doctrine of John Wycliffe." *Canadian Historical Association Historical Papers*, 1969, 157–65.

Gilchrist, Roberta, and Marilyn Oliva. *Religious Women in Medieval East Anglia*. Studies in East Anglian History, 1. Norwich: Centre of East Anglian Studies, 1993.

Goheen, R. B. "Peasant Politics? Village Community and the Crown in Fifteenth-Century England." *American Historical Review* 96 (1991): 42–62.

Goldberg, P. J. P. "Marriage, Migration, Servanthood, and Life-Cycle in Yorkshire Towns of the Later Middle Ages: Some York Cause Paper Evidence." *Continuity and Change* 1 (1986): 141–69.

———. "Women in Fifteenth-Century Town Life." In *Towns and Townspeople in the Fifteenth Century*, edited by John A. F. Thomson, 107–28. Gloucester: Sutton, 1988.

———. *Women, Work and Life Cycle in a Medieval Economy: Women in York and Yorkshire, c. 1300–1520*. Oxford: Clarendon, 1992.

Gowing, Laura. "Gender and the Language of Insult." *History Workshop* 35 (1993): 1–21.

———. "Women, Sex and Honour: The London Church Courts, 1572–1640." Ph.D. diss., University of London, 1993.

Granovetter, Mark S. "The Strength of Weak Ties." *American Journal of Sociology* 78 (1973): 1360–80.

———. "The Strength of Weak Ties: A Network Theory Revisited." In *Social Structure and Network Analysis*, edited by Peter V. Marsden and Nan Lin, 105–30. Beverly Hills, Calif.: Sage, 1982.

Greenblatt, Stephen. *Renaissance Self-Fashioning: From More to Shakespeare*. Chicago: University of Chicago Press, 1980.

Grosz, Elizabeth. *Volatile Bodies: Toward a Corporeal Feminism*. Bloomington: Indiana University Press, 1994.

Grundmann, Herbert. *Religiöse Bewegungen im Mittelalter*. 2nd ed. Hildesheim: Olms, 1961.

Haas, Louis. "Social Connections Between Parents and Godparents in Late Medieval Yorkshire." *Medieval Prosopography* 10 (1989): 1–21.

Hampshire, Annette P. and James A. Beckford. "Religious Sects and the Concept of Deviance: The Mormons and the Moonies." *British Journal of Sociology* 34 (1983): 208–29.

Hanawalt, Barbara A. *The Ties That Bound: Peasant Families in Medieval England*. New York: Oxford University Press, 1986.

Hanawalt, Barbara A., and Ben R. McRee. "The Guilds of *Homo Prudens* in Late Medieval England." *Continuity and Change* 7 (1992): 163–79.

Hargreaves, Henry. "Sir John Oldcastle and Wycliffite Views on Clerical Marriage." *Medium Aevum* 42 (1973): 141–46.

Härtel, Helmar. "Lollardische Lehrelemente im 14. und 15. Jahrhundert." Ph.D. diss., Universität Göttingen, 1969.

Hasted, Edward. *The History and Topographical Survey of the County of Kent*. 12 vols. Canterbury: Bristow, 1797–1801. Reprint, Wakefield: E.P. Publishing, 1972.

Haywood, Carol Lois. "The Authority and Empowerment of Women among Spiritualist Groups." *Journal for the Scientific Study of Religion* 22 (1983): 157–66.

Herlihy, David. *Opera Muliebria: Women and Work in Medieval Europe*. New York: McGraw-Hill, 1990.

———. *Women in Medieval Society*. Smith History Lecture. Houston, Tex.: University of St. Thomas, 1971.

Higgs, Laquita Mae Alexander. "Lay Piety in the Borough of Colchester, 1485–1558." Ph.D. diss., University of Michigan, 1983.

Horner, Patrick J. " 'The King Taught Us the Lesson': Benedictine Support for Henry V's Suppression of the Lollards." *Mediaeval Studies* 52 (1990): 190–220.

Hoskins, W. G. "English Provincial Towns in the Early Sixteenth Century." *Transactions of the Royal Historical Society*, 5th ser., 6 (1956): 4–19.

Houlbrooke, Ralph A. *The English Family, 1450–1700*. London: Longman, 1984.

Howell, Martha C. *Women, Production and Patriarchy in Late Medieval Cities*. Chicago: University of Chicago Press, 1986.

Hsia, R. Po-Chia. "Civic Wills as Sources for the Study of Piety in Muenster, 1530–1618." *Sixteenth Century Journal* 14 (1983): 321–48.

Hudson, Anne. *Lollards and Their Books*. London: Hambledon, 1985.

———. *The Premature Reformation: Wycliffite Texts and Lollard History*. Oxford: Clarendon, 1988.

———. "Wycliffism in Oxford, 1381–1411." In *Wyclif in His Times*, edited by Anthony Kenny, 67–84. Oxford: Clarendon, 1986.

Hutchison, Ann M. "Devotional Reading in the Monastery and in the Late Medieval Household." In *De Cella in Seculum: Religious and Secular Life and Devotion in Late Medieval England*, edited by Michael G. Sargent, 215–28. Woodbridge, Suffolk: Boydell and Brewer, 1989.

Ingram, Martin. "Spousals Litigation in the English Ecclesiastical Courts, c. 1350–1640." In *Marriage and Society: Studies in the Social History of Marriage*, edited by R. B. Outhwaite, 35–57. London: Europa, 1981.

James, Mervyn. "Ritual, Drama and Social Body in the Late Medieval English Town." *Past and Present* 98 (1983): 3–29.

Jedin, Hubert, Kenneth Scott Latourette, and Jochen Martin, eds. *Atlas zur Kirchengeschichte*. Freiburg: Herder, 1987.

Johnson, Penelope D. *Equal in Monastic Profession: Religious Women in Medieval France*. Chicago: University of Chicago Press, 1991.

Jones, W.R. "Lollards and Images: The Defense of Religious Art in Later Medieval England." *Journal of the History of Ideas* 34 (1973): 27–50.

Julien, Lucienne. "Le catharisme et la femme." *Cahiers d'études cathares* 27 (1976): 29–37.

Karant-Nunn, Susan C. "Continuity and Change: Some Effects of the Reformation on the Women of Zwickau." *Sixteenth Century Journal* 12 (1982): 17–42.

Keen, Maurice. "Wyclif, the Bible, and Transubstantiation." In *Wyclif in His Times*, edited by Anthony Kenny, 1–16. Oxford: Clarendon, 1986.

Kenny, Anthony. *Wyclif*. Oxford: Oxford University Press, 1985.

Kieckhefer, Richard. *Unquiet Souls: Fourteenth-Century Saints and Their Religious Milieu*. Chicago: University of Chicago Press, 1984.

Kightly, Charles. "The Early Lollards: A Survey of Popular Lollard Activity in England, 1382–1428." D.Phil. diss., University of York, 1975.

King, Margaret L. *Women of the Renaissance*. Chicago: University of Chicago Press, 1991.

Klapisch-Zuber, Christiane, ed. *A History of Women in the West*. Vol. 2, *Silences of the Middle Ages*. Cambridge, Mass.: Belknap Press of Harvard University Press, 1992.

Klassen, John. "Women and Religious Reform in Late Medieval Bohemia." *Renaissance and Reformation* 17 (1981): 203–21.

Knowles, David, and R. Neville Hadcock. *Medieval Religious Houses, England and Wales*. London: Longmans, Green, 1953.

Koch, Gottfried. *Frauenfrage und Ketzertum im Mittelalter*. Berlin: Akademie-Verlag, 1962.

Kowaleski, Maryanne. "The Commercial Dominance of a Medieval Provincial Oligarchy: Exeter in the Late Fourteenth Century." *Mediaeval Studies* 46 (1984): 355–84.

——. "The History of Urban Families in Medieval England." *Journal of Medieval History* 14 (1988): 47–64.

Lambert, Malcolm. *Medieval Heresy: Popular Movements from the Gregorian Reform to the Reformation*. 2nd ed. Oxford: Blackwell, 1992.

Le Roy Ladurie, Emmanuel. *Montaillou: The Promised Land of Error*. Translated by Barbara Bray. New York: Vintage, 1979.

Lees, Clare A. ed. *Medieval Masculinities: Regarding Men in the Middle Ages*. Minneapolis: University of Minnesota Press, 1994.

Lerner, Gerda. *Women and History*. 2 vols. Vol. 1, *The Creation of Patriarchy*. Vol. 2, *The Creation of Feminist Consciousness: From the Middle Ages to Eighteen-Seventy*. New York: Oxford University Press, 1986–93.

Levin, Carole. "Women in *The Book of Martyrs* as Models of Behavior in Tudor England." *International Journal of Women's Studies* 4 (1981): 196–207.

Luxton, Imogen. "The Lichfield Court Book: A Postscript." *Bulletin of the Institute of Historical Research* 44 (1971): 120–25.

———. "The Reformation and Popular Culture." In *Church and Society in England: Henry VIII to James I*, edited by Felicity Heal and Rosemary O'Day, 57–77. London: Macmillan, 1977.

Macek, Ellen. "The Emergence of a Feminine Spirituality in *The Book of Martyrs*." *Sixteenth Century Journal* 19 (1988): 63–80.

Macfarlane, Alan. *Marriage and Love in England: Modes of Reproduction, 1300–1840*. Oxford: Blackwell, 1986.

Mack, Phyllis. "Women as Prophets during the English Civil War." *Feminist Studies* 8 (1982): 19–47.

Malmgreen, Gail. "Domestic Discords: Women and the Family in East Cheshire Methodism, 1750–1830." In *Disciplines of Faith: Religion, Patriarchy, and Politics*, edited by James Obelkevich, Lyndal Roper, and Raphael Samuel, 55–70. London: Routledge and Kegan Paul, 1986.

Marshall [Wyntjes], Sherrin. "Women and Religious Choices in the Sixteenth-Century Netherlands." *Archiv für Reformationsgeschichte* 75 (1984): 276–89.

———. "Women in the Reformation Era." In *Becoming Visible: Women in European History*, 1st ed., edited by Renate Bridenthal and Claudia Koonz, 165–86. New York: Houghton Mifflin, 1977.

———, ed. *Women in Reformation and Counter-Reformation Europe*. Bloomington: Indiana University Press, 1989.

Martin, J.W. *Religious Radicals in Tudor England*. London: Hambledon, 1989.

Martin, John. "Popular Culture and the Shaping of Popular Heresy in Renaissance Venice." In *Inquisition and Society in Early Modern Europe*, edited by Stephen Haliczer, 115–28. Totawa: Barnes and Noble, 1987.

McFarlane, K.B. *John Wycliffe and the Beginnings of English Nonconformity*. London: English Universities Press, 1952.

———. *Lancastrian Kings and Lollard Knights*. Oxford: Clarendon, 1972.

McLaughlin, Eleanor. "Equality of Souls, Inequality of Sexes: Woman in Medieval Theology." In *Religion and Sexism: Images of Woman in the Jewish and Christian Traditions*, edited by Rosemary Radford Ruether, 213–66. New York: Simon and Shuster, 1974.

———. "Les femmes et l'hérésie médiévale: Un problème dans l'histoire de la spiritualité." *Concilium (Nijmegen)* 111 (1976): 73–90.

McNamara, Jo Ann. "The *Herrenfrage*: The Restructuring of the Gender System, 1050–1150." In *Medieval Masculinities: Regarding Men in the Middle Ages*, edited by Clare A. Lees, 3–29. Minneapolis: University of Minnesota Press, 1994.

McNiven, Peter. *Heresy and Politics in the Reign of Henry IV: The Burning of John Badby*. Woodbridge, Suffolk: Boydell, 1987.

McRee, Ben R. "Religious Gilds and Civic Order: The Case of Norwich in the Later Middle Ages." *Speculum* 67 (1992): 69–97.

——. "Religious Gilds and Regulation of Behavior in Late Medieval Towns." In *People, Politics and Community in the Later Middle Ages*, edited by Joel T. Rosenthal and Colin Richmond, 108–22. New York: St. Martin, 1987.

McSheffrey, Shannon. "Literacy and the Gender Gap in the Late Middle Ages: Women and Reading in Lollard Communities." In *Women, The Book and the Word*, edited by Jane H. M. Taylor and Lesley Smith, 157–70. Woodbridge, Suffolk: Boydell and Brewer, 1995.

——. "Women and Lollardy: A Reassessment." *Canadian Journal of History* 26 (1991): 199–223.

——. "Women in Lollardy, 1420–1530: Gender and Class in Heretical Communities." Ph.D. diss., University of Toronto, 1992.

Milsom, S. F. C. "Richard Hunne's 'Praemunire.'" *English Historical Review* 76 (1961): 80–82.

Mitchell, Linda E. "The Lady Is a Lord: Noble Widows and Land in Thirteenth-Century Britain." *Historical Reflections/Réflexions historiques* 18 (1992): 71–97.

Monter, E. William. "Protestant Wives, Catholic Saints, and the Devil's Handmaid: Women in the Age of the Reformations." In *Becoming Visible: Women in European History*, 2nd ed., edited by Renate Bridenthal, Claudia Koonz, and Susan Stuard, 203–19. Boston: Houghton Mifflin, 1987.

Moore, R. I. *The Origins of European Dissent*. London: Allen Lane, 1977.

Moran, Jo Ann Hoeppner. *The Growth of English Schooling, 1340–1548: Learning, Literacy, and Laicization in Pre-Reformation York Diocese*. Princeton, N.J.: Princeton University Press, 1985.

Morant, Philip. *The History and Antiquities of the County of Essex, Compiled from the Best and Most Ancient Historians*. London: Osborne, 1768. Reprint, Chelmsford: Meggy and Chalk, 1816.

Mundy, John Hine. "Le mariage et les femmes à Toulouse au temps des cathares." *Annales: Economies, Sociétés, Civilisations* 42 (1987): 117–34.

——. *Men and Women at Toulouse in the Age of the Cathars*. Toronto: Pontifical Institute of Mediaeval Studies, 1990.

Nelson, Janet L. "Society, Theodicy and the Origins of Heresy: Towards a Reassessment of the Medieval Evidence." *Studies in Church History* 9 (1972): 65–77.

Niles, Philip. "Baptism and the Naming of Children in Late Medieval England." *Medieval Prosopography* 3 (1982): 95–108.

Orme, Nicholas. *English Schools in the Middle Ages*. London: Methuen, 1973.

Partner, Nancy F. "No Sex, No Gender." *Speculum* 68 (1993): 419–44.

Perry, Mary Elizabeth. "Beatas and the Inquisition in Early Modern Seville." In *Inquisition and Society in Early Modern Europe*, edited by Stephen Haliczer, 147–68. Totawa, N.J.: Barnes and Noble, 1987.

Phillips, Heather. "John Wyclif and the Optics of the Eucharist." In *From Ockham to Wyclif*, edited by Anne Hudson and Michael Wilks, 245–58. Studies in Church History, Subsidia, 5. Oxford: Blackwell, 1987.

Phythian-Adams, Charles. "Ceremony and the Citizen: The Communal Year at Coventry, 1450–1550." In *Crisis and Order in English Towns, 1500–1700*, edited by Peter Clark and Paul Slack, 57–85. London: Routledge and Kegan Paul, 1972.

———. *Desolation of a City: Coventry and the Urban Crisis of the Late Middle Ages.* Cambridge: Cambridge University Press, 1979.

Plumb, Derek. "The Social and Economic Spread of Rural Lollardy: A Reappraisal." *Studies in Church History* 23 (1986): 111–30.

Poos, L. R. *A Rural Society After the Black Death: Essex, 1350–1525.* Cambridge: Cambridge University Press, 1991.

———. "Sex, Lies, and the Church Courts of Pre-Reformation England," *Journal of Interdisciplinary History*. Forthcoming.

Porterfield, Amanda. "Women's Attraction to Puritanism." *Church History* 60 (1991): 196–209.

Potter, Mary. "Gender Equality and Gender Hierarchy in Calvin's Theology." *Signs* 11 (1986): 725–39.

Rigby, Stephen. "Urban 'Oligarchy' in Late Medieval England." In *Towns and Townspeople in the Fifteenth Century*, edited by John A. F. Thomson, 62–86. Gloucester: Sutton, 1988.

Riley, Denise. *"Am I That Name?": Feminism and the Category of "Women" in History.* Minneapolis: University of Minnesota, 1988.

Roelker, Nancy Lyman. "The Appeal of Calvinism to French Noblewomen in the Sixteenth Century." *Journal of Interdisciplinary History* 2 (1971–72): 391–418.

———. "The Role of Noblewomen in the French Reformation." *Archiv für Reformationsgeschichte* 63 (1972): 168–95.

Roper, Lyndal. *The Holy Household: Women and Morals in Reformation Augsburg.* Oxford: Clarendon, 1989.

———. *Oedipus and the Devil: Witchcraft, Sexuality and Religion in Early Modern Europe.* London: Routledge, 1994.

Rosenthal, Joel T. *Patriarchy and Families of Privilege in Fifteenth-Century England.* Philadelphia: University of Pennsylvania Press, 1991.

Rosser, Gervase. "Going to the Fraternity Feast: Commensality and Social Relations in Late Medieval England." *Journal of British Studies* 33 (1994): 430–46.

Rowlands, Marie B. "Recusant Women, 1560–1640." In *Women in English Society, 1500–1800*, edited by Mary Prior, 149–80. London: Methuen, 1985.

Rubin, Miri. *Corpus Christi: The Eucharist in Late Medieval Culture.* Cambridge: Cambridge University Press, 1991.

Ruggiero, Guido. "'Più che la vita caro': Onore, matrimonio e reputazione femminile nel tardo Rinascimento." *Quaderni Storici*, n.s., 66 (1987): 753–75.

Rupp, E. G. *Studies in the Making of the English Protestant Tradition.* Cambridge: Cambridge University Press, 1947.

Scarisbrick, J. J. *The Reformation and the English People.* Oxford: Blackwell, 1984.

Scott, Joan W. *Gender and the Politics of History.* New York: Columbia University Press, 1988.

Scribner, R. W. *Popular Culture and Popular Movements in Reformation Germany.* London: Hambledon, 1987.

Shahar, Shulamith. "De quelques aspects de la femme dans la pensée et la communauté religieuses aux XIIe et XIIIe siècles." *Revue de l'histoire des religions* 185 (1974): 29–77.

———. *The Fourth Estate: A History of Women in the Middle Ages*. Translated by Chaya Galai. London: Methuen, 1983.

Shaw, David Gary. *The Creation of a Community: The City of Wells in the Middle Ages*. Oxford: Clarendon, 1993.

Sheehan, Michael M., and Jacqueline Murray. *Domestic Society in Medieval Europe: A Select Bibliography*. Toronto: Pontifical Institute of Mediaeval Studies, 1990.

Sheehan, Michael M. *The Will in Medieval England from the Conversion of the Anglo-Saxons to the End of the Thirteenth Century*. Toronto: Pontifical Institute of Mediaeval Studies, 1963.

Shorter, Edward. *The Making of the Modern Family*. New York: Basic Books, 1975.

Smart, Stefan J. "John Foxe and 'The Story of Richard Hun, Martyr.'" *Journal of Ecclesiastical History* 37 (1986): 1–14.

Smith, David M. *Guide to Bishops' Registers of England and Wales: A Survey from the Middle Ages to the Abolition of Episcopacy in 1646*. London: Royal Historical Society, 1981.

Smith, J. Challenor C., ed. *Index of Wills Proved in the Prerogative Court of Canterbury 1383–1558*. Index Library, 10–11. London: n.p., 1893. Reprint, Nendeln: Kraus Reprint, 1968.

Snow, David A., Louis A. Zurcher, and Sheldon Ekland-Olson. "Social Networks and Social Movements: A Microstructural Approach to Differential Recruitment." *American Sociological Review* 45 (1980): 787–801.

Spufford, Margaret. *Contrasting Communities: English Villagers in the Sixteenth and Seventeenth Centuries*. Cambridge: Cambridge University Press, 1974.

Stark, Rodney, and William Sims Bainbridge. "Networks of Faith: Interpersonal Bonds and Recruitment to Cults and Sects." *American Journal of Sociology* 85 (1980): 1376–95.

Stock, Brian. *The Implications of Literacy: Written Language and Models of Interpretation in the Eleventh and Twelfth Centuries*. Princeton, N.J.: Princeton University Press, 1983.

Stone, Lawrence. *The Family, Sex and Marriage in England, 1500–1800*. London: Weidenfeld and Nicolson, 1977.

Stuard, Susan. "The Dominion of Gender: Women's Fortunes in the High Middle Ages." In *Becoming Visible: Women in European History*, 2nd ed., edited by Renate Bridenthal, Claudia Koonz, and Susan Stuard, 153–72. Boston: Houghton Mifflin, 1987.

Summers, W. H. *The Lollards of the Chiltern Hills*. London: Griffiths, 1906.

Swanson, R. N. *Church and Society in Late Medieval England*. Oxford: Blackwell, 1989.

Tanner, Norman P. *The Church in Late Medieval Norwich, 1370–1532*. Toronto: Pontifical Institute of Mediaeval Studies, 1984.

Thomas, Keith. *Religion and the Decline of Magic*. London: Weidenfeld and Nicholson, 1971.

———. "Women and the Civil War Sects." *Past and Present* 13 (1958): 42–62.

Thomson, John A. F. "John Foxe and Some Sources for Lollard History: Notes for a Critical Appraisal." *Studies in Church History* 2 (1965): 251–57.

———. *The Later Lollards, 1414–1520*. London: Oxford University Press, 1965.

———. "Orthodox Religion and the Origins of Lollardy." *History* 74 (1989): 39–55.

Thrupp, Sylvia. *The Merchant Class of Medieval London (1300–1500)*. Ann Arbor: University of Michigan Press, 1948.

Vale, M. G. A. *Piety, Charity and Literacy among the Yorkshire Gentry, 1370–1480*. York: Borthwick Papers, no. 50, 1976.

Van Engen, John. "The Christian Middle Ages as an Historiographical Problem." *American Historical Review* 91 (1986): 519–52.

Vauchez, André. *The Laity in the Middle Ages: Religious Beliefs and Devotional Practices*. Edited by Daniel J. Bornstein. Translated by Margery J. Schneider. Notre Dame: University of Notre Dame Press, 1993.

———. *La Sainteté en occident aux derniers siècles du moyen âge*. Bibliothèque des études françaises d'Athènes et de Rome, 241. Rome: Ecole Française de Rome, 1981.

The Victoria History of the County of Berkshire. 5 vols. Edited by William Page and P. H. Ditchfield. London: Institute for Historical Research, 1972.

The Victoria History of the County of Buckingham. 5 vols. Edited by William Page. London: Institute for Historical Research, University of London, 1905–27. Reprint, London: Institute for Historical Research, 1969.

The Victoria History of the County of Middlesex. 3 vols. Edited by J. S. Cockburn. London: Institute for Historical Research, 1970.

The Victoria History of the County of Oxford. 12 vols. Edited by L. F. Salzman. London: Institute for Historical Research, 1907–90.

The Victoria History of the County of Warwick. 8 vols. Edited by H. Arthur Doubleday and William Page. London: Constable, 1904–69.

Von Nolcken, Christina. "Another Kind of Saint: A Lollard Perception of John Wyclif." In *From Ockham to Wyclif*, edited by Anne Hudson and Michael Wilks, 429–43. Studies in Church History, Subsidia, 5. Oxford: Blackwell, 1987.

Weber, Max. *The Sociology of Religion*. Translated by Ephraim Fischoff. Boston: Beacon, 1964.

Wedgwood, Josiah Clement. *History of Parliament, 1439–1509*. Vol. 2, *Biographies*. London: His Majesty's Stationery Office, 1936.

Weinstein, Donald, and Rudolph M. Bell. *Saints and Society: The Two Worlds of Western Christendom, 1000–1700*. Chicago: University of Chicago Press, 1982.

Welch, Edwin. "Some Suffolk Lollards." *Suffolk Institute of Archaeology Proceedings* 29 (1962): 154–65.

Wiesner, Merry E. "Beyond Women and the Family: Towards a Gender Analysis of the Reformation." *Sixteenth Century Journal* 18 (1987): 311–21.

———. "Luther and Women: The Death of Two Marys." In *Disciplines of Faith: Religion, Patriarchy, and Politics*, edited by James Obelkevich, Raphael Samuel, and Lyndal Roper, 295–308. London: Routledge and Kegan Paul, 1986.

———. "Women's Response to the Reformation." In *The German People and the Reformation*, edited by R. Po-Chia Hsia, 148–71. Ithaca, N.Y.: Cornell University Press, 1988.

Willen, Diane. "Godly Women in Early Modern England: Puritanism and Gender." *Journal of Ecclesiastical History* 43 (1992): 561–80.

———. "Women in the Public Sphere in Early Modern England: The Case of the Urban Working Poor." *Sixteenth Century Journal* 19 (1988): 559–75.

Wilson, Bryan. *Religion in Sociological Perspective.* Oxford: Oxford University Press, 1982.

Wiltenburg, Joy. *Disorderly Women and Female Power in the Street Literature of Early Modern England and Germany.* Charlottesville: University Press of Virginia, 1992.

Wunderli, Richard. *London Church Courts and Society on the Eve of the Reformation.* Cambridge, Mass.: Medieval Academy of America, 1981.

———. "Pre-Reformation London Summoners and the Murder of Richard Hunne." *Journal of Ecclesiastical History* 33 (1982): 209–24.

Zell, Michael L. "Fifteenth- and Sixteenth-Century Wills as Historical Sources." *Archives* 14 (1979): 67–74.

———. "The Use of Religious Preambles as a Measure of Religious Belief in the Sixteenth Century." *Bulletin of the Institute of Historical Research* 50 (1977): 246–49.

Zika, Charles. "Hosts, Processions and Pilgrimages: Controlling the Sacred in Fifteenth-Century Germany." *Past and Present* 118 (1988): 25–64.

Index

University of Pennsylvania Press
MIDDLE AGES SERIES
Ruth Mazo Karras and Edward Peters, General Editors

F. R. P. Akehurst, trans. *The* Coutumes de Beauvaisis *of Philippe de Beaumanoir*. 1992

Peter L. Allen. *The Art of Love: Amatory Fiction from Ovid to the* Romance of the Rose. 1992

David Anderson. *Before the Knight's Tale: Imitation of Classical Epic in Boccaccio's* Teseida. 1988

Benjamin Arnold. *Count and Bishop in Medieval Germany: A Study of Regional Power, 1100–1350*. 1991

Mark C. Bartusis. *The Late Byzantine Army: Arms and Society, 1204–1453*. 1992

Thomas N. Bisson, ed. *Cultures of Power: Lordship, Status, and Process in Twelfth-Century Europe*. 1995

Uta-Renate Blumenthal. *The Investiture Controversy: Church and Monarchy from the Ninth to the Twelfth Century*. 1988

Gerald A. Bond. *The Loving Subject: Desire, Eloquence, and Power in Romanesque France*. 1995

Daniel Bornstein, trans. *Dino Compagni's* Chronicle *of Florence*. 1986

Maureen Boulton. *The Song in the Story: Lyric Insertions in French Narrative Fiction, 1200–1400*. 1993

Betsy Bowden. *Chaucer Aloud: The Varieties of Textual Interpretation*. 1987

Charles R. Bowlus. *Franks, Moravians, and Magyars: The Struggle for the Middle Danube, 788–907*. 1995

James William Brodman. *Ransoming Captives in Crusader Spain: The Order of Merced on the Christian-Islamic Frontier*. 1986

Kevin Brownlee and Sylvia Huot, eds. *Rethinking the* Romance of the Rose*: Text, Image, Reception*. 1992

Matilda Tomaryn Bruckner. *Shaping Romance: Interpretation, Truth, and Closure in Twelfth-Century French Fictions*. 1993

Otto Brunner (Howard Kaminsky and James Van Horn Melton, eds. and trans.). Land *and Lordship: Structures of Governance in Medieval Austria*. 1992

Robert I. Burns, S.J., ed. *Emperor of Culture: Alfonso X the Learned of Castile and His Thirteenth-Century Renaissance*. 1990

David Burr. *Olivi and Franciscan Poverty: The Origins of the* Usus Pauper *Controversy*. 1989

David Burr. *Olivi's Peaceable Kingdom: A Reading of the Apocalypse Commentary*. 1993

Thomas Cable. *The English Alliterative Tradition*. 1991

Anthony K. Cassell and Victoria Kirkham, eds. and trans. *Diana's Hunt/Caccia di Diana: Boccaccio's First Fiction*. 1991

John C. Cavadini. *The Last Christology of the West: Adoptionism in Spain and Gaul, 785–820.* 1993

Brigitte Cazelles. *The Lady as Saint: A Collection of French Hagiographic Romances of the Thirteenth Century.* 1991

Karen Cherewatuk and Ulrike Wiethaus, eds. *Dear Sister: Medieval Women and the Epistolary Genre.* 1993

Anne L. Clark. *Elisabeth of Schönau: A Twelfth-Century Visionary.* 1992

Willene B. Clark and Meradith T. McMunn, eds. *Beasts and Birds of the Middle Ages: The Bestiary and Its Legacy.* 1989

Richard C. Dales. *The Scientific Achievement of the Middle Ages.* 1973

Charles T. Davis. *Dante's Italy and Other Essays.* 1984

William J. Dohar. *The Black Death and Pastoral Leadership: The Diocese of Hereford in the Fourteenth Century.* 1994

Katherine Fischer Drew, trans. *The Burgundian Code.* 1972

Katherine Fischer Drew, trans. *The Laws of the Salian Franks.* 1991

Katherine Fischer Drew, trans. *The Lombard Laws.* 1973

Nancy Edwards. *The Archaeology of Early Medieval Ireland.* 1990

Richard K. Emmerson and Ronald B. Herzman. *The Apocalyptic Imagination in Medieval Literature.* 1992

Theodore Evergates. *Feudal Society in Medieval France: Documents from the County of Champagne.* 1993

Felipe Fernández-Armesto. *Before Columbus: Exploration and Colonization from the Mediterranean to the Atlantic, 1229–1492.* 1987

Jerold C. Frakes. *Brides and Doom: Gender, Property, and Power in Medieval Women's Epic.* 1994

R. D. Fulk. *A History of Old English Meter.* 1992

Patrick J. Geary. *Aristocracy in Provence: The Rhône Basin at the Dawn of the Carolingian Age.* 1985

Peter Heath. *Allegory and Philosophy in Avicenna (Ibn Sînâ), with a Translation of the Book of the Prophet Muhammad's Ascent to Heaven.* 1992

J. N. Hillgarth, ed. *Christianity and Paganism, 350–750: The Conversion of Western Europe.* 1986

Richard C. Hoffmann. *Land, Liberties, and Lordship in a Late Medieval Countryside: Agrarian Structures and Change in the Duchy of Wrocław.* 1990

Robert Hollander. *Boccaccio's Last Fiction:* Il Corbaccio. 1988

John Y. B. Hood. *Aquinas and the Jews.* 1995

Edward B. Irving, Jr. *Rereading* Beowulf. 1989

Richard A. Jackson, ed. Ordines Coronationis Franciae: *Texts and Ordines for the Coronation of Frankish and French Kings and Queens in the Middle Ages, Vol. I.* 1995

C. Stephen Jaeger. *The Envy of Angels: Cathedral Schools and Social Ideals in Medieval Europe, 950–1200.* 1994

C. Stephen Jaeger. *The Origins of Courtliness: Civilizing Trends and the Formation of Courtly Ideals, 939–1210.* 1985

Donald J. Kagay, trans. *The Usatges of Barcelona: The Fundamental Law of Catalonia.* 1994

Richard Kay. *Dante's Christian Astrology*. 1994

Ellen E. Kittell. *From* Ad Hoc *to Routine: A Case Study in Medieval Bureaucracy*. 1991

Alan C. Kors and Edward Peters, eds. *Witchcraft in Europe, 1100- 1700: A Documentary History*. 1972

Barbara M. Kreutz. *Before the Normans: Southern Italy in the Ninth and Tenth Centuries*. 1992

Michael P. Kuczynski. *Prophetic Song: The Psalms as Moral Discourse in Late Medieval England*. 1995

E. Ann Matter. *The Voice of My Beloved: The Song of Songs in Western Medieval Christianity*. 1990

Shannon McSheffrey. *Gender and Heresy: Women and Men in Lollard Communities, 1420–1530*. 1995

A. J. Minnis. *Medieval Theory of Authorship*. 1988

Lawrence Nees. *A Tainted Mantle: Hercules and the Classical Tradition at the Carolingian Court*. 1991

Lynn H. Nelson, trans. *The Chronicle of San Juan de la Peña: A Fourteenth-Century Official History of the Crown of Aragon*. 1991

Barbara Newman. *From Virile Woman to WomanChrist: Studies in Medieval Religion and Literature*. 1995

Joseph F. O'Callaghan. *The Learned King: The Reign of Alfonso X of Castile*. 1993

Odo of Tournai (Irven M. Resnick, trans.). *Two Theological Treatises:* On Original Sin *and* A Disputation with the Jew, Leo, Concerning the Advent of Christ, the Son of God. 1994

David M. Olster. *Roman Defeat, Christian Response, and the Literary Construction of the Jew*. 1994

William D. Paden, ed. *The Voice of the Trobairitz: Perspectives on the Women Troubadours*. 1989

Edward Peters. *The Magician, the Witch, and the Law*. 1982

Edward Peters, ed. *Christian Society and the Crusades, 1198-1229: Sources in Translation, including* The Capture of Damietta *by Oliver of Paderborn*. 1971

Edward Peters, ed. *The First Crusade: The* Chronicle of Fulcher of Chartres *and Other Source Materials*. 1971

Edward Peters, ed. *Heresy and Authority in Medieval Europe*. 1980

James M. Powell. *Albertanus of Brescia: The Pursuit of Happiness in the Early Thirteenth Century*. 1992

James M. Powell. *Anatomy of a Crusade, 1213–1221*. 1986

Susan A. Rabe. *Faith, Art, and Politics at Saint-Riquier: The Symbolic Vision of Angilbert*. 1995

Jean Renart (Patricia Terry and Nancy Vine Durling, trans.). *The Romance of the Rose or Guillaume de Dole*. 1993

Michael Resler, trans. Erec *by Hartmann von Aue*. 1987

Pierre Riché (Michael Idomir Allen, trans.). *The Carolingians: A Family Who Forged Europe*. 1993

Pierre Riché (Jo Ann McNamara, trans.). *Daily Life in the World of Charlemagne*. 1978

Jonathan Riley-Smith. *The First Crusade and the Idea of Crusading*. 1986

Joel T. Rosenthal. *Patriarchy and Families of Privilege in Fifteenth-Century England.* 1991

Teofilo F. Ruiz. *Crisis and Continuity: Land and Town in Late Medieval Castile.* 1994

James A. Rushing, Jr. *Images of Adventure: Ywain in the Visual Arts.* 1995

James A. Schultz. *The Knowledge of Childhood in the German Middle Ages, 1100–1350.* 1995

Pamela Sheingorn, ed. and trans. *The Book of Sainte Foy.* 1995

Robin Chapman Stacey. *The Road to Judgment: From Custom to Court in Medieval Ireland and Wales.* 1994

Sarah Stanbury. *Seeing the* Gawain-*Poet: Description and the Act of Perception.* 1992

Robert D. Stevick. *The Earliest Irish and English Bookarts: Visual and Poetic Forms Before A.D. 1000.* 1994

Thomas C. Stillinger. *The Song of Troilus: Lyric Authority in the Medieval Book.* 1992

Susan Mosher Stuard. *A State of Deference: Ragusa/Dubrovnik in the Medieval Centuries.* 1992

Susan Mosher Stuard, ed. *Women in Medieval History and Historiography.* 1987

Susan Mosher Stuard, ed. *Women in Medieval Society.* 1976

Jonathan Sumption. *The Hundred Years War: Trial by Battle.* 1992

Ronald E. Surtz. *The Guitar of God: Gender, Power, and Authority in the Visionary World of Mother Juana de la Cruz (1481–1534).* 1990

Ronald E. Surtz. *Writing Women in Late Medieval and Early Modern Spain: The Mothers of Saint Teresa of Avila.* 1995

Del Sweeney, ed. *Agriculture in the Middle Ages.* 1995

William H. TeBrake. *A Plague of Insurrection: Popular Politics and Peasant Revolt in Flanders, 1323–1328.* 1993

Patricia Terry, trans. *Poems of the Elder Edda.* 1990

Hugh M. Thomas. *Vassals, Heiresses, Crusaders, and Thugs: The Gentry of Angevin Yorkshire, 1154–1216.* 1993

Mary F. Wack. *Lovesickness in the Middle Ages: The* Viaticum *and Its Commentaries.* 1990

Benedicta Ward. *Miracles and the Medieval Mind: Theory, Record, and Event, 1000–1215.* 1982

Suzanne Fonay Wemple. *Women in Frankish Society: Marriage and the Cloister, 500–900.* 1981

Kenneth Baxter Wolf. *Making History: The Normans and Their Historians in Eleventh-Century Italy.* 1995

Jan M. Ziolkowski. *Talking Animals: Medieval Latin Beast Poetry, 750–1150.* 1993

This book has been set in Linotron Galliard. Galliard was designed for Mergenthaler in 1978 by Matthew Carter. Galliard retains many of the features of a sixteenth-century typeface cut by Robert Granjon but has some modifications that give it a more contemporary look.

Printed on acid-free paper.